Linguistische Arbeiten

543

Herausgegeben von Klaus von Heusinger, Gereon Müller,
Ingo Plag, Beatrice Primus, Elisabeth Stark und Richard Wiese

Klaus Abels

Phases

An essay on cyclicity in syntax

De Gruyter

ISBN   978-3-11-048211-9
e-ISBN 978-3-11-028422-5
ISSN   0344-6727

Library of Congress Cataloging-in-Publication Data
A CIP catalog record for this book has been applied for at the Library of Congress.

Bibliographic information published by the Deutsche Nationalbibliothek
The Deutsche Nationalbibliothek lists this publication in the Deutsche Nationalbibliografie;
detailed bibliographic data are available in the Internet at http://dnb.d-nb.de.

Gesamtherstellung: Hubert & Co. GmbH & Co. KG, Göttingen
∞ Gedruckt auf säurefreiem Papier

Printed in Germany

www.degruyter.com

Contents

List of glosses used

1, 2,3,...	noun class one, two, three,...	GEN	genitive case
		GO	Irish neutral complementizer
1st, 2nd, 3rd	first, second, third person	ICP	incompletive aspect
		INDEF	indefinite
A	Tzotzil set A affix	INF	infinitive
A	Lakhota agent agreement	INST	instrumental case
ABL	ablative case	IV	instrumental voice
ABS	absolutive case	LNK	linker
ACC	accusative case	LOC	locative
AGR	agreement	M	masculine
AL	Irish leniting complementizer	NE	French initial part of bipartite negation
AN	Irish nasalizing complementizer		
AM	Malagasy agent marker	N	neuter
APPL	applicative	NMLZ	nominalizer
ART	article	NOM	nominative case
ASP	aspectual auxiliary	OBJ	object case
aux	auxiliary	OV	objective voice
AV	agentive voice	P	pre- or postposition
B	Tzotzil set B affix	PASS	passive voice
BV	benefactive voice	PERF	perfect
CAUS	causative	PL	plural
COMP	complementizer	POSS	possessive
COND	conditional	PRS	present tense
CP	completive aspect	PROG	progressive aspect
DAT	dative case	PST	past tense
DEF	definite	PRT	particle
DEM	demonstrative	PV	Hungarian preverb
DIR	directional	Q	interrogative marker
DR	German filler morpheme used with prepositions	REFL	reflexive
		REL	relative marker
DV	dative voice	SG	singular
ENC	enclitic	SM	subject marker
ERG	ergative case	SUBJ	subjunctive
F	feminine	T	French marker of subject auxiliary inversion
FOC	focus marker		
FUT	future tense	TM	Malagasy theme marker
FV	final vowel	U	Lakhota theme agreement

1 Introduction

This essay investigates the concept of the phase in minimalist syntax. If the concept of the phase is fundamental to the theory and if it is to to be productive theoretically, it should provide the grounds for a unifying formulation of different aspects of syntactic theory. I try to make some progress on this project, restricting myself to the theory of movement. The investigation focuses on cyclic movement and certain questions connected to it. I ask to what extent a unifying treatment of successive-cyclic movement, partial movement, pied-piping, secondary movement under pied-piping, and Abels's (2003c) stranding generalization is possible and what role the notion of a phase might play in this.

Movement is a characteristic property of human languages. In many languages particular structural positions are associated with particular properties. In English (English being a SVO language) the position immediately after the verb is canonically associated with accusative case on pronouns and, semantically, with the thematic interpretation of patient, (1a). The clause-initial position on the other hand is associated with topics and with question words in constituent questions. When a constituent realizes the thematic role of patient and is the focus of a question or the topic, it is displaced to the front of the clause (1b–c).

(1)   English
       a.   John kicked him.
       b.   Him, John kicked.
       c.   Who did John kick?

There is substantial evidence that such movement is mediated locally. Take for example the description of Belfast English in Henry, 1995. According to Henry, Belfast English exhibits subject-auxiliary inversion of the standard English type in direct questions, (2a). However, unlike standard English, Belfast English also allows inversion in indirect questions, (2b), and, crucially, along the path of Wh-movement, (2c).

(2)   Standard English (SE) and Belfast English (BE)
       a.   ✓SE | ✓BE What have you done?
       b.   * SE | ✓BE She asked who had I seen.   Henry, 1995, p. 106
       c.   * SE | ✓BE Who did John hope would he see?Henry, 1995, p. 108

Effects like these can be given a simple account if the Wh-word *who* in (2c) moves from the canonical object position in the embedded clause to the position where it is pronounced not in one step but in two steps, passing through the initial position of the embedded clause and triggering subject-auxiliary inversion there. Effects like subject-auxiliary inversion in (2c) are usually taken to provide evidence for successive-cyclic movement: long movement proceeding in a series of short steps.

I hasten to add that this interpretation of the evidence is not uncontroversial. Some of the controversy is the topic of chapter 2. For the moment it is sufficient to note that there is evidence suggesting that apparently unbounded movement proceeds in a sequence of short steps. This is the successive-cyclic property of movement.

This property is related to phases here via the assumption that all and only the phase edges along the path of successive-cyclic movement provide intermediate landing sites for movement. This is implemented using features that have an interpretation but—and this is a special property of phase heads—that need not be interpreted on phase heads.

In some languages Wh-phrases are pronounced in positions which, in other languages, are hypothesized to provide intermediate landing sites for movement. For example, Malagasy, an Austronesian VOS language, has two strategies for forming local constituent questions (Sabel, 2006). An *in situ* strategy, where the questioned constituent remains in its canonical position, and a movement strategy, where the questioned constituent moves to the clause-initial position. If the canonical position of a Wh-phrase is separated from the clause with interrogative scope by a clause boundary, a third strategy becomes possible: The Wh-word may remain in situ in the embedded clause, it may move to a left-peripheral position in the embedded clause, or it may move to a left-peripheral position in the interrogative clause itself, (3a–c), respectively. Malagasy allows the same three strategies also in forming indirect questions. I refer to the type of pattern in (3b) as *partial Wh-movement*: the Wh-phrase appears to undergo Wh-movement to a position between its canonical position and its scope position and surfaces where theories of successive-cyclicity would locate an intermediate landing site.

(3) Malagasy   Sabel, 2006, 157 ex. 18

   a. Heverin'   i   Piera fa nividy   inona Rakoto?
       PRS.TM.believe ART Piera that PST.AM.buy what Rakoto

   b. Heverin'   i   Piera fa inona no   novidin-
       PRS.TM.believe ART Piera that what FOC PST.TM.buy
       dRakoto   ___?
       GEN.Rakoto

   c. Inona no heverin'   i   Piera fa novidin
       what FOC PRS.TM.believe ART Piera that PST.TM.buy

dRakoto   ___?
GEN.Rakoto
What does Piera blieve that Rakoto bought?

Talk of *partial Wh-movement* is intended merely as a convenient descriptive label in line with the usage in the literature. The analysis of these patterns in later chapters will not literally involve partial Wh-movement, that is, Wh-movement that does not terminate in the scopal position. Analytically, I follow Sabel, 2006, who suggests that partial Wh-movement instantiates focus movement rather than Wh-movement proper.

A complete theory of Wh-movement must be able to account for such patterns. The theory of phases and features in this book provides just such an analysis. The implementation again rests on features that need not be interpreted on the phase head targeted by partial movement. This ties together the theories of successive-cyclicity with that of partial movement via the unifying concept of the phase.

Movement also has the property of pied-piping. The specific syntax of constituent questions in English generally requires one Wh-word to front. If a word is fronted that does not belong to the narrowly circumscribed class of question words, the particular interrogative syntax of subject-auxiliary inversion is not triggered and no question interpretation is possible, (4). We can informally call this the *Wh-requirement* imposed on the clause-initial position in Wh-questions.

(4)   English
   a.   Who did John kick?
   b.   *Fred did John kick?
   c.   I wonder who John kicked.
   d.   *I wonder Fred John kicked.

Phrases that merely *contain* a Wh-word may frequently satisfy the Wh-requirement. The initial preposition in (5a–b) is not a Wh-word and neither is its noun phrase complement. The Wh-word is relatively deeply buried inside of the prepositional phrase. Yet the entire prepositional phrase satisfies the Wh-requirement. Similarly, the head noun of the initial phrase in (5c–d) is not morphologically a Wh-word. The Wh-word is deeply buried in the possessor. Nevertheless, the entire phrase satisfies the Wh-requirement. Following Ross, 1967, this phenomenon is called *pied-piping* (for a concise overview see Horvath, 2006).

(5)   English
   a.   In what way did he solve the problem?
   b.   I wonder in what way he solved the problem.
   c.   Whose mother's demands could he satisfy?
   d.   I wonder whose mother's demands he could satisfy.

Recent work on pied-piping (Cable, 2007, 2010a,b; Heck, 2004, 2008, 2009) has revealed a number of cross-linguistically valid generalizations. First, to enable pied-piping, the pied-piper must be situated in one of a few canonical pied-piping positions. Second, the definition of such positions is recursive. Third, words and phrases often move to their pied-piping position. Finally, and more controversially, pied-piping is optional.

Regarding the first two points I will claim that the canonical pied-piping positions are the complement and the movement-derived specifier positions of phase heads. Pied-piping is recursive because of iterated agreement from phase head to phase head. Such agreement is mediated by the same features that drive successive-cyclic movement. The analysis rests on the concept of the phase with its specific property that phase heads may bear features not interpreted on them.

The third generalization about pied-piping above requires elaboration. Following Heck, 2004, I refer to movement as *secondary movement*, if it involves placement of a constituent in a particular position to enable pied-piping. A good example of this type comes from Tzotzil, a Mayan VOS language (see Aissen, 1996). Within the noun phrase, the possessor follows the possessed, (6).

(6) Tzotzil   Aissen, 1996, 454 ex. 22, 455 ex. 25

    a.   s-p'in   li Maruch-e
           $A3^{rd}$-pot the Maruch-ENC
           Maruch's pot

    b. *Maruch s-p'in
           Maruch $A3^{rd}$-pot

    c. *li   Maruch s-p'in   ...-e
           the Maruch $A3^{rd}$-pot   -ENC

Wh-words are fronted in Tzotzil:

(7) Tzotzil   Aissen, 1996, 453 ex. 16

    a.   K'usi a-man?
           what $A.2^{nd}$-buy?
           What did you buy?

    b. *A-man k'usi?

In Wh-questions with pied-piping, a Wh-possessor obligatorily fronts across the possessed:

(8) Tzotzil   Aissen, 1996, 457 ex. 32, 35

    a.   Buch'u x-ch'amal i-cham?
           who $A3^{rd}$-child CP-died
           Whose child died?

b. *X-ch'amal buchu i-cham?
   $A3^{rd}$-child who CP-died

This cannot be treated as a simple, local flipping-around of the branches of the tree, leaving the hierarchical structure of the phrase intact. Clear evidence for a movement derivation comes from recursive possessor constructions. The declarative (9a) allows the three interrogative versions in (9b–d). (9c) clearly shows that the Wh-possessor has moved within the pied-piped noun phrase. If the possessor fails to front, pied-piping is impossible.

(9) Tzotzil   Aissen, 1996, 481 ex. 97a, 485 ex. 103
   a. I-'ixtalaj s-kayijonal y-osil   li j-tot-e.
       CP-ruin $A3^{rd}$-firelane $A3^{rd}$-land the A.1st-father-ENC
       The firelane around my father's land was ruined.
   b. Buch'u i-'ixtalaj s-kayijonal   y-osil?
       who   CP-ruin $A3^{rd}$-firelane $A3^{rd}$-land
   c. Buch'u s-kayijonal   y-osil   i-'ixtalaj?
       who $A3^{rd}$-firelane $A3^{rd}$-land CP-ruin
   d. Buch'u y-osil   i-'ixtalaj s-kayijonal?
       who $A3^{rd}$-land CP-ruin $A3^{rd}$-firelane
       The firelane around whose land was ruined?

Regarding secondary movement, I will claim that it is independently motivated movement to a phase edge. It enables pied-piping as a side effect, relying yet again on the privilege of phase heads to bear features not interpreted there.

Pied-piping is often optional, as in (9b–d) above. There are important exceptions to this optionality. Thus, pied-piping may become obligatory if extraction would lead to an island violation.

A particular case of obligatory pied-piping is formulated as the stranding generalization in Abels, 2003c. The stranding generalization says that the complement of a phase head may never move without pied-piping of the immediately containing phase. Thus, a TP embedded under C, for example, cannot move alone but must pied-pipe the entire CP. I argue that this follows as a direct consequence of the theory of successive-cyclicity and the last-resort nature of movement.

To achieve all of this I will assume that phase heads are special in that they and only they are able to bear movement-inducing features that need not be interpreted on them. Universal grammar imposes no further restrictions on the feature content of phase heads, but it does impose such restrictions on interpretation. Particular languages also impose restrictions on the feature content of phase heads.[1]

---

[1] The idea pursued here has a certain similarity to Chomsky's suggestion (Chomsky,

8

The remainder of this chapter gives an overview of the contents of the book by chapter and provides a thumbnail sketch of the theory.

1.1 Overview

Syntacticians working within the Extended Standard Theory, Government and Binding theory, and Minimalism have usually assumed that long distance displacement is mediated by a series of relatively local steps. This assumption has been challenged from various sides. Chapter 2 defends the traditional position in generative grammar. Section 2.2 clarifies the logic of the situation and to make explicit what shape arguments for successive-cyclic movement in the traditional sense would need to take. It is also an attempt to provide such arguments. (This section is a development of Abels, 2003c, chapter 2.1 and of Abels and Bentzen, 2009, 2010. Kristine Bentzen's contributions are hereby gratefully acknowledged.) The evidence reviewed in section 2.2 suggests that there is a landing site for successive-cyclic movement at the edge of vP. Traditionally, the edge of CP is taken to provide another intermediate landing site. However, in a number of papers den Dikken (2006; 2009) has challenged this idea. Section 2.3 discusses this challenge. I suggest that neither den Dikken's arguments nor his counterproposal actually threaten the traditional view. Section 2.4 provides a brief discussion of the tools that will be used to implement successive-cyclicity. Among these are a last-resort condition on movement and movement-type-specific features on select heads, the phase heads. These features drive movement. The section is also a first answer to the charge that these features might be purely theory internal devices to implement movement. It should become clear in later chapters that this is not the case: the features on phase heads that implement successive-cyclic movement have empirical and not just theory internal content. A lot of evidence for this claim is given in later chapters, but the issue is raised in section 2.4 and the lines of later argumentation are foreshadowed.

Chapter 3 is a brief overview of the most salient properties of pied-piping, secondary movement, and partial movement. The chapter summarizes findings already in the literature. The discussion of partial Wh-movement and basic properties of pied-piping illustrates known facts. The examples of partial movement come mostly from Kîîtharaka, and some of them cannot be found in the literature. Regarding secondary movement, I introduce a distinction between *secondary movement proper* and *apparent secondary movement*, which I haven't

---

2008, p. 143) that "I[nternal] M[erge] should only be driven by phase heads." The difference is that in the present system not all movement-inducing features reside on phase heads but only those that are not interpreted.

found in the prior literature. *Apparent secondary movement* is movement of an element to a particular position, where pied-piping is impossible without that movement but where the relevant movement can be shown to exist in the language independently of pied-piping. *Secondary movement proper* is movement of an element to a particular position, where pied-piping is impossible without that movement and the movement does not exist in the language independently of pied-piping. Judging by the examples of secondary movement given in Heck, 2008, secondary movement proper is rare. The theory in this book (chapter 5) derives the prediction, idealized from the facts, that secondary movement proper is altogether impossible.

Chapter 4 is the theoretical companion to chapter 2. The chapter implements and formulates more precisely the ideas sketched in section 2.4. The main idea is that a given feature may be deficient and that this deficiency can be overcome if the feature enters into an agreement relation. I understand agreement as structure-sharing much like Pesetsky and Torrego, 2007. In order to enter into such sharing relations, the heads and phrases bearing the features need to be brought into certain syntactic configurations (section 4.1). Items can be brought into the relevant configurations through application of the operation merge. Merge is subject to a last resort condition (section 4.2): If no feature enters into a structure-sharing relation as a result, merge cannot take place.

To implement successive-cyclicity, I adopt the phase impenetrability condition from Chomsky, 2000. Section 4.3 explains why I do not adopt some of the other phase-related assumptionsfrom Chomsky, 2000. I also point out the lack of a logical relation between phase theory and the theory of islands given current approaches to islands: The existence of islands does not follow from existing conceptions of phases and phase theory is not entailed by the existence of islands. Finally, I show how the stranding generalization follows directly from the joint action of the last resort and the phase impenetrability conditions.

Some of this discussion is very abstract and formal. The final section of chapter 4 therefore explains how the assumptions made in earlier parts of the chapter derive successive-cyclicity. I illustrate how assuming specific features for different movement types accounts for various morphological and syntactic effects of cyclicity. I use Kîîtharaka to illustrate the morphological point, drawing heavily on Abels and Muriungi, 2008. The syntactic point is made through an analysis of the pivot-only restriction of Tagalog. Tagalog, like other Austronesian languages, only allows extraction of a dedicated constituent within each clause, the pivot. Furthermore, extraction is only possible from the pivot itself. I show that the existence of a system like the one found in Tagalog is expected if we assume movement-type-specific features on phase heads and parameterization for the availability of such features. The pivot-only restriction is difficult to capture otherwise and has been a persistent puzzle within Austronesian syntax.

Chapter 5 is the theoretical companion to chapter 3. It develops notions of feature valuation and feature interpretation to accompany the theory from chapter 4. The main superficial aim of sections 5.1 and 5.2 is to account for the fact that the features postulated on intermediate phase heads only have morphological and syntactic effects but seem to be semantically empty. I adopt, adapt and sharpen Adger and Ramchand's (2005, p. 174) condition *Interpret Once under Agreement* as *Interpret Once under Sharing*. The resulting suggestion about feature interpretation also captures those aspects of Rizzi's (2006) Criterial Freezing that seem defensible to me. The suggestions boils down to saying that any given feature is interpreted once under sharing and that an element undergoing movement of type μ determines interpretation exactly at the highest landing site of its μ-movement. To illustrate and possibly clarify the intent of the definitions, section 5.3 illustrates the workings of the system in the abstract using only a single feature. From the discussion it can be seen very clearly that, when only a single feature is considered, the descriptive apparatus made available by the theory is quite limited. This allows a number of generalizations about he system to emerge. Section 5.4 returns to the generalizations from chapter 3 and shows how they are derived or, in the case of partial movement, described. Section 5.5 finally, discusses various strategies of forming Wh-questions found in the languages of the world and shows how they fit into the descriptive apparatus. The descriptions are mere sketches of single-, multiple-, and non-Wh-movement strategies. They are intended mainly as a demonstration of the reasonable fit between the theory and the cross-linguistic record.

The remaining two chapters deal with the stranding generalization. They are revised versions of chapters 3 and 4 of Abels, 2003c. Chapter 6 discusses the observation that light verbs, complementizers, and adpositions are not strandable by their complements. This is expected under the current theory on the assumption that v, C, and P are phase heads. In chapter 7, I discuss the question whether the generalization regarding P carries over to languages that allow adposition stranding.

1.2 Theoretical sketch

I assume a theory of syntax here in which structures are built bottom up by a structure building operation merge. Merge combines two syntactic objects (where both lexical items and the results of merger count as syntactic objects) to create a new one, projecting the label of one of the two objects as the label of the resulting structure. Lexical items are their own label.

Merger can either combine syntactic objects that are not in a part-of relation (external merge) or objects that are in such a relation (internal merge). The operation merge is constrained by a condition, Last Resort, which states that merge is only possible when this lead to at least one feature being shared.

Features may be valued ([F]) or unvalued ([uF]). Unvalued features need to acquire a value in the course of the derivation, otherwise they are illicit interface objects (*[uF] at the interface). When two features are shared, this leads to valuation as long as one of the two features is also valued, but it need not, if both of the shared features are unvalued (see discussion in Pesetsky and Torrego, 2007). Last Resort is formulated in terms of feature-sharing rather than in terms of feature-valuation.

There are certain configurations in which features may be shared. These configurations are defined in terms of the more primitive c-command relation, which underpins syntactic relations in general (Koster, 1987; Neeleman and van de Koot, 2002, 2010). More concretely, a feature borne by a syntactic head H can be shared with the feature borne by a different syntactic object O if either H c-commands O, O c-commands H, H and O c-command each other. Unvalued features are cross-classified by the conditions under which they can be shared. For a feature that can be shared under c-command from H to O, I will write [uF$_\downarrow$]. For a feature that can be shared under c-command from O to H, I will write [uF$_\uparrow$]. Finally, for a feature that requires mutual c-command between H and O, I will write [uF$_{\downarrow\uparrow}$].[2] These three types of unvalued features will be called probes. I make a distinction between unvalued features and probes, because I allow the possibility of unvalued features that do not probe ([uF]).

As mentioned above, Last Resort dictates that an application of merge is never licensed unless a probe enters into a feature-sharing relation that it couldn't have entered into without this application of merge. I will also, albeit more tentatively, assume that internal merge can only be licensed by [uF$_{\downarrow\uparrow}$].

A number of further restrictions apply. Thus, I will adopt the phase impenetrability condition, according to which the complement domain of a phase head is inaccessible for further operations once the phase, that is, the maximal projection of the phase head is complete. I assume that v, C, P, and D are phase heads. Borrowing a term first suggested for a similar concept by Juan Uriagereka, I will also adopt a virus theory of feature-sharing, according to which an unshared probe may never be syntactically embedded without projecting.

These notions are mostly directly adopted or slightly adapted from fairly standard minimalist notions. What is absent here is a notion of edge features, of a specifier-head relation, and of feature strength. What replaces such notions, for the most part, is [uF$_{\downarrow\uparrow}$]. Recall that [uF$_{\downarrow\uparrow}$] is a kind of probe that requires the head that bears it and another syntactic object bearing [F] to c-command each other. Mutual c-command of this type can be achieved in exactly two ways. Ei-

---

[2] My use of the upward and downward arrows has nothing to do with the use that these arrows have in functional equations in Lexical Functional Grammar.

ther H and O are sisters, (10a), or they come to c-command each other by virtue
of internal merge, (10b). Recognizing the connection, Epstein et al., 1998 called
the latter relation 'derivational sisterhood'.

The trees below also introduce a bit of notation that I will use throughout
the book. The official definition of internal merge gives rise to multidominance
structures (see chapter 4). Informal representations are usually sufficient and
in those, I represent unpronounced occurrences (traces, lower copies) by grey
print: this is an unpronounced occurrence.

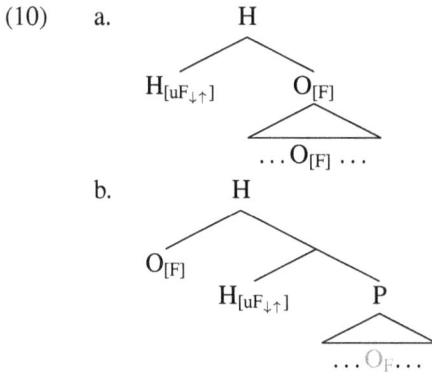

(10)   a.

$$H$$

$$H_{[uF_{\downarrow\uparrow}]} \qquad O_{[F]}$$

$$\ldots O_{[F]} \ldots$$

    b.

$$H$$

$$O_{[F]}$$

$$H_{[uF_{\downarrow\uparrow}]} \qquad P$$

$$\ldots O_F \ldots$$

Not represented in the tree above is the notation for feature-sharing: That [F]
on O and $[uF_{\downarrow\uparrow}]$ on H come to be shared is merely implicit in (10). When it is
relevant to represent sharing explicitly, I will make use of a co-superscripting notation. This notation indicates structure sharing and is borrowed from Pesetsky
and Torrego, 2007, who borrow it from Head-driven Phrase Structure Gram-
mar. Co-superscripted features share a value ($[F^{\boxed{1}}] \ldots [F^{\boxed{1}}]$), while counter-
superscripted features do not share their value ($[F^{\boxed{1}}] \ldots [F^{\boxed{2}}]$), though they may
have type-identical values, of course. When no superscripting is present, the
reader has to infer the relevant interpretation from context. In cases where superscripting is systematically indicated, lack of co-superscripting indicates lack
of sharing. Otherwise it may or may not indicate sharing. In (10), sharing is
intended.

Of course, the mutual c-command relation between a head and an element
moved from its complement domain holds whether the moved element is internally merged locally or at an arbitrarily great distance. The idea of the specifier-
head relation makes the additional claim that a specifier is local to its head—
contained within the head's projection. In the present theory, this local aspect of
feature-sharing results from the virus theory.

The assumptions above entail a particular implementation of successive-cyclicity. Merge, and in particular internal merge, is subject to the last-resort condition. In addition, the phase impenetrability condition limits the structural distance between a moving element and the target of movement. It follows that

long distance movement must be driven by $[uF_{\downarrow\uparrow}]$ on intervening phase heads.

The feature-sharing relation that results between the moving element and the phase head, I will claim, enables pied-piping. We therefore have an account for why pied-piping is possible, in traditional terms, from complement position and from specifier position (assuming the specifier is movement derived): These are the two configurations in which a $[uF_{\downarrow\uparrow}]$ can be satisfied. We also predict that CP, vP, PP, and DP may be pied-piped, since they are phase heads. Finally, the system directly derives Abels's (2003c) stranding generalization. This is the generalization that phase heads may never be stranded by their complements. The predictions follows from the joint action of the last resort and the phase impenetrability conditions.

Chapter 4 develops the ideas just sketched. I argue that the system describes movement as we find it in natural languages to a certain extent, but brief reflection reveals that it considerably overgenerates. A lot of the excess power is taken back in chapter 5, which discusses the question of feature-interpretation.

I assume that shared features must be interpreted. However, I borrow Adger and Ramchand's (2005, p. 174) Interpret Once under Agree, which I call *Interpret Once under Sharing*. It says that a shared feature is interpreted in exactly one position. Interpret Once under Sharing encodes certain aspects of Rizzi's (2006) Criterial Freezing. While Rizzi claims, in essence, that every syntactic object is associated with at most one scope position (a.k.a. criterial position), I suggest that this condition needs to be relativized to features: relative to a given feature, every syntactic object has only one scope position.

I then define the positions where a shared feature is interpreted. For $[uF_{\downarrow}]$ and $[uF_{\uparrow}]$ this is the unique position where the feature is shared and that c-commands all other positions where that feature is shared. For $[uF_{\downarrow\uparrow}]$, it is the highest position where $[uF_{\downarrow\uparrow}]$ triggered merger. Not every position where $[uF_{\downarrow\uparrow}]$ is shared is also one where it triggers merger. The distinction between a feature that triggers merger and one that doesn't (that is, one that gets shared as a free-rider) is drawn in terms of an independently justified restriction on the order in which features must be used. Abels, 2007, 2009; Williams, 2002, 2011 assume that there is a, presumably universal, constraint on the ordering of operations in language. In Abels, 2007, 2009 I call this Universal Constraint on the Ordering of Operations in Language, Williams, 2011 refers to a similar idea as the F-clock. A feature counts as the trigger of merger only if it is the lowest feature on this universal hierarchy that is being shared as the result of an application of merge.

With the help of the ancillary definitions and assumptions just mentioned, Interpret Once under Sharing can be used to derive the empirically correct restrictions on partial and secondary movement.[3]

---

[3] Further restrictions directly relevant to the question of criterial freezing follow from

14

the generalized bans on improper movement formulated in Abels, 2007, 2009; Williams, 2002.

2 On successive-cyclic movement

2.1 Introduction

This chapter investigates the question of how movement dependencies should be modeled. It provides arguments that long-distance dependencies are represented in the grammar as a series of relatively short steps that affect some phrases along the path of movement and leave others unaffected.

I take the question of whether movement dependencies are mediated in a very local, medium-range local, or long-distance manner to be empirical. Investigating this question requires considering effects movement has on the material crossed by that movement. Whether such effects exist at all and where and how they are expressed are all empirical questions.

It is clear, empirically, that the material along the path of movement has an effect on the movement dependency. The most obvious case are island effects: While (1a) is ambiguous between the readings in (1a.i) and (1a.ii), the ambiguity disappears once we replace *that* by *how* along the path of movement, as in (1b). Such effects necessitate some notion of *path of movement*.

(1) English
   a. When did the boy say that he hurt himself?
      (i) When did the boy say [*that* he hurt himself when]?
      (ii) When did the boy say [*that* he hurt himself] when?
   b. When did the boy say how he hurt himself?
      (i) *When did the boy say [*how* he hurt himself when]?
      (ii) When did the boy say [*how* he hurt himself] when?

Example (2) shows that changing *that* to *how* along the linear path between filler and gap does not necessarily give rise to the effect seen in (1). This is why paths must be construed in hierarchical terms. All modern theories of grammar make available the relevant notion of path.

(2) English
   a. When did [the boy who told his mother [*that* he hurt himself]] go to bed when?
   b. When did [the boy who told his mother [*how* he hurt himself]] go to bed when?

Given this much, we might expect to find an influence not only of the path on the dependency but also of the dependency on the path. Whether movement in any given structure, say (3), has an effect on the material between the filler and the gap is again an entirely empirical question.

(3)   Which book

> does John think that Mary said that Frank believes that he should tell the police that it is unlikely that Edward has read

which book

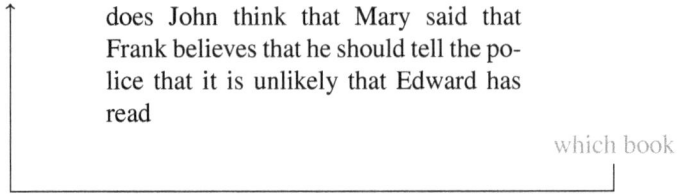

As a matter of empirical fact, we find that movement along a path does exert an influence on the material crossed. This is shown by familiar effects from word order—for example, the famous inversion under question formation in Spanish (Torrego, 1983, 1984; Uribe-Echevarria, 1992)—and from morphology—for example, the alternation in the shape of the complementizer in Irish (McCloskey, 1979, 1990a, 2002; Noonan, 1997), illustrated in (4). Reconstruction effects to places along the path—like the reconstruction effects for binding theory to intermediate landing sites, sometimes called *pit-stop reflexives* (as discussed in Barss, 1986)—show yet another type of interaction between path and moving item.

(4)   Irish   McCloskey, 1990b, p. 205
   a.   Dúirt sé gu-r   bhuail tú é
        said   he GO-PST struck you him
        He said that you struck him
   b.   an rud   a   shíl   mé a   dúirt tú   a   dhéanfá
        the thing AL thought I   AL said you AL do-COND-2^{nd}SG
        the thing that I though you said you would do

I introduce a distinction between two types of theories, which was pointed out in this form first in Abels, 2003c. There, I distinguished between *punctuated* and *uniform* paths. A path will be called punctuated if some but not all nodes along a filler-gap dependency are affected. A path will be called uniform if all nodes along it are affected in the same way. HPSG, Categorial Grammar, and the theory of the Configurational Matrix are examples of theories where paths are treated uniformly: All nodes along the path are affected, and all are affected in the same way. Tree-Adjoining Grammars offer a theory that is uniform in a very different way: the nodes along the movement path remain uniformly unaffected.

On the other hand, theories in the narrower Chomskyan tradition postulate punctuated paths. This is true of the Extended Standard Theory of the seventies, where only selected nodes, namely the COMP nodes, along the path were affected. This is true of the Barriers theory, where intermediate landing sites are available at some nodes along the path while they are unavailable at others. The same is true, of course, also of the more recent idea of vP and CP as phases. Even in theories where landing sites are quite close together, as for example in Chomsky and Lasnik, 1993, Takahashi, 1994a, Stroik, 1999, Boeckx, 2001, 2008, and Bošković, 2007, it still remains true that only the maximal projections along the path are affected, but not intermediate projections.[1]

Most so-called cyclicity effects of the types alluded to above have no direct bearing on the question of punctuated versus uniform paths. The Irish data, for example, are compatible with various uniform and punctuated analyses.

Bouma, Molouf, and Sag (2001), who treat the alternating element, irrelevantly, as a preverbal particle rather than a complementizer, use a theory where paths are uniform. They model the alternation in HPSG using the assumption that the morphological shape of the alternating element depends on whether its sister has an empty or a non-empty SLASH value.[2]

By contrast, the analyses of the same alternation that McCloskey has given over the years (with the exception of McCloskey, 1979) treat the alternation in terms of a punctuational model, in which the shape of the complementizer depends on a local relation with the moving element at various stages of the derivation. The moving element itself 'leapfrogs', leaving many nodes along the path completely untouched.

Finally, we can give a uniform non-local account of the alternation. We could assume the following realization rule for the complementizer in Irish.[3]

(5) a.   Realize an instance of the complementizer C^0 as *aL* (leniting) if there is a movement chain in which the head c-commands C^0 and C^0 c-commands the foot. Otherwise

   b.   realize an instance of the complementizer C^0 as *aN* (nasalizing) if it is locally c-commanded (Spec-Head) by an operator. Otherwise

---

[1]   Abels, 2003c calls theories where the nodes affected by movement are very close together *quasi uniform*. The reason for this terminological move was the assumption that it would be empirically very difficult to distinguish quasi uniform theories from uniform theories, while it seemed at the time easier to distinguish punctuated theories with wide gaps between the affected nodes from the other two types. This assumption was probably wrong.

   We might still end up with a category of quasi-uniform theories. For example Lechner, to appear proposes that every instance of external merge and most (see Lechner's paper for details) instances of internal merge trigger displacement, leading to a theory where there can be several intermediate landing sites within one and the same maximal projection. Still, not every node is affected identically.

[2]   See also Adger and Ramchand, 2005 for an approach without intermediate traces.

[3]   There might be an indirect argument here against a non-local treatment. The rules (5a) and (5b) are not ordered by the elsewhere principle unless "c-commands" is replaced by "locally c-commands" in the formulation of the first condition.

c.   realize an instance of the complementizer C^0 as *go*.

The Irish data therefore do not provide conclusive evidence one way or another.

The existence of reconstruction to positions along the path of movement is often taken as strong evidence for punctuational theories of movement. However, considerations similar to those just rehearsed for the Irish complementizer alternation make even fairly complex arguments demonstrating the existence of reconstruction sites silent on the issue of punctuated versus uniform movement paths; thus, while (6) argues for the existence of a reconstruction site for the topicalized noun phrase in between the position of the subject and the object of *ask*, it does not bear on the question whether all nodes between the subject and object of *ask* can serve as reconstruction sites or just some.

(6)   English   Lebeaux, 1991, see also Fox, 2000, pp. 10–11
  a.   [The papers that he$_1$ wrote for Ms. Brown$_2$] every student$_1$ [$_{VP}$ t' asked her$_2$ to grade t]
  b.   *[The papers that he$_1$ wrote for Ms. Brown$_2$] she$_2$ [t' asked every student$_1$ to revise t]

The aim of this chapter is to improve on this unsatisfactory state of affairs.

The chapter has three further sections. In section 2.2 I argue that movement paths are punctuated. In subsection 2.2.1, I discuss the shape that a true argument for he punctuated path hypothesis would have to take. In section 2.2.2, I investigate whether the argument in Abels, 2003c for the punctuated path hypothesis is compelling, reaching a negative conclusion. In section 2.2.3, I offer a set of data from Norwegian as empirical support in favor of punctuated movement paths. Section 2.2.4 discusses the syntax of the ellipsis of modal complements in Dutch, based on Aelbrecht, 2008, as further evidence. Section 2.2.5 discusses evidence from parasitic gaps and finally 2.2.6 provides a short survey of other configurations that would be involved in constructing prima facie arguments for the punctuated path hypothesis, but for which relevant data has not been investigated yet. The tentative conclusion is that movement paths are indeed punctuated. We can then ask where the intermediate landing sites of movement are. In the clausal domain there is good evidence that there is an intermediate landing site at the periphery of the traditional VP and in the periphery of the clause itself. This state of affairs is as predicted by the models of Chomsky, 1986 and Chomsky, 2000. Evidence will be reviewed in section 2.3. Section 2.4 reflects on the shape of an explanatory analysis of the facts.

2.2 Are movement paths punctuated or uniform?

2.2.1 What constitutes a valid argument for punctuated paths?

The putative arguments for the punctuated nature of movement paths from the previous section can all be construed as arguments from reconstruction: reconstruction for (local) agreement in the case of the Irish complementizer alternation and reconstruction for binding and scope in the case of topicalization. What these arguments seem to show is that some nodes along the path of movement are affected because they act as reconstruction sites. Such arguments do not bear on the question of the punctuated nature of paths, since they are fully compatible with a theory where all nodes along the path serve as reconstruction sites and, hence, are all affected.

To give a true argument for the punctuated nature of paths, we therefore need to show that some nodes along the path are *un*affected by movement while others are affected. As noted for example in Abels, 2003c and Boeckx, 2008, the literature contains little if any convincing empirical evidence for the absence of reconstruction to a particular position. The situation is complicated by the fact that even the lack of reconstruction (construed in the broadest sense) to a particular position is not direct evidence for the punctuated nature of paths; a node might have been affected by movement, yet, for independent reasons, we might be unable to show this. Boeckx (2008, p. 58) expresses this clearly at the end of the following quotation (see also Boeckx and Grohmann (2007, fn. 5)):

> "Whereas the copy theory of movement readily accounts for reconstruction by involving the interpretation of unpronounced copies, we cannot conclude from this that if no reconstruction effect is found, no copy is available at the relevant site. All we can conclude from the absence of reconstruction is either that there is no copy present, or that a copy was created, but for some (perhaps interpretive) reason cannot be interpreted in the relevant position."

A well-known case where reconstruction is blocked is provided by the readings that quantified arguments get when they are extracted from a weak island (for related discussion see also Bianchi and Zamparelli, 2004; Rizzi, 2001b and the references cited there). Consider example (7). There is no reconstruction of the restriction of the Wh-phrase into the weak island in (7b) (Cinque, 1990a; Cresti, 1995; Frampton, 1999; Longobardi, 1991), hence, only a *de re* reading of the Wh-moved NP is available. This could be taken to indicate that there is no copy of the Wh-phrase inside of the weak island. This conclusion would be rash, however—and a different explanation for the lack of reconstruction has to be sought—since there is reconstruction into the island for other properties such as binding (Cinque, 1990a; Starke, 2001).

(7)   English

    a.   How many people do you think that John invited?

    b.   How many people do you wonder whether to invite?

What is striking about this case and others like it is that while reconstructive behavior is not uniform along the entire length of the path, it is monotonic: for some reconstructive property, the path is cut into two contiguous bits one of which allows and the other one of which disallows reconstruction.

Let us make a terminological distinction between uniform, (non-uniform) monotonic, and punctuated reconstruction patterns.

Uniform reconstruction patterns are those where no two points along a path can be distinguished by their reconstructive behavior, that is, either reconstruction is possible to every point along the path or to none. In figure 2.1, a uniform reconstruction pattern would correspond to a situation where either reconstruction is possible at all points along the path between XP and its trace, that is, a situation in which reconstruction to all of α, β, γ, and γ is possible, or else where no reconstruction is possible at all, that is, none of α–γ are available for reconstruction.

On the other hand, non-uniform monotonic patterns are those where the path can be divided into two contiguous bits one of which allows and the other one of which disallows reconstruction. In figure 2.1, this would be the case if reconstruction was available to α and β but not to γ and γ. The weak-island extraction facts are a case of the monotonic sort, where reconstruction of the nominal restriction is possible above the island-inducing element but not below it.[4]

A punctuated reconstruction pattern is one where there are sites for reconstruction both above and below sites that do not allow reconstruction. In figure 2.1, we would speak of a punctuated reconstructive pattern if α and γ were possible reconstruction sites while β and γ were not, if reconstruction sites alternated with non-reconstruction sites, etc.

Different theories of movement give rise to different expectations regarding reconstructive patterns. Uniform theories of movement predict uniform reconstructive patterns and need to invoke additional assumptions to handle non-uniform monotonic and punctuated reconstructive patterns. Theories of movement that predict punctuated movement paths on the other hand give rise to the expectation that we should find punctuated reconstructive patterns. They need additional assumptions to deal with non-uniform monotonic and uniform patterns.

Therefore, if a punctuated reconstructive pattern can be found, this provides a prima facie argument for a punctuated theory of movement paths. Such an argument will fall if an independent reason can be found why reconstruction

---

[4]   Notice that uniform reconstructive patterns are also monotonic, hence the modifier 'non-uniform.'

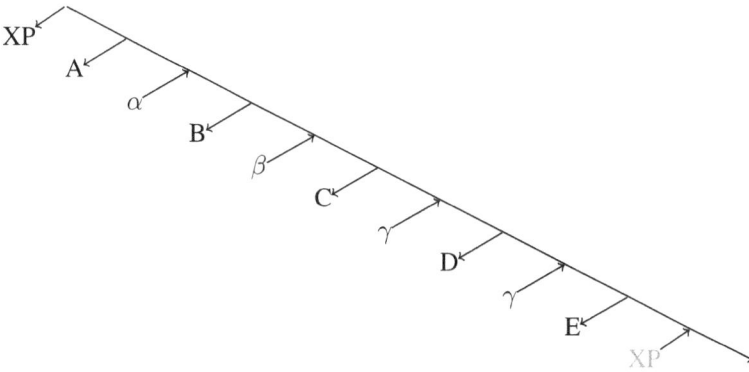

Figure 2.1: Path between XP and XP with four distinct points along the path, α–γ

to particular points along the path is blocked (the second disjunct in the quote from Boeckx above) or if reconstructive behavior for different properties does not align, that is, if a position is not a scope reconstruction site but it is a binding reconstruction site, etc.

These matters have not been investigated in sufficient detail. Below I discuss and reject an argument given in Abels, 2003c to support the assumption that movement paths are punctuated. I then discuss different data from Norwegian, English, and Dutch that suggest that movement paths are punctuated in those languages. Together, these data present a prima facie argument for the punctuated nature of movement paths.

2.2.2 Proposed evidence for punctuated paths (Abels 2003c)

Let us start by looking at a case involving binding condition A. The locality inherent in Principle A of the binding theory allows us to probe for lack of intermediate landing sites. Given that, in a language like English, binding condition A roughly requires the antecedent and the anaphor to be clausemates, binding condition A is a relatively coarse measure of the absence/presence of intermediate landing sites.

The relevant structure is schematized below in figure 2.2. In the structure there is an anaphor contained in a moving phrase, XP. Under the punctuated path hypothesis, there would be various copies of XP, concretely in figure 2.2 there are three. For each of the copies there is a certain local domain within which the anaphor has to be bound if that copy is the one relevant to binding.

This is schematized in figure 2.2 by the nodes labeled 'DomainP' which are co-superscripted with the copy for which they constitute the binding domain. Finally, there are various potential antecedents for the anaphor.

For any given copy, the closest dominating DomainP indicates the maximal possible binding domain of the anaphor contained in the moving constituent. Given this structure, what we should test is whether there are DPs that cannot antecede the anaphor despite the fact that they c-command one or more copies of it, simply because these DPs are not sufficiently local to any of the intermediate copies. This is again illustrated in figure 2.2. Pit-stop binding by Antecedent$_3$ and Antecedent$_1$ ought to be possible, while the same should not be true for Antecedent$_2$.

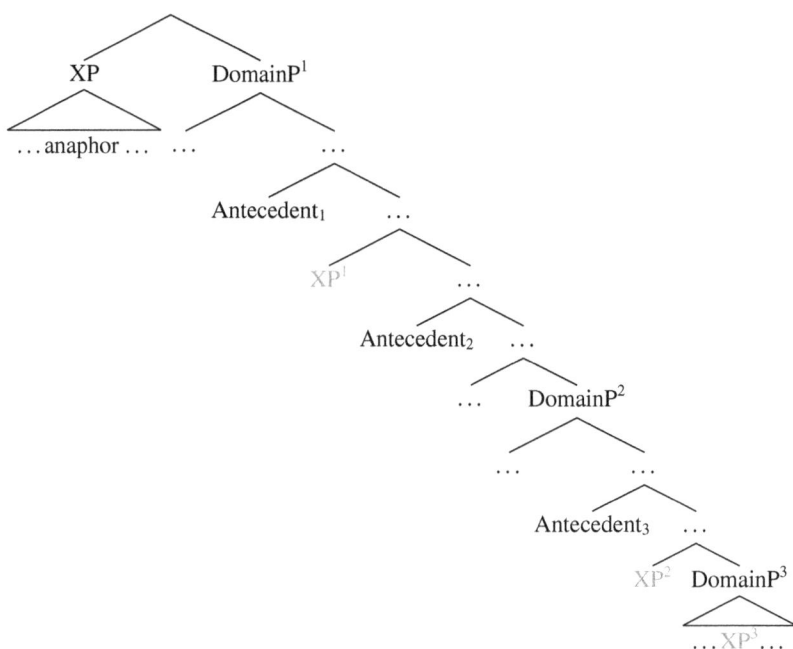

Figure 2.2: Schematic representation of the argument in Abels, 2003c

Abels, 2003c attempts an argument of this shape.

Anaphors may be bound at various points along the movement path (see Barss 1986), as shown in (8). In (8a), the anaphor *himself* within the Wh-phrase is bound by *John* in its surface position. In (8b), *herself* is bound in the base position of the Wh-phrase. In (8c), *himself* is bound by *John* in some intermediate position of the Wh-phrase.

(8)   English
    a.   John$_i$ wonders which pictures of himself$_i$ Mary likes.
    b.   John wonders which pictures of herself$_i$ Mary$_i$ likes.
    c.   Which pictures of himself$_i$ does Jane believe (that) John$_i$ thinks (that) she likes?

As explained in the previous subsection, such examples do not tell us anything about whether paths are uniform or punctuated. A sentence like (8c) can be analyzed in conformity with both hypotheses.

(9)   a.   **Uniform path:**
    [which picture of himself]$_i$ [... John ... [$_{vP}$ t$_i$ v^o [$_{VP}$ t$_i$ thinks [$_{CP}$ t$_i$ that [$_{TP}$ t$_i$ Mary [...]]]]]]
    b.   **Punctuated path:**
    [which picture of himself]$_i$ [... John ... [$_{vP}$ t$_i$ v^o [$_{VP}$ thinks [$_{CP}$ t$_i$ that [$_{TP}$ Mary [...]]]]]]

Crucially, though, Abels, 2003c provides a context in which intermediate binding of a moved anaphor is not possible. Consider the pair in (10). In (10a), the experiencer of *seem* can bind the anaphor in the moved Wh-phrase. In (10b), when *seem* is used as a raising verb, on the other hand, this is not possible.[5]

(10)   English
    a.   Which picture of himself$_i$ did it seem to John$_i$ that Mary liked?
    b.   *Which picture of himself$_i$ did Mary seem to John$_i$ to like?

In Abels (2003c) I claimed that in (10a) there is a copy of the Wh-phrase in the embedded Spec,CP and this copy is local enough for *John* to bind the anaphor. This is shown in (11).

(11)   [Which picture of himself]$_i$ it [$_{VP^1}$ seem [$_{VP^2}$ to John t$_{seem}$ [$_{CP}$ t$_i$ that [$_{TP}$ Mary [$_{VP^3}$ t$_i$ liked t$_i$]]]]]

In (10b) on the other hand, no such copy is available, as seen in (12). The raising infinitive is taken to be a TP rather than a CP, and, following Chomsky, 1986, adjunction to TP is not allowed. Furthermore, the Wh-phrase could not have moved through Spec,TP, as a copy of *Mary* occupies this position.

(12)   [Which picture of himself]$_i$ Mary [$_{VP^1}$ seem [$_{VP^2}$ to John t$_{seem}$ [$_{TP}$ t$_{Mary}$ to [$_{VP^3}$ t$_i$ like t$_i$]]]]

---

[5] Since I ultimately reject the argument based on anaphors in *picture*-NP contexts, I will simply assume here that they are subject to Principle A of the binding theory rather than being logophoric (Pollard and Sag, 1994; Reinhart and Reuland, 1993; Runner, Sussman, and Tanenhaus, 2002).

As we just saw, Abels takes the contrast in (10) as evidence for punctuated paths and constructs his analysis accordingly: the moving element makes intermediate stops only in certain positions, namely in the embedded CP but not in the TP.

I am aware of two potential challenges to this argument. Gereon Müller makes the following observation concerning the two crucial examples: While in (10a) only a single phrase, the Wh-phrase, is moving, there are two moving phrases in (10b). In (10b), the Wh-phrase and the raising subject move along overlapping paths. This raises the possibility that there *is* an intermediate landing site both for the Wh-phrase and the subject above the embedded Spec,TP position but below the experiencer, as schematized in (13).

(13)   [Which picture of himself]$_i$ Mary [$_{VP1}$ seem [$_{VP2}$ to John [t$_{Mary}$ [t$_i$ [t$_{seem}$ [$_{TP}$ t$_{Mary}$ to [$_{VP3}$ t$_i$ like t$_i$]]]]

Notice that all traces of the Wh-phrase below the experiencer in (13) are c-commanded by a trace of the subject below the experiencer. Therefore, if the trace of the subject can be construed as an intervener for the purposes of anaphoric binding, the pattern in (10b) receives a different explanation. Under Müller's assumption, the raised subject would always be the relevant binder for the anaphor in (10b)/(13). In (10a) by contrast, there is an intermediate position where the experiencer is the closest potential binder for the anaphor, since the embedded subject does not raise. Hence, Müller argues, the contrast between (10a) and (10b) does not provide evidence for the punctuated nature of movement paths.

This objection, of course, is only as strong as the binding theoretic assumption that it crucially rests upon, namely, that anaphors in English can only be bound by the closest c-commanding antecedent. This assumption is problematic, as (14) illustrates.

(14)   English
    a.   Mary explained the man to himself.
    b.   Mary explained the man to herself.

As is well-known, the DP object in such examples c-commands into the PP, (14a). However, and this undermines the strength of the objection, in example (14b) the subject can antecede the anaphor despite the fact that it is not the closest potential c-commanding antecedent, which, just as in (14a), is the object.[6]

---

[6]   There might be ways of rescuing the closest c-command theory of anaphor binding; thus, Lechner, to appear, for unrelated reasons, posits an intermediate structure where the subject locally c-commands the second object in a double-object structure. If Lechner's theory is correct and if binding could be read off this structure, then the closest c-command approach to anaphor binding might be workable for English after all.

A second, more damaging problem for the argument is pointed out by Boeckx 2008; Boeckx and Grohmann 2007. If the contrast between (10a) and (10b) were due only to the presence versus absence of a CP below *John*, then we would expect reconstruction for anaphor binding to be possible past the experiencer and into a more deeply embedded intermediate position. This would be the hallmark of a truly punctuated pattern of binding reconstruction. The expectation then is that all examples in (15) should be fine. However, (15c) is ungrammatical. It seems that reconstruction of the moved Wh-phrase to an intermediate landing site below the experiencer in a raising construction is blocked in general.

(15)   English
    a.   Which picture of himself$_i$ did Mary tell John$_i$ that she liked?
    b.   Which picture of himself$_i$ does it seem to Jane that Mary told John$_i$ that she liked?
    c.   *Which picture of himself$_i$ does Mary seem to Jane to have told John$_i$ that she liked?

In the terminology of the previous section, we are dealing with a monotonic reconstruction pattern. We argued that non-uniform monotonic patterns like this one (or the reconstruction of the nominal restriction into a weak island discussed above) require additional assumptions no matter what we assume about the punctuated or uniform movement paths and do not, therefore, provide a direct argument for or against punctuation.[7]

Thus, I agree with Boeckx that when the data in (15) are taken into account, the contrast between (10a) and (10b) does not constitute an argument for punctuated paths. In the next subsections, some facts are presented that do argue for punctuated paths. The first set are reconstruction data from Norwegian (see also Bentzen 2007).

2.2.3   Reconstruction in Norwegian

This section looks at the interaction of scope and variable binding as a source of information about the absence of sites for intermediate reconstruction. The idea

---

On the other hand one might accept as fact that the closest c-command theory of anaphor binding is wrong but assume that binding domains are upward bounded by subjects and that intermediate traces of subjects count as subjects. Under this latter approach (suggested by Winnie Lechner, pers. comm.) Müller's objection would again stand.

I will not pursue these issues here, simply because there is a second, stronger objection to Abels's argument, to which I now turn.

[7] I leave an investigation of what exactly is going on in these examples for future research.

is the following: Suppose a moved quantifier can take either wide or narrow scope with respect to another scope-bearing element. If the quantifier needs to take scope below the other scope-bearing element and simultaneously bind into an even lower XP, this will only be possible if there is a reconstruction site in between the two but not if there is no such reconstruction site between them. The situation is illustrated in Figures 2.3 and 2.4, where the trace (QP) between the scope-bearing element and XP in figure 2.3 marks the availability of a reconstruction site while its absence in Figure 2.4 indicates the absence of such a site. Both figures are concrete instantiations of the abstract schema in the earlier figure 2.1. In figure 2.3 there are reconstruction sites everywhere, while in figure 2.4, a reconstruction site is missing between the scope-bearing element and XP.

The expectations created by the two structures are quite different: given that scope reconstruction of QP is possible below the scope-bearing element by assumption, the structure in Figure 2.3 gives rise to the expectation that narrow scope of QP should be able to go hand in hand with binding into XP; the structure in Figure 2.4 gives rise to the expectation that low scope of QP and binding into XP cannot happen simultaneously.

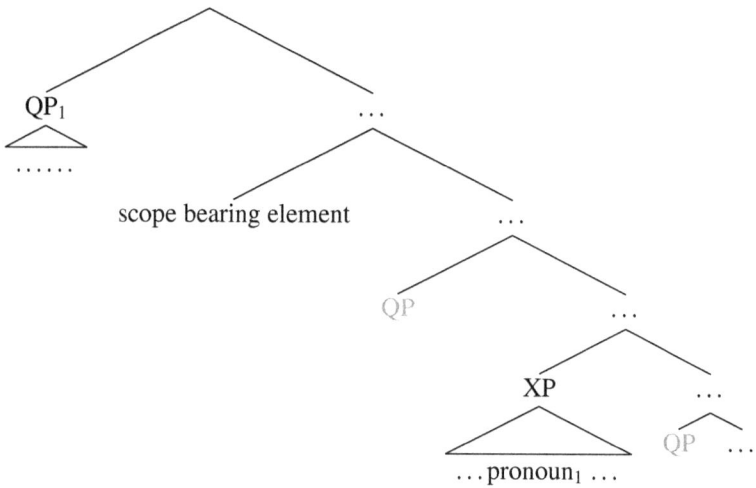

Figure 2.3: Low scope and simultaneous high binding possible with intermediate trace

This logic will now be applied to data from Norwegian, and, as we will see, the observations provide support for the punctuated nature of movement paths.

First consider example (16). There are two readings for this example, one in which the quantified DP *some girls* has surface wide-scope over the adverb

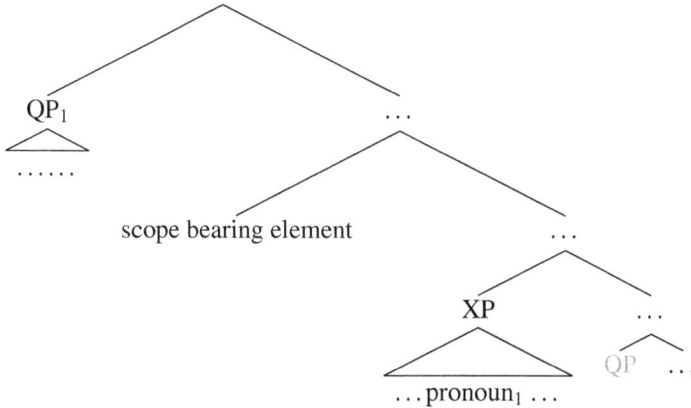

Figure 2.4: Low scope and simultaneous high binding impossible without intermediate trace

probably, yielding the reading that *some girls are probably such that they will come to the party*. Alternatively, the quantified DP may be reconstructed into a position between *probably* and *come* (indicated by **t** in the gloss), yielding the reading that *it is probable that some girls are such that they will come to the party*.

(16)   Norwegian

Noen jenter vil   sannsynligvis   komme på festen.
some girls   will probably   **t** come   on party.the
Some girls will probably come to the party.

In (16) it is not clear exactly where the reconstruction site is located; it could either be the DP's base position (presumably in Spec,vP), or some intermediate position. Thus, to probe whether or not an intermediate reconstruction site is indeed available, we need to construct a context in which reconstruction into the base position can be excluded semantically. (17) provides exactly such a context.

(17)   Norwegian

. . . at   noen gutter sannsynligvis   må   ha   dratt til Roma.
. . . that some boys   probably   **t′** must have **t** gone to Rome
. . . that some boys probably must have gone to Rome.

Example (17) is three-ways ambiguous. The quantified DP *some boys* may get a surface wide-scope reading: *Some boys are such that they probably must have gone to Rome*. A second reading is possible if the DP reconstructs into a position between the adverb *probably* and the modal *must*. This yields the reading that *it is probable that some boys are such that they must have gone to Rome*. In the third reading, then, the DP reconstructs below *must*, yielding the reading that *it is probable that it must be the case that some boys have gone to Rome*.

Of course, what is of interest is the availability of the intermediate reading in (17), associated with the copy t'. The availability of the intermediate reading, or its absence, provides information about the availability (or lack thereof) of an intermediate site for scope reconstruction of the moved subject. This is the first ingredient in the crucial example that follows.[8]

The second ingredient involves variable binding. Since binding requires scope, we can force the subject to take scope at least as high as some other phrase, by forcing the subject to bind into that other phrase. The relevant phrase is the PP *på eget initiativ*—'on their own initiative' in (18).

(18)   Norwegian

Noen jenter vil   sannsynligvis   på eget initiativ   komme på
some girls   will probably   *t' on own initiative *t come   on
festen.
party.the
Some girls will probably on their own initiative come to the party.

In (18) reconstruction into the DP's base position is blocked for reasons of binding. This is indicated by the asterisk on t; the DP needs to bind the reflexive *own* inside the adverb *on their own initiative*. If paths were uniform, it should still be possible to reconstruct the subject to a position in between *sannsynligvis* and *på eget initiativ*. However, it turns out that only a wide-scope reading of the DP is available in (18), suggesting that there is no reconstruction site for the subject in between *sannsynligvis* and *på eget initiativ*. The example thus shows that there is no intermediate reconstruction site for the subject in the position of t', and, in conjunction with the observation that intermediate reconstruction is available in (17), this constitutes support for the assumption that paths are punctuated. Note that the observation in these two clauses cannot be accounted for by simply assuming monotonic (non-uniform) paths.

The starred trace t is there, but cannot be used for reasons of binding, while the starred trace t' must be assumed to be absent.

A possibly even more telling contrast is that between (17) and (19). The examples form a minimal pair; the only difference is the addition of *mot sin*

---

[8]   A potential challenge to this argument might come from the treatment of scope phenomena in the absence of syntactic scope by way of quantification over semantic objects of higher types (see Chierchia, 1993; Engdahl, 1980, 1986; Kratzer, 1998; Sauerland, 1998, 2004 and in particular the application of these ideas to scopal interactions between quantifiers and modals in Abels and Martí, 2010).

vilje—'against his own will' to the right of *sannsynligvis* in (19).

(19)   Norwegian

    ... at   noen gutter sannsynligvis **t″** mot   sin   vilje **t′** må
    ... that some boys   probably   against REFL will   must
    ha   **t** dratt til Roma.
    have   gone to Rome
    ...that some boys probably must have gone to Rome against their will.

Reconstruction of the subject to a position below the added PP is impossible, since this would leave the possessive anaphor unbound. This explains why reconstruction to **t** is impossible. Structurally, both t' and t'' in (19) are in a position corresponding to t' in (17). However, we know that reconstruction to t' is impossible in (19) for binding reasons—a restriction not found in (17). If there were an intermediate landing site in the position of t'', (19) should still be ambiguous, though, between a reading where the subject takes scope over *sannsynligvis* and a reading where *sannsynligivs* takes scope over the subject. However, the example is unambiguous; only the wide-scope reading for the subject is available. This suggests, again, that there is no trace in the position of t'', which in turn suggests—together with the three way ambiguity of (17)—that paths are punctuated. There is no reconstruction site at t''; there are reconstruction sites at t' and t, but they are useless in (19) because of binding. These Norwegian constructions constitute the appropriate kind of test case for the availability of intermediate reconstruction sites. The data illustrated here provide real support for the claim that movement paths are punctuated rather than uniform.

2.2.4   Evidence from ellipsis

A different line of argumentation for the punctuated nature of movement paths comes from Aelbrecht, 2010; Baltin, 2010. Both authors are concerned with patterns where phrases are missing and typical diagnostics for the presence of covert syntactic structure yield contradictory results. Baltin discusses properties of British English *do* in constructions like (20a) (Algeo, 2006; Baker, 1984; Baltin, 2007; Haddican, 2007; Huddleston and Pullum, 2002; Joos, 1964; Miller, 2000, 2002; Pullum and Wilson, 1977; Thoms, to appear); Aelbrecht's focus are the properties of null complements of modals in Dutch, (21). The properties of (20a) differ in interesting ways from those of VP ellipsis, (20b), and *do it* anaphora, (20c).

(20)   English
    a.   John will visit Sally, and Fred will do, too.
    b.   John will visit Sally, and Fred will, too.

    c.   John will visit Sally, and Fred will do it, too.

(21)   Dutch

    Wie wast   ere   vanavond af? B: Ik kan niet
    Who washes there tonight   off? B: I can not
    Who is doing the dishes tonight? – I can't.

As is well known, VP ellipsis differs from *do it* anaphora in a number of syntactic and semantic respects. For example, VP ellipsis is compatible with a construal inside of the missing verbal constituent of topics, Wh-traces (see Shuyler, 2002, for important discussion), traces of comparative operators, as well as traces of subjects in clauses with passivized, unaccusative, and raising predicates. *Do it* anaphora are incompatible with all of the above:[9]

(22)   English

    a.   Hazelnuts, I like. Peanuts, I don't (*do it)
    b.   I know who John will visit but I don't know who he won't (*do it).
    c.   I have read more books than Joe has (*done it)
    d.   John might be visited by Sally, and Fred might be (*done it), too.
    e.   John might die, and Fred might (*do it), too.
    f.   John might seem to enjoy it, and Fred might (*do it), too.

Generative accounts usually treat these facts by assuming that the missing verbal constituent in VP ellipsis has internal syntactic structure while the nominal pro-form *it* of *do it* anaphora lacks such structure (see Johnson, 2001, for discussion). This difference can then be used to account for the diverging behavior seen in (22).

Dutch modal complement ellipsis and British English *do* do not fit neatly into this dichotomy. Both constructions show some evidence for internal structure at the ellipsis site but do not allow the full range of extractions from the missing constituent that we find with English VP ellipsis. Both Baltin and Aelbrecht resolve the apparent paradox by assuming analyses that posit an unpronounced verbal constituent at the ellipsis site. In explaining the restrictions on extraction from the ellipsis site, both make crucial use of the assumption that movement paths are punctuated.

Below, I give a brief summary of the core generalizations that Aelbrecht's analysis is intended to capture and then outline of the logic of her account. Before doing so, however, I briefly explain why I set aside British English *do*. Baltin's account and the argument it makes for punctuated paths is built on the generalization that $\overline{\text{A}}$-movement cannot escape from the domain of British English *do*. There are reasons to think that this generalization is incorrect. While it

---

[9]   Toosarvandani, 2009 argues that Farsi has a similar ellipsis process.

seems to be true that Wh-movement is blocked from the domain of British English *do*, other $\overline{\text{A}}$-extractions are possible. Thus, we find Wh-extraction in (23a) contrasting with extraction of a comparative operator, (23b),[10] relative clause formation, (23c),[11] topicalization, (23d), and quantifier raising, (23e–f).[12]

(23) British English
    a.   *Although I don't know who Fred will visit, I do know who John will do.
    b.   He ate more than he should have done. Algeo, 2006; Baker, 1984; Huddleston and Pullum, 2002; Miller, 2002
    c.   A man who steals does not incur the same measure of public reprobation which he would have done in the past.
                                         Algeo, 2006; Baker, 1984
    d.   ?Hazelnuts, he won't eat, but Almonds he might do.
                  Haddican, 2007 gives a more strongly deviant judgment
    e.   Some man must read every book and some woman must do, too.
         $\exists > \forall, \forall > \exists$ G. Ramchand and G. Thoms, pers. comm.
    f.   Rab won't finish more than two thirds of the exam. Morag won't do either.
         $\neg > 2/3+, 2/3+ > \neg$ Thoms, 2011

It is hard to see how to accommodate these examples while maintaining Baltin's generalization or his account. Thoms's 2011 suggestion, according to which the domain of British English *do* allows extraction but not reconstruction into it, seems closer to the mark. As supporting evidence, consider the following. Bianchi, 2004 argues that reconstruction is obligatory in amount relatives, free relatives, and relatives with idiomatic heads. Thoms's claim that reconstruction into the domain of British English *do* is blocked therefore predicts that these types of relative clause should not be compatible with British English *do*. This expectation appears to be met, as (24) shows.

(24) British English

---

[10] Examples like these are also acceptable in standard American English, which otherwise does not allow British English *do*. The example might therefore represent a different construction and hence be irrelevant to the discussion.

[11] British English *do* occurs with relative clause formation particularly easily in antecedent-contained deletion contexts. I do not know why this is so.

[12] Example (23e) contrasts minimally with the following from Baltin, 2007, 2010:

    (i)   British English
          Some man will read every book, and some woman will do, too.

For reasons I don't understand, Baltin's example appears only to have the surface scope reading.

a. Amount relative
   (i)   I put in my pocket all the money I could.   VP ellipsis
   (ii) ??I put in my pocket all the money I could do. British English
      do

b. Free relative
   (i)   He buys what he can.   VP ellipsis
   (ii) *He buys what he can do.   British English *do*

c. Idiomatic head
   (i)   It's easy to spend your time regretting that you haven't taken advantage of every opportunity that you should have. VP ellipsis
   (ii) ??It's easy to spend your time regretting that you haven't taken advantage of every opportunity that you should have done. British English *do*

British English *do* seems to allow quite a broad range of extraction, which makes it unsuitable for the argument that I make in this section. I therefore concentrate on Dutch modal complement ellipsis from here on; it allows a much more narrowly circumscribed range of extraction.

Aelbrecht, 2010 argues that those modals that allow their complements to be elided are raising verbs in the language. The argument in favor of analyzing the relevant modals as raising predicates comes from truth conditional equivalence between active and passive complements, the compatibility with impersonal passives, and the possibility of occurring with weather-*it* as the subject (the reader is referred to Aelbrecht, 2010, sect. 2.1.2 for the relevant data). Crucially, modal complement ellipsis is compatible not only with transitive and unergative verbs but also with passive and unaccusative predicates. This is shown in (25).

(25)   Dutch   Aelbrecht, 2010, 60–61 ex. 78

a. Die broek MOET nog niet gewassen worden, maar hij MAG
those pants must still not washed become but he may
al   wel.
already PRT
Those pants don't have to be washed yet, but they can be.

b. Erik is al   langsgekomen, maar Jenneke moet nog
Erik is already by.passed   but Jenneke must still
Erik has already passed by, but Jenneke still has to.

Such data strongly suggest that there is unpronounced structure at the ellipsis site. Importantly, the arguments for treating the modal verbs involved as raising predicates remain valid in examples with modal complement ellipsis, as the compatibility of impersonal passives and *weather* verbs with modal complement ellipsis in (26) indicates.[13]

(26)   Dutch   Lobke Aelbrecht, pers. comm.

    a.   A: Denk je   dat het gaat   regenen?
                 think you that it   going.to rain
                 Do you think that it is going to rain?
       B: Het moet (regenen)!
                It   must rain
                It must (rain)!
    b.   Er   kan gedanst worden, maar er   moet niet.
         There can danced become, but   there must not
         Roughly: Dancing is permitted but not required

We therefore have evidence for A-movement from the domain of modal complement ellipsis. On the other hand, there is also evidence that not all types of movement can escape the elliptical domain. Aelbrecht claims, for example, that scrambling from the elliptical domain is ruled out:

(27)   Dutch   Aelbrecht, 2010, 65 ex. 84a–b

    a.   Ik WIL je   wel helpen, maar ik KAN (*je) niet.
         I want you PRT help   but   I can   you not
    b.   Ik WIL je   wel helpen, maar ik KAN je   niet helpen.
         I want you PRT help   but   I can you not help
         I *want* to help you, but I *can't* help you.

The examples in (27) illustrate Aelbrecht's point for pronominal objects, those in (28)—for focused objects.

(28)   Dutch   Aelbrecht, 2010, 65 ex. 86a–b

    a.   *Ik kan MAX wel helpen, maar ik kan ADAM niet.
         I can Max PRT help,   but I can Adam not
    b.   Ik kan MAX wel helpen, maar ik kan ADAM niet helpen.
         I can Max PRT help,   but I can Adam not help
         I can help *Max*, but I can't help *Adam*.

Similarly, topicalization from the domain of modal complement ellipsis is also ruled out:

(29)   Dutch   Aelbrecht, 2010, 72 ex. 95a

    Ik kan de boodschappen doen, maar de afwas kan ik niet *(doen).
    I can the shopping   do   but   the dishes can i not   do
    I can do the shopping, but the dishes, I can't.

---

[13] Ad Neeleman and Hans van de Koot (pers. comm.) reject (26), suggesting that for them, modal complement ellipsis is built around a control construal of the modal.

34

Finally, on the basis of (30) Aelbrecht claims that Wh-extraction from the domain of modal complement ellipsis is ruled out.

(30)   Dutch

    ?*Ik weet niet wie Kaat WOU   uitnodigen, maar ik weet wel   wie
    I know not who Kaat wanted invite,   but I do know who
    ze MOEST *(uitnodigen).
    she had.to invite
    I don't know who Kaat wanted to invited, but I do know who she had to.

The analytical challenge is how to capture the ellipsis site's selective transparency for extraction. The issue is not limited to Dutch. German has a very similar modal complement ellipsis construction. Houser, Mikkelsen, and Toosarvandani, 2007 describe a similar state of affairs for Danish, where the verb phrase is not elided but replaced by a nominal pro-form (see also Bentzen, Merchant, and Svenonius, 2012 for Norwegian). The Danish facts are illustrated in (31).

(31)   Danish   Houser, Mikkelsen, and Toosarvandani, 2007

    Han siger han kan hækle, men selvfølgelig kan han ikke det.
    he says he can crochet but of.course can he not that
    He says he can crochet, but of course he can't.

According to Houser, Mikkelsen, and Toosarvandani verb phrase pronominalization supports A-movement with passive, unaccusative, and raising verbs from the domain of the missing VP. Wh-movement on the other hand is blocked, (32).[14]

(32)   Danish   Houser, Mikkelsen, and Toosarvandani, 2007

    *Jeg ved hvem Susan kildede, men jeg ved ikke hvem Palle gjorde
    I know who Susan tickled but I know not who Palle did
    det.
    that
    intended: I know who Susan tickled, but I don't know who Palle did.

---

[14] To accommodate the A-movement facts and a number of other observations not discussed here, Houser, Mikkelsen, and Toosarvandani, 2007 assume that *det* is a surface anaphor standing in for a syntactically present verb phrase (vP). The difference between A-movement and Ā-movement is captured by Houser, Mikkelsen, and Toosarvandani's account in terms of locality and without appealing to punctuated paths. After explaining Aelbrecht's account of modal complement ellipsis, I discuss Houser, Mikkelsen, and Toosarvandani's solution and provide some reasons to be skeptical about it.

Returning to Dutch modal complement ellipsis, Aelbrecht claims that it allows A-movement but blocks $\overline{\text{A}}$-movement from the elliptical domain. I should point out that the situation here is a little less than clear-cut. There are cases where an operator can be $\overline{\text{A}}$-extracted from the ellipsis site. Aelbrecht's discussion of antecedent-contained deletion, (33), is the prime example of this (Aelbrecht, 2010, pp. 137–142), though we will see below that comparative operators can escape the elliptical domain as well. Under antecedent-contained deletion, the relative operator escapes the domain of modal complement ellipsis, (33).

(33)   Dutch   Aelbrecht, 2010, 139 ex. 93b
    a.   Olaf heeft elk   boek gelezen dat hij moest.
          Olaf has   every book read   that he must.PST
          Olaf read every book he had to.
    b.   Olaf zal   uitnodigen wie hij mag.
          Olaf will invite   who he is.allowed
          Olaf will invite who he's allowed to.

Interestingly, when there is clear evidence for extraction of overt material from the ellipsis site, for example when a preposition is pied-piped to the beginning of the relative clause the examples degrade:

(34)   Dutch   Aelbrecht, pers. comm.
    ??/?*Hij praat met alle mensen met wie   hij kan.
          He talks with all people with whom he can
          He talks with everybody that he can

Comparative operators, which are null, can also be extracted from the elliptical domain:

(35)   Dutch   Aelbrecht, pers. comm.
    Hij moet meer (boeken) lezen dan hij kan.
    He must more (books)   read than he can
    He has to read more books than he can.

The examples of $\overline{\text{A}}$-extraction from the elliptical domain lend further support to the claim that there is normal if unpronounced syntactic structure at the ellipsis site. However, these examples are problematic for the generalization that all $\overline{\text{A}}$-movement is blocked from the domain of modal complement ellipsis. The contrast between (33) and (35) on the one hand and (34) on the other suggests that $\overline{\text{A}}$-extraction is licit only if the moving operator is null.[15]

---

[15] This claim requires an analysis of *wie*—'who' in (33b) is a complementizer agreeing in certain features with a null relative operator rather than the moved operator itself.

Despite the slight complication for Aelbrecht's original generalization, according to which A-extraction is possible from the ellipsis site in modal complement ellipsis while all $\overline{\text{A}}$-extraction is impossible, I now present Aelbrecht's own analysis and then make a preliminary suggestion how the problematic facts might be integrated into the account.

Aelbrecht's account of extraction from elliptical domains and, in particular, of the A-/$\overline{\text{A}}$-extraction asymmetry requires paths to be punctuated. She formulates her proposal in a derivational framework and assumes that ellipsis makes material inside of the elliptical constituent unavailable to syntactic manipulations. Whether a given element can be extracted from an ellipsis site depends on whether ellipsis happens before or after extraction. This is schematized in (36). In (36a), extraction of Y happens before ZP is elided and its contents made inaccessible to syntactic operations. In (36b) on the other hand, ZP is elided first, making Y inaccessible for further syntactic operations.

(36) a. Licit extraction from ellipsis site:
   (i) [X [$_{ZP}$ Y Z]]   movement of Y
   (ii) [Y [X [$_{ZP}$ Y Z]]]   ellipsis of ZP
   (iii) [Y [X $_{ZP}$ Y Z]]]
  b. Illicit extraction from ellipsis site:
   (i) [X [$_{ZP}$ Y Z]]   ellipsis of ZP
   (ii) [X $_{ZP}$ Y Z]]   movement of Y blocked
   (iii) *[Y [X $_{ZP}$ Y Z]]]

Notice that under such an approach, ellipsis cannot happen after syntactic structure building is complete. If it did, all instances of ellipsis would have to follow all instances of (overt) movement and a distinction between different kinds of overt movement could not be drawn. Indeed, Aelbrecht assumes that ellipsis is licensed by certain heads and happens as part of the set of operations triggered by those heads. Concretely, Aelbrecht claims that the kind of ellipsis that she studies is licensed only by modals. She further assumes that the complement of Dutch modals are TPs. Evidence for this assumption comes from that fact that modal complements allow independent temporal modification:

(37) Dutch   Aelbrecht, 2010, 33, ex. 33a
   Gisteren moest   ik nog volgende week optrede, en nu   zij de
   yesterday must.PST I   still next   week perform and now are the
   plannen alweer een week opgeschoven
   plans   again a   week delayed

The degraded status of (34), where the presence of the pied-piped preposition makes an analysis in terms of an overt operator unavoidable, lends support to this line of analysis.

Yesterday I still had to perform next week, and now the plans have been delayed by another week.

Since independent temporal modifiers but not lower modifiers such as manner adverbs may remain even when ellipsis happens, (38), Aelbrecht claims that what is elided is not literally the complement of the modal, which would be the TP, but the complement of T.[16]

(38)   Dutch   Aelbrecht, 2010, 74 ex. 99a, p. 75–76 ex. 100d

    a.   Gisteren moest   ik nog volgende week optreden en nu
        yesterday must.PST I   still next   week perform and now
        moet ik pas de week erna.
        must I   only the week there.after
        Yesterday I still had to perform next week, and now I only have to
        the week after that.

    b.   *Je   hoeft niet per se snel te schrijven; je   moet vooral
        you need not per se fast to write   you must most.of.all
        mooi.
        beautifully

The relevant structure for modal complement ellipsis can then be given as in figure 2.1.

The extraction asymmetry between A-movement, which is allowed from the ellipsis site, and $\overline{\text{A}}$-movement, which is disallowed can now be explained on the assumption that A-movement makes an intermediate stopover in Spec,TP but that there is no (intermdiate) $\overline{\text{A}}$-trace either within TP or within ModP. A-movement then instantiates (36a), while $\overline{\text{A}}$-movement instantiates (36b).

---

[16] The assumption that a head—here the modal—can license ellipsis of a phrase which is not its complement may be non-standard, but it is necessary (see for extensive discussion Aelbrecht, 2010). A simple way of making the argument comes from the following considerations. In English, VP ellipsis is not licensed by non-finite auxiliaries but only by (certain instances) of the tense head (and by negation). The first point is demonstrated by (ia), the second—by (ib). (ic) is the crucial example:

(i)   English
    a.   *I hadn't been thinking about it, but I recall Morgan having been.
    b.   I wasn't thinking about it, but Morgan was.
    c.   I hadn't been thinking about that. – Well, you should have been!

The ellipsis site is the complement of *been*, which was shown in (iia) not to be a licensor of ellipsis by itself; ellipsis in (iic) is licensed not by *been* but by the tense head. The conclusion seems unavoidable that the tense head may license ellipsis at a distance (under agreement in Aelbrecht's implementation).

```
              ModP
            /      \
        Mod          TP
        modal      /    \
               AdvP        TP
               time adverbial  /  \
                                  T'
                                /   \
                             T    ┌───────┐
                                  │  ...  │  → ellipsis
                                  └───────┘
```

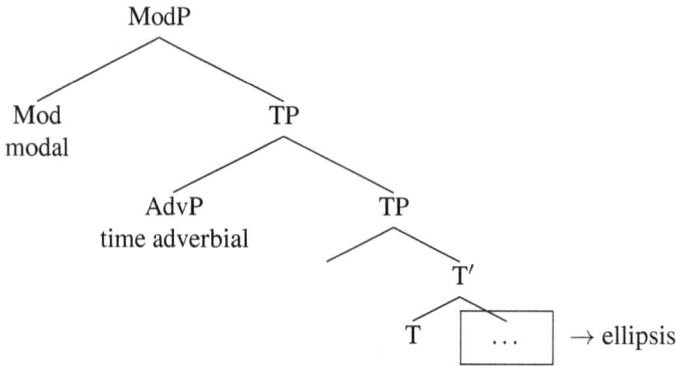

Table 2.1: Structure of Dutch modal complement ellipsis according to Aelbrecht, 2010, p. 93 ex. 13

The further asymmetry between $\overline{\text{A}}$-extraction of pronounced material versus null operators, (34)–(35) above, falls into place if we assume that ellipsis deletes phonological features of elements rather than rendering them altogether inaccessible for syntactic operations but that originally overt operators cannot be moved after deletion, because this would render them (locally) non-recoverable. (I must leave elaboration of this idea to a different occasion.)

Recall that English VP ellipsis allows both A-extraction and $\overline{\text{A}}$-extraction from the ellipsis site. To account for this, Aelbrecht, 2010, ch. 3 suggests that the licensing head of VP ellipsis is T, that the elided constituent is vP, and that VoiceP is a phase.[17] On these assumptions, the extraction facts follow directly.

The explanation runs as follows. Chomsky's phase impenetrability condition (discussed in detail below) requires any movement out of a given phase to pass through the phase's edge, where the edge is understood as all positions not c-commanded by the head of the phase. Long-distance movement is implemented by assuming that phases provide landing sites (and any triggers necessary) to enable movement through the edge of the phase. Given that ellipsis is triggered by T, both A- and $\overline{\text{A}}$-extraction to Spec,VoiceP happens before ellipsis. Both types of operation instantiate schema (36a) and are therefore licit.

---

[17] VoiceP as the phase replaces the more usual assumption of vP as a phase. See Aelbrecht, 2010 for justification. The account of extraction from the ellipsis site is unaffected by this choice. We could also make vP the phase and assume that VP ellipsis elides VP. I follow Aelbrecht's designation using vP and VoiceP here, though elsewhere in this book I follow common usage and call the phase projected above the verb phrase vP rather VoiceP. In other words, everywhere in this book, except here in the discussion of Aelbrecht's proposal, vP refers to the phase above the verb phrase whatever the exact other properties of v under this usage may be.

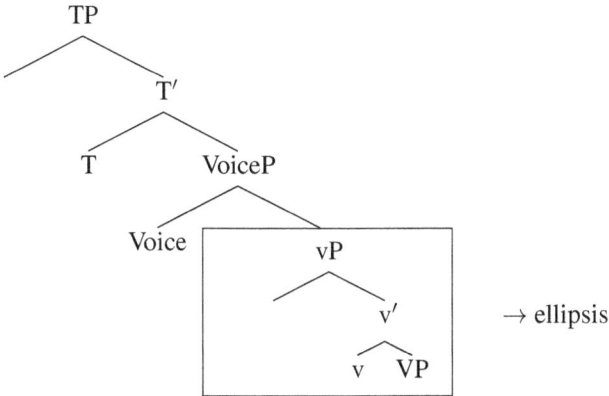

→ ellipsis

Table 2.2: Structure for English VP ellipsis

Although it should be clear from the discussion so far that and how Aelbrecht's account relies on the assumption that movement paths are punctuated, I
will give a representational restatement to bring out the point even more clearly.
Aelbrecht's account derives the following generalization:[18]

(39)   Aelbrecht's Generalization:
       Movement (of overt material) from an ellipsis site may be licensed only
       if there is a landing site (intermediate or final) for the moving element
       that is both
       a.   outside of the ellipsis site and
       b.   dominated by the maximal projection of the head which triggers
            or licenses ellipsis.

In the case of Dutch modal complement ellipsis, A-movement out of the ellipsis site passes through a position which is both dominated by the maximal projection of the licensor (ModP) and outside of the ellipsis site proper: Spec,TP.
For $\overline{\text{A}}$-extraction, there is no available landing site. At the other end of the spec-
trum, VP ellipsis is compatible with all kinds of extraction because there is an
intermediate landing site for all types of extraction within VoiceP; this landing
site is both dominated by the maximal projection of the licensor of ellipsis (TP)
and outside of the elliptical domain (vP).

Notice that the configurations for ellipsis in the English and the Dutch constructions are rather similar. There is a licensing head (Mod and T, respectively)
separated from the elided constituents by one phrase (TP and VoiceP, respectively). If movement paths were uniform, this intermediate structure should have

---

[18] Baltin's account derives the same generalization, though its application to British English *do* is suspect, as we saw.

the same effect on $\overline{\text{A}}$-extraction in both cases: it should either be possible in both configurations or impossible. The idea that movement paths are punctuated and that there is an intermediate landing site of $\overline{\text{A}}$-movement in VoiceP but not in TP is what allows the constructions in the two languages to be distinguished. Furthermore, the distinction between A-movement and $\overline{\text{A}}$-movement in Dutch modal complement ellipsis follows from the analysis above, which distinguishes A-movement paths from $\overline{\text{A}}$-movement paths in terms of the intermediate landing sites. Again, the distinction does not find a natural account under analyses where movement paths are uniform.[19]

To the extent that Baltin's and Aelbrecht's analyses are on the right track, they provide evidence for the punctuated nature of movement paths.

It is now time to return to the Danish phenomenon of verb phrase pronominalization introduced above. As mentioned, Houser, Mikkelsen, and Toosarvandani, 2007 take the availability of A-movement with passive, unaccusative, and raising verbs in the construction as evidence for the syntactic complexity of the ellipsis site. What needs to be explained is the asymmetry between the possibility of A-extraction from the missing VP and the impossibility of Wh-extraction. It should be immediately clear how Aelbrecht's account of modal complement ellipsis can be extended to the Danish pattern. All that is required is to identify the syntactic head realized by *det*—'it' or to assume that *det* spells out entire verb phrases. I omit the details.

Houser, Mikkelsen, and Toosarvandani, 2007 propose a different account of the asymmetry. Their account does not rely on the punctuated paths hypothesis but on locality theory. If the account were tenable, then Danish VP pronominalization would not furnish an argument for the punctuated paths hypothesis. Moreover, the possibility of such an account would reduce our confidence in Aelbrecht's account of Dutch modal complement ellipsis. I argue below that Houser, Mikkelsen, and Toosarvandani's account cannot be maintained.

To account for the lack of Wh-movement from the ellipsis site in Danish VP pronominalization, Houser, Mikkelsen, and Toosarvandani invoke locality. The structure they assume is given in figure 2.3 on the next page (their ex. 16).

Houser, Mikkelsen, and Toosarvandani assume that the elided vP is systematically topical in this construction. This is indicated in figure 2.3 by the '[top]' subscript on the vP node. They further assume that topics intervene for the purposes of locality with Wh-movement and that a feature on a containing phrase (vP) may block extraction: a topical vP, on these assumptions, is an island for Wh-extraction of *hvem*—'who'. Example (32) can therefore be ruled out with-

---

[19] These conclusions appear to me to be quite general and independent of the stance one takes on derivations versus representations and on the exact triggering regime for movement assumed. Boeckx, 2008; Neeleman and van de Koot, 2002; Stroik, 1999 represent very different approaches to the issues mentioned in this footnote, yet, the text conclusion holds regardless.

CP
 C′
  C   TP
  [uĀ]
     Palle   T′
          gjorde   vP[top] → *det*
               <Palle>   v′
                       v   VP
                           kilde   <hvem>
                                    [wh]

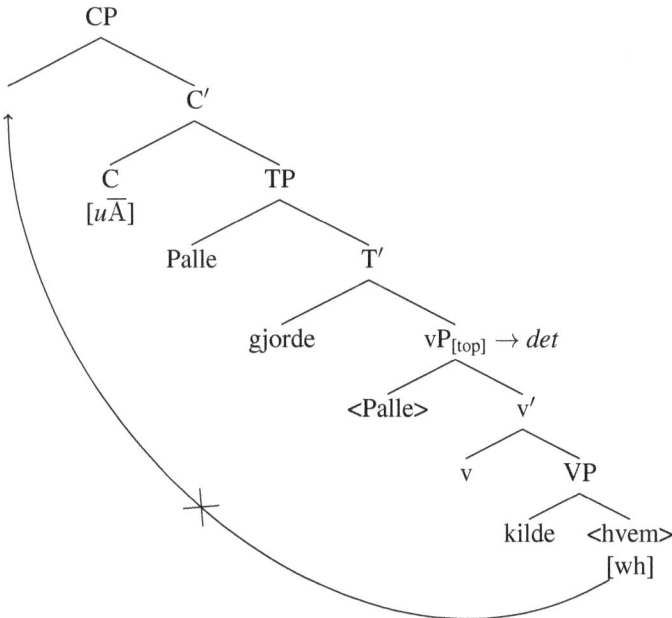

Table 2.3: The structure of Danish VP ellipsis according to Houser, Mikkelsen, and Toosarvandani, 2007

out compromising the otherwise motivated assumption that the missing verb phrase is structurally represented.

Appealing though this explanation is, it is also problematic. The problem has to do with a generalization which is due to Müller, 1996a. According to Müller, in remnant movement constructions, the remnant-creating movement and remnant movement may not be of the same type. Thus, if the remnant creating movement is scrambling, remnant scrambling is blocked. If remnant creating movement is Wh-movement, remnant Wh-movement is blocked, etc. This generalization is sometimes accounted for in terms of locality theory, more precisely in terms of intervention of the kind that Houser, Mikkelsen, and Toosarvandani appeal to in their account of why extraction of *hvem* in figure 2.3 is bad. For relevant discussion see among others Abels, 2007; Fukui, 1997; Kitahara, 1997; Müller, 1996a, 1998; Takano, 2000. Contrary to the conclusion necessary for Houser, Mikkelsen, and Toosarvandani's account to go through, however, Müller's reasoning leads to the conclusion that Wh-extraction from a topical verb phrase is possible. This is illustrated in (40a-b). In (40a), a verb phrase has been topicalized out of an indirect question, which leads to a certain degradation. (40b) is a case of remnant topicalization, where the object *was*—'what' has been extracted from the verb phrase which is later topicalized. The first step is exactly the kind of operation which needs to be banned under Houser, Mikkelsen, and

Toosarvandani's account. However, the example is no better and, crucially, no worse than (40a).

(40) German   Müller, 1996a, p. 384

    a. ??Bücher zu lesen weiß ich nicht warum sie versucht hat
        books to read know I not why she tried has
        I don't know why she tried to read books.

    b. ??Zu lesen weiß ich nicht was sie versucht hat
        to read know I not what she tried has
        I don't know what she has tried to read.

In this respect, (40b) contrasts with examples that actually violate Müller's generalization in that they show, for example, remnant Wh-movement of a phrase that has been Wh-moved out of. Thus, (41a–b), both of which involve Wh-extraction contrast quite clearly.

(41) German   Müller, 1996a, p. 374

    a. ?*Welches Buch über die Liebe weißt du nicht wann du lesen
        which book about the love know you not when you read
        sollst?
        should
        Which book about love don't you know when you should read?

    b. *Welches Buch weißt du nicht über wen du lesen sollst?
        Which book know you not about who you read should
        Which book about whom don't you know about whom you should
        read

Thus, while it is plausible to account for (41b) in terms of a locality prohibition against extracting a Wh-phrase from a Wh-phrase, the fact that there is no contrast between (40a) and (40b) suggests that extraction of a Wh-phrase from a topic is actually licit. The account fatally undergenerates for examples like (40b).

The same problem arises even more sharply if we tried to generalize Houser, Mikkelsen, and Toosarvandani's account to Dutch. Recall that in Dutch modal complement ellipsis neither scrambling nor Wh-movement are licit. To extend Houser, Mikkelsen, and Toosarvandani's account, the topic feature on the elided constituent should block scrambling as well as Wh-movement. However, there is ample evidence (see for example Müller, 1996b, 1998) that a topical verb phrase can be scrambled out of, (42). There seems to be no way of accounting for (42) on the one hand and (27) and (28) on the other in a unified way.

(42) German

    Gelesen hat {das Buch | es} keiner.
    read has the book it nobody

Nobody has read the book/it

Finally, the observation that modal complement ellipsis is compatible with antecedent-contained deletion, (33a)—so long as no overt material is moved from the VP, (30)—and with comparative-operator movement, (35), is not easily accounted for under the locality approach.

These reasons should suffice to favor Aelbrecht's account over Houser, Mikkelsen, and Toosarvandani's.

2.2.5 Parasitic gaps (Nissenbaum, 2001)

Nissenbaum, 2001 argues that the syntax of parasitic gaps provides an argument against theories positing uniform paths (which he calls 'path based'). Nissenbaum is interested in the inter-related questions of what the syntax of parasitic gaps is and how they are interpreted.[20] A typical example of a parasitic gap structure is provided in (43), where the complement position of the verb *file* is the real gap, the complement of the verb *read*—the parasitic gap, and the entire adjunct introduced by *with*—the parasitic domain. The parasitic domain (PD) is the maximal constituent containing the parasitic gap which is not included in the path between the real gap and the filler.

(43)   What did you file without reading.

The assumption that there is a movement dependency between the parasitic gap and the structural edge of the parasitic domain is standard. It is supported by the existence of a range of island effects inside of the parasitic domain. Nissenbaum observes that movement structures are characterized semantically by the creation of derived predicates that can then be used by various operators. He suggests that parasitic domains are, semantically speaking, simply derived predicates much like relative clauses. They combine with another predicate (via predicate modification à la Heim and Kratzer, 1998) to yield a predicate. By assumption, interpretive rules like predicate modification apply strictly locally under sisterhood. These assumptions are sufficient to derive two well-known restrictions on parasitic gaps, according to which (i) the real gap must not c-command the parasitic gap and (ii) the parasitic gap must be c-commanded by the filler of the real gap. The two generalizations are violated in (44a–b), respectively.

(44)   a.   [filler [... [$_X$ filler [$_{PD}$ ...PG ...]]]]
        b.   [[...[filler [$_Y$ ... filler...]]] [$_{PD}$ ...PG ...]]

---

[20] For a very solid overview of the syntactic literature on the issue, see Culicover, 2001.

Neither of these structures would lead to the desired interpretation. In (44a), which violates (i) above, the parasitic domain is attached directly to the real gap. But the gap is, on standard assumptions, not interpreted as a predicate but as an individual variable. This entails that X will have a propositional interpretation rather than being a predicate.[21] In (44b), which violates (ii) above, the parasitic domain is attached above the landing site of the filler and can therefore never modify a derived predicate created by the movement of the filler. The largest constituent with that interpretive possibility is Y. The other main property of parasitic gaps, that they are licensed only by $\overline{\text{A}}$-movement can be accounted for if we assume that the trace within the parasitic domain is subject to principle C of the binding theory or that the moving operator is subject to principle B or principle C.

Nissenbaum, 2001, ch. 2.1 argues that in examples like (43), the adjunct hosting the parasitic gap is adjoined to vP, vP being the label assumed by Nissenbaum for the phasal projection through which successive-cyclic movement passes. He analyzes the generally free alternation between a parasitic gap and a pronoun, (45), by assuming that adjunction is possible either above or below the intermediate trace of Wh-movement.

(45)   English
        a.   These are the reports that I filed without reading.
        b.   These are the reports that I filed without reading them.

The space of logical possibilities is shown in (46), however, Nissenbaum argues that only (46a) and (46d) are interpretable structures.

(46)   a.   [$_{vP}$ t [$_{vP}$ [$_{vP}$ filed t] [OP [without reading PG]]]]
        b.   [$_{vP}$ t [$_{vP}$ [$_{vP}$ filed t] [without reading them]]]
        c.   [$_{vP}$ [$_{vP}$ t [$_{vP}$ filed t]] [OP [without reading PG]]]
        d.   [$_{vP}$ [$_{vP}$ t [$_{vP}$ filed t]] [without reading them]]

Nissenbaum assumes that the intermediate trace in Spec,vP is interpreted via function application. It acts as the argument to a predicate abstract created by movement. He further assumes "that predicate abstraction created by movement ignores adjuncts. One way of making this assumption explicit is by stating predicate abstraction as a rule that type-shifts the lowest saturated projection of the head that attracts the moving phrase, from type τ to (e,τ)" (Nissenbaum, 2001, p. 46 fn. 21).

We are now ready to tackle (46). While all structures in (46) are syntactically well-formed, only (46a) and (46d) are interpretable. (46b–c) are semantically ill-formed because of a type mismatch. In (46a), the parasitic domain and its

---

[21]   Sufficiently abstractly, (44a) might be the structure relevant for *tough*-movement constructions.

sister are predicates, which enables the application of predicate modification while in (46d), the adjunct and its sister are of a propositional type which allows a conjunctive interpretation. But in (46b–c), the adjunct is of a different type from its sister and interpretation fails because of the type mismatch.

The apparent optionality of parasitic gaps is thus analyzed in terms of the variable attachment site of the adjunct.[22]

Confirmation for this view comes from the following paradigm. As just discussed parasitic gaps (in rightward adjuncts) usually alternate freely with pronouns. However, according to Nissenbaum, (47) shows that when more than one adjunct to vP is present, the presence of a parasitic gap in the more peripheral (linearly subsequent) adjunct forces the presence of a parasitic gap in the less peripheral (linearly preceding) one(s).

(47)   Examples and sketched analysis from Nissenbaum, 2001, p. 82-83

    a.   Who did you [vP who [vP [vP [vP praise who to the sky vP] [after criticizing *PG*] vP] [in order to surprise *PG*] vP] vP]?

    b.   Who did you [vP [vP [vP who [vP praise who to the sky vP] vP] [after criticizing *him*] vP] [in order to surprise *the poor man*] vP]?

    c.   Who did you [vP [vP who [vP [vP praise who to the sky vP] [after criticizing *PG*] vP] vP] [in order to surprise *him*] vP]?

    d.   *Who did you [vP [vP [vP praise who to the sky vP] [after criticizing *him*] vP] [in order to surprise *PG*] vP]?

---

[22] Nissenbaum tries to give independent motivation for this analysis using examples involving heavy NP shift.

  (i)   English

    a.   John insulted deeply – by not recognizing (*him) immediately – his favorite uncle from Cleveland.

    b.   John insulted deeply his favorite uncle from Cleveland by not recognizing *(him) immediately.

Both (ia) and (ib) involve heavy-NP shift. Nissenbaum assumes that in both cases the shifted phrase adjoins to vP. The *by*-phrase can be attached below, (ia), or above, (ib), the landing site of heavy-NP shift. On the assumption that the gap in the adjunct in (ia) is a parasitic gap, we now see that parasitic gaps are not optional but obligatory when the adjunct attaches below the heavy-shifted phrase and impossible (unsurprisingly) when it attaches above it. The apparent optionality of parasitic gaps reduces to the choice of attachment sites for the adjunct: above or below the landing site of heavy-NP shift.

Unfortunately, it is not at all clear that (ia) involves a parasitic gap. Postal, 1994 argues at length that these are instances of non-coordinate right-node raising and should not be collapsed with parasitic gaps.

The generalization is schematized in (48). It follows directly from Nissenbaum's analysis of the alternation between parasitic gaps and pronouns sketched above. Example (47a) is the case where both adjuncts are attached below the intermediate trace. (47b) the case where the inner adjunct is below and the outer adjunct above the intermediate trace. (47c) is the situation where both adjuncts are adjoined above the intermediate trace. The ungrammatical example in (47d) cannot arise, because it would require the inner adjunct to be above and the outer adjunct to be below the intermediate trace; but this is impossible in a layered, rightward-ascending vP. Therefore, there is no interpretable position for the intermediate trace and the judgments given by Nissenbaum follow.

(48) Generalization about obligatory parasitic gaps   Nissenbaum, 2001, p. 62
      A movement that targets vP will force the appearance of a parasitic gap inside a vP-modifier adjoined below the landing site.
      V ([... PG]) ([... PG]) [... no PG] (*[... PG]) ([... no PG])

Of course, when two adjuncts are attached to different vPs along the path of successive-cyclic movement, the appearance and disappearance of parasitic gaps in those adjuncts is again independent. This is illustrated by the contrast between (49a) and (49b). The two adjuncts are construed as modifying different verbs in (49a) and the appearance of parasitic gaps in them is independent. The two adjuncts are construed as modifying the same verb in (49b) and the appearance of parasitic gaps in them is therefore subject to the generalization (48) above.

(49) English   Nissenbaum, 2001, 70 ex. 79
      a. John's the guy they [[said they'll [hire [if I criticize him publicly]]] [in order to get me to praise]]
      b. *John's the guy they'll [[[hire][if I criticize him publicly]][in order to console]]

Nissenbaum's account makes crucial use of the distinction between adjunction above and adjunction below the intermediate copy. Such a distinction is not available in accounts of parasitic gaps such as those in HPSG (going back ultimately to Sag, 1983) that rely on the possibility of combining two separate, uniform percolation paths of slash features. Since such percolation paths are uniform, the kind of asymmetry discussed by Nissenbaum is unexpected.

To the extent that it is empirically and theoretically sound, Nissenbaum's analysis provides a further argument for the punctuated nature of paths. His account relies crucially on a distinction being available between nodes that lie between the intermediate copy and the λ-binder and those that lie above the intermediate copy. A uniform theory of paths, where all nodes are treated the same way lacks the power of making such a distinction. Since the distinction is needed, not every node along the path can be treated as identically affected by the movement, hence, we have a prima facie argument for punctuated paths.

2.2.6   A point of logic: Condition C and scope for binding

Certain interactions between scope for binding and condition C of the binding theory are potentially informative regarding the punctuated nature of paths. Recall examples (6), repeated as (50). In the good example, (50a), the quantifier that binds into the moved phrase c-commands the pronoun which potentially interacts with the R-expression in the moved phrase via condition C: *her₂*. In the bad example, (50b), the c-command relations are reversed. The pronoun c-commands the quantifier. Hence, if the quantifier binds into the moved phrase, so does the pronoun.

(50)   English   Lebeaux, 1991, see also Fox, 2000, pp. 10–11
      a.   [The papers that he₁ wrote for Ms. Brown₂] every student₁ [$_{VP}$ t' asked her₂ to grade t]
      b.   *[The papers that he₁ wrote for Ms. Brown₂] she₂ [t' asked every student₁ to revise t]

Now, if an example just like the acceptable example, (50a), could be found that was unacceptable so long as the quantifier and the pronoun were structurally very close, but which improved once the structural distance between them was increased, this would be an argument for the punctuated nature of paths.

In the hypothetical case, represented in figure 2.5, there is no possible intermediate node from which the moving element could take scope below the quantifier—which it needs to to allow binding into XP—and above *her₂*—which it needs to to avoid a violation of Binding Condition C. This situation would then be remedied if the quantifer and the pronoun are structurally separated, as in figure 2.6. The structure in figure 2.6 does make an intermediate reconstruction site available.

Whether such cases exist, needs to be investigated.

2.2.7   Conclusion

This section has scrutinized the logic that arguments should take which purport to argue for punctuated and against uniform movement paths. In particular, punctuated reconstruction patterns can lend support to the position that movement paths are punctuated, a position that has long formed part of the orthodoxy of Chomskyan syntactic theory without being backed by truly decisive arguments.

48

*

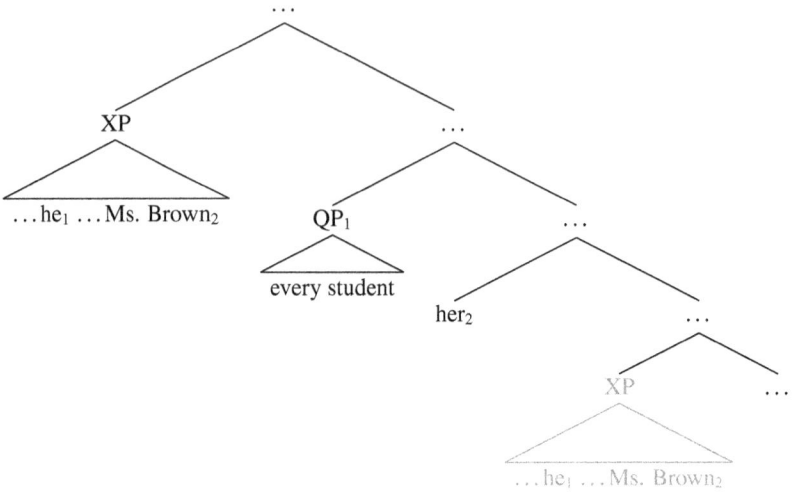

Figure 2.5: A hypothetical unacceptable variant of (50a)

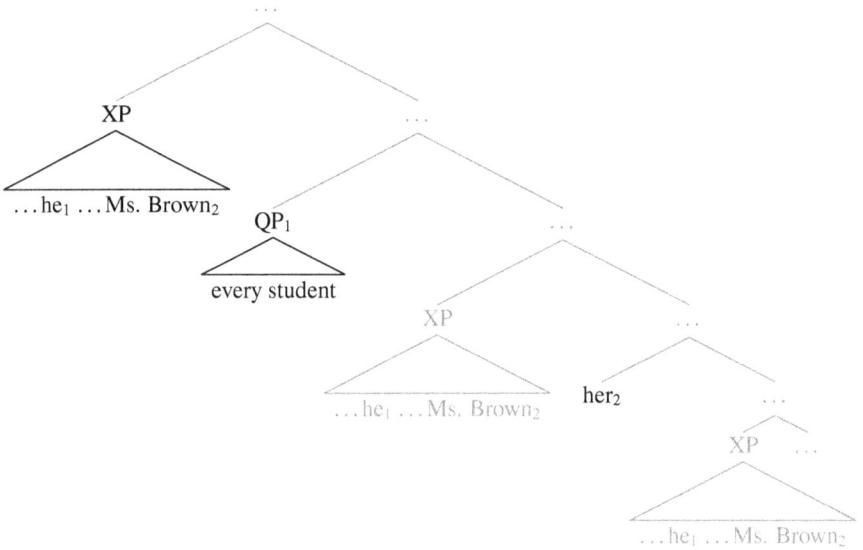

Figure 2.6: Hypothetical repair of the example in Figure 2.5

The evidence for punctuated paths originally proposed in Abels, 2003c does not to stand up to scrutiny, but the argument can still be made. Three potential cases were presented: The interaction of scope reconstruction and binding in Norwegian; the argument from ellipsis based on Aelbrecht, 2010; and finally Nissenbaum's 2001 argument from parasitic-gap licensing in English.

To complete the argument for the punctuated nature of movement in its general form, one would have to show that different properties cluster in their reconstructive behavior: If the positions involved in morphosyntactic changes under movement were limited in a cross-linguistic perspective, if they coincided with the positions crucially involved in cyclic extraction, and if those same nodes were the only possible reconstruction sites, then this would constitute very strong evidence for the punctuated nature of paths. For the moment our knowledge, especially that of lacking reconstruction sites, is too limited to warrant such conclusions in any strong way.

It should also be pointed out that the Norwegian facts discussed here are fairly subtle and subject to a certain amount of variation. Although the true issues involved in the punctuated paths hypothesis have barely been probed, I proceed in what follows on the assumption that paths are punctuated.

2.3   The edge of CP as a landing site of successive-cyclic movement

The discussion in the previous section was meant to lend plausibility to the punctuated-paths hypothesis. The intermediate copies of $\overline{A}$-movement that we were led to postulate in subsections 2.2.4 and 2.2.5 are located at the edge of the traditional verb phrase.[23] This conclusion fits nicely with theories that endorse punctuated movement paths, since these typically follow the lead of Chomsky, 1986, 2000 in assuming that intermediate landing sites of movement exist at the edge of the traditional VP (vP in the terminology used here) and at the edge of the clause (CP).

While the arguments given in the previous section suggested that there is indeed a landing site for Wh-movement at the edge of vP, we have not seen comparable evidence for the existence of an intermediate landing site at the edge

---

[23] On the basis of the evidence discussed in subsection 2.2.3, Abels and Bentzen, 2010; Bentzen, 2007 posit a further intermediate landing site for A-movement at the immediate edge of the phrase projected by a finite verb. This is presumably Spec,TP.

den Dikken, 2006a, whose work on cyclicity will be discussed below, disputes the validity of Nissenbaum's argument from parasitic gaps presented in subsection 2.2.5. Nevertheless, in other work den Dikken acknowledges the existence of (other) evidence for successive-cyclic movement specifically through the edge of vP.

of CP above.

Such an argument, one which is parallel to Nissenbaum's in many ways, could potentially be based on parasitic gaps in Bavarian. Felix, 1983 discusses parasitic gap-constructions of the following type in Bavarian. The sites marked by underscores are the real and the parasitic gaps.

(51)   Bavarian   Lutz, 2001, p. 237

    Den wann i derwisch ___, derschlog i ___.
    that when I catch   kill   I
    When I find that one, I'll kill him.

Lutz, 2001 argues that an analysis of such constructions should involve movement of an empty operator in the *if*-clause and movement of the topic to the clause-initial position in the main clause:

(52)   [$_{CP}$ filler [[OP [$_{if}$ ... PG ...]] ... filler...]]

Generally, adjacency is required between the moved element and the adverbial clause hosting the parasitic gap. This can reasonably be expected under Nissenbaum's analysis of parasitic gaps discussed above. The adverbial clause must be adjoined just below the moved phrase for reasons of interpretability. In this context it is interesting to observe that Lutz reports the following type of example as a problem for the adjacency generalization. It is a problem, because the usual adjacency requirement between the moved element and the adverbial clause is broken, yet, the example is fairly acceptable in sharp contrast to other examples where the adjacency generalization is violated.

(53)   Bavarian   Lutz, 2001, 247–248 fn. 141

    ?Den   Peter {glaube ich | meint er | sagt er} wenn er sieht ___,
    the.ACC Peter believe I   thinks he says he when he sees
    schlägt er   ___.
    beats   he.
    Peter {I believe | he thinks | he says} he will beat ___when he sees ___.

Under Nissenbaum's analysis of parasitic gaps, this type of example falls into place directly as a parasitic gap licensed under successive-cyclic movement through the specifier of CP:

(54)   [$_{CP}$ filler [... [CP filler [[OP [if ... PG...]] [... filler...]]]]]

The many unresolved puzzles surrounding this construction (see Lutz, 2001, chapter 3.3 and the references given there) prevent me from offering this as a very strong argument, however.

Likewise, I am unaware of an argument for an intermediate landing site of Wh-movement in Spec,CP that would run parallel to Aelbrecht's argument for a landing site at the edge of vP.

Nevertheless, the assumption that an intermediate landing site at the edge of CP exists enjoys a strong tradition in generative grammar and is supported in other ways. In work of the 1970s, the intermediate stopover at the edge of the clause was guaranteed by the formulation of the rule of Wh-movement, which targeted the COMP node, and the subjacency condition. Together, they guaranteed that long Wh-movement had to go COMP to COMP. A crucial piece of evidence for this line of argumentation came from Wh-islands, which seemed to show that once a COMP position is filled, extraction from the relevant domain is impossible.

None of these simple supporting arguments for successive-cyclic movement through the clausal periphery survive. Intermediate landing positions for Wh-movements are now assumed to be much more varied than simple COMP-to-COMP movement would suggest. Indeed we saw evidence for movement through the edge of vP above. In addition, it is now customary, following the logic of Rizzi, 1990, to subsume Wh-islands under the very general constraint against crossing of sufficiently similar elements: Relativized Minimality or its feature based formulation Attract Closest. These accounts say that a constituent X in class α or with feature $[\alpha]$ cannot cross another constituent Y in the same class or with the same feature. A clausal edge filled by a Wh-element counts as an intervener for Wh-movement, but an unfilled clausal edge does not. Crossing happens whether intermediate copies are present or not, therefore, Relativized Minimality and Attract Closest do not guarantee that movement pass through the clausal edge.[24]

These remarks should not undermine our confidence in the assumption that there is an intermediate landing site of Wh-movement at the edge of the clause. There is a wealth of additional arguments for this assumption. Boeckx, 2008 provides an overview, useful discussion, and many references. (See also some of the work mentioned in section 2.1.) I follow this body of work in assuming that intermediate landing sites in the clausal edge (Spec,CP) exist.

The strength of this customary assumption can maybe best be appreciated by assessing a recent challenge to it. den Dikken, 2009a points out a number of ways in which traditional arguments for successive-cyclic movement through Spec,CP are not entirely watertight. He claims (p. 89) that "[t]o the extent that any of these arguments implicate SpecCP at all, they never make reference to SpecCP as an intermediate stopover point: they are arguments either for terminal movement to a subordinate SpecCP or for successive-cyclic movement via intermediate stopovers in positions other than SpecCP."[25]

---

[24] Note that Rizzi, 1990 formulated Relativized Minimality in terms of (potential) positions rather than in terms of interveners. In this way, the original formulation does guarantee successive-cyclic movement through the edge of the clause.

[25] Den Dikken's attempt to analyze away intermediate traces in Spec,CP is ultimately driven by the aim of making exceptionless the generalization that movement to an

$\overline{\text{A}}$-specifier position is terminal (see Rizzi's 2006 notion of Criterial Freezing). Recalcitrant counterexamples to this generalization come from scrambling in Japanese. Saito, 1992 famously claimed "that scrambling in Japanese, even when it moves a constituent 'long distance', can be literally undone in the LF component." The claim is based on the fact that scrambling reconstructs for Wh-scope, (i).

(i)   Japanese

    a.   [Masao-ga [$_{CP}$ [$_{IP}$ Hanako-ga   dono hon-o   tosyokan-kara
           Masao-NOM   Hanako-NOM which book-ACC library-from
           karidasita] ka] siritagatteiru] koto
           checked-out Q   want-to-know fact
           the fact that Masao wants to know [Q [Hanako checked out which book from the library]]
           the fact that Masao wants to know which book Hanako checked out from the library

    b.   ?[dono hon-o$_i$ [Masao-ga [$_{CP}$ [$_{IP}$ Hanako-ga   t$_i$ tosyokan-kara
           which book-ACC Masao-NOM   Hanako-NOM   library-from
           karidasita] ka] siritagatteiru] koto
           checked-out Q   want-to-know fact
           the fact that which book, Masao wants to know [Q [Hanako checked out which book from the library]]
           the fact that Masao wants to know which book Hanako checked out from the library

Japanese might turn out not to be a counterexample to Criterial Freezing in the end, as one might deny that in Japanese Wh-question formation or scrambling (or both) involve movement to an $\overline{\text{A}}$-specifier. However, we face the same situation for German examples, where a Wh-moved constituent is topicalized, (ii). Reis and Rosengren, 1992 argue that Wh-movement of the object in (iib) feeds topicalization of that very object in (iia).

(ii)   German   Reis and Rosengren, 1992

    a.   Wen   stell   dir   vor, dass Peter besucht hat!
           whom.ACC imagine yourself PRT that Peter visited has
           Imagine who Peter visited!

    b.   Stell   dir   vor, wen   Peter besucht hat!
           imagine yourself PRT whomACC Peter visited has
           Imagine who Peter visited!

Such examples cast some doubt on the generalization that provides the impetus for den Dikken's analysis. See Abels, 2007 for an alternative generalization, which directly accommodates the facts in (ii). Abels, 2007 actually fails to acknowledge the existence of examples like (ii). The assumed absence of cases where Wh-movement feeds topicalization led to a complication in the theory presented there. This complication is of course superfluous if examples like (ii) are true instances of topicalization of a Wh-moved constituent.

A simple illustration comes from den Dikken's discussion of embedded subject-auxiliary inversion in Belfast English (Henry, 1995, ch. 5), already mentioned in chapter 1. As mentioned there, unlike standard English (SE), which allows subject auxiliary inversion only in direct questions, Belfast English (BE) also allows inversion in indirect questions, and, crucially, along the path of Wh-movement.[26]

(55)   Standard English and Belfast English
    a.   ✓SE | ✓BE What have you done?
    b.   * SE | ✓BE She asked who had I seen.   Henry, 1995, p. 106
    c.   * SE | ✓BE Who did John hope would he see?   Henry, 1995, p. 108

However, movement of a relative pronoun to Spec,CP does not give rise to inversion, neither at the final landing site nor along the path of movement.

(56)   Belfast English   Henry, 1995, p. 120
    a.   *This is the man who John claimed did I see.
    b.   This is the man who John claimed that I saw.

Den Dikken takes the examples in (56) to argue that inversion is not a property of successive-cyclic movement through Spec,CP *per se*. He furthermore interprets (55a–b) as showing that inversion is triggered by Wh-movement terminating in the specifier of a Wh-complementizer.

The first conclusion is certainly true. The examples make the important point that if we are to interpret embedded inversion as a consequence of successive-cyclic movement, inversion must be cued specifically to movement of a Wh-phrase. This is not difficult to achieve if successive-cyclic movement is triggered by a Wh-feature on the embedded complementizer, as I will be assuming. It might be more difficult to make the embedded complementizer sensitive to the content of the moving phrase under accounts that assume a generic (EP)P feature on the embedded complementizer to trigger successive-cyclic movement (or no feature at all). To the extent that this is difficult, den Dikken's discussion of Belfast English provides an argument against theories where intermediate movement steps are triggered by a generic (EP)P-feature or no feature at all.[27]

The examples of partial Wh-movemement discussed elsewhere in this book might also provide counterexamples to Criterial Freezing, if the partially moved phrases land in specifier positions. Similarly, cases where Wh-phrases are scrambled (Abels (2007); Beck (1996); Fanselow (2001, 2004); Sauerland (1996)) may provide further counterexamples if it is assumed that scrambling targets $\overline{\text{A}}$-specifier positions.

[26] Torrego, 1984 claims that Spanish has similar subject-auxiliary inversion effects along the path of Wh-movement. Ortiz de Urbina, 1989, chapter 4 makes a similar claim for Basque Wh-movement and focalization.

On the basis of his second conclusion, that inversion is triggered only by terminal Wh-movement, den Dikken suggests that (55c) does not involve successive-cyclic movement through the embedded Spec,CP, as in the traditional analysis (57a), but instead Wh-movement in the embedded clause terminating in Spec,CP. The terminal Wh-movement chain in the embedded clause remains unpronounced. Only the chain in the matrix clause is phonetically realized, (57b). The fact that there are two chains in (57b) is indicated via superscripting. Non-pronunciation of lower copies within a chain is indicated by graying out, as before. The unpronounced occurrence of *who^1* in the embedded Spec,CP also remains unpronounced. Since this cannot be due to it being a lower copy in a chain it is not grayed out but instead ~~struck out~~ to indicate non-pronunciation.

(57) a. Who^1 did John hope [$_{CP}$ who^1 would he see who^1]?
      b. Who^2 did John hope who^2 [$_{CP}$ ~~who^1~~ would he see who^1]?

den Dikken, 2009a,b calls structures like (57b) 'full-concordial scope marking,' assimilating them terminologically to scope-marking constructions like (58). This assimilation remains terminological, however, since, as we will see, substantial empirical and analytic differences remain between scope marking and 'full-concordial scope marking.'

(58) German

      Was glaubst du, wen Hans gesehen hat?
      what believe you who Hans seen   has
      Who do you think Hans saw

Under den Dikken's analysis, the difference between the two structures is that the scope marker and the Wh-phrase in the embedded Spec,CP are identical in (57b) and non-identical in (58). This, according to den Dikken, leads to obligatory deletion of *who* in (57b) and to preservation of *wen*—'who' in (58). The same analysis in terms of 'full-concordial scope marking' is also invoked for much more complex Wh-phrases. Replacing *who* in (57b) by *how many girls* would give rise to the structure in (59). For ease of reference, all occurrences of *how many girls* have been subscripted separately.

(59) How many girls$_1$ did John hope how many girls$_2$ [$_{CP}$ ~~how many girls$_3$~~ would he see how many girls$_4$]?

---

[27] The facts of *meng* deletion in Malay, as discussed in Cole and Hermon, 1998, will be seen later to make the same point under the analysis advocated here, namely, that the morphology can be sensitive to the type of feature triggering intermediate steps of movement. This contrasts with Cole and Hermon's analysis, where the morphosyntax is sensitive to the timing of the movement (overt vs. covert) rather than the feature content.

The following considerations make this analysis suspect. First, invoking concord to create full copies of syntactic phrases is unprecedented theoretically. It is also, as far as I know, empirically unmotivated in concord systems, where concord usually involves ϕ-features and features related to polarity only. Notice that for examples like (59), not only the Wh-word *how* but the entire pied-piped phrase would have to be recreated under concord, thus endowing concord with the key movement property of pied-piping.

Second, to explain why occurrences 2 and 4 are silent, den Dikken 2009, p. 18 invokes the type of reasoning present in Nunes, 2004 (building on Kayne, 1994) according to which the elements of a chain are non-distinct and pronouncing both would lead to a violation of the linear-correspondence axiom. Items are non-distinct iff they are copies (of copies) of token-identical items in the numeration. Den Dikken suggests that the same considerations could explain why occurrence 3 is silent: Occurrence 3 must be silent because occurrences 2 and 3 are 'identical twins' created by concord. Even if we accept for the sake of the argument the premise that concord can recreate complex phrases, occurrences 2 and 3 in (59) are type identical and featurally identical, but it is not obvious that they are copies of the same elements in the numeration. Indeed, occurrence 2 is created *ex nihilo* by concord and does not bear the copy relation to any elements in the numeration. Therefore, we are led to assume that occurrences 2 and 3 are actually distinct. They should therefore be treated like type-identical syntactic objects, that is, objects which happen to have identical feature sets. Such pairs are not subject to deletion:

(60) a. He says that he is happy.
      b. *He says that ~~he~~ is happy.

To avoid this conclusion, concord must further be assimilated to movement: both 'concord' and movement create copies. Of course, this analytic move makes the analysis of (55c) in terms of 'full-concordial scope marking' nearly indistinguishable from the traditional movement analysis.

At the same time, non-pronunciation of occurrence 3 in (59) sets 'full-concordial scope marking' apart, empirically, from regular scope marking; in general, scope marking constructions are well-known for exhibiting multiple scope markers. This is illustrated by the multiple occurrences of the scope marker *was* in (61).

(61) German

Was glaubst du, was er gesagt hat, wen er getroffen hat.
what believe you what he said has who he met   has
Who do you believe he said he met?

In the context of his analysis of (59), examples like (61) create a knotty technical problem for den Dikken, 2009b: the two occurrences of *was* are 'identical twins' created by concord and should therefore be subject to deletion if the analysis of (59) is to be maintained. To solve this problem den Dikken suggests (fn. 24, p. 18) that multiple occurrences of scope markers as in (61) are licit and, despite their identity, can escape from deletion under identity imposed by the Linear Correspondence Axiom because the various instances of *was*—'what' do not c-command each other.

It is unclear how this suggestion is supposed to address the problem. The linear-correspondence axiom demands that there be a linear order on terminals. If the two instances of *was* in (61) were non-distinct copies, one of which precedes *glaubst du* and one which follows *glaubst du*, then the Linear Correspondence Axiom should rule out the example precisely because there is no linear order on (non-distinct) terminals. This is true whether the non-distinct copies of *was* are in a symmetric, an asymmetric, or no c-command relation to each other. Under den Dikken's own assumptions, therefore, regular cases of scope marking—unlike 'full-concordial scope marking'—must not involve copies created by concord.[28]

For purposes of linearization, 'full-concordial scope marking' thus behaves like movement and not like scope marking or concord. As we saw, it also behaves like movement in creating full copies and supporting pied-piping. 'Full-concordial scope marking' further patterns with uncontested cases of movement and against clear cases of scope marking also when it comes to presuppositionality and (in)consistent belief contexts (see den Dikken, 2009b, for discussion). All of this raises the suspicion that 'full-concordial scope marking' is no more than a new label for movement through Spec,CP.

Indeed, the only more or less direct evidence for the existence of 'full-concordial scope marking' comes from the interplay of case and agreement in Hungarian. Under extraction from an embedded clause, an extracted subject may surprisingly be realized in the accusative. In that case the extracted phrase triggers indefinite agreement on the matrix verb, (62). All other combinations of case and matrix agreement are impossible. Den Dikken interprets (62b) as evidence that there is no movement chain connecting the embedded subject po-

---

[28] Alternatively, if den Dikken's idea that c-command between terminals somehow mattered for the Linear Correspondence Axiom could be maintained, then the lower copies of *how many girls* in (59) should be pronounced, since here the terminals in the higher copy do not c-command those in the lower copy. This is clearly an unwanted conclusion.

Either way, den Dikken's suggestion involving lack of c-command between terminals fails to make the intended cut between 'full-concordial scope marking,' where the lower copy is deleted, and plain scope marking, where it is not. There is no obvious non-stipulative way around this problem that does not assimilate 'full-concordial scope marker' even further to movement and makes it less similar to regular scope marking.

sition to the matrix Wh-phrase. Rather, the Wh-phrase is the object of the matrix verb, which explains both the appearance of accusative case and the indefinite inflection on the verb. This object is in a full-concord relation with a silent copy of *how many girls* in the embedded Spec,CP.

(62) Hungarian   den Dikken, 2009b, p. 7 ex. 12a, p. 8 ex. 14c

a. (?)?hány   lány-∅   akar-od   hogy
how.many girl-NOM want-2^{nd}SG.DEF that
eljöjjönn
PV.come.SUBJ.3^{rd}SG

b.   ?hány   lány-t   akar-sz   hogy
how.many girl-ACC want-2^{nd}SG.INDEF that
eljöjjönn
PV.come.SUBJ.3^{rd}SG
How many girls do you wish should come

Den Dikken's account predicts, that the case switch to accusative should be able to affect any Wh-phrase moved from the embedded clause into the matrix, since nothing restricts the 'full-concordial scope marking' strategy to embedded subjects. However, the case switch strategy in (62b) is limited to nominatives; oblique objects never show up in the accusative when extracted and do not trigger indefinite agreement.

(63) Hungarian   É. Kiss, 2001, 107 ex. 16

a.   Kitől   szeretnéd   hogy ajándékot kapj?
who-ABL you-would-like that gift-ACC you-receive
From whom would you like that you should receive a gift?

b. *Kit   szeretnél,   hogy ajándeékot kapj?
who-ACC you-would-like that gift-ACC   you-receive
Whom would you like that you should receive a gift?

É. Kiss, 2001 makes the plausible suggestion that (62b) involves exceptional case marking along the path of Wh-movement, a phenomenon that has been observed elsewhere (Postal, 1974, Rizzi, 1982, ch. 3, Kayne, 1984, ch. 5.3, Pesetsky, 1992, Bošković, 1997c, Lohndal 2011, esp. fn. 24, Georgopoulos, 1991, among others). Exceptional case marking is presumably fed by suppression of nominative (but not subject-verb agreement) in the embedded domain.

Despite den Dikken's valiant attempt to analyze it away, it seems safe to conclude that successive-cyclic movement through Spec,CP exists. Den Dikken's charge against the argument carries little force for the three reasons discussed in the preceding paragraphs: (i) the prime argument for the existence of 'full-concordial scope marking' is built on a misanalysis of long extraction in Hungarian; (ii) den Dikken's reanalysis of cyclicity effects in terms of 'full-concordial scope marking' is the old movement analysis under a new name, since the core empirical properties of 'full-concordial scope marking' do not fall out from the analysis or from general properties of scope marking or concord; and (iii) the generalization in the background, according to which movement to an $\overline{\text{A}}$-scope position is always terminal is dubious. While the skepticism with which den Dikken, 2009a approaches many of the traditional arguments for successive-cyclic movement through Spec,CP seem both healthy and warranted to some measure, I hope to have shown here that his overall conclusion that there are no valid arguments for successive-cyclic movement through Spec,CP is far too strong and that the arguments survive intact.

2.4   Reflection

Section 2.2 of this chapter discussed the question of whether movement paths are punctuated or uniform. The chapter summarizes the existing evidence for the punctuated paths hypothesis from scope and binding interactions in Norwegian (Abels and Bentzen, 2009, 2010), from parasitic gaps (Nissenbaum, 2001), and from Dutch modal complement ellipsis (Aelbrecht, 2009, 2010). It was shown that the hypothesis that movement paths are punctuated is supported, though, admittedly, there is far less truly decisive evidence for punctuation than tradition would have us assume.

The facts from modal complement ellipsis and from parasitic gaps also pro-vided evidence that Wh-movement creates intermediate landing sites at the edge of vP. In section 2.3 I investigated the challenges in den Dikken, 2009a to the hypothesis that successive-cyclic Wh-movement passes through the edge of CP. As it turns out, den Dikken's challenge has little merit. It seems safe to assume that successive-cyclic movement passes through the edge of vP and the edge of CP.

In later parts of this book I will assume that extraction from DP and extraction from PP passes through the edges of those phrases as well. The very sophisti-cated type of argument discussed in this chapter is not available for extraction through the edge of DP and PP. Such arguments will therefore have to come from elsewhere (secondary movement, pied-piping, and the stranding generalization) and will be given in due course.

As mentioned already, the findings of this chapter align nicely with the tra-dition that assumes that successive-cyclic movement passes through the edge of the verb phrase and the edge of the clause but skips other positions (Chomsky, 1986, 2000, 2001, 2004, 2008). I implement this by assuming that the phrases providing intermediate landing sites are special; they are special in that they al-low non-terminal movement through their edge because they are endowed with the relevant features; they are also special in that they enforce movement through their edge by the phase impenetrability condition. These special phrases are the phases that this essay is about. To derive the punctuated nature of movement paths, that is, the fact that only phases provide intermediate landing sites, I assume that movement is not free but a last-resort operation.

Much of the discussion that follows concerns the nature and interpretation of the features triggering intermediate movement steps. I argue below that the property of the phase head which triggers the movement is a bona-fide feature—a Wh-feature for Wh-movement, a Foc-feature for focus movement, etc.—rather than a generic (EP)P-feature or property. The assumption that there is a movement-type-specific feature on the phase head does not follow directly from the punctuated nature of paths. Instead of being triggered by a Wh-feature, successive cyclic movement of a Wh-phrase could instead be triggered by some form of expulsion from the phase. Under such a view successive-cyclic movement is simply a by-product of the dynamics of the syntactic derivation: an element has to be iteratively expelled from a certain domain as a consequence of how bottom-up structure building proceeds. For example, successive-cyclic movement might be a response to the need to spell out a domain without fatal violations. Ideas along these lines have been suggested in in Bošković, 2007; Putnam, 2009; Stroik, 1999, 2009. These theories explicitly avoid postulating specific features on phase heads that would trigger the relevant movements. In fact, they even avoid the more generic optional (EP)P-features on phase heads as triggers: no features on the phase heads are needed at all to trigger intermediate movement steps.[29]

Movement-type-specific triggering features for intermediate steps have sometimes been called 'spurious' features. The main reason for the negative epithet 'spurious' is that these features are not semantically interpreted. As we have

---

[29] The even stronger statement that no features are needed at all to trigger intermediate movement steps would be false. Expulsion theories usually locate the trigger for movement as a feature in the moving item.

Following this line of analysis, Bošković, 2007, pp. 631-633 proposes that English Wh-words come in two flavors, one of which has an uninterpretable, movement-triggering feature [uF] while the other one does not. The assumption is a key ingredient in Bošković's account of languages like English that have obligatory single Wh-fronting but where additional Wh-phrases in multiple Wh-questions remain in situ. No evidence from English or any other language is given by Bošković to show that adding [uF] to a Wh-word has morphological effect. Nor is evidence of a semantic effect given, but given that [F] is unintepretable, this comes as no surprise. In particular, no evidence is presented of a language where the optional [uF] is morphologically represented. Without such evidence the feature, being uninterpretable, is strictly a movement trigger and nothing else. If no evidence is forthcoming, the theory introduces a spurious ambiguity that it would be good to avoid.

60

already seen, these features are not spurious at all from the perspective of the morphosyntax. Consider yet again examples (64a-b), which have been discussed several times now, and the versions without embedded subject auxiliary inversion, (64c–d).

(64)   Belfast English and Standard English
    a.   * SE | ✓BE Who did John hope would he see?
    b.   * SE | * BE This is the man who John claimed did I see.
    c.   ✓SE | ✓BE Who did John hope that he would see?
    d.   ✓SE | ✓BE This is the man who John claimed that I saw.

Under the interpretation suggested here, the embedded complementizer is endowed with a Wh-feature in (64a) and (64c) and with a Rel-feature in (64b) and (64d). In no case does this lead to a semantic interpretation of the embedded clause as a question or a relative clause, respectively. Morphosyntactically, however, the presence of the intermediate Wh-feature on the embedded complementizer is all but spurious. In (64a) it is precisely this feature which gives rise to subject auxiliary inversion.

Assuming that the Wh-feature on the embedded complementizer in (64) is morphosyntactically as real as the on the matrix complementizer, what is needed is an explanation for the morphosyntax-semantics asymmetry. In chapter 5, an explanation will be provided in the form of a theory of feature interpretation which is cued to relational properties, the configuration that a feature finds itself in. Such a theory contrasts with the more standard view of feature interpretability as an inherent property.[30]

The argument for a Wh-feature on the intermediate C in Belfast English comes from the fact that embedded subject-auxiliary inversion is not a general property of successive-cyclic movement but selectively targets Wh-extraction. These facts fall into place, if we assume that Belfast English has one complementizer C_1 with features to trigger Wh-movement and subject-auxiliary inversion. There must also be other complementizers in the language. One has a feature to trigger movement of a relative operator C_2, another one, C_3, which triggers no movement at all, and one, C_4, which triggers Wh-movement but no subject-auxiliary inversion,... Let me simply write these properties as [wh], [rel], and [SAI] here, since a serious theory of features has not been introduced: $C_{1\,[wh,\,SAI]}$, $C_{2\,[rel]}$ /that/, C_3 /that/, $C_{4\,[wh]}$. The clear advantage of this type of

---

[30] The last sentence is a bit of an overstatement, actually, since it is often assumed that certain features are interpretable on one class of items but not on another class. ϕ-features are a case in point: interpretable on nouns but uninterpretable on T. The relational context taken into account is much smaller under the standard view than under that to be proposed below, though. For related ideas on feature interpretation see Pesetsky and Torrego, 2007.

analysis is that it provides fine-grained control over the transparency of a particular phase for intermediate movement of a particular type. The disadvantage is that it seems to lead to a proliferation of lexical entries and spurious ambiguity.

The movement-triggering features on C, or any other phase head for that matter, encode the potential transparency of that phase for a particular type of movement. Postulating different triggering features for different movement types allows us, by means of a lexical stipulation, to make a particular domain transparent for one kind of movement but opaque for a different kind. The descriptive power inherent in this seems necessary, as a few, more or less randomly chosen examples may illustrate: In English, Wh-movement and relative-operator movement can cross finite CPs but *tough*-movement for many speakers cannot. In Russian, scrambling can cross CPs, but Wh-movement cannot (Müller and Sternefeld, 1994). In Georgian, relativization can cross clause boundaries but Wh-movement cannot (Harris, 1993). In Malagasy relativization is strictly local and is launched from the clause-final 'subject' position while movement to that clause-final position (whether this is A- or $\overline{\text{A}}$-movement is controversial but irrelevant to the point under discussion, see Hyams, Ntelitheos, and Manorohanta, 2006 for a good overview and references) itself can cross finite clause boundaries (Keenan, 2008, pp. 488–491). Kikuyu topicalization may be clause bound (Bergvall, 1987; Schwarz, 2003) while Wh-movement and relativization are not. Many speakers of (predominantly northern varieties of) German disallow Wh-movement across finite CPs, using the scope-marking construction instead, but do allow topicalization across finite clause boundaries. Such discrepancies between different movement types are easily accommodated and indeed expected if successive-cyclic movement is triggered by specific lexically coded features on intermediate phase heads.

Such movement type asymmetries are unexpected under expulsion theories, since for them successive-cyclic movement is an automatic by-product of syntactic structure building. Movement is therefore not under lexical control of elements along the path. The only lexical parameterization that is possible concerns the moving element and the target element themselves. Since Minimalism generally eschews any form of non-lexical parameterization, this leaves expulsion theories without any means of describing the differences between different types of movement just mentioned.

In fact, the criticism just leveled against expulsion theories of movement applies to a somewhat broader range of theories. Theories that implement successive-cyclic movement with a generic EPP feature on phase heads for example rob themselves of the necessary fine-grained parameterization. Similarly, Boeckx, 2008 proposes that intermediate traces of movement are constructed late, as a by-product of terminal movement. Terminal movement is controlled by properties of the moving element and the target of movement and must be allowed by locality. In the problematic cases where different movement operations pattern differently, suitable targets and moving elements are available in the language and locality is not an issue. Therefore, distinctions between types of movement are again unexpected. Finally, Heck and Müller, 2000 present a theory of phase balance where triggering features are added to phase heads in order to balance a phase and prevent items that eventually need to move from getting trapped. Although these features are specific to the movement type, there is no indication that the addition of features is in any way under the lexical control of the phase head. Therefore, the kind of fine-grained parametric variation needed cannot be encoded in the theory.[31]

The necessary descriptive power is clearly an advantage of the system suggested here. The drawback is that it appears to lead to a proliferation of lexical entries and rampant lexical ambiguity. The traditional lexicalist answer to the problem of functional syncretism is to assume lexical entries with optional features: C – ([wh]) ([rel]) /that/. Realizational models of morphology on the other hand usually do not require a perfect match between the syntactic structure and the morpheme that realizes it. The morpheme may be over- or underspecified with respect to the syntactic insertion context. If we want to replace the parenthesis notation for optionality from the traditional lexical entry by a more systematic device, Nanosyntax (Abels and Muriungi, 2008; Caha, 2009; Taraldsen, 2010, as well as Starke, 2009 and the other papers in that volume of Nordlyd) provides a particularly appealing solution.

Like the better-known Distributed Morphology (Embick and Noyer, 2007; Halle and Marantz, 1993; Harley and Noyer, 1999), Nanosyntax is a realizational theory of the syntax-morphology interface. An important property of Distributed Morphology is that it can deal with morphological defaults realizing dif-

---

[31] It is difficult to discern clearly what Chomsky's position on the question is. Chomsky, 2000, p. 109 suggests the following:

(i)   "The head H of phase Ph may be assigned an EPP-feature."

This EPP feature is then held responsible for the intermediate steps in successive-cyclic movement (Chomsky's indirectly feature-driven movement). As the accompanying text makes clear (p. 108), Chomsky uses the term EPP feature as a cover term for ϕ-features, force, topic focus,... The features triggering movement, both terminal and intermediate steps, are therefore specific to the type of movement. In the footnote accompanying the sentence just quoted Chomsky (2000, 144 fn. 50) acknowledges the need for parameterization when he states that "[p]arametrically varying properties of H enter into the application of [(i)]." But this suggestion is not given an implementation and is not clear how the assignment of features can be under the control of parametrically varying properties of H other than saying that, as a lexical property, H does or does not have the relevant feature.

If this is the intended interpretation, then my proposal in in line with Chomsky's suggestion.

ferent syntactic feature specifications by assuming that there can be mismatches between the syntactic insertion context and the specification on the lexically stored morphological form. In particular, Distributed Morphology assumes that an item is a candidate for insertion in a particular syntactic context if and only if it is specified for a (not necessarily proper) subset of the features in the syntactic context. When more than one morpheme is a candidate for insertion, then competition is regulated by a closest-fit metric, according to which that item wins the competition that is the least underspecified, that is, that item which has the biggest subset of the features specified in the syntactic insertion context.

Nanosyntax puts these assumptions upside down. In Nanosyntax a morpheme is a candidate for insertion into a particular syntactic context if and only if it is specified for a (not necessarily proper) superset of the features in the syntactic context. When more than one morpheme is a candidate for insertion, then competition is regulated by a closest-fit metric, according to which that item wins the competition that is the least overspecified, that is, that item which has the smallest superset of the features specified in the syntactic insertion context.[32]

A hypothetical lexical entry like $C_{[wh]\,[rel]}$ /gnarf/ will therefore be able to be a candidate for insertion in the syntactic context of Wh-movement, of relative-operator movement, of both, and of neither. But it will not be a candidate for insertion in the context of focus movement. Whether the item is actually inserted in the contexts where it is a candidate then depends on the inventory of other complementizers. This is exactly the kind of lexical control that is needed to encode the distinctions between movement types seen above. Note that Distributed Morphology by contrast does not give us an easy handle on these facts. A complementizer like *gnarf* above that can be inserted in the context of Wh-movement, relative operator movement, both, and none would have to take the maximally impoverished default specification C /gnarf/. By the subset principle, however, this complementizer is automatically a candidate for insertion also in the context of focus movement. To avoid overgeneration, Distributed Morphology needs to invoke a second, syntactic lexicon that can limit the syntactic structures available in the language.

Given the simple solutions to the problem of the proliferation of lexical entries provided by Nanosyntax and, to a lesser extent, Distributed Morphology, I will set this issue aside.

To recap, the observation that paths are punctuated will be implemented by assuming that the phrases providing intermediate landing sites are special: they are the phases. To derive the fact that other phrases do not provide intermediate landing sites, I assume that movement is not free but is a last-resort operation. The trigger for this operation resides on the head of the phase but not on other

---

[32] This paragraph is a great oversimplification and covers only the single aspect of Nanosyntax that is of interest here. The reader is referred to the literature mentioned above for further discussion.

64

heads. I assume that the property of the phase head which triggers the movement is a bona-fide feature—a Wh-feature for Wh-movement, a Foc-feature for focus movement, etc. Together these assumptions derive punctuated paths, predict the possibility of (general or movement-type-specific) morphological effects on phase heads along the path of movement, and predict the existence of language internal and cross-linguistic differences in the availability of long successive-cyclic movement by movement type.

3 Some properties of movement

3.1 Introduction

This chapter reviews key generalizations regarding partial Wh-movement, pied-piping, and secondary Wh-movement. The phenomena were briefly introduced in chapter 1 and relevant generalizations taken from the literature (mainly Sabel, 2006 for partial Wh-movement and Heck, 2008 for pied-piping) will be discussed in the following sections.

At the end of the previous chapter, the puzzle was raised how the features that trigger intermediate movement steps can be simultaneously morphosyntactically active and semantically inert. The facts reviewed in this chapter bear on this question more or less directly. The possibility to pied-pipe phrasal categories strengthens the argument for the morphosyntactic reality of movement-type-specific features on phase heads even when those phase heads do not express this property morphologically or semantically. The generalizations regarding partial and secondary movement will be used to sharpen the theory of feature interpretability. The chapter therefore concludes with an informal outline of the approach to feature interpretability that will be developed more rigorously in chapter 5.

Before taking up these issues, a brief comment on the question of the optionality of pied-piping is in order. Heck, 2004, 2008, 2009 proposes a theory of pied-piping which disallows true optionality in pied-piping. As discussed at length in Heck's work, there are many cases of that appear to be optional (see Cable, 2010b, pp. 166–170 for a summary list of cases). Heck suggests various ways of tackling these counterexamples to his claim. In contrast to Heck, I will take data like example (9) in Chapter 1 on page 7 above or (1) and (19) below at face value and assume that they involve truly optional pied-piping.

(1)   German   Heck, 2008, p. 156
    a.   Fritz weiß wieviel   Meter die Mauer zu hoch war.
           Fritz knows how.many meters the wall   too high was
           Fritz knows how many meters too high the wall was.
    b.   Fritz weiß wieviel   Meter zu hoch die Mauer war.
           Fritz knows how.many meters too high the wall   was
           Fritz knows how many meters too high the wall was.

3.2   Partial movement

Core cases of partial Wh-movement are those where a Wh-element is pronounced in a position that is higher than the highest thematic or case position for that item but lower than the interrogative scope position for that item. In chapter 1, partial Wh-movement was exemplified on the basis of Malagasy. Here I give examples from Kîîtharaka (SVO, Bantu, E54, Kenyan), which behaves in relevant respects like Malagasy. Kîîtharaka allows Wh-in-situ in direct questions:

(2)   Kîîtharaka   Muriungi, 2005, p. 45
    a.   Maria   a-k-ir-e   mbi?
        1.Maria 1SM-build-PERF-FV what
        What did Maria build?
    b.   I-mbi   Maria   a-k-ir-e?
        FOC-what 1.Maria 1SM-build-PERF-FV
        What did Maria buy?

In addition it has a partial-movement strategy in long distance questions. This is shown in (3b). (3a) and (3c) are the in-situ and full-movement variants of the same question.

(3)   Kîîtharaka   Muriungi, 2005, pp. 47–48
    a.   G-ug-ir-e   ati   John a-ring-ir-e   mbi?
        2^{nd}SG-say-PERF-FV that John 1SM-beat-PERF-FV what
    b.   G-ug-ir-e   ati   i-mbi   John a-ring-ir-e?
        2^{nd}SG-say-PERF-FV that FOC-what John 1SM-beat-PERF-FV
    c.   I-mbi   g-ug-ir-e   ati   John n-a-ring-ir-e?
        FOC-what 2^{nd}SG-say-PERF-FV that John FOC-1SM-beat-PERF-FV
        What did you say that John beat?

Unlike for example French, which has optional Wh-in-situ only in direct questions, (4),

(4)   French   Sabel, 2006, p. 152
    a.   (i)   Elle a   rencontré qui?
            she has met   who
      (ii) Qui a-t   elle rencontré
            who has-T she met
            Who has she met?
    b.   (i)   *Je ne sais   pas elle a   rencontré qui.
            I NE know not she has met   who

(ii) Je ne sais pas qui elle a   rencontré.
      I NE know not who she has met
      I don't know who she has met.

Kîîtharaka allows all three strategies also in indirect questions:

(5)   Kîîtharaka   Peter Muriungi, pers. comm.

  a. M-bur-ir-i-e   gu-ug-ir-e   John
      1[st]SG-ask-PERF-CAUS-FV 2[nd]SG-say-PERF-FV 1.John
      a-ring-ir-e   mbi
      1SM-beat-PERF-FV what

  b. M-bur-ir-i-e   gu-ug-ir-e   i-mbi   John
      1[st]SG-ask-PERF-CAUS-FV 2[nd]SG-say-PERF-FV FOC-what 1.John
      a-ring-ir-e
      1SM-beat-PERF-FV

  c. M-bur-ir-i-e   i-mbi   gu-ug-ir-e   John
      1[st]SG-ask-PERF-CAUS-FV FOC-what 2[nd]SG-say-PERF-FV 1.John
      n-a-ring-ir-e
      FOC-1SM-beat-PERF-FV
      I asked what you said John beat.

According to Sabel, 2006, p. 157, we find optional Wh-in-situ in indirect questions co-occurring with partial Wh-movement also in Gurune, Kikuyu, Malagasy, Malay, Ancash Quechua, Babine-Witsuwit'en, West Apache, Slave, Tuki, and Zulu. Sabel claims that the possibility of having optional Wh-in-situ in indirect questions entails the possibility of having partial Wh-movement. This may in fact be incorrect; Wong, 2012 shows that Manglish, an English based creole spoken in Malaysia, allows optional Wh-in-situ in indirect questions yet disallows partial Wh-movement. If Wong is correct about Manglish, then there is no entailment from optional Wh-in-situ to partial Wh-movement. I am not aware of counterexamples to the implication in the other direction.

Sabel analyzes these partial-movement patterns not as instances of literal partial Wh-movement but rather as instances of movement triggered by focus features.[1] He gives two main arguments for this assumption.

First, many languages show focus marking of moved Wh-phrases or focus marking along the path of Wh-movement. These languages include among others Sinhala, Hausa, Kikuyu, Duala, Tuki, Ngizim, Bade, Duwai, Toba Batak, Tagalog, Malagasy, and Malay. The pattern is illustrated below for Kîîtharaka with the marker n/i—'FOC', which already appeared in the examples above.[2]

---

[1] Of course, some connection between focalization and Wh-question formation is postulated very frequently (e.g. Beck and Kim, 2006; Bošković, 1999; Kratzer and Shimoyama, 2002; Miyagawa, 2010; Van Valin and LaPolla, 1997) and seems uncontroversial.

68

(6) Kîîtharaka

    a. Maria a-k-ir-e   mbi?
        1.Maria 1SM-build-PERF-FV what
        What did Maria build?

    b. *Maria n-a-k-ir-e   mbi?
        1.Maria FOC-1SM-build-PERF-FV what

    c. *Maria a-k-ir-e   i-mbi?
        1.Maria 1SM-build-PERF-FV FOC-what

    d. I-mbi   Maria a-k-ir-e?
        FOC-what 1.Maria 1SM-build-PERF-FV
        What did Maria build?

    e. *Mbi Maria a-k-ir-e?
        What 1.Maria 1SM-build-PERF-FV

    f. *Mbi Maria n-a-k-ir-e?
        What 1.Maria FOC-1SM-build-PERF-FV

The sentences that correspond to the grammatical Wh-questions (6a,d) with a non-Wh-object require object focus (Abels and Muriungi, 2008; Muriungi, 2005).

(7) Kîîtharaka

    a. Maria a-k-ir-e   nyomba.
        1.Maria 1SM-build-PERF-FV house.
        Maria built a HOUSE.

    b. I-nyomba Maria a-k-ir-e.
        FOC-house 1.Maria 1SM-build-PERF-FV
        It was a house that Maria built.

As can be seen by inspecting examples (3c) and (5c), the focus marker appears not only on the moved Wh-phrase but also preverbally along the path of Wh-movement. This is shown systematically in (8). (8a) is the Wh-in-situ variant of the question with no focus marker present, (8b) shows short movement of the Wh-word, which becomes marked with FOC. (8c–d) are two further possible ways of expressing the question with partial Wh-movement. Notice the appearance of FOC on all verbs between the overt position of the Wh-word, which is boxed for ease of reading, and the original, sentence-final extraction site. Finally, (8e) shows movement of the Wh-word to the main clause, the clause which is interpreted as a Wh-question throughout. FOC is now obligatory along the entire movement path.

---

[2] In Kîîtharaka, FOC undergoes a phonologically conditioned allomorphy such that *n* appears before vowel initial words and *i*—before consonant initial ones. In the language, FOC appears obligatorily on fronted Wh-phrases, (6d)–(6f), and is impossible on in situ Wh-phrases, (6a)–(6c).

(8) Kîîtharaka   Abels, 2007, pp. 83–84

    a. U-ri-thugania   atî John a-ug-ir-e   atî Pat
        2ndSG-PRS-think that John 1SM-say-PERF-FV that Pat

        a-ug-ir-e   Lucy a-ring-ir-e | ûû |
        1SM-say-PRS-FV Lucy 1SM-beat-PERF-FV who
        Who do you think that John said that Pat said that Lucy beat?

    b. U-ri-thugania   atî John a-ug-ir-e   atî Pat
        2ndSG-PRS-think that John 1SM-say-PERF-FV that Pat

        a-ug-ir-e   n-| ûû | Lucy a-ring-ir-e
        1SM-say-PRS-FV FOC-who Lucy 1SM-beat-PERF-FV
        Who do you think that John said that Pat said that Lucy beat?

    c. U-ri-thugania   atî John a-ug-ir-e   atî n-| ûû | Pat
        2ndSG-PRS-think that John 1SM-say-PERF-FV that FOC-who Pat

        a-ug-ir-e   Lucy n-a-ring-ir-e
        1SM-say-PRS-FV Lucy FOC-1SM-beat-PERF-FV
        Who do you think that John said that Pat said that Lucy beat?

    d. U-ri-thugania   atî n-| ûû | John a-ug-ir-e   atî Pat
        2ndSG-PRS-think that FOC-who John 1SM-say-PERF-FV that Pat

        n-a-ug-ir-e   Lucy n-a-ring-ir-e
        FOC-1SM-say-PRS-FV Lucy FOC-1SM-beat-PERF-FV
        Who do you think that John said that Pat said that Lucy beat?

    e. N-| ûû | u-ku-thugania   atî John n-a-ug-ir-e   atî
        FOC-who 2ndSG-PRS-think that John FOC-1SM-say-PERF-FV that

        Pat n-a-ug-ir-e   Lucy n-a-ring-ir-e
        Pat FOC-1SM-say-PRS-FV Lucy FOC-1SM-beat-PERF-FV
        Who do you think that John said that Pat said that Lucy beat?

The morphosyntactic similarity of focus movement and question formation seen in the above patterns is the first reason Sabel gives for the assumption that apparent Wh-movement in partial-movement languages is really focus movement.

    The second of Sabel's arguments comes from the fact that in many languages there is a restriction according to which only a single focus may appear left-peripherally and foci and Wh-phrases compete for the relevant position.[3] Again, Kîîtharaka can be used to illustrate the generalization. Example (9a) illustrates the restriction to a single focus per clause. Example (9b) shows that moved Wh-phrases participate in this restriction like any other focus.[4]

---

[3] In Abels, 2012, I interpret such facts from a different perspective invoking locality rather than templatic restrictions on positions. However, this does not change the core of the argument as it leaves the fundamental similarity between focus movement and Wh-movement untouched.

(9) Kîîtharaka   Abels and Muriungi, 2008, p. 691

    a. *N-î-buku* (*i-)Maria (*n-)a-gûr-î-îr-e
       FOC-5-book FOC-1.Maria FOC-1SM-buy-APPL-PERF-FV
       (*i-)mw-arimû
        FOC-1-teacher
       Maria bought the teacher a book.

    b. *I-mbi* (*i-)Maria (*n-)a-gûr-î-îr-e
       FOC-what FOC-1.Maria FOC-1SM-buy-APPL-PERF-FV
       (*i-)mw-arimû
        FOC-1-teacher
       What did Maria buy for the teacher?

These are strongly suggestive arguments and I will assume that the movement we see in partial-Wh-movement languages is not driven by a Wh-feature but by a focus feature.[5]

A further important consideration to bear in mind in what follows is that full movement in Kîîtharaka is sensitive to islandhood in a fairly standard way (Muriungi, 2003, pp. 37–45). Example (10e) illustrates this for a complex-NP island. Wh-in-situ, on the other hand, is insensitive to islands, (10a). Partial Wh-movement is sensitive to islands both along the path between the gap and the landing site of partial movement, (10d), and along the path from the landing site of partial movement to the Wh-scope position, (10b–c). All examples in (10) are intended to have the meaning given for (10a).[6]

(10) Kîîtharaka   Peter Muriungi, pers. comm.

---

[4] Sabel, 2006 suggests that languages like German have partial Wh-movement driven by a Wh-feature and exemplified by the scope-marking construction. My analysis will exclude this type of analysis for the scope-marking construction and allow only what is known as the indirect-dependency approach to scope-marking constructions (see the papers in Lutz, Müller, and Stechow, 2000, den Dikken, 2009b; Fanselow, 2006; Felser, 2001).

[5] The implementation that I will give does not rely crucially on the other feature being a focus feature. It does rely crucially on the trigger for partial movement being different from a Wh-feature.

[6] For comparable facts from Malay, a very similarly behaved language, see Cole and Hermon, 1998.
Example (10c) is ungrammatical for independent reasons, anyway, as the focus marker never occurs in the topmost clause of a relative (see Abels and Muriungi, 2008). For the other examples, locality of movement seems to be the deciding factor.

a. û-rî-thûgan-i-a   n-ding-ir-e   mw-arî û-ra
2^{nd}SG-PRS-think-CAUS-FV 1^{st}SG-hit-PERF-FV 2-girl 2-that
a-ug-ir-e   ati Peter a-gur-ir-e   ûû
SM-say-PERF-FV that 1.Peter SM-marry-PERF-FV who
Who$_k$ do you think that I hit the girl$_m$ who$_m$ said that Peter will
marry her$_k$?

b. *û-rî-thûgan-i-a   n-ding-ir-e   mw-arî û-ra
2^{nd}SG-PRS-think-CAUS-FV 1^{st}SG-hit-PERF-FV 2-girl 2-that
a-ug-ir-e   ati n-ûû   Peter a-gur-ir-e
SM-say-PERF-FV that FOC-who 1.Peter SM-marry-PERF-FV

c. *û-rî-thûgan-i-a   n-ding-ir-e   mw-arî û-ra
2^{nd}SG-PRS-think-CAUS-FV 1^{st}SG-hit-PERF-FV 2-girl 2-that
n-ûû   a-ug-ir-e   ati Peter n-a-gur-ir-e
FOC-who SM-say-PERF-FV that 1.Peter FOC-SM-marry-PERF-FV

d. *û-rî-thûgan-i-a   n-ûû   n-ding-ir-e   mw-arî
2^{nd}SG-PRS-think-CAUS-FV FOC-who 1^{st}SG-hit-PERF-FV 2-girl
û-ra a-ug-ir-e   ati Peter n-a-gur-ir-e
2-that SM-say-PERF-FV that 1.Peter FOC-SM-marry-PERF-FV

e. *N-ûû   û-kû-thûgan-i-a   i-n-ding-ir-e
FOC-who 2^{nd}SG-PRS-think-CAUS-FV FOC-1^{st}SG-hit-PERF-FV
mw-arî û-ra n-a-ug-ir-e   ati Peter
2-girl 2-that FOC-SM-say-PERF-FV that 1.Peter
n-a-gur-ir-e
FOC-SM-marry-PERF-FV

3.3 Pied-piping

Another important property of movement has to do with the size of the moving element. The specific syntax of constituent questions in English generally requires a Wh-word to front. If a word is fronted that does not belong to the narrowly circumscribed class of question words, the particular interrogative syntax of subject-auxiliary inversion is not triggered and no question interpretation is possible, (11).

(11)   English
    a. Who did John kick?
    b. *Fred did John kick?
    c. I wonder who John kicked.

    d. *I wonder Fred John kicked.

However, in some cases phrases that merely contain a Wh-word may satisfy the relevant requirement on the clause-initial position. Thus the preposition in (12a–b) is not morphologically a Wh-word and neither is its noun phrase complement. The Wh-word is relatively deeply buried inside of the prepositional phrase. Yet, syntactically, the entire prepositional phrase satisfies the relevant requirement on the clause initial position. Similarly, the head noun in (12c–d) is not morphologically a Wh-word. The Wh-word is deeply buried in the possessor phrase. Nevertheless, the entire phrase satisfies the Wh-requirement on the clause-initial position.

(12)   English
    a. In what way did he solve the problem?
    b. I wonder in what way he solved the problem.
    c. Whose mother's demands could he satisfy?
    d. I wonder whose mother's demands he could satisfy.

Important recent work on pied-piping (Cable, 2007, 2010a,b; Heck, 2004, 2008, 2009) has revealed a number of cross-linguistically valid generalization concerning pied-piping.

First, pied-piping is recursive. Heck, 2008, p. 76 formulates the relevant generalization as follows:

(13)   Generalization on recursive pied-piping
    If a Wh-phrase α can pied-pipe a constituent β, and if β is in a canonical position to pied-pipe γ, then α can also pied-pipe γ.

Specifiers, particularly specifiers of DP, are probably *the* canonical position for pied-piping. In (14), the Wh-word occupies the specifier position within DP and the entire DP can be pied-piped.[7]

(14)   English
    Whose mother did you invite?

It follows from (13) that specifiers of specifiers of DP should be able to pied-pipe the largest DP, as in (15).

(15)   English
    Whose mother's friends did you invite?

---

[7] Here and throughout I abstract away from the cases discussed in the literature under the label of massive pied-piping, which occurs in echo questions and has a somewhat different syntax from the more restricted application of pied-piping found in true questions and relative clauses. For discussion, see Cable, 2007; Heck, 2004, 2008.

As is well-known, pied-piping by possessors is recursive in English. Heck exemplifies recursion of this type also using Danish, Russian, Polish, German, and French examples.

Another typical position from which pied-piping is possible, is the complement position of a preposition. In languages disallowing preposition stranding, moving Wh-words often pied-pipe the preposition. This is illustrated in (16) for German. (16a) represents pied-piping of a PP by the Wh-complement of that preposition, while (16b) shows pied-piping of a PP (headed by *bis*—'until') recursively by the complement of its complement.

(16)   German   Heck, 2008, p. 85
    a.   Fritz fragt sich mit wem sie gesprochen hat.
            Fritz asks REFL with whom she spoken   has
            Fritz wonders who she talked to.
    b.   Fritz weiß bis zu welchem Punkt er gehen kann
            Fritz knows until to which   point he go   can
            Fritz knows how far he can go.

As predicted by (13) pied-piping from specifier and from complement position can happen simultaneously as in (17), which illustrates pied-piping of PP by the specifier of P's complement.

(17)   German
    Ich frage mich mit wessen Mutter du gesprochen hast.
    I   ask REFL with whose mother you spoken   have
    I wonder whose mother you talked to.

Heck notes that in some cases recursivity breaks down, citing Icelandic and various Mayan languages, including Tzotzil, which features in the discussion in the next section.

I will implement pied-piping in terms of feature transmission via agreement with phase heads. The first consequence of this is that only phases are potential pied-pipees. Given that DPs and PPs are regularly pied-piped, I conclude that DP and PP must be phases. A problem for most agreement based theories of pied-piping is that they fail to unify pied-piping by a specifier, for examples the possessor in DPs, with pied-piping by a complement, since the specifier-head configuration is often seen as crucial for agreement (Heck, 2004). This problem will be solved by stating the configuration which licenses agreement in terms of more primitive c-command requirements. These, it will be shown, are met by the head-complement relation as well. This move provides the required unification of agreement configurations, making an agreement-based theory of pied-piping possible. The second problem of agreement-based accounts of pied-piping is the apparent absence of independent evidence for the existence of the features in question on the heads that would need to agree for these features (Heck, 2008, pp. 56–58): The agreeing features on the heads of the pied-piped phrases are accused of being spurious. I would like this entire essay and the theory it contains to be understood as a plausibility argument against this suggestion.

A direct prediction from the idea that phases are potential pied-pipees is that vPs and CPs should be able to be pied-piped. A possible example of CP pied-piping comes from Basque (see Ortiz de Urbina, 1989). Basque has two strategies for forming questions. In one strategy the Wh-phrase moves to the position immediately to the left of the inflected verb within the clause where it takes scope, (18a). In the other strategy, the Wh-word moves to the corresponding position in the clause where it originates and the entire clause then moves to the position where the Wh-word itself moves in the first strategy, (18b).

(18)   Basque   Arregi, 2003, p. 118

    a.   Se   pentzate su [$_{CP}$ esan dabela Mirenek   [$_{CP}$ se idatzi rabela
        what you.think   said has   Miren.ERG   written has
        Jonek]]?
        Jon.ERG
        What do you think Miren said Jon wrote?

    b.   [$_{CP_1}$ Se idatzi   rabela Jonek]   pentzate su [$_{CP_2}$ esan dabela
                what written has   Jon.ERG you.think   said has
        Mirenek t$_{CP_1}$]?
        Miren.ERG
        What do you think Miren said Jon wrote?

While the exact position occupied by the Wh-word itself is subject to some controversy,[8] it is clear that the category undergoing movement here is CP. Other languages for which pied-piping of CPs has been proposed include Imbabura Quechua (Hermon, 1985), Cuzco Quechua (Ortiz de Urbina, 1989), Latin, and German. See Heck, 2004 for detailed and Heck, 2008 for more cursory discussion. To this list we might add Tlingit (Cable, 2007, 2010a,b) and Sinhala (Kishimoto, 2005).

In sum, pied-piping of CP is robustly attested.

Pied-piping of vP appears to be rare cross-linguistically. The most plausible cases that I am familiar with come from a construction in German (Trissler, 2000, pp. 41–42, 145–146, Reis, 2006, Heck, 2008, pp. 157–160) where participles and infinitives with and without *zu*—'to' are pied-piped by a degree phrase. Pied-piping is optional here.

---

[8]   Ortiz de Urbina, 1989 reverses his earlier analysis where Wh-phrases are located low and argues for placement in Spec,CP. Arregi, 2002 argues, essentially, for a return to the older position with placement of Wh-phrases in Spec,vP.

    An analysis with pied-piping of CP by an element in a vP-peripheral focus position, an analysis similar to Arregi's analysis of Basque, that is, is also suggested for Malayalam in Jayaseelan, 2001, 2003, 2004.

(19)　German　　　　　　　　　　　　based on examples in Reis, 2006

    a.   Weißt du, wie schön　　geschrieben man haben muss, um
        know you how beautifully written　　one have　must in.order
        eine Eins zu bekommen?
        a　one to get
        Do you know how beautifully one must have written in order to
        get an A?

    b.   Weißt du, wie schön　　man geschrieben haben muss, um
        know you how beautifully one written　　have　must in.order
        eine Eins zu bekommen?
        a　one to get
        Do you know how beautifully one must have written in order to
        get an A?

    c.   Ich weiß nicht, wie gut　zu sehen ein Verkehrsschild sein muss.
        I　know not　how good to see　a　traffic.sign　be　must
        I don't know how visible a traffic sign must be.

    d.   Ich weiß nicht, wie gut　ein Verkehrsschild zu sehen sein muss.
        I　know not　how good a　traffic.sign　to see　be　must
        I don't know how visible a traffic sign must be.

    e. ?Ich habe ihn gefragt, wie schrecklich laut　singen er sie
        I　have him asked　how horribly　loudly sing　he her
        gehört hat.
        heard has
        I asked him how terribly loudly he had heard her sing.

    f.   Ich habe ihn gefragt, wie schrecklich laut　er sie singen
        I　have him asked　how horribly　loudly he her sing
        {gehört | hören} hat.
        heard　hear　has
        I asked him how terribly loudly he had heard her sing.

These examples are at least plausible candidates for pied-piping of vP.[9]

I develop a theory of pied-piping that relies on feature transmission from the pied-piper to the pied-pipee via agreement. Under such a theory, those categories that can be pied-piped can also bear the relevant features, even if they are not expressed morphologically or interpreted semantically. In this perspective, pied-piping provides another argument for movement-type-specific features on phases.

---

[9] I would speculate that the difficulty in finding examples of vP pied piping is connected to the absence of Wh-verbs in the better-studied languages. For discussion of interrogative (pro-)verbs. See Cysouw, 2004; Hagège, 2008; Mackenzie, 2009 and references given there.

3.4 Secondary movement

I refer to movement as secondary (Wh-)movement, if it involves placement of a constituent in a particular position to enable pied-piping. Typically, this special position is the specifier position of the pied-piped phrase. A good example of this type comes from Tzotzil, a Mayan VOS language (see Aissen, 1996). Within the noun phrase, the possessor usually follows the possessed, (20).

(20)   Tzotzil   Aissen, 1996, 454 ex. 22, 455 ex. 25

        a.   s-p'in   li   Maruch-e
             A3^{rd}-pot the Maruch-ENC
             Maruch's pot
        b. *Maruch s-p'in
             Maruch A3^{rd}-pot
        c. *li   Maruch s-p'in   ... -e
             the Maruch A3^{rd}-pot   -ENC

Wh-words are fronted in Tzotzil.

(21)   Tzotzil   Aissen, 1996, 453 ex. 16

        a.   K'usi a-man?
             what A.2nd-buy?
             What did you buy?
        b. *A-man k'usi?

In Wh-questions with pied-piping, a Wh-possessor obligatorily fronts across the possessed:

(22)   Tzotzil   Aissen, 1996, 457 ex. 32, 35

        a.   Buch'u x-ch'amal i-cham?
             who   A3^{rd}-child CP-died
             Whose child died?
        b. *X-ch'amal buchu i-cham?

This is true also in recursive possessor constructions. The declarative (23a) allows the three interrogative versions in (23b–d). (23c) shows clear evidence that the Wh-possessor is fronted within its noun phrase.

(23)   Tzotzil   Aissen, 1996, 481 ex. 97a and 485 ex. 103

        a.   I-'ixtalaj s-kayijonal   y-osil   li   j-tot-e.
             CP-ruin A3^{rd}-firelane A3^{rd}-land the A.1st-father-ENC
             The firelane around my father's land was ruined.

b. Buch'u i-'ixtalaj s-kayijonal   y-osil?
    who   CP-ruin $A3^{rd}$-firelane $A3^{rd}$-land
c. Buch'u s-kayijonal   y-osil   i-'ixtalaj?
    who $A3^{rd}$-firelane $A3^{rd}$-land CP-ruin
d. Buch'u y-osil   i-'ixtalaj s-kayijonal?
    who $A3^{rd}$-land CP-ruin $A3^{rd}$-firelane
    The firelane of whose land was ruined?

Secondary Wh-movement is like partial Wh-movement discussed in section 3.2 in that it does not terminate in the scope position of the Wh-word. To facilitate the discussion below, let me introduce a terminological distinction not found in Heck, 2004, 2008, 2009, on whose work much of the following discussion relies otherwise. Consider (23c) again. In the example, the Wh-word is moved within the containing DP and the entire DP is moved to the beginning of the sentence, (24a). The variant in (24b), where the Wh-element remains in situ while the containing DP moves, is ungrammatical.

(24)   a. $[_{CP} [_{DP}$ *wh* $[\dots$ wh $]] [\dots$ DP $]]$
       b.   *$[_{CP} [_{DP} [\dots wh]] [\dots$ DP $]]$

Heck calls every pattern secondary movement where pied-piping of a larger phrase depends on a particular word order within that phrase. While this is a useful descriptive label to have, we can ask whether a given type of word order alternation is allowed independently of whether the containing phrase moves or not (and potentially contains no Wh-element at all). Applied to Tzotzil this is the question of whether a possessor can front to the left edge of DP independently of the (Wh-)fronting of the containing DP. The terminological distinction I make is as follows: I call those cases *secondary movement proper* where the word order alternation in question depends on the simultaneous fronting of the larger pied-piped structure. If, on the other hand, the type of alternation within the moved constituent exists independently of pied-piping, I speak of *apparent secondary movement*:

(25)   X is the target of the movement operation, Y is the containing, pied-piped constituent
       a.   Secondary movement proper: X can only pied-pipe Y given a particular order O within Y; the order type O is not attested in the language independently of pied-piping of Y.
       b.   Apparent secondary movement: X can only pied-pipe Y given a particular order O within Y; the order type O is attested in the language independently of pied-piping of Y.

The distinction is of potentially great analytic importance. The analytically simpler case is that of apparent secondary movement. It has as its basis an independent word order alternation. All that needs to be explained is why pied-piping is possible with one order but not with the other. The explanation of the order alternation itself can therefore be kept independent of the theory of, for example, Wh-movement or relativization or pied-piping. Instances of secondary movement proper present a greater challenge, since they require not only an explanation of why pied-piping is impossible under one order but also require a movement operation within the pied-piped constituent that is not otherwise present in the language.

If we investigate the examples in Heck, 2004, 2008 in this light, we note that most instances of secondary movement he gives are cases of apparent secondary movement. For simplicity, let me start with an example discussed in Cable, 2010b. Cable, 2010b, p. 177 says that the (ii)-examples of the following English pairs involve secondary Wh-movement in Heck's sense. The (i)-examples are more or less strongly deviant instances of pied-piping.[10]

(26)   English

    a.   (i)   ?I wonder pictures of who John bought.
        (ii)   I wonder whose pictures John bought.
    b.   (i)   *I wonder a how big boat John bought.
        (ii)   I wonder how big a boat John bought.

Clearly, these examples fit the description of secondary movement: pied-piping requires a particular word order in the pied-piped constituent. Equally clearly, though, we are not dealing here with secondary movement proper: possessors may (*John's picture*) and certain degree expressions must (*too big a boat*) appear at the left edge of the DP in English anyway.

The same is true for a quite a few of Heck's own examples of secondary Wh-movement. Heck, 2008 lists German genitive possessors as an instance of secondary Wh-movement. In German, non-Wh-possessors in the genitive case may appear postnominally, but Wh-possessors are restricted to prenominal position, (27a–b).

(27)   German   Heck, 2008, p. 91

    a.   die Bilder   des   Künstlers
        the paintings the.GEN artist.GEN
        the artist's paintings
    b.   Ich weiß, {*die Bilder   wessen | wessen Bilder}   du
        I   know   the paintings whose.GEN   whose paintings you
        kaufen würdest.
        buy   would

---

[10]   In contrast to Cable, 2010b, I am using embedded versions of the examples to avoid echo construals of these questions in which the constraints on pied-piping are different (see Cable, 2010b; Heck, 2004, 2008; Horvath, 2006).

I know whose paintings you would buy.

However, since DP-initial genitive possessors are possible (if marked stylistically) in German, (28), the pattern we see in (27) is apparent secondary movement rather than secondary movement proper. As a consequence, the theory of Wh-movement or pied-piping need not be burdened with an explanation of the possibility of prenominal genitives. All that needs to be explained is why pied-piping from post-nominal position is blocked.

(28) German

  des Künstlers Bilder
  the artist.GEN paintings
  the artist's paintings

Similarly, in Hungarian pied-piping by possessors is possible only if the possessor is in the dative case. Nominative possessors do not induce pied-piping, (29).

(29) Hungarian   Heck, 2008, p. 92

  a. Kinek   a   vendégét ismertétek?
      who.DAT the guest   you knew
      Whose guest did you know?
  b. *Ki   vendégét ismertétek
      who.NOM guest   you knew

Again, the positioning (before the article) and case marking of the possessor is independent of Wh-movement in Hungarian, where we find a regular alternation between nominative and dative possessors, (30). We are thus dealing with a case of apparent secondary movement.

(30) Hungarian   Szabolcsi, 1994

  a. (a) Mari   kalap-ja-i-$\emptyset$
      the Mari.NOM hat-POSS-PL-3^{rd}SG
      Mari's hats
  b. Mari-nak a   kalap-ja-i-$\emptyset$
      Mari-DAT the hat-POSS-PL-3^{rd}SG
      Mari's hats

The same considerations apply to genitives in Polish. According to Heck, 2008, p. 93 only prenominal genitives support pied-piping. Genitives may appear both pre- and postnominally in Polish (Rappaport, 2001), therefore this is another case of apparent secondary movement.

For Rumanian, we are again faced with a similar situation. According to Heck, 2008, pp. 94-96, as a first approximation, only prenominal possessors induce pied-piping in Rumanian while postnominal ones do not, (31).

(31)   Rumanian   Heck, 2008, p. 95

      a.   vecinul   pe a cărui fată   am   văzut-o
          neighbor.the pe P whose daughter have.1^{st}SG seen-her
          the neighbor whose daughter I saw

      b.   *vecinul   pe fată   a cărui am   văzut-o
          neighbor.the pe daughter whose have.1^{st}SG seen-her

The language allows prenominal genitives outside of movement contexts, though they are stylistically marked (Grosu, 1988, fn 3), (32c). The preposition *a* appearing on the prenominal possessor both in (31a) and in (32c) is crucial in allowing prenominal placement of the possessor.

(32)   Rumanian   Grosu, 1988, pp. 933–934

      a.   portret-ul   rege-l-ui
          portrait-ART king-ART-GEN
          the king's portait

      b.   *rege-l-ui   portret(-ul)
          king-ART-GEN portret-ART

      c.   a-l   regel-ui   portret
          P-ART king-GEN portrait
          the king's portrait

In fact, the same considerations show that almost all of Heck's cases of secondary Wh-movement instantiate apparent secondary movement. The clearest cases of secondary movement proper come from French *dont*—'of who' and from Tzotzil.

Regarding French, note first that PPs follow the noun they modify or are and argument of.

(33)   French   Heck, 2008, p. 96

      a.   le comportement de son mari
          the behavior   of her husband
          her husband's behavior

      b.   *de son mari   le comportement
          of her husband the behavior

Relativization of such PPs uses the relative pro-PP *dont*—'of who'. Just in case its extraction is possible, *dont* is extracted from the containing DP. (See the literature cited below for examples and discussion.) In the crucial example below, *dont* will be trapped inside a subject, an island for extraction. The islandhood of subjects can be illustrated with examples like those in (34a–b) and by the impossibility of long *dont* extraction from subjects, (34c) (see Tellier, 1990 and Sportiche, 1998, p. 133 for discussion).

(34)   French   Tellier, 1990, pp. 307, 310 and Sportiche, 1998, p. 132
    a. ?*le diplomate de qui   la secrétaire t'   a   téléphoné
       the diplomate of whom the secretary you has called
       intended: the diplomat whose secretary has called you
    b. ??un homme dont   je refuse que le fils vous fréquente
       a man   of.whom I refuse that the son you   associate.with
       intended: a man who I refuse that the son of him associate with
       you
    c. *la ville de laquelle   la destruction serait   entreprise
       the city of the.which the destruction would.be undertaken
       intended: the city whose destruction would be undertaken

When extraction of *dont* is impossible, it must move to a left-peripheral position within the containing DP. Heck, 2008 interprets such data as involving
secondary movement proper of *dont*, which co-occurs with pied-piping of the
subject.

(35)   French   Heck, 2008, p. 96
    a. un homme dont   le comportement devient drôle
        a man   of.who the behavior   becomes weird
        a man whose behavior becomes weird
    b. *un homme le comportement dont   devient drôle
        a man   the behavior   of.who becomes weird

Heck's analysis is complicated by the fact that secondary Wh-movement must
be restricted to *dont*; if it were available for other PPs as well, examples (34a–b)
would be acceptable. A further complication comes from the fact that long pied-
piping by *dont* is unacceptable, (36).

(36)   French   Heck, 2008, 100 fn. 95
    *un homme dont   le fils je refuse que vous fréquente
    a man   of.whom the son I refuse that you visits
    intended: a man whose son I refuse that he visits you

Despite these complications, the advantage of Heck's proposal is that it turns
a problem of undergeneration into a more tractable problem of overgeneration.
The problem of undergeneration arises under many previous analyses of *dont*,
because they do not allow *dont* to pied-pipe the containing NP but only to extract. This leads to a theoretical impasse when examples like (34) are considered together with (35a). The problem of overgeneration that Heck's analysis
creates is twofold. First, the secondary movement strategy must be restricted
to *dont* since no other prepositional phrase is able to pied-pipe a DP in French
from pre-nominal position. Second, even for *dont*, long pied-piping must be
blocked. Since *dont* shows a positioning within DP not otherwise allowed for

PPs in French, we are dealing with a case of secondary movement proper under Heck's analysis.

The second reasonably clear case of secondary movement proper comes from the Tzotzil data discussed above.[11] As we saw, Aissen, 1996 argues that possessors in Tzotzil are obligatorily postnominal, (20). This pattern may and must be broken when the possessed DP undergoes movement via pied-piping by the possessor, (22). That we are truly dealing with movement of the possessor is strongly suggested by the pattern for complex DPs, (23), in particular by (23c), where possessor and possessed are not adjacent. That we are dealing with movement *internal* to the DP is suggested by the fact that when the DP is an island, for example, the subject of an unergative or transitive verb, the possessor cannot extract and the entire DP fronts, (37).

(37) Tzotzil   Aissen, 1996, p. 460

    a. Buch'u x-ch'amal y-elk'an   chij?
        whose $A3^{rd}$-child $A3^{rd}$-steal sheep?
        Whose child stole sheep?

    b. *Buch'u y-elk'an   chij   x-ch'amal
        whose $A3^{rd}$-steal sheep $A3^{rd}$-child

Unlike the French pattern with *dont*, which is restricted to a single lexical item, possessor fronting in Tzotzil is productive. According to Aissen, it is also not restricted to Wh-movement. She claims (Aissen, 1996, p. 473) that foci are also fronted to the clausal left periphery in Tzotzil and that focus-fronted DPs also allow internal possessor fronting, (38). However, possessor fronting in focal DPs is limited to first and second person pronouns (Aissen, 1996, 473 fn. 26).

(38) Tzotzil   Aissen, 1996, p. 473

    a. Vo'ot a-krem   i-p'aj yalel
        you $A.2^{nd}$-son CP-fall down
        It's *your* son that fell down.

    b. Vo'on j-malal   i-y-ik'-ik   ech'el
        I $A.1^{st}$-husband CP-$A3^{rd}$-take-3^{rd}PL away
        It's *my* husband that they took away.

Overall, we find that possessor fronting in Tzotzil is restricted to contexts where the containing phrase undergoes pied-piping. Possessor fronting in the language therefore presents a bona fide case of secondary movement proper.

I take the preponderance of apparent secondary movement over secondary movement proper to show that secondary movement is triggered by a feature dif-

---

[11] Other languages that show this type of pattern are Chol (Coon, 2009), San Dionico Zapotec (Broadwell, 2001), and possibly also Kaqchikel (Broadwell, 2005, section 4.3).

ferent from the feature driving primary movement. Indeed, this will be encoded in the theory of feature interpretability introduced informally in the next section. The few cases where secondary movement proper does seem to exist must also be analyzed in terms of two different features: one driving the secondary movement and the other driving the primary movement. For Wh-movement for example, this requires splitting the Wh-relation into two separate components, which roughly correspond to a focus-like relation and the Wh-relation proper. The same move is required anyway for an analysis of partial-Wh-movement constructions, as mentioned above.

In their discussion of the Tzotzil pattern, Coon, 2009 and Cable, 2010b, chapter 5.4 particularly emphasize the impossibility of successive possessor roll-up (also known as, snowballing movement), (39). The impossibility of roll-up is predicted by Cable's theory of pied-piping but not by the traditional analysis. Translated into present terminology, the observation is that secondary movement proper never allows roll-up movement.

(39) Tzotzil   Aissen, 1996, p. 481

*Buch'u y-osil   s-kayijonal   i-'ixtalaj?
who   A3rd-land A3rd-firelane CP-ruin
Whose land's firelane was ruined?

This generalization will be captured by the current theory.[12] The expectation of the system developed below is that all and only phase edges can be targeted by secondary movement, because only phase heads carry the necessary movement-inducing, uninterpreted features.

3.5 Reflection

At the end of the last chapter I concluded not only that movement paths are punctuated but also that successive-cyclic movement is triggered by features on certain heads, the phase heads, along the path of movement. Recall that subject-auxiliary inversion along the path of movement in Belfast English is restricted to cyclic movement of Wh-phrases and is impossible under cyclic relativization. On the basis of such facts, I concluded that the features responsible for intermediate movement steps are not all-purpose movement triggers but specific features: a Wh-feature for Wh-movement, a Rel-feature for relativization,... A

---

[12] Cable's generalization provides a new argument in favor of Abels and Neeleman's (2012) account of the word order within DP and against Cinque's (2005) account in terms of roll-up movement implemented as pied-piping.

question that remained open in the previous chapter had to do with the semantic interpretation of these features, their apparent semantic vacuity.

Belfast English suggests that in a sequence of phase heads triggering successive-cyclic Wh-movement, only the head hosting the last step of Wh-movement is interpreted. As a first approximation we could postulate the following condition on semantic interpretation of features: only those features that give rise to a terminal movement step are semantically interpreted.

Obviously, this condition is far too strong. Most features don't rely on triggering movement for their interpretation. Some features are intrinsically valued; others require a syntactic dependency that does not involve movement (for example agreement) for interpretation. Alluding to early minimalist terminology, I will, for the present discussion, call those features that rely on movement for a particular interpretation *strongly deficient*.[13]

We can sharpen the idea from the previous paragraph and assume that strongly deficient features are only interpreted if they give rise to a terminal movement step.

It should be intuitively clear that the contrast between (40a) and (40b) can be captured in these terms: The Wh-feature on the embedded complementizer is interpretable in (40a) because the Wh-phrase terminates in its specifier position. In (40b) on the other hand, the Wh-phrase does not terminate in that position, hence, the Wh-feature on the embedded complementizer is not interpreted semantically, hence, the subcategorization requirement of *wonder* is violated.

(40) a. I wonder when he arrived.
      b. *When do you wonder when he arrived?

This discussion is still not sufficiently fine-grained however. I pointed out above (footnote 25 in Chapter 2 on page 51) that the Wh-operator position need not be the final landing site for a Wh-phrase. Relevant evidence came from the Wh-imperative construction in German (Reis and Rosengren, 1992) and from scrambling past the target Wh-operator position in Japanese (Saito, 1992). The German facts are repeated here as an illustration.

---

[13] I make this terminological move with some trepidation since it misrepresents the ultimate theory somewhat. Eventually I will actually suggest that deficient features may be downward looking, upward looking, or both, where these notions are defined in terms of c-command. Those features that look both upward and downward can be satisfied either by their sister or by a moved specifier. The ultimate notion of graded deficiency is quite distinct from feature weakness/strength since it does not involve movement or the specifier-head relation as a primitive.

These matters will be taken up later when the theory sketched here informally will be implemented. For the time being I use the term 'strongly deficient' at the peril of being somewhat misleading.

(41)   German

    a.   Wen   stell   dir   vor, dass Peter besucht hat!
        whom.ACC imagine yourself PRT that Peter visited   has
        Imagine who Peter visited!

    b.   Stell   dir   vor, wen   Peter besucht hat!
        imagine yourself PRT whom.ACC Peter visited   has
        Imagine who Peter visited!

Under Reis and Rosengren's (1992) analysis the Wh-phrase in (41a) is situated in the specifier of the main CP. Here, the generalization that the Wh-feature is interpreted semantically on the head that triggers the final movement step is obviously violated. It is the embedded clause that is interpreted as a question not the main clause. We can rectify this situation by relativizing the notion of a final landing site to the features being checked under movement. On the assumption (Reis and Rosengren, 1992) that the Wh-phrase is a topic in the main clause, we can say that a Wh-feature drives movement to the edge of the embedded clause and a Top-feature drives movement to the edge of the matrix. *Wen* in (41a) therefore makes its terminal step of Wh-movement to the embedded Spec,CP. This allows the embedded CP to be interpreted as a question. *Wen* makes a terminal step of topicalization to the specifier of the main CP.[14] The final formulation of the condition on semantic interpretation of a feature can therefore be given as follows:

(42)   Condition on feature interpretation:
    A strongly deficient feature F is semantically interpreted if and only if it is the trigger of terminal F-movement for some constituent.

This chapter has provided a brief bird's eye view of a large amount of data regarding partial Wh-movement and pied-piping. The main reason for discussing this data is that it bears on the question of the interpretation of features and what might be meant by a terminal movement step. Condition (42) has obvious consequences for the analysis of partial movement and secondary movement. Recall that in partial-Wh-movement structures, the Wh-phrase moves only part of the way to its interrogative-scope position. The overt landing site lies below the

---

[14] An obvious worry at this point is how the feeding-bleeding relations between different movement types are to be regulated. Abels, 2007, 2009, following Williams, 2002 (see also Williams, 2011), suggests that any two movement types are ordered asymmetrically with respect to each other and that movement operations generally are ordered linearly. I call this ordering the universal constraint on operational ordering in language. Evidence for this constraint comes from the type of feeding-bleeding relations under discussion here as well as the feeding-bleeding relations found in remnant movement and in extraction from moved constituents.

interrogative-scope position (just as in (41) it lay above it). (42) precludes analyzing partial-Wh-movement structures as involving movement driven by Wh-
features but where the Wh-movement terminates part of the way to the actual
target. If these movements were triggered by Wh-features, the last overt step
of movement would determine Wh-scope. (42) thus forces the type of analysis adopted on independent grounds by Sabel, where partial Wh-movement is
triggered by a focus feature rather than a Wh-feature.

I will implement pied-piping by assuming feature transmission via (often abstract) with features on phase heads. The recursiveness generalization regarding
pied-piping will be implemented in terms of iterated agreement. Nothing surprising needs to be said here. Regarding secondary movement, (42) precludes
secondary movement triggered by the same feature that triggers movement of
the contained phrase. To see this, consider the following structure.

(43) $[_{AP} [_{BP}$ *wh* $B_{[wh]} [\ldots wh \ldots]] A_{[wh]} [\ldots BP \ldots]]$

Movement of *wh* in this structure is what I have called secondary movement.
If such movement were triggered by a Wh-feature it would count as terminal,
since *wh* does not move on past the specifier of BP and the Wh-feature on B
would have to be interpreted semantically as interrogative. The intent of the
structure, however, is to interpret the Wh-feature on A. At the same time, B must
have the Wh-feature to enable pied-piping. Given (42), movement of *wh* to the
specifier of BP will not count as terminal Wh-movement just in case the movement is triggered by a feature other than [wh]. In light of this, the observation
that most cases of secondary movement instantiate apparent secondary movement is relevant. In all cases of apparent secondary movement an independent
trigger for the (non-Wh-)movement of the Wh-word can be found. Therefore,
by (42), this movement is not terminal Wh-movement and the Wh-feature on
the pied-pipee (B in the structure above) need not be interpreted semantically.
Consider again example (29), repeated here.

(44)   Hungarian   Heck, 2008, p. 92
    a.   Kinek   a   vendégét ismertétek?
        who.DAT the guest   you knew
        Whose guest did you know?
    b. *Ki   vendégét ismertétek
        who.NOM guest   you knew

The derivation of (44a) involves a D-head which has two (strongly) deficient
features. One of them is case related and is responsible for the fact that the
possessor in (44a) appears in the dative. Let me call this feature [dat]. The other
is a strongly deficient Wh-feature. Movement of *kinek* within its containing DP
will satisfy and value both of these features on D. The valuation of D's Wh-
feature allows the entire DP to count as a Wh-phrase and undergo subsequent

Wh-movement to the clausal periphery. Crucially, movement of *kinek* to the edge of DP is not triggered by the Wh-feature since there is another feature, [dat], present on D which is satisfied by the movement.

The discussion would be grossly simplified without bringing up the following issue. While I intend to say that movement of *kinek* is not triggered by the Wh-feature because D also has a strongly deficient dative feature, I would claim that the opposite is not true. That is, movement of *kinek is* triggered by the dative feature despite the presence of a strongly deficient Wh-feature. The asymmetry is the familiar asymmetry between A- and $\overline{\text{A}}$-movements, according to which case-triggered movement of an item must be concluded before operator-triggered movement may happen. As mentioned above (footnote 14 on page 85), Abels, 2007, 2009; Williams, 2002 generalize this reasoning from the binary A-/$\overline{\text{A}}$-distinction to a more fine-grained typology of movement operations. Technically then, when a movement operations satisfies several features simultaneously, the movement is *triggered* only by that feature which determines the lowest movement operation on Abels's (2007; 2009) hierarchy of operations given as the universal constraint on the ordering of operations in language. A suitable definition of *trigger* will be developed in chapter 5

We can now return to (44). (44b) can be ruled out by assuming that there is an inaudible determiner in (44b) which does not have a deficient Wh-feature (but a non-deficient feature valued [-wh]). A DP headed by such a determiner will not be able to be pied-piped, because it cannot acquire the relevant feature value [+wh]. Nor will it be transparent for Wh-extraction, since extraction past a phase head requires a movement-triggering feature on the phase head. As far as I can see, this correctly characterizes the situation in Hungarian.

Other instances of apparent secondary movement will be dealt with on the same model.

As seen in section 3.4, there are a few potential examples of secondary movement proper. These will be analyzed along the same lines as apparent secondary movement, that is, they require the assumption that the secondary movement is triggered by a different feature from the primary movement. Recall now that partial Wh-movement crucially involves a non-Wh-feature as the trigger for overt movement. Similarly, secondary Wh-movement proper will be analyzed as involving a first movement step which is triggered by a feature different from [wh]. (For Tzotzil this feature is plausibly [foc], the feature that is also involved in partial Wh-movement according to Sabel, 2006.) This movement values (as a free-rider) a strongly deficient Wh-feature on the target of secondary movement, which allows pied-piping of the target phrase. Put more bluntly, I claim that secondary movement is always triggered by a feature different from that which drives pied-piping and that it is, in that sense, only apparent.

To conclude, let me summarize again. In the previous chapter, the idea was introduced and defended that successive-cyclic movement is triggered by movement-type-specific features on the heads of intermediate phases. These features are under fine-grained parametric, lexical control and they are morphosyntactically real. However, they are not interpreted semantically. This suggests condition (42) as a condition on feature interpretation. This condition entails that partial movement is only apparent and must be triggered by a feature different from that which would trigger full movement; arguably this is the correct interpretation of the facts anyway. The condition also entails that secondary movement proper cannot exist in a strict theoretical sense.

4 The theory of cyclicity and phases

It is now time to introduce a more technical formulation of the theory that has been developed informally in the previous chapters. In this chapter, I introduce the implementation of the assumptions from chapter 2. I show how the account deals with basic facts of cyclicity, the morphological effects of cyclic movement, how it solves a long-standing puzzle of Austronesian syntax: the restriction in some languages that extraction may only target the pivot and constituents contained therein, and how the account derives the anti-locality constraint from Abels, 2003c, p. 12, (1). The anti-locality constraint says that a phrase merged as the complement of a head may not move within the projection of that head.

(1)   Anti-locality constraint:

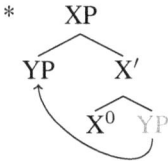

Together with the phase impenetrability condition the anti-locality constraint immediately derives what I called the stranding generalization in Abels, 2003c. The stranding generalization claims that the complements of phase heads can never move by themselves, stranding their embedding phase head, but must always pied-pipe that phase head.

(2)   Stranding generalization
      Given a phase head H and a constituent X in H's c-command domain, the following configurations are, respectively,
      a.   possible to derive: $[X \ldots [H [\ldots X \ldots]] \ldots]$ and
      b.   impossible to derive: $[X \ldots [H X] \ldots]$.

The condition on feature interpretation (42) in Chapter 3 on page 85 will be formulated precisely and discussed only in chapter 5.

Based on the discussion in chapter 2, I take it as a fact that movement paths are punctuated. In section 2.4, I argued that punctuation is the result of a number of simultaneous assumptions. First, movement is a last-resort operation that requires a specific feature to drive movement. This assumption is intended to rule out intermediate landing sites everywhere along the path of movement. Specific triggers may be present only on some heads, the phase heads v, C, D, and P.

What was said in section 2.4 *allows* successive-cyclic movement through phase edges but it does not force such movement. Chomsky, 2000, 2001, 2004,

2008 has suggested that phases have an additional property that forces movement through the phase edge. This additional property is the phase impenetrability condition. The phase impenetrability condition says the following:[1]

(3) Phase impenetrability condition   Chomsky, 2000, p. 108
     In phase α with head H, the domain of H is not accessible to operations outside α, only H and its edge are accessible to such operations.[2]

The phase impenetrability condition was introduced by the name of head constraint first by Riemsdijk:

(4) Head constraint   Riemsdijk, 1978a, p. 169
     No rule may involve X_i (X_j) and Y in the structure $\ldots X_i$ [$_\alpha$ $\ldots$ Y $\ldots$] $\ldots X_j \ldots$
     if Y is c-commanded by the head of α.
     α ranges over V''', N''', A''', P'''

I will assume that the phase impenetrability condition holds. Nevertheless, I dedicate a subsection to the discussion of the (lack of a) relation between phase impenetrability and the theory of islands.

The beginning of the present chapter, section 4.1, gives a precise characterization of configurations under which feature-sharing is possible. The initial discussion is necessarily somewhat technical and abstract, since issues in the definition of syntactic relations, in particular c-command, that arise under multidominance theories need to be taken into account. The section also addresses the issue of whether a sui generis (EP)P or edge property is necessary over and above the assumption that features can be shared and ultimately satisfied only in certain configurations. The second half of section 4.1 discusses, and ultimately dismisses, the argument in Lasnik, 2001a for the assumption of a sui generis EPP.

Section 4.2 shows how the anti-locality constraint falls out as a special case from more general consideerations of the last-resort nature of movement. The section also discusses Grohmann's (2000; 2003) alternative conception of anti-locality.

Section 4.3 restates the phase impenetrability condition in current terms taking account of the refined definitions of c-command discussed in section 4.1. In three successive subsections, I remind the reader that the phase impenetrability

---

[1] Actually, Chomsky has provided two formulations of the phase impenetrability condition. What I paraphrase here is the version from Chomsky, 2000. For relevant discussion of both versions see Grewendorf and Kremers, 2009; Richards, 2007, 2011.

[2] The domain of an element is made up of all constituents that that element c-commands. The edge of a head are all and only those constituents which are dominated by a projection of the head and which asymmetrically c-command the head.

condition is logically independent of and much better supported than the device of sub-numerations, that the phase impenetrability condition does not and cannot deliver a theory of syntactic islands but only of cyclicity, and show how the stranding generalization follows from the joint action of the anti-locality constraint and the phase impenetrability condition.

The final section of the chapter is more directly empirical. It first shows in the abstract how successive cyclicity is implemented here. The next subsection discusses some issues of morphological parameterization of phase heads. The discussion illustrates the descriptive power that the assumption of fine-grained, movement-type specific features on phase heads gives us. At the same time, the cases discussed support the necessity of assuming the relevant features. The final subsection shows how the assumptions about fine-grained featural distinctions between phase heads solve a long-standing puzzle of Austronesian syntax: the problem of the pivot-only restriction on extraction and subextraction.

4.1 Configurations for feature-sharing

In line with much work in minimalist syntax, I assume that there are syntactic heads with unvalued features. Such unvalued features are deficient in that they must be valued in the course of the syntactic derivation for a well-formed object to result. Where relevant, I use the notation [uF]–[F] or [uF]–[+/-F] for unvalued and valued (positively or negatively valued) instances of a feature. As should be clear from the discussion at the end of chapter 3, The notion of valuation must be kept distinct from the notion of interpretation.

Syntactic features inhere in—I will sometimes say are 'borne' by—heads and phrases. Following bare phrase structure (Chomsky, 1995a), I assume that a head bears all of its features and that a complex syntactic object bears all and only the features of the head labeling it.

In line with the assumptions in Brody, 1997; Frampton and Gutmann, 2000; Pesetsky and Torrego, 2007; Pollard, 1984, I assume that feature valuation involves feature-sharing. Pesetsky and Torrego, 2007 point out that under this view, valuing a previously unvalued feature presupposes feature-sharing, but that features can be shared without this leading directly to valuation. This possibility is realized just in case two unvalued features are shared. Shared features will be indicated by a common, boxed superscript. Thus, $[F^{\boxed{7}}]$ and $[F^{\boxed{7}}]$ are shared features but $[F^{\boxed{2}}]$ and $[F^{\boxed{5}}]$ are not and neither are [F] and [F] or [F] and $[F^{\boxed{3}}]$. The indices are not part of the theory but merely a notational convenience. Two features that are shared are the same object and we could try to indicate sharing with a link in a graph (the same way that I show multidominance in constituent structures below). Unfortunately, such notations are very unwieldy and so I resort to the superscript indices. There is no appeal to indices as theoretical devices here, a move that is barred under the guidelines of Chomsky's 1995 inclusiveness condition anyway.

In the spirit of standard approaches to agreement, I assume that feature-sharing and therefore also feature valuation requires the creation of a syntactic dependency between a head bearing an unvalued probing feature and some other syntactic object bearing a corresponding feature. If feature-sharing is to lead to feature valuation, one of the features involved has to be valued. It is a very strong generalization that syntactic dependencies require c-command between the elements involved (see Koster, 1987; Neeleman and van de Koot, 2002, 2010, for discussion). Feature sharing will therefore involve c-command. Ideally, feature sharing should involve nothing else.

C-command, of course, has two directions. A head H with an unvalued feature may c-command a syntactic object bearing the corresponding valued feature or it may be c-commanded by such an object (or both). I construe features as specified for the type of relation that they must bear with the corresponding feature. An unvalued feature that requires a downward syntactic relation with a bearer of [F] will be written as $[uF_\downarrow]$; an unvalued feature that requires an upward syntactic relation with a bearer of [F] will be written as $[uF_\uparrow]$; an unvalued feature that requires both an upward and a downward syntactic relation with a bearer of [F] will be written as $[uF_{\downarrow\uparrow}]$; finally, a feature that is not specified either way will be written as [uF]. I will call $[uF_\downarrow]$, $[uF_{\downarrow\uparrow}]$, and $[uF_\uparrow]$ *probes*.[3] [uF] is unvalued but not a probe.

Ideally this is all we say about feature-sharing. Indeed, we can come quite close to this ideal.

As discussed in slightly different terms in Abels, 2003c, the minimalist distinction between strong and weak features can be recast in terms that involve only c-command. Transparently, $[uF_\downarrow]$ is a weak feature, since it can be shared under c-command and movement is not required for sharing or valuation. The following two configurations are therefore configurations in which $[uF_\downarrow]$ can be shared since in both the unvalued feature on the head c-commands the corresponding feature on another syntactic object, figure 4.1.

$[uF_{\downarrow\uparrow}]$ replace the strong features. Such features can be shared in the two configurations shown in figure 4.2. This requires slightly more discussion. The head-complement relation, (a) in figure 4.2, is clearly one satisfying the c-command requirements of $[uF_{\downarrow\uparrow}]$ since H's complement is both c-commanded by and c-commands H. Under the re-merge or multidominance theory of move-

---

³ Rizzi, 2001c makes a similar upward/downward distinction calling the relevant relations agreement and government, respectively. Rizzi adds the important qualification that locality (Relativized Minimality) has to be observed for upward and downward dependencies to be licit. I assume that this is true.

a.

H$_{[uF\boxed{1}\downarrow]}$ $\ldots[F^{\boxed{1}}]\ldots$

b.

H$_{[uF\boxed{2}\downarrow]}$ $\ldots[F^{\boxed{2}}]\ldots$

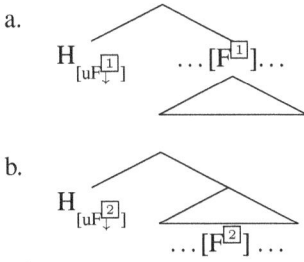

Table 4.1: Sharing configuration for [uF$_\downarrow$]

ment H also c-commands and is c-commanded by any phrase that moves from a position contained in H's complement to a position c-commanding H, (b) in 4.2. Epstein et al., 1998 call this relation derivational sisterhood for exactly this reason.[4]

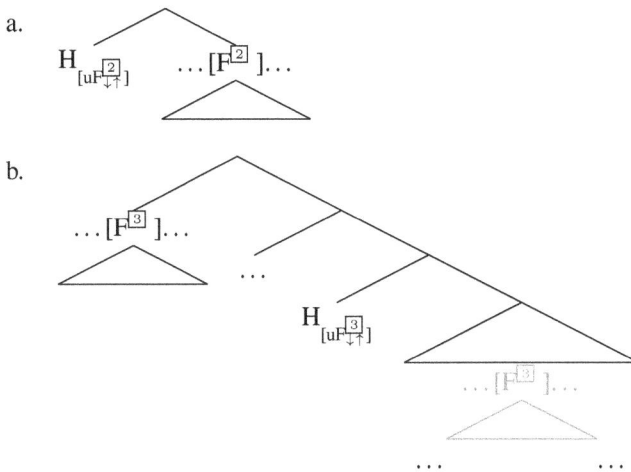

a.

H$_{[uF\boxed{2}\downarrow\uparrow]}$ $\ldots[F^{\boxed{2}}]\ldots$

b.

$\ldots[F^{\boxed{3}}]\ldots$ $\ldots$

H$_{[uF\boxed{3}\downarrow\uparrow]}$

$\ldots[F^{\boxed{3}}]\ldots$

$\ldots$ $\ldots$

Table 4.2: Sharing configurations for [uF$_{\downarrow\uparrow}$]

---

[4] Under a literal copy theory of movement things are less clear-cut. We would need a definition of a syntactic object bearing a feature to include, essentially, a sequence of non-distinct copies. This object, a chain, could then enter into c-command relations with other constituents. I assume here and throughout that the re-merge/multidominance view of movement is correct.

See Stabler, 2004 for a cautioning against the generative power that comes with the type of unbounded copying required under the literal interpretation of the copy theory.

The (b)-structure in figure 4.2 subsumes the relation between a head and its moved specifier as a special case which is derived if the landing site of syntactic object bearing [F] falls within the projection of H. On the assumption that all unvalued features of a head must be shared within that head's projection (along the lines of the virus theory of feature strength), (5), the (b)-structure in figure 4.2 has the relation of a head to its moved specifier or adjunct as the only case.

(5)   Virus theory of feature-sharing.
       A probe on H must be shared before a projection of H may be embedded under the projection of a different head.

Together with (5), figure 4.2 approximates without exactly recreating minimalist notions of feature strength, (EP)P-features, and edge features.[5] The important difference for my purposes is that the standard notions always create a category exclusively for non-complements (specifiers, edge elements). On the other hand the configurations for sharing $[uF_{\downarrow\uparrow}]$ unify complements and moved specifiers in a simple and natural way.

There is substantial empirical support for the unification of complements with movement-derived specifiers and adjuncts. First, in chapter 3 we reviewed properties of pied-piping. We saw that pied-piping by complements of phase heads and by specifiers of phase heads is possible. These specifiers reach their surface position through movement. The definition in 4.2 therefore allows a unified approach to pied-piping. As laid out above, the main question facing the theory of pied-piping is how come a phrase not headed by a Wh-word comes to act as a Wh-constituent. If we assume that the heads of phases that undergo pied-piping bear $[uWh_{\downarrow\uparrow}]$, then any [+Wh]-complement of such a head or a moved [+Wh]-specifier will be able to share and value the head's feature in accordance with 4.2. The entire phase then comes to bear the valued Wh-feature, which allows it to act as a Wh-phrase and thus explains why it can be pied-piped.[6]

Second, as discussed already in Abels, 2003c, the proposed theory of feature-sharing also contributes to our understanding of case-licensing configurations. The view in government and binding theory was that there are three different case licensing configurations: (i) the head-complement relation, (ii) the specifier-head relation, and (iii) the head specifier-of-complement relation. The latter was involved in exceptional case marking. Empirical arguments (Davies

---

[5]   In addition to the virus theory, (5), we will also need a condition banning unvalued features from the interfaces. The virus theory is partly redundant with this interface condition together with the phase impenetrability condition, which I will assume below. I do not try to address this potential inelegance here.

[6]   The structures in figure 4.2 explain how a shared and valued feature ends up on the phase allowing pied-piping. As it stands the system overgenerates substantially, but much of this excess power will be taken back by the theory of feature interpretation later in this chapter.

and Dubinsky, 2004; Lasnik and Saito, 1991; Postal, 1974) suggest that configuration (iii) might not be relevant after all, since, under the revamped raising-to-object analysis, exceptional case marking turns out to require configuration (ii) rather than (iii).[7] The core instances of case licensing then involve the complementation relation (complement of P, complement of V) and moved specifiers (specifier of T for nominative and specifier of v for accusative under exceptional case marking). These configurations are unified, as desired, if we assume that the case licensors bear [uCase$_{\downarrow\uparrow}$].

The third type of probe has an upward looking deficiency: [uF$_\uparrow$]. Such features are shared in the three configurations, shown in figure 4.3. Taking into account the virus theory, these three configurations represent the head-complement relation, the relation between a head and its moved specifier and the relation between a head and its externally-merged specifier. In each case the head bearing [uF$_\uparrow$] is c-commanded by a syntactic object bearing [F].[8]

As can be seen easily, [uF$_\uparrow$] are slightly more permissive regarding the configurations for valuation than [uF$_{\downarrow\uparrow}$]. The issue whether one or the other or sometimes one and sometime the other is the correct theoretical expression of feature strength is subtle. For example the idea that case-licensing configurations are unified as the configurations for valuing [uF$_{\downarrow\uparrow}$] entails that expletive subjects either are not case-licensed or are not directly inserted in the specifier of T. Both positions, caseless expletives and moved expletives, exist in the literature. If it turns out that we must assume that expletives are both case licensed and directly inserted in the specifier of TP, then case licensing might actually be unified using [uF$_\uparrow$]. The issue is too involved to be decided here. Having noted the point, I will use [uF$_{\downarrow\uparrow}$] as the theoretical reconstruction of feature strength henceforth.

Finally, there are simple unvalued features [uF]. These do not bear any instructions regarding the type of configuration under which they can be shared. These features do not act as probes, they do not trigger applications of merge, and are not subject to the virus theory of feature valuation. However, according to the assumption that no unvalued features are tolerated at the interfaces, all [uF] must be shared and eventually valued. The structures above illustrated probes in feature-sharing configurations with valued features, but the configurations could just as well have been illustrated using unvalued features [uF]. [uF] that are not probes play an important role in the account of multiple-Wh-fronting languages

---

[7] It is not clear that exceptional case marking by prepositional complementizers falls under this claim. As discussed in Rizzi, 2001c, the government configuration involved might involve a downward looking dependency only [uCase$_\downarrow$] with further constraints coming from locality theory.

[8] A more exotic configuration that would value [uF$_\uparrow$] is extraction from the specifier/adjunct of H to an outer specifier/adjunct of H. See fn. 17 for some discussion of issues surrounding this configuration.

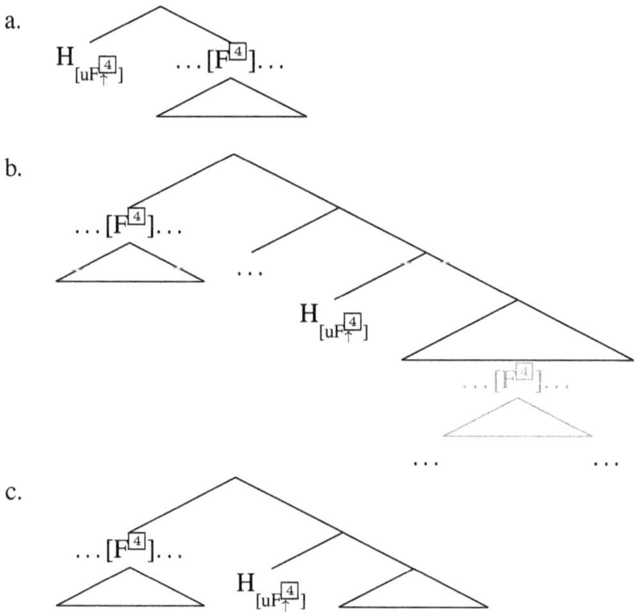

a.

H $_{[uF\boxed{4}_\uparrow]}$ $\ldots[F\boxed{4}]\ldots$

b.

$\ldots[F\boxed{4}]\ldots$

$\ldots$

H $_{[uF\boxed{4}_\uparrow]}$

$\ldots[F\boxed{4}]\ldots$

$\ldots$ $\ldots$

c.

$\ldots[F\boxed{4}]\ldots$

H $_{[uF\boxed{4}_\uparrow]}$

Table 4.3: Sharing configurations for [uF$_\uparrow$]

below, largely because they allow us to implement something like greedy movement.

Conceptually the present reformulation of feature strength in terms of $[uF_{\downarrow\uparrow}]$ seems to be commended by its simplicity. As shown, it also yields immediate insights in the theory of case-licensing and pied-piping in that it automatically unifies configurations that come out as distinct under other approaches. Notwithstanding all of this, it has been claimed that there are empirical reasons to view movement to specifier positions (at least in some cases) as distinct from feature strength. If such arguments are convincing, we would have to abandon the position developed above on empirical grounds and admit the existence of (EP)P features, edge features, traditional feature strength, or something like it.

The remainder of this subsection argues that the arguments in the literature for a sui generis (EP)P or edge property distinct from feature strength are not compelling.

Lasnik, 2001a; Lasnik and Park, 2003 give a number of empirical arguments against treating the EPP as a requirement on valuing strong features. (For discussion from a rather different perspective see Craenenbroeck and den Dikken, 2006.) Lasnik's 2001 argument is built on the claim that otherwise obligatory movement may and must sometimes be suppressed if it originates within an ellipsis site. Lasnik lists two constructions that behave this way: main-clause sluicing and pseudogapping. A relevant example of sluicing in (6) illustrates this.

(6)   English
       Mary will see someone.
       a.   Who will she see?
       b.   *Who she will see?
       c.   Who?
       d.   Who will?   * with *who* as the object

On the assumption that examples like (6c) involve sluicing (Lasnik, 2001b; Merchant, 2001) and that sluicing involves IP ellipsis, the expected form is (6d) with I-to-C movement rather than (6c).[9] Lasnik explains the lack of subject-

---

[9]   Lasnik, 2001a claims that pseudogapping (Jayaseelan, 1990; Johnson, 2001; Lasnik, 1995a; Levin, 1978, 1986) behaves in abstractly the same way. This claim is crucially built on the assumption that material which is not elided in pseudogapping, *Bob* in (i), is in its normal syntactic position and that all elided material, including exceptionally the verb, remains below that position.

On Lasnik's assumptions the structure of (ia) is (ib) with elision of the lower VP.

(i)   English
       a.   You might not believe me, but you will Bob.

auxiliary inversion in sluicing on the basis of the PF-crash theory of strong features. Strong features are those that usually require overt satisfaction and, in particular, overt movement. The PF-crash theory of feature strength explains this in terms of a PF violation that ensues just in case the strong feature is not satisfied (through movement) overtly. Lasnik's version of the PF-crash theory of feature strength localizes the PF violation in the moving element itself (see Lasnik, 1999; Ochi, 1998 for discussion). This view entails that example (6b) is ruled out as a PF violation and that the locus of the violation is the auxiliary *will*. This violation can be avoided in (6c), because here *will* remains unpronounced, hence, invisible to PF.

In Lasnik, 2001a, the behavior of the auxiliary in sluicing is contrasted with the behavior of the subject in VP ellipsis. While in sluicing otherwise obligatory movement (of the auxiliary) out of the ellipsis site is prohibited, such movement (this time movement of the subject from its VP-internal thematic position) remains mandatory under VP ellipsis.

(7)   English

    a.   Mary said she can't swim,

    b.   ...even though she (really) can.

---

        b.   ...but [$_{AgrsP}$ you [Agrs [$_{TP}$ [$_T$ will [$_{VP}$ you [V [$_{AgroP}$ Bob [Agr$_O$ [$_{VP}$ [$_V$ believe] Bob]]]]]]]]]

        c.   ...but [$_{AgrsP}$ you [Agrs [$_{TP}$ [$_T$ will [$_{VP}$ you [believe+Agr$_O$ +V [$_{AgroP}$ Bob [believe+Agr$_O$ [$_{VP}$ [$_V$ believe] Bob]]]]]]]]]

Based on the contrast between (iia) and (iib), the overt realizations of (ib) and (ic) respectively, Lasnik claims that there are two derivational continuations of (ib). Either VP elides or V raises, but not both. On this view, pseudogapping raises the same question as matrix sluicing, where the auxiliary's maximal projection must either elide, or the auxiliary must raise to C, but not both.

(ii)   English

    a.   *You will Bob believe.

    b.   You will believe Bob.

However, examples like the following (Johnson, 2001, 461 ex. 79c, based on Levin, 1986, see also Lasnik, 1999, 205–206 fn. 12) strongly suggest that the unelided material in pseudogapping moves to an exceptionally high position rather than staying in its regular low position that it should occupy according to Lasnik.

(iii)   English

    While Truman doesn't want to visit every city, he does—Barcelona.

For this reason, I will not discuss the argument from pseudogapping in the text.

c. *...even though (really) can.

Under Lasnik's PF-crash theory of feature strength where the crash is triggered by the moving item, this contrast is mysterious. Indeed, Lasnik concludes that the grammatical property that drives movement of the subject, the EPP, is not a strong feature at all but the requirement that Agr$_S$ must project a specifier.

As formulated by Lasnik, the theory entails that there is a first dichotomy between head movement, which is always feature driven, and phrasal movement to specifier positions, which may be driven by strong features or by the EPP. Feature-driven movement is always subject to the strategy of repair by ellipsis, while EPP-driven movement is not. Failure to do head movement should therefore always be reparable by ellipsis. This is empirically incorrect, as the existence of V-stranding VP ellipsis in languages like Irish, Hebrew, and Swahili suggests (Doron, 1999; Goldberg, 2005; McCloskey, 1990a; Ngonyani, 1998). The second dichotomy inherent in Lasnik's theory is that between phrasal movement driven by strong features and phrasal movement driven by the EPP. Both are usually obligatory, but failure to do movement driven by strong features should be ameliorated by ellipsis while failure to do EPP-driven movement should not. To illustrate the logic, suppose that Wh-movement were driven by a strong feature rather than the EPP. We would predict that Wh-phrases could remain in situ and elide as long as their content is recoverable.

(8)   English
   a.   I remember what Joe ordered, but I can't remember what Sally did order what.
   b.   *I remember what Joe ordered, but I can't remember Sally did order what.

I am not aware of the existence of cases that would instantiate this logic and assume that they do not exist. If this is true, Lasnik would be forced to assume that all phrasal movement is EPP-driven. This severely weakens the PF-crash theory of strong features advocated by Lasnik. It now applies only to those cases of obligatory head movement that become non-obligatory or impossible under ellipsis of the launching site. The only example of this type we have seen so far comes from the failure to observe subject-auxiliary inversion under sluicing.

In fact, this one case supporting the PF-theory of strong features and the strict independence of the EPP and feature strength can be dealt with quite easily. The argument, recall, comes from the lack of subject-auxiliary inversion in matrix sluicing. Merchant, 2001, section 2.2.2 shows that the failure to observe subject-auxiliary inversion in English sluicing is part of a larger generalization, which turns out to be independent of head movement. Sluicing is generally incompatible with the realization of material other than the Wh-operator in the C-domain. Merchant, 2001, p. 62 calls this the sluicing-COMP generalization which says that "[i]n sluicing, no non-operator material may appear in COMP."

This applies both to material base-generated in C and to material moved there. Merchant gives examples from German, Bavarian, Dutch, Frisian, Slovene, and Norwegian.

(9)   Southern dialects of Dutch   Merchant, 2001, 74 ex. 97a

    a.   Ik weet niet, wie (of) (dat) hij gezien heeft.
           I know not who if that he seen has
           I don't know who he has seen.

    b.   Hij heeft iemand gezien, maar ik wee niet
           he has someone seen but I know not
        (i)   wie.
        (ii) *wie of.
        (iii) *wie dat.
        (iv) *wie of dat.
            who if that
        He has seen someone, but I don't know who.

On the assumption that complementizers are pronounced in their base positions, these data are not amenable to Lasnik's account in terms of the PF-crash theory of strong features. Instead, the facts suggest that in sluicing all material below the moved phrase elides, that is, they suggest that sluicing is not IP ellipsis but C' ellipsis.[10]

This suggestion receives support from the one counterexample to the sluicing-COMP generalization discussed by Merchant. The examples come from Hungarian, where, unlike in Dutch, the Wh-phrase follows the complementizer, (10a). This complementizer is preserved under sluicing. These facts follow

---

[10] Alternatively, one could assume that in sluicing the Wh-phrase moves to an exceptionally high position. The Wh-phrase might then make use of a higher specifier in a more articulated complementizer structure. What gets elided would be the regular CP containing the inverted auxiliary in English. This suggestion might then be connected to the otherwise mysterious fact that the Wh-phrase must be contrastive in sluicing, (i).

(i)   English
    a.   I know what John bought and you know when.
    b.   *I know what John bought and you also know what.

An account that allows movement of the Wh-phrase to a particularly high position would assimilate sluicing to pseudogapping (see fn. 9). Unusually high placement of the Wh-element in sluicing might also be required for the analysis of sluicing in Japanese (Fukaya, 2007 and the literature referenced there, in particular Takahashi, 1994b). I do not pursue this option here, having shown in Abels, 2012 that the existence of many dedicated heads in an exploded CP layer is dubious.

directly if sluicing involves ellipsis of the sister of the Wh-phrase rather than ellipsis of IP.

(10) Hungarian   Merchant, 2001, 81–2 ex. 116–7

    a. Nem emléksem, (hogy) kivel   talákoztak a   gyerekek.
       not I.remember that   who.with met   the children
       I don't remember who the kids met with.

    b. A   gyerekek találkoztak valakivel   de nem emlékszem,
       The children met   someone.with but not I.remember
       (hogy) kivel.
       that   who.with
       The kids met with someone, but I don't remember who.

Consequently, it is theoretically less costly to assume that Lasnik's PF-crash theory of strong features is wrong. This removes the necessity of a sui generis requirement that certain heads must project specifiers.[11]

In conclusion, the arguments in Lasnik, 2001a do not seriously threaten the reductionist view of feature valuation proposed here and, in particular, they fail to make the argument for an EPP requirement distinct from feature valuation.

The current position is further supported by the observation that EPP satisfaction never happens by an entirely arbitrary (phrasal) constituent. Expletives, in particular, are not arbitrary elements and cannot be replaced arbitrarily by different constituents. A purely configurational notion of the EPP, which is not linked to feature valuation, has no way of expressing this. The configurational EPP would therefore always have to be supplemented with a concomitant feature-valuation requirement. As we just saw, the theory that has only feature valuation and no EPP fares quite well on its own leaving the separate EPP as an assumption without empirical support.

Towards a precise formulation

The discussion of feature-sharing configurations above proceeded on the basis of examples. I hoped that this would be clear enough to get the idea across, but I will now give a more rigorous statement of the configurations in which an unvalued probe can be shared. This gives me a chance also to be a bit more precise about the notions of c-command involved in the different configurations.

---

[11] Lasnik and Park, 2003 present another argument that the EPP cannot be driven by a strong feature. The argument relies crucially on the PF-crash theory of feature strength, which we have seen to be poorly motivated. It also rests on the dubious assumption that sluicing repairs island violations. See also fn 13 in Chapter 6 on page 203.

Extra precision is necessary since, as discussed at some length in Gärtner, 2002, the concept of c-commands splits under the re-merge/multidominance view of movement.

I begin with the concept of c-command in a multidominance theory. Two structures shall suffice to illustrate the issues.

(11)   a.

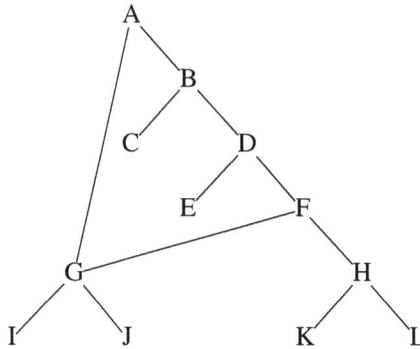

   b.

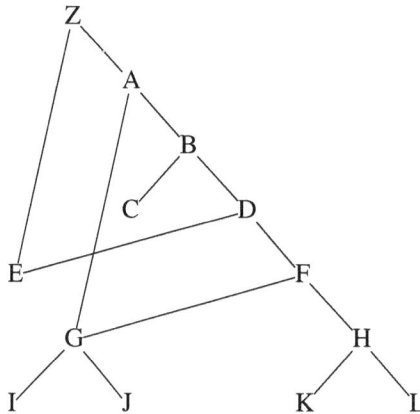

Any definition of c-command rests on the notion of dominance, but in a structure with multidominance, there are two dominance relations: partial and total dominance.[12]

(12)   In a rooted structure, given two nodes α and β,

   a. α *totally dominates* β iff α is contained in every path from β to the root.[13]

   b. α *partially dominates* β iff α is contained in some path from β to the root.

---

[12] For more in-depth treatment, see Gärtner, 2002.

[13] A path from some node γ to the root is an ordered set of nodes $P=n_1 \ldots, n_i \ldots, n_n$ such that $n_1 = \gamma$, n_n is the root, and for any n_k, n_{k+1}, n_{k+1} is a mother of n_k.

In a tree without multidominance both of these definitions collapse. Similarly for c-command. It can be defined either in terms of existential quantification or in terms of universal quantification. For structures obeying the single-mother condition, the result is the same. But the definitions diverge in their scope once we assume multidominance. (13ci-v) are to be interpreted as alternative to each other:

(13) α c-commands β if and only if

    a. α does not dominate β, and

    b. β does not dominate α, and

    c.   (i)   the mother of α properly dominates β.[14]

          (ii)   there is a mother of α that properly partially dominates β.[15]

          (iii) there is a mother of α that properly totally dominates β.

          (iv) every mother of α properly partially dominates β.

          (v)   every mother of α properly totally dominates β.

In a standard tree obeying the single-mother condition, all definitions above give the same result. In a multidominance structure (13c.i) is not defined in all cases, since there is no guarantee that every node has a unique mother. The explicitly quantificational statements in (13c.ii–c.v) give identical results for singly-dominated nodes (C always c-commands K in the structures above), but they give different results for multidominated nodes. Consider the relation between nodes E and G in (11a) and (11b) respectively.

(14)

Definition	Structure (11a)		Structure (11b)		
	E cc's G	G cc's E	E cc's G	G cc's E	Name
(13c.i)	NA	NA	NA	NA	
(13c.ii)	yes	yes	yes	yes	c-command
(13c.iii)	no	yes	yes	no	final c-command
(13c.iv)	yes	no	yes	no	first c-command
(13c.v)	no	no	no	no	first and final c-command

I have given names to the different kinds of c-command relation that we can define in multidominance structures using existential and universal quantification. I will usually use 'c-command' to be defined in the most permissive way,

---

[14] I use *proper* (total|partial) domination to exclude all types of reflexive domination.

[15] The point here has to do with quantification over relations. The same point could have been made using the sister-containment definition of c-command.

(13c.ii). I will use a qualifier if I intend to refer to a different definition, as below in (27), in my rendition of the phase impenetrability condition.

Recall that I use the notion of bearing a feature in the following sense: Any terminal H bears all and only its inherent features. A syntactic object formed by merge bears all and only the features borne by its head.

We can now define the configurations for potential feature-sharing precisely. These configurations are potential in the sense that actual feature-sharing requires locality and the phase impenetrability condition to be satisfied as well. Locality will be understood, in the spirit of Relativized Minimality, to ban sharing with a further-away target, when a closer one is available. As usual, closeness is understood in terms of (some kind of) c-command. The details of locality are irrelevant for what follows.

(15) Potential feature-sharing configurations:

    a. A probing feature $[uF_\downarrow]$ borne by terminal H is in a potential feature-sharing configuration with syntactic object O bearing an F-feature, if and only if H c-commands O.

    b. A probing feature $[uF_\uparrow]$ born by terminal H is in a potential feature-sharing configuration with syntactic object O bearing an F-feature, if and only if O c-commands H.

    c. A probing feature $[uF_{\downarrow\uparrow}]$ born by terminal H is in a potential feature-sharing configuration with syntactic object O bearing an F-feature, if and only if O c-commands H and H c-commands O.

The virus theory of feature-sharing is repeated here from above. It is somewhat vaguer than one would like it to be: What is meant by 'embed'? What exactly is meant by 'before'? The exact answers one gives will depend on the answers to questions such as the following: Is adjunction driven by features of the adjunct or by features of the adjoined-to category? Can complementation lead to sharing of probes borne by the complement? The resolution of such questions is as important for this theory as it is for any other, but I shall set them aside here.

(16) Virus theory of feature valuation
    A probing feature on H must be shared before a projection of H may be embedded under the projection of a different head.

Finally, the interface condition banning unvalued features from the interfaces mentioned in footnote 5 can simply be formulated as follows.

(17) No structure may contain unvalued features at the interfaces.

4.2 Movement and last resort

The previous subsection introduced the configurations in which probes can be shared, (15). I will assume that the presence of an F-probe on a head may trigger the application of the operation merge, which creates a new syntactic object from the current maximal projection of H and another syntactic object bearing [F], projecting H. This is the entirely standard notion of root-extending merge (Chomsky, 1995a,b). If the syntactic object bearing [F] is already contained in H's projection, we speak of internal merge or movement. If the syntactic object bearing [F] is not yet contained in H's projection, we speak of external merge.

I will assume that merge is subject to the following last resort condition which demands that merge generally and internal merge (movement) in particular must bring about feature-sharing.

(18)   *Last Resort*
        A constituent α may only be merged—internally or externally—if that
        leads to the immediate sharing of a feature.[16]

---

[16] A slightly more precise rendition would take the following form:

(i)   Last Resort
       Given two (atomic or derived) syntactic objects α and β, Merge(α, β) is illicit,
       unless either (a) or (b):
       a.   A   The head of α bears a probing feature ([uF$_\downarrow$], [uF$_\uparrow$], or [uF$_{\downarrow\uparrow}$])
                 and β bears a corresponding feature [F] and
            B   the result of Merge(α, β) is a structure in which the probe on the
                 head of α is in a potential feature-sharing configuration with β
                 satisfying locality and the phase impenetrability condition.
       b.   A   The head of β bears a probing feature ([uF$_\downarrow$], [uF$_\uparrow$], or [uF$_{\downarrow\uparrow}$])
                 and α bears a corresponding feature [F] and
            B   the result of Merge(α, β) is a structure in which the probe on the
                 head of β is in a potential feature-sharing configuration with α
                 satisfying locality and the phase impenetrability condition.

We further need to maximize sharing, which can be achieved with the following condition:

(ii)   Immediate Sharing:
       At any stage of the derivation, if a probing feature [F] on head H is in a potential feature-sharing configuration with a corresponding feature borne by O satisfying locality and the phase impenetrability condition, then [F] is shared.

Valuation and interpretation of features are discussed in the next chapter.

This assumption is a key ingredient in the account of the punctuated nature of movement paths. Since movement must be triggered by a probe, it can only target positions projected by heads bearing them. The phase heads (v, C, D, and P) may bear the relevant probes to implement successive-cyclic movement. Other heads may not. Together these assumptions account for the fact that movement may be successive cyclic and may target phases along the path of movement. They also explain why non-phases may not be targeted by successive-cyclic movement. We still do not have an explanation for why movement *must* target intermediate phases. The explanation for this comes from the phase impenetrability condition, which will be recast for the present theory in the next subsection.

Before moving on to the phase impenetrability condition, let's observe an immediate consequence of (18): No syntactic object may be merged with a projection of the same head more than once:

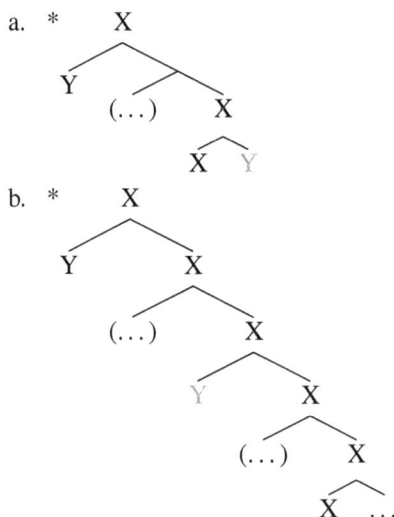

Table 4.4: Illicit second merger within the same projection

Structure (a) in figure 4.4 is intended to illustrate movement of a head or phrase Y from the complement position of a head X to a specifier or adjoined position projected by X. Structure (b) of the same figure is intended to illustrate movement of a head or phrase Y from a specifier or adjoined position within X's projection to another specifier or adjoined position within X's projection.

The illicit structures in figure 4.4 should be contrasted with those in figure 4.5 which are not banned in general, though, of course, many factors may interfere in particular circumstances.

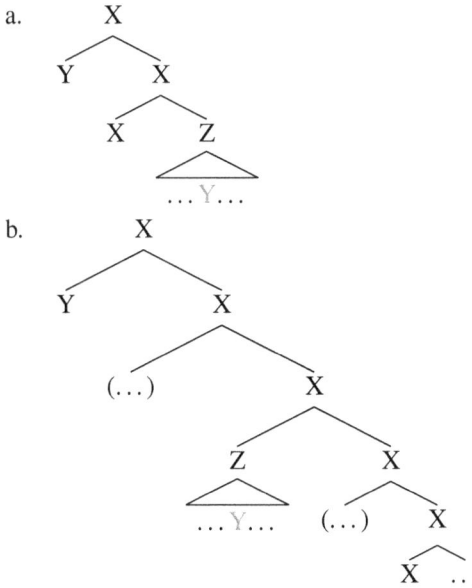

Table 4.5: Licit second merger within the projection of a different head

Structure (a) in figure 4.5 is intended to illustrate movement of a head or phrase Y from the domain of the complement Z of a head X into a specifier or adjoined position projected by X. Structure (b) shows movement from the domain of Z, a specifier or adjunct to X, to a specifier or adjoined position within X's projection.[17]

Essentially, 4.4 says that movement cannot be too short. This idea has been suggested a number of times in the literature. A condition ruling out movement within the same XP has been invoked for example in Bošković (1994, 1997c); Saito and Murasugi (1999), and Kayne (2005, p. 272, 331). These authors also develop some of the consequences of that ban.[18]

---

[17] While extraction from non-complements, structure (b) in figure 4.5, is ruled out categorically by some theories, essentially following Cattell, 1979 (see Chomsky, 1986; Cinque, 1990b; Hornstein, Lasnik, and Uriagereka, (2003) 2007; Huang, 1982; Uriagereka, 1999), there are many examples where extraction from non-complement position appears to be possible (Abels, 2007; Chomsky, 2008; Müller, 2010; Stepanov, 2007; Truswell, 2007a,b). Indeed, Müller, 2010 allows not only extraction from non-complements but explicitly rules in relevant structures, provided that Z and the landing site of Y are separated by some material. Such structures are involved in his 'melting effects.'

[18] Grohmann, 2000, 2003 makes the suggestion that movement within the same 'domain'

In order to understand why last resort rules out 4.4 but allows 4.5, we need to consider for each of the four structures in 4.4–4.5 separately three scenarios: (i) Y bears [F] and the head X bears [uF$_\downarrow$], (ii) Y bears [F] and the head X bears [uF$_{\downarrow\uparrow}$], and (iii) Y bears [F] and the head X bears [uF$_\uparrow$]. We need not consider cases where the head X and Y do not bear corresponding features, because in that case movement could not possible lead to feature-sharing and would therefore always violate last resort.

In structure (a) of figure 4.4, before remerger Y is in a position to share any unvalued feature borne by the head X. This is so, because Y is the complement of the head X and the complement both c-commands and is c-commanded by the head. Therefore, Y can share all three types of probes. Given that feature-sharing is an automatic and immediate consequence of merge, all features that X and Y have in common are shared immediately upon external merge of X with Y. Remerge of Y therefore necessarily violates the last resort condition. Last Resort thus rules out structure (a) of figure 4.4.

Likewise in structure (b) in figure 4.4. Before re-merger of Y, Y c-commands the head X but is not c-commanded by it. Therefore, Y may only share [uF$_\uparrow$] borne by the head X. This situation is not altered by remerging Y. Therefore, re-merger does not lead to the possibility of any new features being shared and is therefore ruled out by Last Resort.

The situation is different in 4.5. In structure (a) of figure 4.5, prior to re-merger of Y, Y may value only [uF$_\downarrow$] borne by the head X, since X asymmetrically c-commands Y. After re-merger of Y, the head X c-commands Y and Y c-commands the head X, therefore [uF$_{\downarrow\uparrow}$] and [uF$_\uparrow$] borne by the head X can be shared. Therefore, if the relevant features are present on X and Y, movement of Y is licit. Similarly in structure (b) of figure 4.5. Prior to re-merger, Y may value no features borne by the head X since it does not c-command Y and Y does not c-command it. Remerger of Y leads to asymmetric c-command of the head X by Y. This enables [uF$_\uparrow$] but no other kind of probe born by the head X to be shared. The presence of relevant features will thus license structure (b) in figure 4.5.

The ban against the configuration in structure (a) of figure 4.4 is what I called the anti-locality constraint in Abels, 2003c. Movement is too short to deliver the kind of change in the c-command relations that would allow features to be shared that couldn't be shared before. Since the same reasoning also blocks structure (b) in figure 4.4, the ban against this configuration should be covered by the term anti-locality as well. The anti-locality constraint follows directly from the assumptions about feature valuation together with the last-resort nature of merge.[19]

---

is ruled out. Since Grohmann's domains are much bigger than the projection of a given head, Grohmann's theory is, in some sense, considerably stronger than the theory of anti-locality pursued here. I discuss Grohmann's theory at the end of this section.

Excursus: An interface view of anti-locality (Grohmann, 2003)

Before closing this section, let me digress briefly and compare the current view of anti-locality to that developed in work by Kleanthes Grohmann. In his Ph.D. thesis (Grohmann, 2000) and a book based on it (Grohmann, 2003), Grohmann develops a rather different view of anti-locality from the one entertained here. He suggests that clauses are divided into three domains: the thematic domain at the bottom (Θ), the agreement domain above it (Φ), and the discourse domain (Ω) at the top. Every syntactic head has a 'context value,' where context values range over Θ, Φ, and Ω. A clause is made up of an uninterrupted sequence of heads and their projections whose context value is Θ at the bottom, followed by an uninterrupted sequence of heads and their projections whose context value is Φ, followed by an uninterrupted sequence of heads and their projections whose context value is Ω:

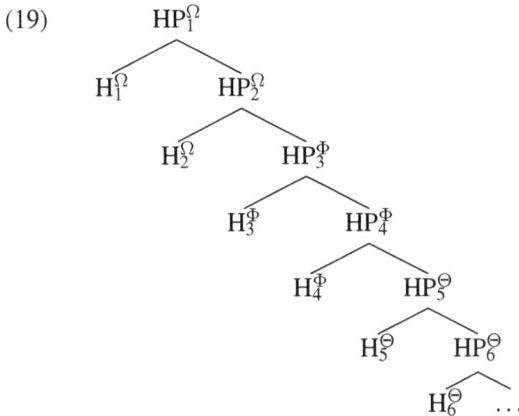

(19)

$$
\begin{array}{l}
\text{HP}_1^{\Omega} \\
\quad \text{H}_1^{\Omega} \quad \text{HP}_2^{\Omega} \\
\qquad \text{H}_2^{\Omega} \quad \text{HP}_3^{\Phi} \\
\qquad\quad \text{H}_3^{\Phi} \quad \text{HP}_4^{\Phi} \\
\qquad\qquad \text{H}_4^{\Phi} \quad \text{HP}_5^{\Theta} \\
\qquad\qquad\quad \text{H}_5^{\Theta} \quad \text{HP}_6^{\Theta} \\
\qquad\qquad\qquad \text{H}_6^{\Theta} \quad \ldots
\end{array}
$$

All adjacent projections with the same context value are said to make up a 'domain' (Δ). Grohmann's anti-locality constraint takes the form of the Condition on domain exclusivity:

(20)   Condition on domain exclusivity   Grohmann, 2003, 78 #35
        For a given prolific domain $\Pi\Delta$, an object O in the phrase marker must receive an exclusive interpretation at the interfaces, unless duplicity of O yields a drastic effect on the output of O.

The intention behind this condition is, under normal circumstances, to ban multiple merger of a single syntactic object within a given domain. To make

---

[19] Snowballing or roll-up movements from complement to specifier of the same head, postulated in a lot of the early work inspired by Kayne, 1994, are impossible under the approach advocated here, since they violate last resort. See Abels and Neeleman, 2012b for extensive discussion compatible with the views taken here.

this slightly more perspicuous and easier to compare with the present theory, let me reformulate both anti-locality constraints in comparable terms. I begin by stating my own constraint in terms of m-command.

(21)   M-command:
        A node α m-commands another node β iff
        a. α does not dominate β;
        b. β does not dominate α;
        c.   the minimal maximal projection dominating α also dominates β.

We note that in the illicit structures in 4.4, the two occurrences of Y m-command each other, while in 4.5, m-command between the two occurrences of Y is asymmetric. In other words, the system of feature-sharing together with Last Resort derives the constraint that no two occurrences of any given syntactic object may be in a symmetric m-command relation.

In a perfectly parallel way, we can define a notion of Δ-command, (23), based on the notion of a maximal Δ-projection, (22). (See Barker and Pullum, 1990 for background.)

(22)   Maximal Δ-projection
        Node α is a maximal Δ-projection iff for every node β immediately dominating α, the context value of α is different from the context value of β.

This definition ensures that in (19) HP_1^{Ω}, HP_3^{Φ}, and HP_5^{Θ} and no other nodes are maximal Δ-projections. The definition of Δ-command now goes as follows:

(23) Δ-command:
        A node α Δ-commands another node β iff
        a. α does not dominate β;
        b. β does not dominate α;
        c.   the minimal maximal Δ-projection dominating α also dominates β.

Grohmann's condition on domain exclusivity now demands that, under normal circumstances, there can be no two occurrences of the same syntactic object in a symmetric Δ-command relation. Since Δ-command domains are strictly bigger than m-command domains, it seems at first that every structure ruled out under the current conception of anti-locality is also ruled out under Grohmann's, but not vice versa. In the limiting case, where there is only a single syntactic head per prolific domain, the two concepts of anti-locality collapse into one.

A question that obviously arises is which of the two notions of anti-locality is empirically more adequate. Boeckx, 2008, ch. 4–5 suggests that the comparison between the syntax of ditransitive verbs in languages that allow both objects to undergo passivization and those that allow only one object to undergo passivization provides an argument for the current view of anti-locality and against Grohmann's. The reader is referred to Boeckx' work for discussion.

However, in addition to being stronger, Grohmann's notion of anti-locality is also weaker than the present formulation. This is so because Grohmann's version of anti-locality is defeasible ("unless duplicity of O yields a drastic effect on the output of O") while (18), crucially, is not. Indeed, the bulk of Grohmann's work is a defense of the notion that pronominalization can be understood as repair a strategy, a way of providing a "drastic effect on the output" of an element that has undergone movement that would otherwise violate (20). The effects discussed in this book under the heading of anti-locality are not generally amenable to this kind of repair strategy so that anti-locality as defined here is a very different notion indeed from Grohmann's. One could, of course, modify Grohmann's version of anti-locality, so that when two members of a chain merely Δ-command each other, this is a reparable anti-locality violation, but if they m-command each other, repair is impossible. However, careful inspection of Grohmann's analyses reveals technical problems and contradictions, which would first need to be resolved.

According to Grohmann, anti-locality violations in the Θ-domain lead to reflexivization. The basic example is the derivation of the sentence *John likes himself*, for which Grohmann (p. 113) suggests the derivation in (24). The idea is that movement of *John* in (24b–c) violates the condition on domain exclusivity. Therefore, the lower copy of *John* is replaced at PF, (24d), by *himself* to guarantee a "drastic effect on output."

(24) a. Lexical Array = {John, like, v, AgrO, I}
      b. [$_V$ likes John]
      c. [$_V$ John [$_V$ likes John]]
      d. [$_V$ John [$_V$ likes himself]]
      e. [$_I$ John I [$_{AgrO}$ (himself) [AgrO [$_V$ John v [$_V$ likes himself]]]]]

Elegant though this may seem, the step between (24c–d) as well as the continuation of the derivation pose an unrecognized architectural challenge for Grohmann's theory. He explicitly endorses the idea that replacement of *John* by *himself* happens at PF and does not feed back into the syntax. According to Grohmann, such feedback would violate the inclusiveness condition (2003, p. 302). In other words, the true syntactic derivation and structure of the example is as follows:

(25) a. Lexical Array = {John, like, v, AgrO, I}
      b. [$_V$ likes John]
      c. [$_V$ John [$_V$ likes John]]
      d. [$_V$ John [$_V$ likes John]]
      e. [$_I$ John I [$_{AgrO}$ (John) [AgrO [$_V$ John v [$_V$ likes John]]]]]

When submitted to PF, (25) evidently contains two violations of the condition on domain exclusivity as *John* appears twice in the Θ-domain and twice in the Φ-domain! Contrary to fact, this should lead to two applications of pronominalization. There is no obvious way of remedying this problem. Similarly thorny problems arise for Grohmann's other analyses.

A final important difference between Grohmann's theory and the present one lies in the way anti-locality is grounded. While the ban on anti-local movement is derived here from the independently supported last-resort nature of merge, Grohmann (chapter 8) states the condition on domain exclusivity as an output condition, which remains a stipulation.

I now return to the main line of argumentation.

4.3   Phase impenetrability

The combined action of the last-resort condition and the assumption that phase heads may bear movement-triggering features *allows* successive-cyclic movement through the edges of phases. But it does not *force* such movement to happen. While the optional construction of intermediate traces is sufficient to explain the facts discussed in chapter 2, there are good reasons to believe that cyclic movement through phase edges is obligatory. Many languages that show morphological reflexes of cyclic movement do so obligatorily. Thus, we saw above that in Kîîtharaka, the appearance of the focus marker is obligatory along the path of overt movement, (8) in Chapter 3. If we interpret the appearance of the focus marker as the reflex of feature-sharing or valuation along the path of movement, the obligatory presence of the marker indicates that intermediate steps not only may but must be taken. The phase impenetrability condition is there to guarantee this.

(26)   Phase impenetrability condition   Chomsky, 2000, p. 108
        In phase α with head H, the domain of H is not accessible to operations
        outside α, only H and its edge are accessible to such operations.

When first introducing the phase impenetrability condition I noted (footnote 2 on page 90) that the domain of an element is made up of all constituents that that element strictly c-commands. The edge of a head are all and only those constituents which are dominated by a projection of the head and which asymmetrically c-command the head. Such a definition raises the question whether the notion of an edge, the non-complement, is necessary after all. If it were, this would slightly weaken the argument given above against positing (EP)P properties or edge features. The following reformulation shows that the notion of edge plays no role in the statement of the phase impenetrability condition. The formulation also takes into account the complications in the c-command relation under a multidominance view:

(27) Phase impenetrability condition:
In phase α with head H, syntactic objects are not accessible to operations outside of α if and only if they are finally c-commanded by H.

By familiar reasoning, the condition enforces movement through the edge of each phase along the path of movement because that element would otherwise be rendered inaccessible.

Before proceeding, a number of remarks regarding the position of (27) in the overall theory are in order.

4.3.1 Phases and sub-numerations

First, Chomsky, 2000 introduces the notion of phases and the phase impenetrability condition together with the device of sub-numerations. The numeration, a multi-set of lexical tokens, was introduced in Chomsky, 1995b to provide a basis for economy-based comparisons of convergent derivations. Only those derivations entered into the comparison that were based on the same numeration.

Thus, for example, (28a) is not compared for the purposes of economy considerations with (28b–c) because it uses a different set of lexical items, while (28b–c) use the same lexical items and are thus compared for the purposes of economy.

(28) English
   a.   A man seems to be in the room.
   b.   There seems to be a man in the room.
   c.   *There seems a man to be in the room.

The relevant economy condition distinguishing (28b) from (28c), according to Chomsky, 1995b, was the merge-over-move preference. Assuming that all of (28a–c) involve step (29a) in their respective derivations, (28a) only has one possible continuation: internally merging *a man* to satisfy the subject requirement of what ends up as the embedded infinitive, (29b.ii). This subject requirement was viewed in Chomsky, 1995b as a strong D-feature borne by T (*to*). Having the additional element *there* in their respective numerations, (29b) and (29c) allow two derivational continuations beyond (29a): (29b.i) and (29b.ii). (29b.i) ultimately leads to the grammatical sentence (28b) while (29b.ii) leads to the ungrammatical (28c). The derivation of (28a), which involves (29b.ii), shows that this step cannot be categorically ruled out. Instead it is ruled out by the merge-over-move

114

preference, according to which external merge preempts internal merge. This principle chooses (29b.i) over (29b.ii) when given the choice.

(29)   a.   [to [be [a man] in the room]]
       b.   (i)   External merge of *there*
                  [there [to [be [a man] in the room]]]
            (ii) Internal merge (move) of *[a man]*
                  [[a man] [to [be a man in the room]]]

The merge-over-move metric has to apply locally, since the derivations of (28b) and (28c) involve the same number of external and internal mergers when viewed globally.

For slightly more complicated examples, the merge-over-move preference leads to wrong predictions. Consider the following pair:

(30)   English
       a.   Evidence that there was a man in the room exists.
       b.   There exists evidence that a man was in the room.

On the assumption that the embedded clause in (30) is necessarily derived before the main clause, both of these sentence involve the step in (31a). The remaining numeration at this step is indicated. From here two continuations are possible, as shown in (31b.i) and (31b.ii). The former ultimately leads to (30a), the latter—to (30b). The same reasoning that forced the choice of (29b.i) over (29b.ii) before should now force the same choice. Therefore, (30b) should be ungrammatical, beaten by competition with (30a).

(31)   a.   [was [a man] in the room]]   Num = {there, exist, T, D, evidence, that}
       b.   (i)   External merge of *there*
                  [there [was [a man] in the room]]
            (ii) Internal merge (move) of *a man*
                  [[a man] [was a man in the room]]

Chomsky, 2000 suggests that this misprediction can be avoided if the numerations leading to (30a) and (30b) are different. He proceeds to introduce further structure in numerations. According to this idea, (30a) derives from differently structured numerations Num={{that, there, T, be, a, man, in, the, room},{D, evidence, T, exist}} while (30b) derives from something like Num={{that, T, be, a, man, in, the, room},{there, D, evidence, T, exist}}. During any given part of the derivation of a sentence, only one particular sub-numeration is accessible for operations. Therefore, the stages in the derivations of (30) are really the following:

(32)   a.   Derivational step for (30a)
          [was [a man] in the room]]   sub-num = {that, there}
       b.   (i)   External merge of *there*
                 [there [was [a man] in the room]]
          (ii) Internal merge (move) of *a man*
                 [[a man] [was a man in the room]]   *by merge-over-move
                 preference

(33)   Derivational step for (30b)
      [was [a man] in the room]]   Subnum = {that}
       a.   (i)   *There* cannot be externally merged since it is not in the sub-
                 numeration
          (ii) Internal merge (move) of *a man*
                 [[a man] [was a man in the room]]

This solves the undergeneration problem raised by (30b). In order to avoid structured numerations that would allow (28c) back in (Num={{there, T, seem},{a, man, to be}}), Chomsky, 2000 suggests that (i) each sub-numeration contains the lexical items to complete the next phase and (ii) neither the embedded infinitive nor the raising predicate are phases.

These considerations established a tight link between phases and sub-numerations.

There are good reasons to be skeptical about this solution. It raises a number of un-answered questions: Why can the computation draw on only one sub-numeration at any given time? Is there any evidence, independent of the examples discussed so far, that the numeration has to be divided in this way?... In addition, the claim that there are no phase boundaries at the edge of raising predicates has been called into question (Legate, 2003, though see den Dikken, 2006a for critical remarks). The validity of the merge-over-move preference has been called into question (Castillo, Drury, and Grohmann, 1999, 2009; Shima, 2000). The existence of economy conditions themselves is problematic, since they substantially complicate both the theoretical apparatus and the determination of what counts as an acceptable output. The need for numerations disappears together with economy conditions. (Notice that the principle of last resort, (18), is not an economy condition in the sense of the present discussion since it imposes an inviolable condition on the applicability of merge.)

An account of the contrast between (28b) and (28c) that is not based on economy principles is therefore preferable on general grounds. Indeed, such accounts exist. The following account illustrates the logic. It does not need the merge-over-move preference in particular or economy conditions in general (but it is compatible with having them elsewhere in the grammar). For ease of comparison with Chomsky's account, I mention numerations but they play no actual part in the account.

Suppose that we accept Chomsky's idea that the problematic examples (30) are built from different numerations but that the difference lies not in the structure of the numeration but in the verbs. Adopting the well-known partitive hypothesis (Belletti (1988); Bošković (1997c, 2002a); Epstein and Seely (1999); Lasnik (1995b,c); Martin (1992) among others), we could say that the numeration for (30a) is (34a) and the numeration for (30b) is (34b), that is, we give the analysis of these structures suggested in Shima (2000) (see also Bošković (2002a)).

(34)   a. $Num_{(30a)}$ = {that, T, a, man, $be_{partitive}$, in, the, garden, there, T, exist, proof}

        b. $Num_{(30b)}$ = {that, T, a, man, be, in, the, garden, there, T, exist $_{partitive}$, proof}

$V_{partitive}$ assigns inherent partitive case. In (30a) *be* assigns partitive case to its object. Since case-marked arguments usually do not undergo further A-movement (setting aside quirky case in some languages), the object will stay put. The expletive must appear in Spec,TP, presumably because T needs to assign case to something. Since T's case cannot be discharged to *a man* and there is no caseless argument, the expletive *there* is assigned T's case. *Exist* in the main clause in (30a) does not assign partitive case to its object, which therefore has to move to the matrix Spec,TP. Mutatis mutandis, the same account also works for (30b).

Of course, this entails that we have to slightly change the numeration assumed for the original examples (28b) and (28c), which motivated the merge-over-move preference to begin with. If we are to allow the expletive at all, then *be* must be able to assign partitive case, that is, it must be $be_{partitive}$. This means that *a man* will be marked by *be* with inherent case and thus immobilized. Notice that now we do not need the merge-over-move preference at all any more to explain why (28c) is ungrammatical. *A man* can't undergo case-driven movement.[20]

In example (28a) of course, the numeration would not contain expletive *there* nor would it contain $be_{partitive}$. Rather, it would contain *be*. As we see, the difference between the examples in (30) is located more naturally in an ambiguity in the verbs involved. Once this ambiguity is recognized, we have an automatic

---

[20] The question whether *there* at some stage occupies the specifier of the embedded, infinitival TP (see Bošković, 2002a,b; Castillo, Drury, and Grohmann, 1999, 2009 for arguments that it does not) and if so whether it is externally merged there, as assumed in Chomsky's work, or moves from a lower, predicate internal position (Moro, 2000; Sabel, 2000) is orthogonal. I will not discuss it here.

In the model proposed here, we can view the driving force of raising through embedded infinitival TP, if such raising exists, as [uCase$_{\downarrow\uparrow}$] on T. Nominative is the morphological reflex of terminal movement triggered by a case probe on T.

account also of (28b) and (28c) and no longer any use for the economy principle itself. This is a welcome result, since it is a simplification of the theory.

An additional gain of this move is that we are now able to explain why (35a) is ungrammatical and that we can describe the facts in (35b–d). In Chomsky's system all of (35a–d) are expected to be well-formed. Under present assumptions, (35a) is ruled out, because *there* in the embedded Spec,TP position remains caseless. The facts in (35b–d) can be described by denying the verbs the ability to assign partitive case.

(35)   English

    a. *There seem there to be three men in the garden. Chomsky, 1995b, Chomsky, 2000, 149n193, Bošković, 1997c, pp. 98-99

    b. *There has a man read a book.

    c. *There was told a long story to Peter.

    d. *There boiled water on the stove.

If the partitive diacritic were not available, then, to take just example (35b), the subject *a man* could be assigned nominative case in situ (as in the standard expletive constructions under Chomsky's theory) and *there* would be introduced in Spec,TP for the usual reasons. Given the partitive diacritic and the assumption that *there* needs case, we rule out (35b) because *a man* remains caseless.

The upshot of this discussion is that sub-numerations (phase-sized or otherwise) are not necessary to account for the problematic examples (30). The alternative, case-based account is empirically superior and more elegant. I know of no compelling reasons to assume sub-numerations of whatever size and I will have no use for the concept.

4.3.2 Phase impenetrability and islands

The main objective of this subsection is to clarify a point frequently missed or at least not acknowledged explicitly even in the specialist literature. This point is that modern theories posit no relation between the theory of islands and successive cyclicity.[21] Locality and successive cyclicity are independent of each other[22] and have been independent at least since the influential publication of Cinque, 1990a and Rizzi, 1990. Cinque, 1990a reformulates Chomsky's (1986)

---

[21] Surprisingly, even Boeckx and Grohmann, 2007 seem confused on this point, stating, as they do, a "dissatisfaction with the *particular form* of current locality theory, viz. its phase-based implementation" (p. 219). This is curious since Boeckx and Grohmann, 2007, p. 212–214 discuss the separation between locality and cyclicity in no uncertain terms.

[22] Müller's work (e.g., Müller, 2004, 2010) is exceptional in this regard.

and Huang's (1982) condition on extraction domains—workthat built originally on Cattell, 1976. Rizzi, 1990 unified several locality phenomena under the general order preservation principle of Relativized Minimality, which states that likes do not cross likes. Neither of the two reformulations of locality principles makes crucial use of cyclicity.

In the days of the Extended Standard Theory the situation was different. A fairly tight relation between cyclicity and locality held. Island effects with all types of Wh-movement—understood in the full generality given that term in Chomsky, 1977—were explained in terms of the assumptions (i) that Wh-movement targeted a single position (COMP, later Spec,CP) and no other position, (ii) that this position was unique per clause, and (iii) that there was an upper limit on the number of bounding nodes that could be skipped in any given step. These assumptions have largely been given up. Work on the left periphery of the clause (starting with Rizzi, 1997) has shown that the conjunction of (i) and (ii) cannot be maintained:[23] To accommodate the simultaneous occurrence of several phrasal elements in the left periphery of the same clause, we must assume that these movements target inherently different positions and/or that they target similar positions but that more than one of these can occur per clause. Assumption (iii) involves counting and is usually considered to be dubious for that reason alone.[24]

Chomsky's notion of phases (Chomsky, 2000, 2001, 2004, 2008) and in particular the phase impenetrability condition entails an update of assumption (iii) in that extraction from the c-command domain of a phase head must pass through a position contained in the projection of that head and not c-commanded by the head itself. This is an improvement, since the dubious counting is replaced by a derivational explanation. The assumption is that the phase impenetrability condition holds because syntactic structure is transferred to the conceptual-intentional and sensorimotor interfaces piecemeal and that, when it is so transferred, it is removed from the purview of the syntactic computation. The pieces undergoing transfer are the c-command domains of the phase heads. Extraction from the domain of a phase head is possible only before it has been transferred

---

[23] Indeed, we saw above that Wh-movement is probably densely cyclic in the sense that it passes not only through the clausal periphery but also through the edge of vP, DP, and PP. This fairly obviously challenges the notion that there is a single designated (intermediate) target position for Wh-movement.

[24] Chomsky, 1986 is probably the last serious attempt to build locality theory on successive cyclicity. This turns out to be the source of one of the inelegancies of the Barriers system; lexically governed phrases (i.e., θ-marked complements) are not inherent barriers whereas adjuncts are. This alone should make complements transparent for extraction and adjuncts opaque. However, given the possibility of voiding barriers by cyclic adjunction, the opaqueness of adjuncts must be stipulated a second time in the form of the ban on adjunction to adjuncts.

and impossible afterwards.[25] However, and this is crucial, absent constraints on the number and type of phase edge position from which extraction is possible, phase theory imposes only cyclicity but no locality constraints on movement.

In light of the direction in which locality theory has developed, it would be pointless to try to ground locality in successive cyclicity. Modern theories of locality usually assume that every successful extraction must obey two types of condition: (i) extraction must proceed from a transparent domain (Cattell, 1976; Cinque, 1978; Hornstein, Lasnik, and Uriagereka, (2003) 2007; Huang, 1982; Kayne, 1983; Rackowski and Richards, 2005; Uriagereka, 1999, among many others); and (ii) extraction is subject to an order preservation principle like Relativized Minimality (Abels, 2012; Boeckx and Jeong, 2004; Chomsky, 1993, 1995b; Fitzpatrick, 2002; Rizzi, 1990, 2001c; Starke, 2001, among many others). As a first approximation, condition (i) says that complements are (or may be) transparent for extraction and that nothing else is and condition (ii) says that likes do not cross likes.

Transparency of a domain is construed in terms of the relation a phrase enters with material external to it. Consequently, the boxed branch in (36) counts as transparent for extraction or as opaque depending on the relation the boxed constituent has to external material. Its transparency is independent of the presence or absence of an intermediate X_2.

(36)

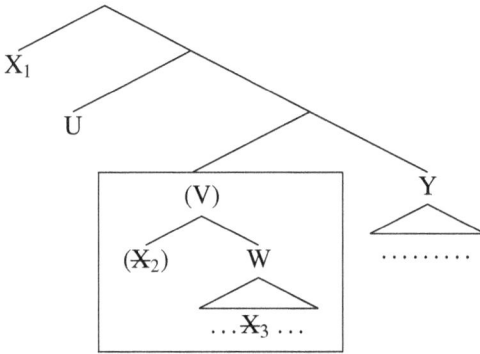

Similarly, whether the potentially intervening U in (36) counts as like or unlike X, that is, whether it counts as an intervener for the relationship between X_1 and X_3 is independent of the presence or absence of the intermediate X_2.

If the arguments reviewed in chapters 2 and 3 are accepted, then successive cyclicity is real, but it never enters into locality explanations.[26]

---

[25] The case for the assumption that the domains of transfer coincide neatly with the targets of successive-cyclic movement is empirically weak. See Boeckx and Grohmann, 2007, section 5 for a brief overview of the issues and references.

[26] In Abels, 2003c I attempted to reverse the direction of explanation and derive cyclicity

4.3.3 The stranding generalization

At the beginning of this chapter I introduced the stranding generalization from Abels, 2003c, repeated here:

(37) Stranding generalization
Given a phase head H and a constituent X in H's c-command domain, the following configurations are, respectively,

a. possible to derive: $[X \ldots [H [\ldots X \ldots]] \ldots]$ and
b. impossible to derive: $[X \ldots [H X] \ldots]$.

The stranding generalization follows directly from the system developed so far. Consider (37b) first. It claims that the complement of a phase head can never be extracted from that phase.

Recall that in section 4.2, we derived the prohibition against movement within the same maximal projection. Together with the phase impenetrability condition, we can then directly derive (37). To derive (37b), note that an unmoved complement of a phase head is finally c-commanded by the phase head and is therefore inaccessible to operations outside of the phase. Movement to a specifier position projected by the phase head is ruled out by Last Resort; such movement would be too local, since the complement of the phase head can already share all of the head's features without moving. This derives (37b).

Notice furthermore that phase head H can share any relevant $[uF_{\downarrow\uparrow}]$ with its complement. If H has such features, they can be used to share and possibly value unvalued features of other heads higher up in the structure. If a higher head bears $[uF_{\downarrow\uparrow}]$ it will attract HP instead of H's complement. Such pied-piping is automatic unless H bears no F-probe.

Consider (37a) now. It claims that, in principle, extraction from the complement of a phase head is possible. Familiar instances of movement like subject and object extraction, raising, etc. are of this type. For this type of movement to be possible, H must bear a relevant $[uF_{\downarrow\uparrow}]$. This will trigger internal merge of the moving element for feature-sharing. Internal merge is necessary to create the sharing configuration and is therefore licit under Last Resort. As a by-product

---

from locality by assuming that phase heads always have full sets of features. These features could be used to (a) trigger successive-cyclic movement, (b) derive the phase impenetrability condition as a special case of Relativized Minimality, (c) implement morphological effects along the path of movement. Otherwise these features were inert. The associated theory of features, default values, interpretation, and interpretability was not spelled out in Abels, 2003c in detail and is, in any case, incompatible with the assumptions made here. The main aim was to explain the otherwise stipulated correlation between creating an opaque domain and providing an escape hatch. It seems to me now that the theory of features, values, and interpretation required was too complicated to count as an explanation.

of internal merge, H no longer finally c-commands the moved element which therefore remains accessible to operations outside of HP according to the phase impenetrability condition. Both the moved X and HP now bear a valued F-feature. This should allow higher heads to value their own probes with either X or HP as a target. If X is chosen, successive-cyclic movement is the result. If HP is chosen—pied-piping.

Empirical justification for the stranding generalization will be given in later chapters, where various consequences will also be discussed.

4.4   Phase heads and their features

In the preceding sections I spelled out a theory of the configurations under which feature-sharing is possible, the last resort nature of movement, and the outwardly opaque domains created by the phase impenetrability condition. The final set of assumptions needed for an account of successive-cyclic movement has to do with the features that phase heads bear. I will assume that universal grammar allows phase heads (but not other heads) to bear any probe. If present, these probes may drive movement if that creates the necessary configuration for sharing of $[uF_{\downarrow\uparrow}]$ and $[uF_\uparrow]$.[27] This is not to say that only phase heads ever bear unvalued features or that only phase heads bear probes (a position contemplated in Chomsky, 2008). Other heads may and often do bear such features. The idea here is that the choice of features that can possibly be borne by a head is restricted for non-phase heads and unrestricted for phase heads.

In the context of the assumption developed so far, it should be clear that languages may choose to lexicalize certain feature combinations and not make use of others. Only those structures will be permitted for which the language in ques-

---

[27] Recall from the discussion of figure 4.1 that $[uF_\downarrow]$ generally does not drive movement and must be shared in situ.

I say 'generally', because there is one type of configuration where $[uF_\downarrow]$ can drive head movement: this may happen if H bears $[uF_\downarrow]$ matched by a corresponding feature on an externally merged specifier or adjunct of H. In that case, nothing prevents movement of H to a position within its own projection where it c-commands that specifier or adjunct. $[uF_{\downarrow\uparrow}]$ may drive projection-internal head movement in the same way:

(i) $[H_{[uF_\downarrow, uG_\downarrow, uH_\uparrow]} [X_{[F, H]} \ldots [H_{[uF_\downarrow, uG_\downarrow, uH_\uparrow]} Y_{[G]}]]]$

The prior external merger, of course, must itself be motivated by a different feature. I suggest below that this slightly exotic pattern is involved in the analysis of the focus marker in Kîîtharaka.

tion provides the appropriate lexical resources and, of course, those resources must then be used.

4.4.1 Implementing successive cyclicity

With all relevant assumptions in place now, we can see how successive-cyclic movement is implemented. I ignore pied-piping for the moment, as this will be discussed in the next chapter. For reasons of clarity of exposition, I restrict myself here to two phase heads (C and v). I take it to be obvious (and technically trivial) to see how the system extends to D and P.

A language may provide $C_{[uWh_{\downarrow\uparrow}]}$ and $v_{[uWh_{\downarrow\uparrow}]}$ (or various versions thereof) as lexical resources. Such a language will allow (i) movement of a local Wh-phrase to Spec,CP, (38a), and (ii) movement of a local Wh-phrase to Spec,vP, (38b). These movements can, of course, be chained together, yielding cases of successive-cyclic movement like (38c.i–iv), which could obviously be continued with additional C and v phases on top, (38c.v–viii). I take it that English is such a language.

(38)   a.   Wh-movement to Spec,CP

        (i) $[_C\ C_{[uWh_{\downarrow\uparrow}]}\ [\ \ldots\ [_{XP_{[Wh]}}\ \ldots X_{[Wh]}\ \ldots]\ \ldots]\ ]$

        (ii) $[_C\ [_{XP_{[Wh\boxed{2}]}}\ \ldots X_{[Wh\boxed{2}]}\ \ldots]\ [_C\ C_{[Wh\boxed{2}_{\downarrow\uparrow}]}\ [\ \ldots XP\ \ldots]\ ]\ ]$

    b.   Wh-movement to Spec,vP

        (i) $[_v\ v_{[uWh_{\downarrow\uparrow}]}\ [\ \ldots\ [_{XP_{[Wh]}}\ \ldots X_{[Wh]}\ \ldots]\ \ldots]\ ]$

        (ii) $[_v\ [_{XP_{[Wh\boxed{3}]}}\ \ldots X_{[Wh\boxed{3}]}\ \ldots]\ [_v\ v_{[Wh\boxed{3}_{\downarrow\uparrow}]}\ [\ \ldots XP\ \ldots]\ ]\ ]$

    c.   Successive cyclic Wh-movement

        (i) $[_v\ v_{[uWh_{\downarrow\uparrow}]}\ [\ \ldots\ [_{XP_{[Wh]}}\ \ldots X_{[Wh]}\ \ldots]\ \ldots]\ ]$

        (ii) $[_v\ [_{XP_{[Wh\boxed{2}]}}\ \ldots X_{[Wh\boxed{2}]}\ \ldots]\ [_v\ v_{[Wh\boxed{2}_{\downarrow\uparrow}]}\ [\ \ldots XP\ \ldots]\ ]\ ]$

        (iii) $[_C\ C_{[uWh_{\downarrow\uparrow}]}\ [\ \ldots\ [_v\ [_{XP_{[Wh\boxed{2}]}}\ \ldots X_{[Wh\boxed{2}]}\ \ldots]\ [_v\ v_{[Wh\boxed{2}_{\downarrow\uparrow}]}\ [$
             $\ldots XP\ \ldots]\ ]\ ]\ \ldots]\ ]$

        (iv) $[_C\ [_{XP_{[Wh\boxed{2}]}}\ \ldots X_{[Wh\boxed{2}]}\ \ldots]\ [_C\ C_{[Wh\boxed{2}_{\downarrow\uparrow}]}\ [\ \ldots\ [_v\ XP\ [_v\ v_{[Wh\boxed{2}_{\downarrow\uparrow}]}$
             $[\ \ldots XP\ \ldots]\ ]\ ]\ ]\ \ldots]\ ]\ ]$

        (v) $[_v\ v_{[uWh_{\downarrow\uparrow}]}\ [\ \ldots\ [_C\ [_{XP_{[Wh\boxed{2}]}}\ \ldots X_{[Wh\boxed{2}]}\ \ldots]\ [_C\ C_{[Wh\boxed{2}_{\downarrow\uparrow}]}\ [\ \ldots$
             $[_v\ XP\ [_v\ v_{[Wh\boxed{2}_{\downarrow\uparrow}]}\ [\ \ldots XP\ \ldots]\ ]\ ]\ \ldots]\ ]\ ]\ \ldots]\ ]$

        (vi) $[_v\ [_{XP_{[Wh\boxed{2}]}}\ \ldots X_{[Wh\boxed{2}]}\ \ldots]\ [_v\ v_{[uWh\boxed{2}_{\downarrow\uparrow}]}\ [\ \ldots\ [_C\ XP\ [_C\ C_{[Wh\boxed{2}]}}$
             $[\ \ldots\ [_v\ XP\ [_v\ v_{[Wh\boxed{2}_{\downarrow\uparrow}]}\ [\ \ldots XP\ \ldots]\ ]\ ]\ \ldots]\ ]\ ]\ \ldots]\ ]\ ]$

        (vii) $[_C\ C_{[uWh_{\downarrow\uparrow}]}\ [\ \ldots\ [_v\ [_{XP_{[Wh\boxed{2}]}}\ \ldots X_{[Wh\boxed{2}]}\ \ldots]\ [_v\ v_{[uWh\boxed{2}_{\downarrow\uparrow}]}\ [\ \ldots$
             $[_C\ XP\ [_C\ C_{[Wh\boxed{2}_{\downarrow\uparrow}]}\ [\ \ldots\ [_v\ XP\ [_v\ v_{[Wh\boxed{2}_{\downarrow\uparrow}]}\ [\ \ldots XP\ \ldots]\ ]\ ]\ \ldots]$
             $]\ ]\ \ldots]\ ]\ ]\ \ldots]\ ]$

(viii) $[_C [_{XP_{[Wh\boxed{2}]}} \ldots X_{[Wh\boxed{2}]} \ldots] [_C C_{[uWh\boxed{2}_{\downarrow\uparrow}]} [\ldots [_v XP [_v v_{[uWh\boxed{2}_{\downarrow\uparrow}]}$
$[\ldots [_C XP [_C C_{[Wh\boxed{2}_{\downarrow\uparrow}]} [\ldots [_v XP [_v v_{[Wh\boxed{2}_{\downarrow\uparrow}]} [\ldots XP \ldots]]$
$] \ldots]]] \ldots]]] \ldots]]$

Each step of movement is licensed by the last-resort condition, as every step leads to the sharing (and valuation) of a Wh-probe. The notation above shows this in two ways. First, the u from $[uF_{\downarrow\uparrow}]$ on C and v is deleted as the features become valued. Sharing is also indicated by co-superscripting. From the perspective of last resort, the sharing relation is curical, not valuation. The movements shown here would be equally licit if XP bore an unvalued Wh-feature.

It is now easy to see that the system not only allows successive-cyclic movement, it enforces it. Movement at one fell swoop is disallowed in the following way: Consider a variant of (38c.iv) created without the intermediate trace in Spec,vP. (39) gives the two relevant versions of the resulting structure. (39a) shows direct movement of the Wh-phrase XP to Spec,CP and a version of v is used that has no unvalued Wh-feature. The structure is ruled out by the phase impenetrability condition. Prior to its movement to Spec,CP, XP is finally c-commanded by the phase head v. XP is therefore inaccessible to C. (39b) shows direct movement of the Wh-phrase XP to Spec,CP using $v_{[uWh_{\downarrow\uparrow}]}$. Again this structure is illicit and cannot be built. There are two reasons for this. First, the embedding vP bearing $[uWh_{\downarrow\uparrow}]$ violates the virus theory of feature-sharing. Second, extraction of XP violates the phase impenetrability condition as before.

(39)   Violations of the phase impenetrability condition

a. $*[_C [_{XP_{[Wh\boxed{5}]}} \ldots X_{[Wh\boxed{5}]} \ldots] [_C C_{[Wh\boxed{5}_{\downarrow\uparrow}]} [\ldots [_v v [\ldots XP \ldots]]$
$\ldots]]]$

b. $*[_C [_{XP_{[Wh\boxed{5}]}} \ldots X_{[Wh\boxed{5}]} \ldots] [_C C_{[Wh\boxed{5}_{\downarrow\uparrow}]} [\ldots [_v v_{[uWh\boxed{5}_{\downarrow\uparrow}]} [\ldots XP$
$\ldots]] \ldots]]]$

A version of the derivation with an intermediate step in Spec,vP where v does not bear a Wh-probe is illicit, because movement to Spec,vP violates the Last Resort, (40).[28]

(40)   Violations of Last Resort at vP

a. $*[_C [_{XP_{[Wh\boxed{5}]}} \ldots X_{[Wh\boxed{5}]} \ldots] [_C C_{[Wh\boxed{5}_{\downarrow\uparrow}]} [\ldots [_v XP [_v v [\ldots XP \ldots]$
$]] \ldots]]]$

b. $*[_C [_{XP_{[Wh\boxed{5}]}} \ldots X_{[Wh\boxed{5}]} \ldots] [_C C_{[Wh\boxed{5}_{\downarrow\uparrow}]} [\ldots [_v XP [_v v_{[uWh\boxed{5}_{\downarrow}]} [$
$\ldots XP \ldots]]] \ldots]]]$

---

[28] Of course, the structure is only ruled out if v bears no other feature that might drive movement of XP. Indeed it is exactly the presence of such ulterior features that will be invoked in the account of secondary movement below.

Finally, movement to other positions in addition to those projected by the phase heads is ruled out by Last Resort unless the heads projecting them are independently bearers of the specific feature in question.

As it stands, the system overgenerates rather dramatically and does not resemble the Wh-grammar of English much. Unlike English, the system allows Wh-movement to terminate in Spec,vP, (38b). Unlike English, the system allows a Wh-probe on C to be satisfied by movement of vP, followed by pied-piping. This is shown in (41). (41) recapitulates the first three steps of the licit derivation for successive-cyclic movement, (38c), and continues this with movement of vP. This step satisfies $[uWh_{\downarrow\uparrow}]$ on C since vP can share this Wh-feature with C.

(41) a. $[_v \ v_{[uWh_{\downarrow\uparrow}]} \ [\ \dots \ [_{XP_{[Wh]}} \ \dots X_{[Wh]} \ \dots] \ \dots] \ ]$

b. $[_v \ [_{XP_{[Wh\boxed{7}]}} \ \dots X_{[Wh\boxed{7}]} \ \dots] \ [_v \ v_{[Wh\boxed{7}_{\downarrow\uparrow}]} \ [\ \dots XP \ \dots] \ ] \ ]$

c. $[_C \ C_{[uWh_{\downarrow\uparrow}]} \ [\ \dots \ [_v \ [_{XP_{[Wh\boxed{7}]}} \ \dots X_{[Wh\boxed{7}]} \ \dots] \ [_v \ v_{[Wh\boxed{7}_{\downarrow\uparrow}]} \ [\ \dots XP$
$\dots] \ ] \ ] \ \dots] \ ]$

d. $[_C \ [_v \ [_{XP_{[Wh\boxed{7}]}} \ \dots X_{[Wh\boxed{7}]} \ \dots] \ [_v \ v_{[Wh\boxed{7}_{\downarrow\uparrow}]} \ [\ \dots XP \ \dots] \ ] \ ] \ [_C \ C$
$_{[Wh\boxed{7}_{\downarrow\uparrow}]} \ [\ \dots \ vP \ \dots] \ ]$

The theory of feature interpretation in the next chapter will address these and a number of other overgeneration issues. Before tackling those, I would like to illustrate the range of parameterization allowed by the system. It provides a powerful descriptive tool and delivers some surprising results. The case studies of fine-grained featural control can be seen as further arguments for the reality of the types of features on phase heads that the current theory predicts to be there.

4.4.2 Morphological parameterization

A straightforward case of morphological parameterization of C is the difference between English and Irish. Whereas English complementizers are invariant under the presence of a (non-terminal) Wh-dependency passing them, Irish complementizers register the difference. According to the standard analysis (McCloskey, 1979, 1990b, 2002), the regular declarative complementizer in Irish is *go*, glossed as GO. It shows up in (42a) with the past tense marker *r* attached to it. When movement past or to a particular complementizer position takes place, the complementizer is realized as the particle *a*, causing lenition. The pattern is shown in the abstract in (42b) and illustrated in (42c–d). The relevant particle is glossed as AL.

(42) Irish   McCloskey, 2002, p. 185

a. Creidim gu-r   inis sé bréag
    I.believe GO-PST tell he lie

I believe that he told a lie.

b. XP [$_{CP}$ AL... [$_{CP}$ AL... [$_{CP}$ AL... XP...]]]

c. an t-ainm a hinnseadh dúinn a bhí ar an áit
the name AL was.told to.us AL was on the place
the name that we were told was on the place

d. cuid den fhilíocht a chualaís ag do sheanmháthair
some of.the poetry AL heard.2^{nd}SG by your grandmother
á rá a cheap an sagart úd
being said AL composed the priest DEM
some of the poetry that you heard your grandmother saying that
that priest composed

There is a third form of the complementizer, again realized as the particle *a* but this time causing nazalization and glossed as AN. This form of the complementizer shows up with an operator binding a resumptive pronoun lower down. (43a) illustrates a dependency with a gap and the complementizer AL again. In (43b) the dependency is with the complement of a preposition. As complements of prepositions may not be extracted, a resumptive pronoun is present. Consequently, the complementizer changes to AN. The path between the the operator and the resumptive pronoun is populated by the unmarked GO-complementizer. This is shown in the abstract in (43c) and illustrated in (43d). (For discussion of more complicated cases see Adger and Ramchand, 2005; Boeckx, 2001; McCloskey, 2002.)

(43) Irish   McCloskey, 2002, p. 189, McCloskey, 1990b, p. 211

a. Céacu ceann a dhíol tú
which one AL sold you
Which one did you sell?

b. Céacu ceann a bhfuil dúil agat ann?
which one AN is liking at.you in.it
Which one do you like?

c. DP [$_{CP}$ AN... [$_{CP}$ GO...*pronoun*...]]

d. Cé are shil tu gur dhúirt sé go bpósfadh Máire
who AN thought you GO.PST said he GO would.marry Mary
é?
him
Who do you think that he said that Mary would marry?

Under the view adopted here, the difference between GO and AL is simply that GO carries no unvalued operator-related features while AL carries [uOp$_{\downarrow\uparrow}$].[29]

---

[29] I use Op here on the assumption that features are categorized into classes and that the values of generic class features are the more specific features such as [Wh], [Rel], [Top]. For a concrete proposal regarding such a feature structure, see Abels,

The distribution of AN is slightly more challenging to describe. One approach might be to invoke an intrinsic difference between the operators undergoing movement and those used in the resumptive strategy. The complementizer AN would then carry the feature $[\text{uRes}_\uparrow]$, which is valued by the special property distinguishing resumptive-binding operators from trace-binding ones. The Res-feature here is characterized as $\uparrow$ rather than as $\downarrow\uparrow$. This characterization of the feature is forced under the view that resumptive chains are base generated by external merge of the operator in the target position, since an externally merged specifier is not c-commanded by its head and would therefore not be in the necessary configuration to share $[\text{uF}_{\downarrow\uparrow}]$.

There is also a way of characterizing AN in purely relational terms. One could assume that only $[\text{uF}_{\downarrow\uparrow}]$ ever triggers movement and that $[\text{uF}_\uparrow]$ cannot do so. A rationale for this assumption might be sought on analogy with Chomsky's probe-goal system where an initial downward-looking relation between probe and goal is a necessary precondition for movement. If such a downward-looking initial relation is a precondition for movement, the feature content of AN and AL could be identical with the one difference that AN would bear $[\text{uOp}_\uparrow]$ while AL bore $[\text{uOp}_{\downarrow\uparrow}]$. This last suggestion comes close to a restatement of McCloskey's 2002 account of the relevant facts. For more details the reader is referred to McCloskey's paper.

A similar account can be given of the distribution of FOC in Kîîtharaka and of similar focus particles elsewhere. Abels and Muriungi, 2008; Muriungi, 2005 analyze FOC as the realization of a low complementizer position (Foc) within Rizzi's (1997) articulated left periphery. I will identify this position with the phase head C here. This is licit, since I have argued elsewhere (Abels, 2012) that a sequence of projections is not necessary to derive the order of phrasal elements in the left periphery and, indeed, represent a weakening of the theory. Like Irish AL in the discussion above, FOC as a cyclicity marker can be viewed as $C_{[\text{uOp}_{\downarrow\uparrow}]}$.

A complete analysis of this morpheme has to answer a number of further questions.

First, FOC has three distinct uses in Kîîtharaka. We need to understand what the relation between these uses is. This question is the topic of Abels and Muriungi, 2008. The main idea is that the three usages reflect increasingly more content of FOC. It can signal the presence of a focus-related element (including a Wh-phrase) in its c-command domain. Abels and Muriungi, 2008 endow this version of FOC also with a feature triggering movement of the subject to account for its immediately preverbal position. (Other analytic options would be to assume verb movement, for which there is no independent motivation in the language, as Abels and Muriungi, 2008 note, or affix hopping from C onto

---

2012. This feature structure seems necessary independently to capture relativized-minimality effects (Boeckx and Jeong, 2004; Rizzi, 2001a, 2004a; Starke, 2001).

the verb.) The second, more complex flavor of FOC triggers operator movement in addition. This is the version that we see along the path of movement in the examples in (8) in Chapter 3 on page 69. The most complex version of FOC appears at the landing site of Wh- and focus movement and induces exhaustivity in addition. This third version is not pro-clitic on the verb but on the moved focus or Wh-phrase.

Abels and Muriungi's analysis of the three uses and the analysis of its position can easily be translated into present terms. In its simplest use, where FOC simply indicates the presence of a focus-related element in its c-command domain, FOC would simply bear [uFoc$_\downarrow$]. To account for the position of the subject before FOC, we would have to assume a [u$\phi_{\downarrow\uparrow}$] in addition. This is shown in (44).

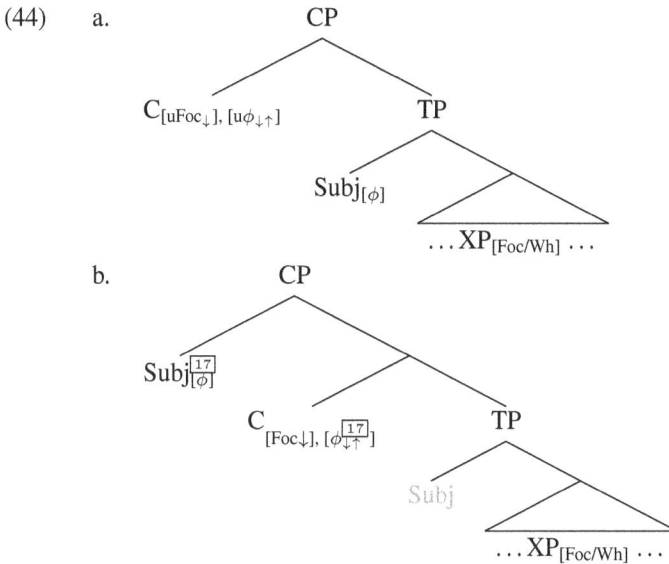

(44)   a.

b.

The use of FOC which serves as a trigger for cyclic movement has those two features and [uOp$_{\downarrow\uparrow}$] in addition, (45).

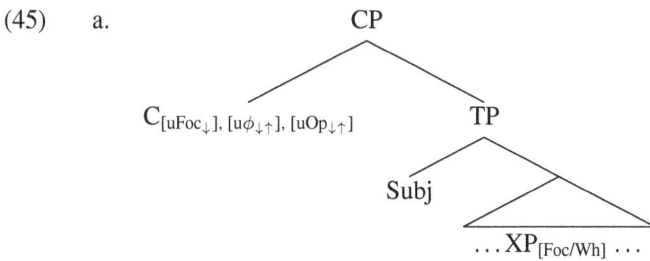

(45)   a.

b.

CP

XP$_{[Foc/Wh\boxed{2}]}$

Subj$_{[\phi\boxed{17}]}$

C$_{[Foc\boxed{2}_\downarrow], [\phi\boxed{17}_{\downarrow\uparrow}], [Op\boxed{2}_{\downarrow\uparrow}]}$

TP

Subj

…XP…

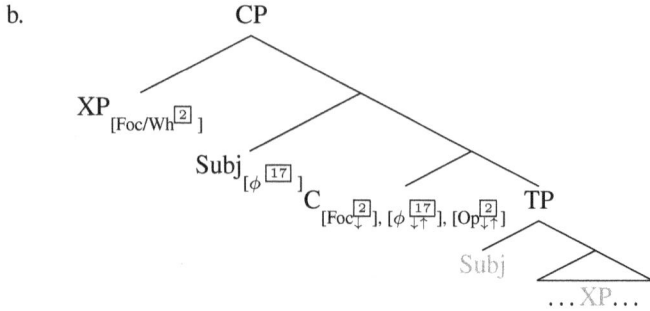

The third use of FOC differs semantically from the first two in that it adds exhaustivity and syntactically in that the focus marker is placed differently. Making use of the possibility of triggering projection-internal head movement using [uF$_\downarrow$] (see footnote 27 on page 121), we can assume that the interpretable exhaustivity property resides in a null element with a valued exhaustivity feature ([Exh]). In addition it bears another feature licensing its external merger with a projection of C. Let us assume that this is an unvalued category feature [uC$_\downarrow$].

The third and most complex version of FOC itself bears the feature [uExh$_\downarrow$]. This will drive movement of FOC past the externally merged exhaustivity head, (46).[30]

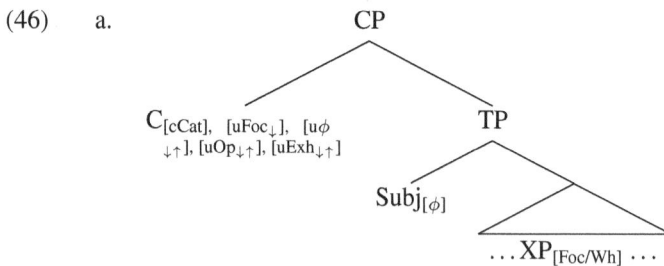

(46)   a.

CP

C$_{[cCat], [uFoc_\downarrow], [u\phi_{\downarrow\uparrow}], [uOp_{\downarrow\uparrow}], [uExh_{\downarrow\uparrow}]}$

TP

Subj$_{[\phi]}$

…XP$_{[Foc/Wh]}$…

---

[30] To guarantee the correct result, the features on a complex head like this need to be ordered. That is not a property particular to the present system and I will not discuss the issue here.

b.

CP

C
$[cCat^{5}][Foc^{2}_{\downarrow}], [\phi^{17}_{\downarrow\uparrow}],$
$[Op^{2}_{\downarrow\uparrow}], [uExh^{1}_{\downarrow\uparrow}]$

H
$[cCat^{6}_{\downarrow}], [Exh^{1}_{\downarrow}]$

XP
$[Foc/Wh^{2}]$

$Subj_{[\phi^{17}]}$

C

Subj

TP

…XP…

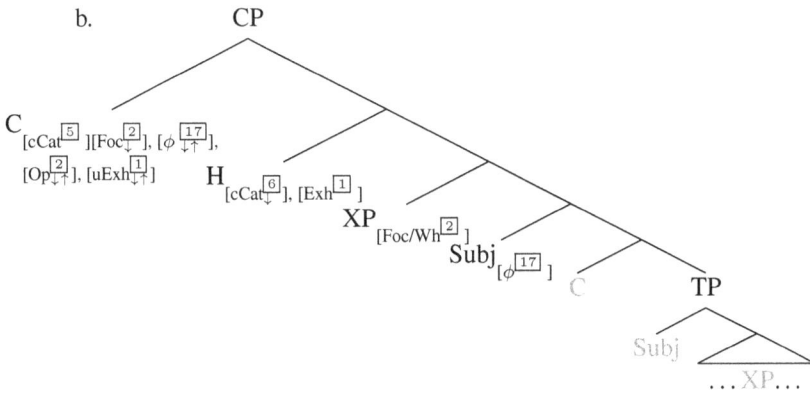

The second question arising in connection with Kîîtharaka has to do with the particle *ati*, which I glossed above as *that*. This seems probelmatic if I am now claiming that FOC is the realization of the complementizer. The issue did not arise in Abels and Muriungi, 2008; Muriungi, 2005, because those analyses are based on the assumption that there is a fine structure of the left periphery, which allowed identifying *ati* with Rizzi's (1997) highest head in the CP domain: Force. As a solution to the questions of what *ati* is and why it is there, I would like to tentatively offer an idea from McCloskey, 2006.

McCloskey, 2006 discusses the fact that adjunction to main CPs is permitted fairly freely, (47a–b), but that adjunction to argumental CPs is not. Thus, (47c) is bad on the interpretation where the temporal adjunct modifies the embedded clause. Instead of being adjoined above the complementizer, the adjunct must appear after the complementizer, as in (47d). McCloskey suggests that these facts exemplify Chomsky's (1986) ban against adjunction to arguments: CP can be adjoined to in principle, but not, if CP acts as an argument.

(47) English
  a. When he got home, he cooked dinner for the children.
  b. When he gets home, will he cook dinner for the children?
  c. *He promised when he got home that he would cook dinner for the children.
  d. He promised that when he got home he would cook dinner for the children.

In light of this, it is interesting that (47d) allows realizing two complementizers, (48a). A partial bracketing of (48a) is given in (48b). It is intended to bring out the fact that CP_1, which is projected by the initial *that*, acts as an argument and therefore falls under the ban on adjunction to arguments. CP_2 on the other hand is not an argument and is therefore exempt from the ban on adjunction. The initial complementizer might be necessary to prevent the structure from running afoul of the ban on adjunction to arguments.

(48)   English
   a.   He promised that when he got home that he would cook dinner for the children.
   b.   He promised [$_{CP_1}$ that [$_{CP_2}$ [when he got home] that he would ...]]

McCloseky points out that it is not clear what the ban on adjunction to arguments might follow from. But since it appears to represent a valid generalization, we can use a superficial formulation as a placeholder for an ultimate account.

Extending the pattern from the English adjunction structures above, Mc-Closkey, 2004 reminds us that the target of clitic left-dislocation in Italian must follow and may not precede the complementizer *che* (Rizzi, 1997). A plausible idea is that the function of *che* is the same that was just suggested for the initial complementizer in (48a), namely, to avoid a violation of the ban on adjunction to arguments. The comparison with Italian is instructive. Rizzi, 1997 locates *che* in Force, the highest head in his template for the left periphery which includes topic positions and a focus position lower down: [Force [Top [Foc [Top [Fin IP]]]]]. Foci therefore also follow *che*. We can explain the presence and position of *che* as part of a strategy to avoid violating the ban on adjunction to arguments.

We can now return to Kîîtharaka *ati*. It behaves like Italian *che*, in that it precedes topics and foci. I would like to suggest that its presence and position, as in Italian, is part of a strategy for avoiding violations of the ban on adjunction to arguments.[31] Apart from fulfilling this function, complementizer like *ati* and *che* are otherwise inert. Notice, for example, that these complementizers do not determine force. This can be seen in (49), where the Spanish complementizer *que*, which behaves in relevant respects like Italian *che*, introduces a Wh-question in which clitic left-dislocation has taken place.

(49)   Spanish   McCloskey, 2004

   Me preguntaron que a Juan$_j$ qué le   habría prometido el decano
   me they.asked that to Juan what him had   promised   the dean
   They asked me what the dean had promised Juan.

I will assume that this type of complementizer is not phasal. For Kîîtharaka then we have the phasal complementizer FOC and the non-phasal *che*-like element *ati* above it.

---

[31] If moved foci are included in the category of adjuncts, as I am doing here, while simultaneously claiming that focus movement is driven by features of the complementizer, the question arises what a useful notion of adjunction might be that would cover all and only the relevant cases and which is required even for the most superficial statement of the ban on adjuncts. The generalization from traditional adjuncts like the temporal modifier in (47) to moved topics, left-dislocated elements, and foci is licit, because none of them are ever selected for.

One final comment is necessary here. In the discussion of Kîîtharaka and of Irish, I have made use of the feature [uOp$_{\downarrow\uparrow}$]. Depending on assumptions about the syntax-morphology interface, this may or may not be the right way to go. As mentioned in the discussion in chapter 2.4, Distributed Morphology requires underspecification of multi-functional, syncretic forms while Nanosyntax requires overspecification. The generic Op feature I used in the discussion above is a useful notation and possibly the correct theoretical analysis under distributed morphology. Under a nanosyntactic approach it would probably have to be replaced by a feature structure (or a list in the worst case) detailing the specific operators falling under Op (Wh, Rel, Foc,...). This concludes my discussion of the core properties of FOC in Kîîtharaka.

I have used Irish and Kîîtharaka to illustrate how the morphological parameterization of phase heads can be employed to describe complex facts. It should at this point be obvious how to deal with Belfast English. Recall that in Belfast English we find subject-auxiliary inversion along the path of movement. This indicates that in this variety there is a complementizer with the features [uWh$_{\downarrow\uparrow}$] and a feature triggering subject-auxiliary inversion. (I will not discuss how to implement subject-auxiliary inversion.) Movement of other operators past C does not give rise to subject-auxiliary inversion. In these cases, the default complementizer *that* or its null variant are used. These facts make a point that the Irish and Kîîtharaka discussion couldn't: The features triggering the intermediate steps of successive-cyclic movement are movement-type specific. We need to invoke a Wh-feature and cannot easily get by with just a generic EPP feature.[32]

Plausibly, there is also parametrization of phase heads for properties of syntactic objects they c-command without attracting them. This is expected if universal grammar allows phase heads to bear all kinds of uninterpretable features including ([uF$_{\downarrow}$]). A possible instance is complementizer agreement. Haegeman, 1992, chapter 2 discusses the shape of complementizers in West Flemish. As illustrated below, the morphological shape of the complementizer differs depending on the number of the subject, whether or not the subject is pronounced adjacent to the complementizer, (50a–b), or not, (50c–f).[33]

(50) West Flemish   Haegeman, 1992, pp. 49–50

    a.   Kpeinzen da   Valère morgen   goat.
          I.think   that.SG Valère tomorrow goes.SG
          I think that Valère will go tomorrow.

---

[32] I leave aside the question why in Belfast English subject-auxiliary inversion along the path competes with insertion of the default complementizer. This optionality might reflect a difference in registers or, given that the complementizer appears in the standard language, dialects which co-exist in these speakers' minds.

[33] The shape of the complementizer in the singular is *da* before consonants and *dat* before vowels (Haegeman, 1992, 218 fn. 5).

    b.   Kpeinzen dan   Valère en Pol morgen   goan
         I.think   that.PL Valère and Pol tomorrow go
         I think that Valère and Pol will go tomorrow.

    c.   Kpeinzen dat-er   nie vee   volk   was.
         I.think   that.SG-there not much people was.SG
         I think that there were not many people.

    d.   Kpeinzen dan-der   nie vele   mensen woaren.
         I.think   that.PL-there not many people were.PL
         I think that there weren't many people

    e.   Hoevee   volk   peinz-je dat-er   doa gisteren   was?
         how.much people think-you that.SG-there there yesterday was.SG
         How many people do you think there were there yesterday?

    f.   Hoevee   mensen peinz-je gie   dan-der   doa
         how.many people think-you you.SG that.PL-there there
         gisteren   woaren?
         yesterday were.PL
         How many people do you think there were there yesterday?

The same alternation also affects the interrogative complementizers *of da* and [o:] and is obligatory.[34] Given the possibility of mismatches between agreement on the verb and agreement on C (van Koppen, 2005), C must be able to enter into a direct relation with the subject rather than with C's complement TP. We therefore posit [uNum$_\downarrow$] on C.

An interesting property of complementizer agreement in Germanic is that it is always with the local subject, never with a subject moved from a non-local position to or past the complementizer. It is not too difficult to understand this, essentially, as an effect of a generalized version of the ban on improper movement. As is well-known, case-licensing interacts with $\overline{\text{A}}$-movement in a very limited way. Movement of a non-case-licensed element to an $\overline{\text{A}}$-position and then to a distinct A-position is ungrammatical, (51). It violates the ban on improper movement.

(51)   a.   *What [$_{IP}$ what seems [$_{CP}$ what that it was said what]].

        b.   *[$_{IP}$ Whose book was asked [$_{CP}$ whose book [$_{IP}$ {whose book | PRO | there} to be read whose book]]]

A-movement is either sequenced before $\overline{\text{A}}$-movement

---

[34] Similar processes can be observed in other Germanic languages and have sometimes been analyzed in terms of complementizer agreement as well (see Bayer, 1984; Carstens, 2003; Fanselow, 1991; Gruber, 2008; Mayr, 2010; Shlonsky, 1994; van Koppen, 2005; Weiß, 1998; Zwart, 2001 among others for discussion). The text focuses on number agreement since this is the strongest case for complementizer *agreement* rather than cliticization to the complementizer.

(52)   English

Who do you think [CP who [IP who was arrested who]]?

or, in what seems to be the limiting case, they coincide in their respective last and first steps. This is what we find with exceptional case marking in Romance:

(53)   French

       a.   *Jules croyait l' homme avoir   épousé ma soeur
            Jules believed the man   to.have married my sister
       b.   L' homme que Jules croyait   avoir   épousé ma soeur était
            the man   that Jules believed to.have married my sister was
            Pierre.
            Pierre.
            The man that Jules believed to have married my sister was Pierre.

A full DP is not allowed in the subject position of the infinitive; the French verb *croire*—'believe', unlike its English counterpart, cannot license case on that subject. Case-licensing of this type becomes possible just in case the subject of the infinitive undergoes independently motivated movement (see Bošković, 1997c). Such exceptional case marking *en passant* is restricted to the local subject, the subject of the complement of *croire*. Any attempt to case-license an argument from a more deeply embedded position *en passant* is illicit. (Informally, what distinguishes (53b) from (54) is that in (54) there is a step of $\overline{\text{A}}$-movement, through the specifier of the most deeply embedded CP, that happens clearly *before* case is licensed.) In (53b) on the other hand, there is no unambiguous $\overline{\text{A}}$-movement step that would precede case-licensing of the moving element.

(54)   French

       *La femme que Jules croit   que tu   as   dit qu' il   était
       The man   that Jules believes that you have said that it/there was
       arresté   est Marie.
       arrested is   Marie
       The man that Jules believes that you have said that there/it was arrested is Marie.

If we take the ban on improper movement to state that A-movement may not follow $\overline{\text{A}}$-movement, rather than making the more stringent demand that A-movement must strictly precede $\overline{\text{A}}$-movement, the facts fall into place.[35]

---

[35] In the current system we can formulate that *croire* and other verbs like it may appear with a v which bears [uOp↓↑] and [uCase↑]. The operator feature triggers movement, the case feature licenses case. Exceptional case marking of the English type can be ruled out if we assume that [uCase↑] cannot itself trigger movement. This is in line with the discussion of the Irish complementizer AN above, where it was suggested that ↑-features never trigger internal merge.

134

Returning now to the question of why number agreement on complementizers is restricted to local subjects, the answer becomes straightforward. Number agreement is part of the A-system. Any phrase valuing such a feature strictly after having undergone Ā-movement would violate a generalization of the ban on improper movement, which would state that improper sequences of operations are barred. This ban would then explain why complementizer agreement in West Flemish is limited to local subjects.[36]

In this subsection, we have seen how fairly complex sets of facts can be described using the tool of movement-type-specific features on phase heads triggering intermediate steps of successive-cyclic movement. The descriptive success of this system provides an indirect justification for the tool used.

The next subsection turns to the pivot-only restriction in Austronesian, which, maybe surprisingly, turns out to represent an entirely expected system under the assumptions argued for here.

---

[36] Kinande is cited in Rizzi, 1990 as an example of language that shows ϕ-feature agreement along the path of Wh-movement. Schneider-Zioga, 2009 argues that this is the wrong analysis and that the complementizer agreement pattern docs not actually involve long extraction. This conclusion is of course forced under the present account of why complementizers agree only with local subjects based on the ban on improper sequences of operations.

I do not agree with Bošković, 2008, who claims, based on Schneider-Zioga's arguments, that there is no clear evidence of a direct relation between the moving element and the complementizers along the path of movement in any language. For Bošković, all apparent cases of agreement along the path of long Ā-movement involve a relationship between the higher v and the embedded C and do not directly involve properties of the moving element at all.

No true argument for this position is provided by Bošković. A real argument would have had to show that, under the criterion for a direct relation used by Bošković, namely ϕ-agreement, intermediate landing sites and final landing sites of long Wh-movement can be distinguished: unlike intermediate landing sites, final landing sites should sometimes exhibit ϕ-agreement. No indication is given in Bošković's paper that the relevant distinction exists. Kinande itself, which is discussed in the paper, does not make the point, because, under Bošković's analysis, Kinande shows either short or no Wh-movement to Spec,CP but never shows long Wh-movement.

Bošković's prediction should be contrast with that of the account based on an improper ordering of operations pursued here. the present theory predicts that there should never be ϕ-agreement with the moving element at the final landing site of long movement. I will tentatively assume that this prediction is correct.

Notice that it is unclear how the Belfast English facts fit with Bošković's claim, since there the embedded complementizer does reflect a specific property of the moving element, to wit, the Wh-nature of the operator.

4.4.3 Extraction in Austronesian

A direct consequence of the proposals above is that a language could allow Wh-movement to pass through Spec,CP but not through other phase peripheries. We can implement this by assuming that, in the relevant hypothetical language, C bears [uWh$_{\downarrow\uparrow}$] but other phase heads do not. Consider the following abstract structure:

(55)

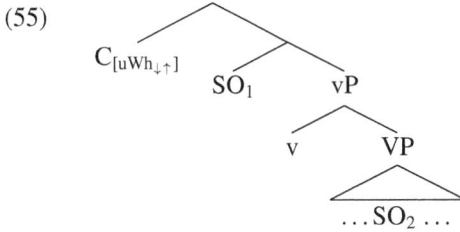

If only C bears [uWh$_{\downarrow\uparrow}$], then an asymmetry regarding extraction is derived for a structure like (55). If SO$_1$, which could be the subject, bears a Wh-feature, it can move to and through Spec,CP, but SO$_2$, which might be the object, cannot do so. SO$_2$ cannot move directly, because that would violate the phase impenetrability condition, and it cannot Wh-move via Spec,vP, because that would violate Last Resort.

Some though not all Austronesian languages appear to have this property (Comrie and Keenan, 1979; Keenan and Comrie, 1977, 1979; Klamer, 2002). Consider the following Tagalog examples.

(56) Tagalog   Kroeger, 1993, p. 211
    a.   Sino ang nagnakaw   ng=kotse mo?
           who NOM PERF.AV.steal GEN=car your.SG
           Who stole your car?
    b. *Ano ang nagnakaw   ang=katulong mo?
           what NOM PERF.AV-steal NOM=maid   your.SG
           Intended: What did your maid steal?

The two examples above are in what Kroeger, 1993 glosses as the active voice, AV, where the agent is the prominent argument marked with *ang*—'NOM'. As the examples show, the *ang*-marked argument can be extracted, the object cannot. It is controversial what the status of the *ang*-marked argument is. Various terms have been proposed: trigger, subject, topic, pivot. I will use the term pivot here. The generalization that (56) is intended to illustrate is that only pivots can be Wh-moved (or relativized).

Tagalog has a rich system of voices, which allows various arguments to act as the pivot. Once a particular element acts as the pivot, it can be Wh-moved (and relativized). The following examples illustrate the voice system and the ability of various arguments to become the pivot.

(57) Tagalog   Kroeger, 1993, pp. 13–14
  a. B-um-ili   ang=lalake ng=isda sa=tindahan.
      -PERF.AV-buy NOM=man GEN=fish DAT=store
      The man bought fish at the store.
  b. B-in-ili   ng=lalake ang=isda sa=tindahan
      -PERF-buy.OV GEN=man NOM=fish DAT=store
      The man bought the fish at the store.
  c. B-in-ilh-an   ng=lalake ng=isda ang=tindahan
      -PERF-buy-DV GEN=man GEN=fish NOM=store
      The man bought fish at the store.
  d. Ip-in-am-bili ng=lalake ng=isda ang=pera
      IV-PERF-buy GEN=man GEN=fish NOM=money
      The man bought fish with the money.
  e. I-b-in-ili   ng=lalake ng=isda ang=bata.
      -BV-PERF-buy GEN=man GEN=fish NOM=child
      The man bought fish for thc child

Pivots can then undergo Wh-movement. (58) shows that the theme, which couldn't be extracted in (56), can be Wh-moved so long as it is the pivot and that the agent, which could be extracted in (56), cannot be so extracted when the theme is the pivot.

(58) Tagalog   Kroeger, 1993, p. 211
  a. *Sino ang ninakaw   ang=kotse mo?
      who NOM PERF.OV.steal NOM=car your.SG
      Intended: Who stole your car?
  b. Ano ang ninakaw   ng=katulong mo?
      what NOM PERF.OV.steal GEN=maid   your.SG
      What did your maid steal.

The examples in (59) illustrate Wh-movement of a benefactive and an instrumental pivot.

(59) Tagalog   Kroeger, 1993, p. 213
  a. Sino ang ibinili   mo   ng=laruan?
      who NOM BV.PERF.buy 2^{nd}SG.GEN GEN=toy
      Who did you buy a/the toy for?
  b. Ano ang ipinangbalot mo   sa=regalo?
      what NOM IV.PERF.wrap 2^{nd}SG.GEN DAT=present
      What did you wrap the presents with?

It is uncontroversial that the pivot is structurally in a prominent position. I follow Rackowski and Richards, 2005 and assume that pivots raise at least to Spec,vP. As in Rackowski and Richards, 2005, the voice marking can be taken as a reflex of movement targeting v. I do not know whether it is more profitable to implement this movement as driven by an unvalued case feature $[uCase_{\downarrow\uparrow}]$ or an unvalued θ-feature $[u\theta_{\downarrow\uparrow}]$ on v. The latter analysis is suggested by the glosses for the voice markers in some of the literature which specifically mention thematic roles.

Two conclusions immediately follow.

The first conclusion is that the Tagalog vP is not, as it were, a locked domain for movement banning extraction entirely. Rather, extraction from vP is cued specifically to the type of movement. Wh-movement may not pass through Spec,vP since v in Tagalog may not (as a lexical property) bear $[uWh_{\downarrow\uparrow}]$. By contrast, the pivot can be lifted from the domain of v with the help $[uCase_{\downarrow\uparrow}]$ (or $[u\theta_{\downarrow\uparrow}]$).

If this is even roughly the correct interpretation of the facts, it provides a powerful argument against two types of theory. First, we cannot claim that phase heads either do or do not have generic edge or (EP)P features. Such an approach would make any phase head either transparent for movement of all types or opaque for movement of all types. It would not allow the selective transparency needed for Tagalog. Second, the data are incompatible with theories where intermediate traces are created as an automatic by-product of chain formation without being specifically licensed (Boeckx, 2001, 2008; Stroik, 1999, 2009, among others). The crucial *selective* transparency of vP in Tagalog can not be handled in such theories.

The second conclusion from the discussion so far takes the form of an empirical expectation. We saw that Wh-extraction of non-pivots is impossible because they remain below v. Their extraction would either violate the phase impenetrability condition or Last Resort. It follows from this, that long extraction *from* non-pivots is equally impossible. Extraction from pivots on the other hand might be possible. To see why, consider figures 4.6 and 4.7. Figure 4.6 shows the configuration of a Wh-phrase that has undergone movement to the embedded Spec,CP.[37] The syntactic object bearing the Wh-feature, $SO_{[Wh]}$, is stuck. It cannot move to Spec,vP, because v does not bear $[uWh_{\downarrow\uparrow}]$. Wh-movement of $SO_{[Wh]}$ to Spec,vP would therefore violate Last Resort. $SO_{[Wh]}$ also cannot undergo case- or θ-driven movement to the matrix Spec,vP. These features are part of the A-system and a violation of the ban on improper movement would ensue. Finally, if $SO_{[Wh]}$ remains in the embedded Spec,CP it will be impossible to extract it directly to the matrix Spec,CP position because of the phase impenetrability

---

[37] For this $SO_{[Wh]}$ of course had to meet the criteria for movement to that position: It had to be the pivot in the embedded clause.

condition. In figure 4.7 on the other hand, the embedded CP undergoes case- or θ-driven movement to matrix Spec,vP and becomes the pivot. As a result, v in the matrix no longer finally c-commands SO$_{[Wh]}$, which therefore remains accessible under the phase impenetrability condition.

The phase impenetrability condition therefore prohibits extraction from non-pivots but allows extraction from pivots. Furthermore, we know that movement to pivot position feeds Wh-movement. Under Abels's (2007) approach to feeding-bleeding relations between movements, we expect Wh-extraction from pivots to be possible. Indeed, this is what we find.

Observe first that subordinate clauses can be pivots and that their grammatical function in the matrix does not put constraints on the voice morphology in the subordinate clause. This is shown in (60).

(60)   Tagalog   Kroeger, 1993, p. 216

$\left\{\begin{array}{lll} \text{Nagsabi} & \text{ako} & \text{kay=Pedro} \\ \text{PERF.AV.say} & 1^{st}\text{SG.NOM} & \text{DAT=Pedro} \\ \text{Sinabihan} & \text{ko} & \text{si=Pedro} \\ \text{PERF.DV.say} & 1^{st}\text{SG.GEN} & \text{NOM=Pedro} \\ \text{Sinabi} & \text{ko} & \text{kay=Pedro} \\ \text{PERF.OV.say} & 1^{st}\text{SG.GEN} & \text{DAT=Pedro} \end{array}\right\}$ $\begin{array}{l} \text{na} \\ \text{COMP} \end{array}$

$\left\{\begin{array}{lll} \text{binili} & \text{ni=Linda} & \text{ang=kotse} \\ \text{PERF.OV.buy} & \text{GEN=Linda} & \text{NOM=car} \\ \text{bumili} & \text{si=Linda} & \text{ng=kotse} \\ \text{PERF.AV.buy} & \text{NOM=Linda} & \text{GEN=car} \end{array}\right\}$

I told Pedro that Linda bought the/a car.

The crucial extraction facts are those in (61). They show that the extractee *aling-na kotse ang*—'which car' must be the pivot in its own clause and must be extracted from a clause that acts as a pivot in the matrix.

(61)   Tagalog   Kroeger, 1993, p. 216

$\begin{array}{lll} \text{Aling=ng} & \text{kotse} & \text{ang} \\ \text{which=LNK} & \text{car} & \text{NOM} \end{array}$

$\left\{\begin{array}{lll} *\text{nagsabi} & \text{ka} & \text{kay=Pedro} \\ \text{PERF.AV.say} & 2^{nd}.\text{SG.NOM} & \text{DAT=Pedro} \\ *\text{sinabihan} & \text{mo} & \text{si=Pedro} \\ \text{PERF.DV.say} & 2^{nd}.\text{SG.GEN} & \text{NOM=Pedro} \\ \text{sinabi} & \text{mo} & \text{kay=Pedro} \\ \text{PERF.OV.say} & 2^{nd}.\text{SG.GEN} & \text{DAT=Pedro} \end{array}\right\}$

$\begin{array}{l} \text{na} \\ \text{COMP} \end{array}$ $\left\{\begin{array}{ll} \text{binili} & \text{ni=Linda} \\ \text{PERF.OV.buy} & \text{GEN=Linda} \\ *\text{bumili} & \text{si=Linda} \\ \text{PERF.AV.buy} & \text{NOM=Linda} \end{array}\right\}$

*

C$_{[uWh_{\downarrow\uparrow}]}$ ... vP

v VP

V CP$_{[Wh_{\downarrow\uparrow}^{[1]}]}$

SO$_{[Wh^{[1]}]}$

C$_{[Wh_{\downarrow\uparrow}^{[1]}]}$ IP

...SO$_{[Wh^{[1]}]}$...

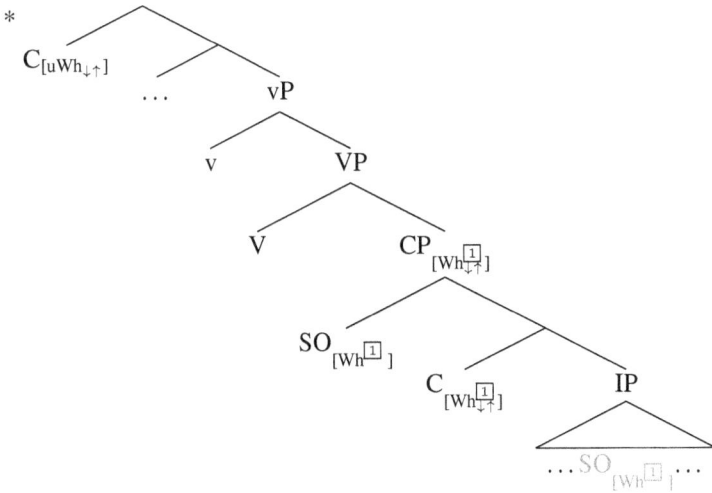

Table 4.6: Extraction from non-pivots is impossible

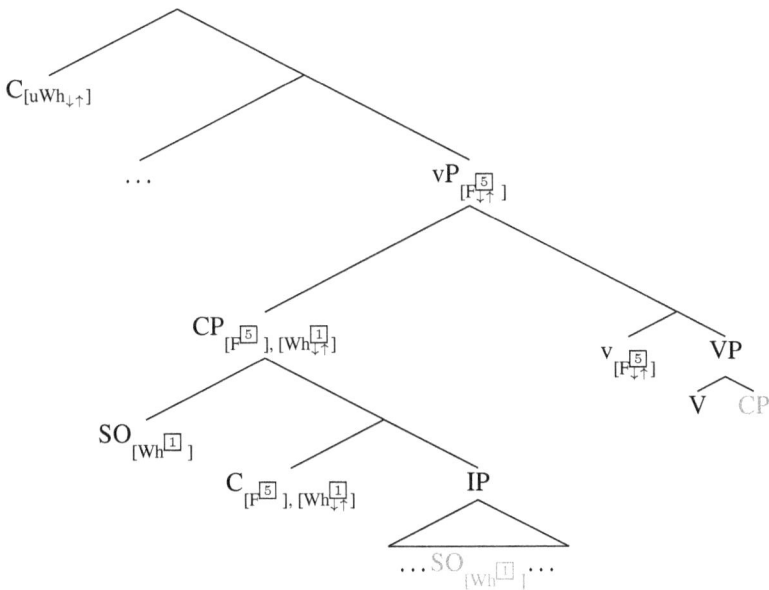

C$_{[uWh_{\downarrow\uparrow}]}$ ... vP$_{[F_{\downarrow\uparrow}^{[5]}]}$

CP$_{[F^{[5]}], [Wh_{\downarrow\uparrow}^{[1]}]}$ v$_{[F_{\downarrow\uparrow}^{[5]}]}$ VP

SO$_{[Wh^{[1]}]}$ V CP

C$_{[F^{[5]}], [Wh_{\downarrow\uparrow}^{[1]}]}$ IP

...SO$_{[Wh^{[1]}]}$...

Table 4.7: Extraction from pivots may be possible

Which car did you tell Pedro that Linda bought?

These facts thus serve to increase our confidence in the theory. In particular, if this analysis is on the right track for Tagalog and the other Austronesian languages that behave like it, our confidence in the crucial claims involved is strengthened: (i) Intermediate movement steps are triggered by features specific to the movement type and that phases can therefore be selectively transparent/opaque. (ii) Different phase heads are independently parameterized.[38]

---

[38] To the extent that the relatively free constituent order in Tagalog is movement-derived, we will have to assume that vP does but CP does not bear the relevant $[uF_{\downarrow\uparrow}]$. This wil account for the clause-boundedness of these movements and constitutes a further potential piece of evidence for the current approach.

Furthermore, these movements must be ordered on the hierarchy of movement operations assumed in Abels's (2007) above Wh-movement and relativization, which will rule out the possibility of $[uF_{\downarrow\uparrow}]$-driven movement feeding extraction or sub-extraction driven by $[uWh_{\downarrow\uparrow}]$ or $[uRel_{\downarrow\uparrow}]$ as cases of improper movement.

5 Feature Values and Interpretation

5.1 Feature interpretation

The most pressing challenge for the account I am developing here is to reconcile the reality of specific intermediate features triggering movement with the evidence that these features are semantically inert. Consider again the following examples.

(1) English
   a. I wonder when he arrived.
   b. *When do you wonder when he arrived?

It appears that the Wh-feature shared by *when* is interpreted in only one position and that the relevant position is the highest position where *when* is merged. If this generalization is true, the status of (1b) follows directly. The verb *to wonder* selects a question, but its complement cannot be interpreted as a question. Further confirmation comes from (2). The example is ambiguous between an embedded and a matrix construal for *when*, but it is uniformly interpreted as a direct question, despite the fact that *tell* optionally selects a question.

(2) English
   When did you tell me that he would arrive.

   = For what time t, you told me at t that he would arrive
   = For what time t, you told me that at t, he would arrive
   ≠ You told me when he would arrive

We have also seen a number of important counterexamples to this simple generalization. We noted , for example, that there are cases where a Wh-phrase is interpreted in a position below its surface position. Relevant examples came from German Wh-imperatives, (3), and the so-called radical reconstruction property of Japanese scrambling.

(3) German   Reis and Rosengren, 1992
   a. Wen   stell   dir   vor, dass Peter besucht hat!
      whom.ACC imagine yourself PRT that Peter visited has
      Imagine who Peter visited!
   b. Stell   dir   vor, wen   Peter besucht hat!
      imagine yourself PRT whom.ACC Peter visited has
      Imagine who Peter visited!

The final step of movement of *wen*—'who' in (3a) does not share $[uWH_{\downarrow\uparrow}]$ on the main complementizer but a topic feature. For reasons that I do not understand this option is blocked in English in general and in German outside of the Wh-imperative construction. Cases like this lead to a first refinement of the generalization about feature interpretation so that it says that a feature [F] on a bearer of [F] is interpreted in the highest position where the bearer of [F] is merged sharing an F-probe.

This still cannot be the final statement of the generalization, however. I suggested informally above that pied-piping involves sharing of features between the pied-piper and the pied-pipee. In a pied-piping structure like (4a), P bears $[uWH_{\downarrow\uparrow}]$. This feature is shared with and valued by P's complement and turns PP into a bearer of a valued Wh-feature. Similarly in (4b), where *whose* shares and values $[uWH_{\downarrow\uparrow}]$ on the head of the immediately containing DP *whose mother*, which in turn values $[uWH_{\downarrow\uparrow}]$ on the head of the eventual pied-pipee *whose mother's friends*. In (4a), the highest position where *wem* is merged sharing a Wh-probe is the complement position of P. In (4b), the highest position where *whose* is merged sharing a Wh-probe is Spec,DP. And the highest position where *whose mother* is merged sharing a Wh-probe is Spec,DP of the larger DP. But this is not where the Wh-features are interpreted. In all cases they are interpreted in Spec,CP of the embedded clause.

(4)   German
    a.   Ich weiß, mit wem   du geredet hast.
          I   know with who.DAT you spoken have
          I know who you talked to.
    b.   I know whose mother's friends you should invite.

I suggest here that the following observation provides the key to understanding this apparently erratic behavior: Merger in the complement position of P and in Spec,DP is motivated independently of the presence of the Wh-feature. *Mit* takes DP complements of all sorts and possessors in English may occupy Spec,DP also when they do not bear a Wh-feature. In the cases of pied-piping, the sharing of the Wh-probe piggy-backs on other features begin shared. This is not the case in (3) and (1), where the Wh-feature is the feature driving merger. We can make this precise by making reference again to an assumed hierarchy in which an item has to undergo operations. For concreteness I will assume Abels's (2007) universal constraint on the ordering of operations in language, given in (5) below. The constraint states that an item must establish its θ-relations before undergoing case-related movement, before undergoing short scrambling, before undergoing Wh-movement, before undergoing topicalization.

If an application of merge leads to the sharing of several different features, we will say that the lowest one on the hierarchy triggers that application of merge while higher ones can be shared as free-riders. Still very informally, we can now formulate that [F] is interpreted in the highest position where [F] triggered merger.

I will now give these ideas a slightly more precise implementation. There are some choices involved that are not determined by the data under discussion. The choices I make seem defensible to me, but many alternative implementations of the intuition sketched in the preceding paragraphs are possible. I then show how simple facts like those discussed above are captured by the system. From there I move on to discuss the generalizations outlined in chapter 3. Finally, I will show how the apparatus introduced in this and the previous chapter can be used to describe the behavior of Wh-movement in various languages.

5.2 Towards a precise formulation

In section 4.1 I discussed the configurations under which feature-sharing is possible. In the spirit of Brody, 1997; Frampton and Gutmann, 2000; Pesetsky and Torrego, 2007, I suggested that feature-sharing (roughly agreement) and valuation are to be kept distinct. Recall that I further assumed that unvalued features are not tolerated at the interfaces, that the derivation proceeds according to the virus theory of feature-sharing, that the phase impenetrability condition holds, and that merge is subject to a last resort.[1]

I will further assume that there is a transitive, asymmetric, possibly total order of features and associated operations.

(5)   The Universal Constraint on the Ordering of Operations in Language
        Abels, 2007, p. 60
        $\theta \ll$ A-mvt $\ll$ Op

I will say that a feature and the associated operation to the left of $\ll$ is lower than features and associated operations to the right.

When a particular application of merge leads to the sharing of more than one feature, then the feature that is the lowest on the hierarchy will count as the trigger of merge and the remaining features will be free-riders. The relevant notion is defined below. As a first step, (6) defines a set of features that come to be shared by merging two syntactic objects α and β, $F^{\alpha\,\beta}_{\text{shared}}$.

(6)   Let γ be a syntactic object created by merging α and β. Let $F^{\alpha\,\beta}_{\text{common}}$ be the set of features (types) borne both by α and β. Let $F^{\alpha\,\beta}_{\text{shared}}$ be the maximal subset of $F^{\alpha\,\beta}_{\text{common}}$ such that for all $f \in F^{\alpha\,\beta}_{\text{shared}}$,

---

[1] I also mentioned there that actual sharing requires that Relativized Minimality be obeyed. To keep things simple, I set Relativized Minimality aside here.

a. f is shared between α and the head of β or between β and the head of α in γ, and

b. f is not shared between α and the head of β or between β and the head of α in α, and

c. f is not shared between α and the head of β or between β and the head of α in β.

Definition (7) then identifies the trigger of merge as the unique element of that set which is lowest on the hierarchy.

(7)   Given a syntactic object γ with daughters α and β, α projecting, the unique member $t \in F_{shared}^{\alpha\,\beta}$ that is ranked lowest on the hierarchy in (5) is the *trigger* for the merger of the non-projecting daughter β.

Very careful readers might object that $F_{common}^{\alpha\,\beta}$ includes only features in the labels of the merged constituents. For this reason the definition of $F_{shared}^{\alpha\,\beta}$ does not cover cases where a head with [uF↓] finds an appropriate feature to share embedded within its complement. To cover this case, the definition would have to be somewhat broader and the statement would be more complicated. In the examples discussed below, features borne not by the complement but only by a constituent embedded within it never need to count as the trigger of merger. I therefore avoid complicating the definition and stick with the simpler version given here.

With the notion of the trigger clarified sufficiently for our purposes, we now want to state the generalization that a feature is interpreted in the highest position where it served as the trigger. To achieve this, we first need to define a notion of the occurrence of a syntactic object. The simple definition used here is that of the object itself and its mother.

(8)   Occurrence:
       An occurrence of a syntactic object α in a syntactic object γ ($Occ_i^{\alpha,\,\gamma}$) is a pair $<\alpha, \beta>$ such that β is a mother of α.

When applied to the structure in figure 5.1, this definition says that C has a single occurrence: <C, B>. E has two occurrence: <E, D> and <E, Z>. Likewise, M has only a single occurrence: <M, J>; while I has two: <I, N> and <I, G>.

The notion of height of an occurrence can now simply be given in terms of partial domination.

(9)   Higher:
       Given two different occurrences of α in syntactic object γ ($Occ_1^{\alpha,\,\gamma} = <\alpha, \beta_1>$ and $Occ_2^{\alpha,\,\gamma} = <\alpha, \beta_2>$), $Occ_1^{\alpha,\,\gamma}$ is *higher* than $Occ_2^{\alpha,\,\gamma}$ if and only if β_1 (partially) dominates β_2.

Returning to the illustration, we find that of the two occurrences of G, <G, A> is higher than <G, F> because A partially (and in fact totally) dominates F. And of

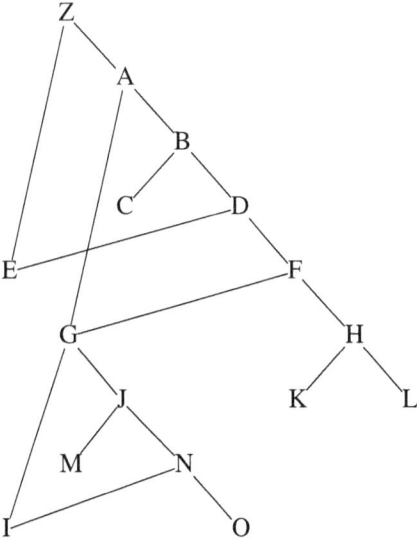

Table 5.1: A multidominance structure for movement

the two occurrences of I, <I, G> is higher than <I, N> because G partially (and in fact totally) dominates N.[2]

The notion of the trigger for an occurrence is given the following definition.

(10) An occurrence $(Occ_i^{\alpha, \gamma} = <\alpha, \beta_i>)$ is triggered by feature [F] if and only if [F] is the trigger of the merger of α to β_i's other daughter.

I will call an occurrence *terminal for [F]* if it is the highest occurrence of a syntactic object whose merger with its sister is triggered by [F].

(11) An occurrence of syntactic object α in γ is *terminal* for [F] if and only if

    a.   it is triggered by [F], and

    b.   there is no higher occurrence of α in γ triggered by [F].

The generalization that a feature is interpreted in the highest position where it triggered merger can now be formulated as follows.

(12) Principle of semantic interpretation at the terminal:

---

[2] Definition (9) mentions partial domination to remain true in remnant movement configurations. For example, if N in figure 5.1 were to be remerged at the root, G would only partially dominate N, yet we would still like to conclude that the occurrence of I as the daughter of G is higher than its occurrence as the daughter of N.

> Let [F] be a feature borne by α in syntactic structure γ, and $\text{Occ}_t^{\alpha, \gamma}$ = <α, β_t>is terminal for [F], then
> a.   F is interpreted on the head of β_t and
> b.   for all occurrence of α in γ $\text{Occ}_j^{\alpha, \gamma}$ = <α, β_j> different from Occ_t $^{\alpha, \gamma}$, [F] is not interpreted on the head of β_j.

The principle of semantic interpretation at the terminal captures what seems to me to be the gist of Rizzi's (2006) Criterial Freezing and related claims discussed above: When an element moves for a specific reason, then the feature involved is interpreted at the final landing site of the relevant movement and nowhere else along the path.[3] For the reasons given in previous chapters, I reject the stronger claim that such an item is frozen and cannot undergo further movement; it can, but such movements have to be triggered by different features and these features must be higher on the hierarchy of operations (5).

I assume that a similar principle also regulates the interpretation of features that are shared without being the triggers for *movement*.

(13)   A [uF$_\downarrow$] (or [uF$_\uparrow$]) probe is terminal for [F], if and only if the head bearing it m-commands all other heads bearing [uF$_\downarrow$] or [uF$_\uparrow$] probes it is in a (transitive) sharing relation with.

We can now extend (12) in the obvious way to all three kinds of probes forcing interpretation at the terminal. I further assume that a feature is interpreted on exactly one of the heads bearing a probe for that feature. We can call this assumption Interpret Once under Sharing (in analogy to the slightly narrower Interpret Once under Agree principle in Adger and Ramchand, 2005, p. 174).

5.3   Possible systems based on a single feature: A dry run

Using a single feature [F] I will now illustrate the types of systems that we expect to find when an element bearing valued or unvalued [F] is combined with phase heads bearing various flavors of probing [F]. We saw above that features come in altogether five different flavors. Features can be valued or unvalued. Valued features do not probe; unvalued features may or may not probe: [uF$_\downarrow$], [uF$_\uparrow$], [uF$_{\downarrow\uparrow}$], or non-probing [uF]. I organize the discussion according to the type of probing features.

---

[3]   I leave deliberately open the possibility that the feature involved may or may not be interpreted on the moving item itself.

5.3.1 [uF$_\downarrow$] probes

When [F] on a probed element X is combined with [uF$_\downarrow$] on phase heads P, the following configuration is licensed.

(14) $[P_{[F_\downarrow^{\boxed{2}}]} \ldots [P_{[F_\downarrow^{\boxed{2}}]} \ldots [P_{[F_\downarrow^{\boxed{2}}]} \ldots X_{[F^{\boxed{2}}]} \ldots]]]$

In this configuration [F] is shared, in the lowest phase, between X and the local phase head. The next phase head up cannot establish a direct relation with X, because of the phase impenetrability condition, and shares its feature with the lowest phase head rather than with X directly.[4] Similarly for all higher phase heads. (An argument for such agreement from phase head to phase head is presented in Preminger, 2009.) [F$^{\boxed{2}}$] will be interpreted on the highest phase head sharing it. Movement of X, whether it is partial movement as in (15a) or full movement as in (15b), is impossible because of the last resort condition. [F] can and therefore must be shared without movement; we are not considering any other features at the moment.

(15) a. *$[P_{[F_\downarrow^{\boxed{2}}]} \ldots [X_{[F^{\boxed{2}}]} [P_{[F_\downarrow^{\boxed{2}}]} \ldots [X_{[F^{\boxed{2}}]} [P_{[F_\downarrow^{\boxed{2}}]} \ldots X_{[F^{\boxed{2}}]} \ldots]]]]]$

    b. *$[X_{[F^{\boxed{2}}]} [P_{[F_\downarrow^{\boxed{2}}]} \ldots [X_{[F^{\boxed{2}}]} [P_{[F_\downarrow^{\boxed{2}}]} \ldots [X_{[F^{\boxed{2}}]} [P_{[F_\downarrow^{\boxed{2}}]} \ldots X_{[F^{\boxed{2}}]} \ldots]]]]]]$

Multiple bearers of [F] are allowed. If all of them are in a feature-sharing configuration with the phase head, all will end up being shared because sharing is automatic.

(16) $P_{[F_\downarrow^{\boxed{2}}]} \ldots [P_{[F_\downarrow^{\boxed{2}}]} \ldots [P_{[F_\downarrow^{\boxed{2}}]} \ldots X_{[F^{\boxed{2}}]} \ldots Y_{[F^{\boxed{2}}]} \ldots]]]$

However, the sequence of agreeing heads in (14) must not be interrupted. If it is interrupted, as in (17), ungrammaticality results, since [uF$_\downarrow$] on the highest phase head cannot be shared and, consequently cannot be valued. There are two problems with this structure: Further embedding of it will lead to a violation of the virus theory of feature-sharing and, at the interface, the structure gives rise to a violation of the ban against unvalued features.

(17) * $[P_{[uF_\downarrow]} \ldots [P \ldots [P_{[F_\downarrow^{\boxed{2}}]} \ldots X_{[F^{\boxed{2}}]} \ldots]]]$

A simple sequence of phase heads with [uF$_\downarrow$] is illicit without a target lower down, (18a). There are two reasons for this. First, The F-probe on the lowest phase head remains unshared until the next higher phase head is introduced. This

---

[4] It should be pointed out that if feature-sharing is implemented as multidominance, then X is inaccessible to operations outside of the lowest phase but [F$^{\boxed{2}}$] borne by X need not be: [F$^{\boxed{2}}$] is not finally c-commanded by the phase head due to its sharing relation with the phase head.

leads to a violation of the virus theory of feature-sharing, since the lowest phase becomes embedded before all of its probes have been shared. In addition, the F-probes remain unvalued at the interface. A structure that solves only one of the two problems remains ungrammatical. Thus, introducing a bearer of valued [F] higher up in the structure, would value all F-probes, (18b), but the most deeply embedded phase still violates the virus theory of feature-sharing. Introducing a bearer of non-probing [uF] in the c-command domain of the lowest phase head, (18c), solves the problem with the virus theory, but now the condition that unvalued features are not tolerated at the interfaces is now violated.

(18)   a. $*[P_{[uF\boxed{2}\downarrow]} \ldots [P_{[uF\boxed{2}\downarrow]} \ldots [P_{[uF\boxed{2}\downarrow]} \ldots \ldots]]]$

       b. $*[P_{[F\boxed{2}\downarrow]} \ldots X_{[F\boxed{2}]} \ldots [P_{[F\boxed{2}\downarrow]} \ldots [P_{[F\boxed{2}\downarrow]} \ldots \ldots]]]$

       c. $*[P_{[uF\boxed{2}\downarrow]} \ldots [P_{[uF\boxed{2}\downarrow]} \ldots [P_{[uF\boxed{2}\downarrow]} \ldots X_{[uF\boxed{2}\downarrow]} \ldots]]]$

The combination of the two strategies from (18b) and (18c) violates neither the virus theory nor the interface ban on unvalued features, as shown in (19). If we assume that merger of $Y_{[F]}$ is triggered (in the technical sense) by [F], then the structure remains ungrammatical, since [F] ends up being interpreted twice, once on the head of the projection into which Y is merged and once on the topmost phase head. On the other hand, if the merger of Y is triggered by a different feature, the structure ought to be licit. Such structures, in other words, are possible, but only in systems that manipulate more than one feature.

(19) $(*)[P_{[F\boxed{2}\downarrow]} \ldots Y_{[F\boxed{2}]} \ldots [P_{[F\boxed{2}\downarrow]} \ldots [P_{[F\boxed{2}\downarrow]} \ldots X_{[uF\boxed{2}]} \ldots]]]$

Finally, if we assume that X bears valued [F], we must also consider the following structure.

(20) $[P \ldots [P \ldots [P \ldots X_{[F]} \ldots]]]$

The structure does not violate any of the constraints that we have encountered and it should be grammatical, but no information about the presence of [F] has been passed up the tree and [F] is interpreted on X but not at the top of the structure.

We have seen how assuming a $[uF_\downarrow]$-probe on phase heads interacts with the assumption of targets bearing [F]. One may wonder whether such systems actually exist. There is a reassuring similarity between the system based on a single feature [F] and a uniform set of $[uF_\downarrow]$ probes on the phase heads and the system of Wh-question formation in Wh-in-situ languages like Japanese. The issue will be explored briefly in section 5.5.3 below.

5.3.2 [uF$_{\downarrow\uparrow}$] probes

While the system discussed above approximates Wh-in-situ-systems, systems with movement involve [uF$_{\downarrow\uparrow}$] probes. A structure directly corresponding to (14) with sharing in-situ is impossible, since the [uF$_{\downarrow\uparrow}$] probes are not in appropriate feature-sharing configurations:

(21)   *[P$_{[uF\downarrow\uparrow]}$ ... [P$_{[uF\downarrow\uparrow]}$ ... [P$_{[uF\downarrow\uparrow]}$ ... X$_{[F]}$ ...]]]

Partial movement, (22a), is again impossible, since any phase heads above the landing site of X cannot share their [uF$_{\downarrow\uparrow}$] probes. Successive-cyclic movement all the way is possible, as in (22b):

(22)   a.   *[P$_{[uF\downarrow\uparrow]}$ ... [X$_{[F\boxed{2}]}$ [P$_{[F\boxed{2}\downarrow\uparrow]}$ ... [X$_{[F\boxed{2}]}$ [P$_{[F\boxed{2}\downarrow\uparrow]}$ ... X$_{[F\boxed{2}]}$ ...]]]]]

   b.   [X$_{[F\boxed{2}]}$ [P$_{[F\boxed{2}\downarrow\uparrow]}$ ... [X$_{[F\boxed{2}]}$ [P$_{[F\boxed{2}\downarrow\uparrow]}$ ... [X$_{[F\boxed{2}]}$ [P$_{[F\boxed{2}\downarrow\uparrow]}$ ... X$_{[F\boxed{2}]}$ ...]]]]]]

Since movement is allowed in principle and since the F-feature is shared between the moving element X and the phase heads along the path, this feature ends up on the phrasal projection of the intermediate phases. It might seem then that we expect a type of pied-piping of the entire phases to be admissible, (23). When iterated, this would give rise to a roll-up derivation with pied-piping of successively larger constituents.

(23)   *[P$^2_{[F\boxed{2}\downarrow\uparrow]}$ [P$^1_{[F\boxed{2}\downarrow\uparrow]}$ X$_{[F\boxed{2}]}$ [P$^1_{[F\boxed{2}\downarrow\uparrow]}$ X]] [P$^2_{[F\boxed{2}\downarrow\uparrow]}$ P^1]]

The expectation that this might be possible is, however, mistaken. In a single-feature system, movement of X is necessarily triggered by the F-feature. The occurrence of X as Spec,PP^1 is the highest occurrence of X triggered by [F]. It is therefore final and [F] must be interpreted on P^1. In and of itself this is, of course, not a problem. However, movement of P^1 to Spec,PP^2 is also triggered by the F-feature. The occurrence of P^1 in Spec,PP^2 is the highest occurrence of P^1 triggered by [F]. It is therefore final and [F] must be interpreted on P^2. Interpreting the same [F] in two places violates the principle Interpret Once under Sharing.

The system developed here therefore rules out roll-up structures in which successively larger constituents are pied-piped and where movement is consistently triggered by the same feature.[5] The following English examples are all ruled out

---

[5]   Such derivations seem to be presupposed in much work based on Kayne's (1994) linear-correspondence axiom. However, Abels and Neeleman, 2012b dispute the necessity of such derivations. If the suggestions here are on the right track, such derivations are not only unnecessary but impossible. This would remove a substantial amount of spurious ambiguity inherent in the account of word order in the extended projection of the noun given in Abels and Neeleman, 2012b.

150

by this reasoning.[6]

(24) English
  a. *[$_{CP}$ What John bought] did you say?
  b. *[$_{vP}$ What bought] did you say that John?
  c. *[$_{vP}$ What say that John bought] did you?

Similarly, a single Wh-phrase cannot do double duty and license a two-questions interpretation in examples like the following, again, because this would run afoul of the principle Interpret Once under Sharing.

(25) English
  *[CP What John bought] do you wonder?

We saw above in the discussion of [uF$_↓$] probes that mixing phase heads bearing a probe with phase heads not bearing a probe leads to ungrammaticality. The same happens with [uF$_{↓↑}$] probes.

(26) a. *[P$^1_{[uF_{↓↑}]}$ ... [P^2 ... [P$^3_{[uF_{↓↑}]}$ X$_{[F]}$]]]
       *, because the probes on P^1 and P^3 remain unvalued

      b. *[P$^1_{[uF_{↓↑}]}$ ... [P^2 ... [X$_{[F⑤]}$ [P$^3_{[F⑤_{↓↑}]}$ X]]]]
       *, because the probe on P^1 remains unvalued

      c. *[P$^1_{[uF_{↓↑}]}$ ... [X$_{[F⑤]}$ [P^2 ... [X [P$^3_{[F⑤_{↓↑}]}$ ... X]]]]]
       *, because movement of X to Spec,PP^2 violates Last Resort and because the probe on P^1 remains unvalued

---

See also fn. 19 in Chapter 4 on page 109 for discussion of a different type of roll-up structures ruled out here.

[6] Consider the following examples, instances of Ross's 1973 *slifting*. The assumption that slifiting involves movement of CP with pied-piping, as in (ic), is incompatible with the theory developed here unless a feature different from [Wh] can be found to trigger movement of the Wh-element to Spec,C$_1$.

(i) English
  a. What did he want do you think?
  b. Who came do you think?
  c. [$_{CP_2}$ [$_{CP_1}$ who [$_{TP}$ who came]] do [$_{TP}$ you think CP$_1$]]

An alternative might be that the slifted clause is externally merged where it is or that the apparent matrix is a parenthetical (possibly with internal null-operator movement, as suggested for *as*-parentheticals in Potts, 2002). A detailed study of slifting would be required to decide these questions.

d. $*[X_{[F\boxed{5}]} [P^1_{[F\boxed{5}]} \ldots [X [P^2 \ldots [(X) [P^3_{[F\boxed{5}]} X]]]]]]$

*, because movement of X to Spec,PP² violates Last Resort, or alternatively because movement from Spec,PP³ to Spec,PP¹ violates the phase impenetrability condition

Furthermore, mixing different types of probes also leads to ungrammaticality. Starting with the structure (27) with alternating $[uF_{\downarrow\uparrow}]$ and $[uF_{\downarrow}]$ probes, there is no configuration that satisfies all constraints.

(27) $*[P^1_{[F_{uF_{\downarrow\uparrow}}]} \ldots [P^2_{[uF_{\downarrow}]}] \ldots [P^3_{[F_{uF_{\downarrow\uparrow}}]}] \ldots X_{[F]} \ldots]]$

X may not remain in situ, since then the probes on P^1 and P^3 are not shared at the interface. In addition PP^2 and PP^3 violate the virus theory and all three probes remain unvalued. If X were to move to Spec,PP³ the probe on P^1 would remain unshared and unvalued. In addition, the F-feature would have to be interpreted both on P^1 and on P^2, since both count as terminal in violation of Interpret Once under Sharing. If X were to move all the way to Spec,PP¹, it would have either to pass through Spec,PP² in violation of Last Resort or to skip this position in violation of the phase impenetrability condition. Finally, any combination of movement of X with movement of a higher phase is ruled out as a violation of Interpret Once under Sharing.

For much the same reasons, the following two structures are also ruled out. (28a) is an attempt to create a partial-movement structure, (28b) is an attempt to create a pied-piping structure. In both cases, the F-feature would have to be interpreted in two places, namely, on P^1 and on P^3, which is ruled out by Interpret Once under Sharing.

(28) a. $*[P^1_{[F\boxed{6}]} \ldots [P^2_{[F\boxed{6}]} \ldots [X_{[F\boxed{6}]} [P^3_{[F\boxed{6}]} \ldots [X [P^4_{[F\boxed{6}]} \ldots X \ldots]]]]]]$

b. $*[[_{PP^3} P^3_{[F\boxed{6}]} \ldots [P^4_{[F\boxed{6}]} \ldots X_{[F\boxed{6}]} \ldots]] [P^1_{[F\boxed{6}]} \ldots [_{PP^3} [P^2_{[F\boxed{6}]} \ldots PP^3$
$\ldots]]]]$

Replacing [F] on X by [uF] doesn't improve any of the examples and renders (22b) ungrammatical. The reason is that all F-features end up being shared but unvalued.

We are now ready to study the slightly more complicated interactions between $[uF_{\downarrow\uparrow}]$ and multiple bearers of an F-feature. If we assume that there are multiple valued F-features, we derive the expectation that multiple movement is possible and optional. To see why it is possible, consider the structure in (29a) (assuming that X and Y are both local to the phase head P in the relevant sense). At this point, either X or Y may be remerged, leading to the sharing of the F-probe on P with F on X, (29b). Crucially, additional movement of Y is still possible, (29c). It does not violate Last Resort since, as a result of merger, a feature is shared that couldn't be shared before: The probing feature mentioned in the formulation of

Last Resort, (18) in Chapter 4, is [F$_{\downarrow\uparrow}$] borne by P which, after movement, is shared between P and Y.

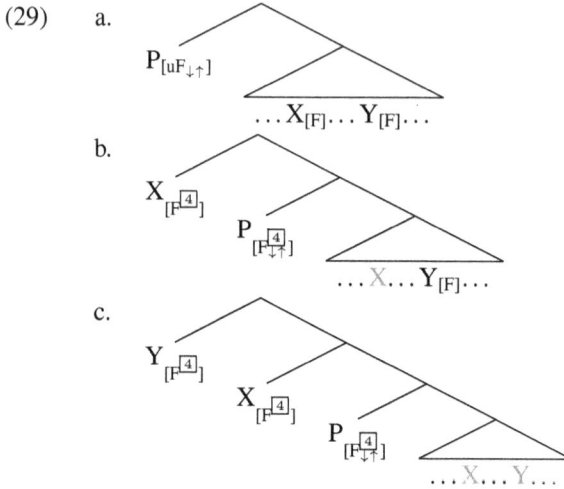

(29)   a.

P$_{[uF_{\downarrow\uparrow}]}$ ...X$_{[F]}$... Y$_{[F]}$...

b.

X$_{[F\boxed{4}]}$ P$_{[F\boxed{4}_{\downarrow\uparrow}]}$ ...X...Y$_{[F]}$...

c.

Y$_{[F\boxed{4}]}$ X$_{[F\boxed{4}]}$ P$_{[F\boxed{4}_{\downarrow\uparrow}]}$ ...X...Y...

Multiple movement to establish sharing configurations with a single probe are allowed in the present system in principle. However, notice that they are not forced. Since, by assumption, the F-feature is valued on X and on Y, X and Y themselves do not lead to violations of the condition banning unvalued features at the interface. Since the probing feature on P becomes valued by movement of X alone, (29b) is sufficient to satisfy the interface ban against unvalued features. (29b) is also sufficient as far as the virus theory of feature-sharing is concerned, because the probing feature borne by P is shared already at (29b). The system thus allows optionality in this circumscribed domain.

It is important to understand that once the multiple-movement option is chosen, the moving items have to move together as long as movement is still triggered by the same feature. They must not end up in different landing sites. This is a consequence of the transitivity of sharing. Consider the two structures below.

In (30a), Y's terminal occurrence for [F] is in Spec,PP^1 and X's terminal occurrence for F is in Spec,PP^2. Therefore, F is interpreted both on P^1 and on P^2 by the principle of semantic interpretation at the terminal, but this violates the principle Interpret Once under Sharing.

In (30b) by contrast, X and Y's terminal occurrence for F is in Spec,PP^1. The F-feature is therefore interpreted on P^1 in accord with the principle of semantic interpretation at the terminal and in accord with the principle Interpret Once under Sharing.

(30) a. *

Y$_{[F\boxed{4}]}$

P$^1_{[F\boxed{4}_{\downarrow\uparrow}]}$ Y

X$_{[F\boxed{4}]}$

P$^2_{[F\boxed{4}_{\downarrow\uparrow}]}$ ...X...Y...

b.

Y$_{[F\boxed{4}]}$

X$_{[F\boxed{4}]}$

P$^1_{[F\boxed{4}_{\downarrow\uparrow}]}$ Y

X

P$^2_{[F\boxed{4}_{\downarrow\uparrow}]}$ ...X...Y...

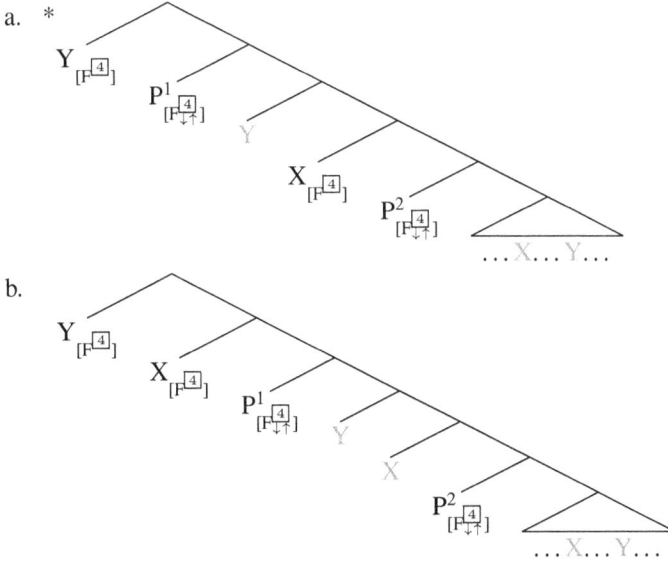

We shall see below in section 5.5.2 how optional multiple movement can be used to implement obligatory multiple movement. In addition, we need a way of blocking multiple movement. Clearly, if Last Resort demanded that merge can only be triggered if a previously unshared *probe* becomes shared as the result of merger, the transition from (29b) to (29c) would be blocked and with it multiple movement. Since both single and multiple movement appears to be empirically necessary, I will assume tentatively that features have an additional second order property which determines whether they are subject to the more permissive version of Last Resort assumed so far, according to which a probe remains active after it has entered into a sharing relation, or whether it becomes inactive as soon as it has entered a sharing relation.[7]

5.3.3 [uF$_\uparrow$] probes

In my discussion of feature-sharing configurations for [uF$_\uparrow$], I pointed out that these features are more permissive than [uF$_{\downarrow\uparrow}$] since [uF$_\uparrow$] can be shared in all configurations where [uF$_{\downarrow\uparrow}$] can be shared. In addition [uF$_\uparrow$] can and [uF$_{\downarrow\uparrow}$] cannot be shared under external merge into non-complement position. I initially left open the question whether [uF$_\uparrow$] may drive internal merge and suggested at various points of the discussion that the answer is no. I continue to make

---

[7] This formulation imports ideas about the possibility of having single or multiple specifiers or checking a feature once or multiple times (see a. o. Adams, 1984; Bošković, 1999, 2000; Pesetsky, 2000; Rudin, 1988a).

this assumption here. Dropping the assumption (and reanalyzing the data that motivate it) would turn [uF↑] into a kind of super-probe that can do everything [uF↓↑] can do and the things described in this section in addition.

Without the power to move elements, [uF↑] is somewhat monadic. The configuration in (31) is possible, but sharing with more than one probe is impossible in a single-feature system.

(31) $[\text{ X}_{[F\boxed{2}]} [\text{ P}_{[F↑\boxed{2}]} \ldots]]$

To see this, consider the following structures. (32a) is impossible because the unvalued probe on P^1 remains unvalued and therefore violates the interface constraint and/or the virus theory. (32b) is impossible because, by assumption [uF↑] probes do not drive internal merge. Finally, (32c) is impossible because its derivation necessarily violates the virus theory.

(32) a. $*[\text{ P}^1_{[uF↑]} [\ldots \text{X}_{[F\boxed{2}]} [\text{ P}^2_{[F↑\boxed{2}]} \ldots]]]$

b. $*[\text{ X}_{[F\boxed{2}]} [\text{ P}^1_{[F\boxed{2}]} [\text{ X } [\text{ P}^2_{[F↑\boxed{2}]} \ldots]]]]$

c. $*[\text{ X}_{[F\boxed{2}]} [\text{ P}^1_{[F\boxed{2}]} [\text{ P}^2_{[F↑\boxed{2}]} \ldots]]]$

Multiple sharing is of course possible in principle.

(33) $[\text{ Y}_{[F\boxed{2}]} [\text{ X}_{[F\boxed{2}]} [\text{ P}_{[F↑\boxed{2}]} \ldots]]]$

Combining [uF↑] probes with other kinds of probes probing the same target leads to violations of the principle Interpret Once under Sharing, as in the previous subsection.

We see that [uF↑] probes do not have very interesting properties by themselves. They are shared only under external merge or as a by-product of merger driven by a different probe. I made use of this option in the discussion of exceptional case marking under Wh-movement in Romance languages above.[8]

In the preceding discussion I tried to clarify the workings of the system on the basis of a single feature. I hope that this has sufficiently elucidated the intended content of the various principles and definitions introduced above. I would like to highlight one point that emerges from the discussion, since it will be important in what follows. Whenever a feature is shared between multiple probes (and a target), the probes must all probe in the same way. They must all be ↓, or all ↑, or all ↓↑probes. If they aren't, the conditions on feature interpretation determine that the relevant feature is interpreted in several places in violation of the principle Interpret Once under Sharing. This property of the system rules

---

[8] It should be noted that the proposed analysis of exceptional case marking *en passant* relied on case as the *trigger* of movement in the technical sense, though this property resided in a [uF↑] probe, which could therefore not *drive* internal merge.

out any implementation of partial movement or pied-piping using only a single feature.

I will now change the mode of the discussion somewhat. Instead of continuing to run systematically through systems containing probes for more than one feature, I will show how the present theory accounts for the major generalizations and facts discussed in chapter 3.

5.4 The generalizations

5.4.1 Partial Movement

In section 3.2, I discussed partial-Wh-movement languages. The discussion followed Sabel, 2006 in the conclusion that partial Wh-movement is, in a sense, a misnomer; partial Wh-movement is actually terminal focus movement of the relevant Wh-elements. It follows from this that movement below the surface position of the Wh-elements implicates Foc-features and that Wh-features are implicated above the landing site of the Wh-elements. The general logic is schematized in (34).

(34) $[P_{\text{[Wh-probe]}} \ldots [P_{\text{[Wh-probe]}} \ldots [\text{Wh-phrase}_{\text{[Foc][Wh]}} [P_{\text{[Foc-probe]}} [\text{Wh-phrase} [P_{\text{[Foc-probe]}} \ldots \text{Wh-phrase} \ldots]]]]]]$

The simplest way of implementing this would be to let the phase heads above the overt landing site bear $[\text{uWh}_\downarrow]$ and the phase heads below the overt landing site bear $[\text{uFoc}_{\downarrow\uparrow}]$.

(35) $[P_{[\text{Wh}\overline{1}_\downarrow]} \ldots [P_{[\text{Wh}\overline{1}_\downarrow]} \ldots [\text{Wh-phrase}_{[\text{Foc}\overline{2}][\text{Wh}\overline{1}]} [P_{[\text{Foc}\overline{2}_{\downarrow\uparrow}]} [\text{Wh-phrase} [P_{[\text{Foc}\overline{2}_{\downarrow\uparrow}]} \ldots \text{Wh-phrase} \ldots]]]]]]$

A language with these properties would allow Wh-in-situ structures both in embedded and main clauses. These would not be sensitive to strong islands, because the relation between the topmost probe and the Wh-phrase is mediated by pure agreement (that is, $[\text{uF}_\downarrow]$ probes) without movement. A language like that would show optional focus movement of Wh-phrases. This movement is expected to be sensitive to all sorts of islands. If the path of focus movement were extended all the way to the Wh-scope position, the semblance of full Wh-movement would result.[9] Finally, in partial-movement structures, the path be-

---

[9] The topmost head would have to be specified as $P_{[\text{uFoc}_{\downarrow\uparrow}]\,[\text{uWh}_\downarrow]}$. Indeed, nothing rules out the option that this is the relevant feature content of the phase heads throughout the overt movement path as long as Foc $\ll$ Wh on the hierarchy in (5).

tween the landing site of focus movement and the Wh-scope position should be insensitive to strong islands, since the relation is mediated by agreement without movement.

But for one detail this characterizes languages like Kîîtharaka and Malay quite well: Both allow Wh-in-situ, Wh-ex-situ, and partial movement strategies in main and embedded clauses. In both languages the Wh-in-situ strategy is island insensitive, overt movement of the Wh-element can be argued to be focus movement because of the presence of focus markers along the path of movement. This movement is sensitive to regular locality constraints. However, we saw above that in Kîîtharaka the path between the overt landing site of the Wh-element and the Wh-scope position is also island sensitive. The same point has been made for Malay by Cole and Hermon, 1998.

To get the correct description of the locality facts, we have to adjust the assumptions as follows. Wh-phrases in these languages are not inherently focal. They become focal by virtue of a null operator that may externally merge with a Wh-phrase. This operator, O, has a valued focus feature and an unvalued Wh-probe: $O_{[Foc]\ [uWh_{\downarrow\uparrow}]}$. The assumption that the relevant languages make use of this operator is the only special thing we need to say. We can otherwise continue to assume that they have phase heads endowed with $[uFoc_{\downarrow\uparrow}]$ to implement focus movement, $[uWh_{\downarrow}]$ to implement Wh-in-situ, and $[uWh_{\downarrow\uparrow}]$ to implement Wh-movement. The operator O has to pied-pipe the Wh-phrase when undergoing focus movement and then obligatorily strands it when undergoing Wh-movement. Consider why.

First, the Wh-probe on O is the only feature that is shared as a result of merging O and the Wh-element. Hence, the Wh-probe borne by O counts as the trigger for merger. Assume that O projects. All of this is shown in (36).

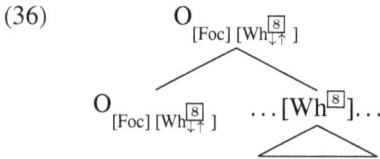

(36)

$$
\begin{array}{c}
O_{[Foc]\ [Wh^{\boxed{8}}_{\downarrow\uparrow}]} \\[2pt]
\diagup\ \diagdown \\
O_{[Foc]\ [Wh^{\boxed{8}}_{\downarrow\uparrow}]} \quad \ldots [Wh^{\boxed{8}}] \ldots
\end{array}
$$

The phrase in (36) has some interesting properties, which derive why O has to undergo Wh-movement by itself. First, it cannot be embedded under $C_{[uWh_{\downarrow}]}$, (37). In (37), the operator O counts as terminal for the Wh-feature, because merger of O was triggered by that feature. At the same time, $C_{[Wh_{\downarrow}]}$ counts as terminal for O, therefore, the Wh-feature would have to be interpreted in both places in violation of the principle Interpret Once under Sharing.

(37) *

$$C_{[\text{Wh}\boxed{8}\downarrow]} \quad \ldots$$
$$O_{[\text{Foc}]\,[\text{Wh}\boxed{8}\downarrow\uparrow]}$$
$$O_{[\text{Foc}]\,[\text{Wh}\boxed{8}\downarrow\uparrow]} \quad \ldots[\text{Wh}\boxed{8}]\ldots$$

Relatedly, it is impossible to Wh-move the entire phrase projected by O to $C_{[\text{uWh}\downarrow\uparrow]}$, (38), as this would again lead to a situation where the Wh-feature must be interpreted in two different positions: C and O.

(38) *

$$O_{[\text{Foc}]\,[\text{Wh}\boxed{8}\downarrow\uparrow]}$$
$$O_{[\text{Foc}]\,[\text{Wh}\boxed{8}\downarrow\uparrow]} \quad \ldots[\text{Wh}\boxed{8}]\ldots \qquad C_{[\text{Wh}\boxed{8}\downarrow\uparrow]} \quad \ldots O\ldots$$

The only option that's left is to move O by itself. The structure violates no constraints.

(39) *

$$O_{[\text{Foc}]\,[\text{Wh}\boxed{8}\downarrow\uparrow]}$$
$$C_{[\text{Wh}\boxed{8}\downarrow\uparrow]} \quad \ldots$$
$$O_{[\text{Foc}]\,[\text{Wh}\boxed{8}\downarrow\uparrow]}$$
$$O \quad \ldots[\text{Wh}\boxed{8}]\ldots$$

Second, observe that focus movement applies in the lower part of the structure while Wh-movement applies in the higher part of the structure. Given the reasoning in Abels, 2007, this entails that Foc ≪ Wh on the hierarchy in (5). Given that the trigger of the merger of O was the Wh-probe, it follows that O itself may not undergo focus movement without violating the generalized ban on improper movement: Since the head O has already been targeted by an operation higher on the hierarchy of operations, it cannot subsequently be targeted by one lower on the hierarchy. The phrase projected by O, however, also carries the

Foc-feature and it has not been targeted by any operation at all yet. It is therefore free to undergo focus movement.

To summarize, these observations about the structure in (36) entail four things: (a) O may and must undergo Wh-movement, (b) O may not undergo focus movement, (c) the phrase projected by O may undergo focus movement, (d) because of the ordering Foc $\ll$ Wh on the hierarchy of operations, (5), focus movement must precede Wh-movement. This is the correct result. With the assumption of O, the facts are correctly captured: The island-insensitive Wh-in-situ option alternates with a partial movement strategy which shows sensitivity to islands along the entire path of movement from the original launching site to the landing site of partial movement and on to the Wh-scope position. The last part of the trip is made exclusively by the operator O, which happens to be null in the languages under discussion.

If the focus marker FOC, is sensitive to the sharing of a Foc-feature, then it is expected to appear along the path of phrasal focus movement and not to appear along the path of null-operator movement. This very simple account of the distribution of FOC gives rise to one last problem, which I would like to discuss now. We have seen that the properties of the partial-movement strategy are correctly encoded using the operator O. We also saw that the Wh-in-situ strategy can be simply characterized by assuming [uWh$_\downarrow$] probes. At this point we are predicting that Wh-phrases without O should be able to participate in the in situ strategy and in a pure Wh-movement strategy without focus. Such an operation should have as its final landing site the Wh-scope position and, as a movement strategy, it should be island-sensitive. Movement along the path should not be marked by the appearance of FOC, since, according to what has just been said FOC tracks the presence of focus movement rather than Wh-movement. The facts of Kîîtharaka discussed above do not fit this prediction; the appearance of FOC is not optional but mandatory along the path of movement. A minor adjustment will fix this problem. Suppose that in addition to [Foc] and [uWh$_{\downarrow\uparrow}$] O bears an additional feature [X] not borne by Wh-phrases without O. Suppose furthermore that there are two features involved in the Wh-movement strategy: [Wh] and [X]. In other words, assume that the heads attracting the operator O bear the features [uWh$_{\downarrow\uparrow}$] and [uX$_{\downarrow\uparrow}$] and that the language does not have the lexical resources to use heads [uWh$_{\downarrow\uparrow}$] that do not also bear [uX$_{\downarrow\uparrow}$]. On this assumption there is now a bi-unique relation between the presence of O and the Wh-movement strategy and the absence of O and the Wh-in-situ strategy, as desired.[10]

---

[10] Another option, one which I will not develop here but which would follow relatively smoothly from the treatment of Wh-movement in Cable, 2007, 2010b, would be to claim that there are no inherent Wh-phrases in languages with partial Wh-movement. We could say that the phase heads along the path bear the feature [uWh$_{\downarrow\uparrow}$], [uFoc$_{\downarrow\uparrow}$], or [uFoc$_\downarrow$]. We would then need an additional null operator that would need to be able

But can this feature [X] be justified? I would suggest, albeit tentatively, that [X] may implement the exhaustivity property (which Abels and Muriungi, 2008 associated with one of the uses of FOC, as discussed above). Exhaustivity is a property of the Wh-movement strategy but not of the Wh-in-situ strategy in Kîîtharaka.[11]

This concludes my discussion of partial Wh-movement. The account developed above fuses the insights of Sabel's work, from where the idea that the lower segment of the path involves focus movement is taken, with the idea from Cole and Hermon, 1998 that the upper part of the path uses null-operator movement. These ideas are expressed in a compact way under the present set of assumptions, which strengthens our confidence in their adequacy.

5.4.2   Pied-piping and secondary movement

Under current assumptions, pied-piping is enabled by the sharing of features between pied-piper and pied-piped category. It is time to make this precise now.

The first point to note is that the generalization according to which complement and movement-derived specifiers are pied-piping positions follows immediately. Pied-piping by definition involves movement. Under present assumptions this entails the presence of $[uF_{\downarrow\uparrow}]$ probes. We saw in the abstract discussion of systems employing only a single feature that all probes probing a particular target must be uniform, otherwise a violation of the principle Interpret Once under Sharing results. Therefore, in pied-piping structures, every probe for the relevant feature (for example, [Wh] or [Rel]) must be $\downarrow\uparrow$. This crucially includes the probe on the pied-piped category. Therefore, if pied-piping is to be allowed at all, it is only possible in a configuration where a $[uF_{\downarrow\uparrow}]$ probe can be shared. $[uF_{\downarrow\uparrow}]$ has two sharing configurations: complement and movement-derived specifier. This derives why complement and movement-derived specifier positions allow pied-piping. The uniformity of all probes also entails that complement and specifier positions are the only pied-piping positions.

Consider the following cases of pied-piping from complement position as

---

to attach to a domain containing a focus and which would introduce the Wh-feature. This operator would undergo Wh-movement.

[11]   Cole and Hermon, 1998 suggest that the appearance of various markers in Malay tracks the overt-covert distinction. Within their set of assumptions this makes sense, but the account is constructed around a single feature. As we saw, this is impossible in the present system. The present system uses separate features to drive the movement of the overt phrase vs. the movement of the null operator. Within this set of assumptions then, the fact that markers appear along the path of focus movement but not along the path of Wh-movement is further evidence for the claim that there are specific rather than generic features triggering intermediate steps of movement.

illustrations:

(40) German
  a. Ich weiß nicht, mit wem du geredet hast.
      I know not   with whom you spoken has.
      I don't know who you talked to.
  b. Fritz weiß, bis   zu welchem Punkt er gehen kann
      Fritz knows until to which   point he go   can
      Fritz knows how far he can go.

Assuming that prepositions are phase heads and that they may bear $[uWh_{\downarrow\uparrow}]$ in German, we have the following as a possible structure for the PP in German. (I am using $[uD_{\downarrow\uparrow}]$ as a placeholder for whatever selectional features the preposition has.) Selectional features are much lower than Wh-features on the hierarchy that orders the application of operations, (5), so the structure encodes that while the Wh-feature is shared between the complement of the preposition, the preposition, and the prepositional phrase, it is not the trigger of merger in (41a). Therefore, the occurrence of the complement of the preposition will not count as terminal for the Wh-feature even if the complement remains in situ. With the Wh-feature shared between the preposition and its complement, the prepositional phrase can act as a Wh-phrase and move, giving rise to what is called pied-piping, (41b).

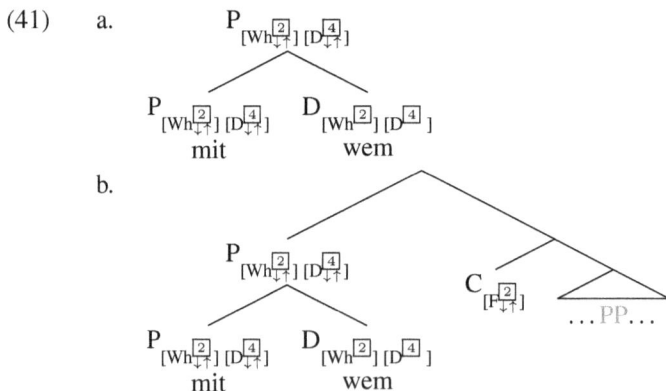

(41) a.
```
              P
              [Wh²↓↑] [D⁴↓↑]
             /        \
        P                  D
        [Wh²↓↑] [D⁴↓↑]     [Wh²] [D⁴]
        mit                wem
```
      b.
```
                P                        C
                [Wh²↓↑] [D⁴↓↑]           [F²↓↑]    ...PP...
               /       \
          P              D
          [Wh²↓↑] [D⁴↓↑] [Wh²] [D⁴]
          mit            wem
```

Notice that the complement of the preposition could not be extracted. This is a simple application of the stranding generalization, which, as we saw, follows from the joint action of Last Resort and the phase impenetrability condition.

Of course, the prepositional phrase itself doesn't *have* to move. If two prepositional phrases are embedded directly within each other, we derive the recursive pied-piping pattern from (40b), which is analyzed in figure 5.2.

Let's turn to simple examples of pied-piping from specifier position now.

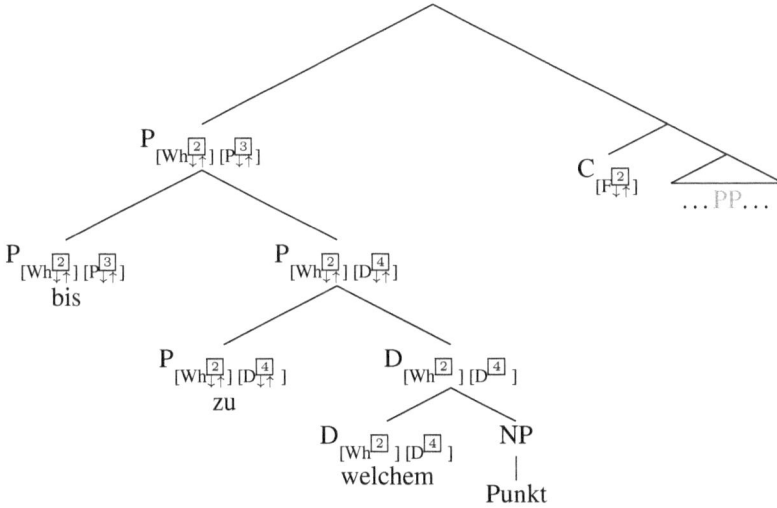

Table 5.2: Structure for recursive pied-piping from complement position

(42)   English
    a.   I wonder whose mother you invited.
    b.   I wonder whose mother's friend you invited.

For (42a), I assume the DP-internal structure in (43a). *Who* shares both a case-feature and a Wh-feature with D. The case feature is the trigger and the Wh-feature the free-rider. The occurrence of *who* in Spec,DP is thus not terminal for the Wh-feature and need not be interpreted. As a consequence the containing DP is able to undergo Wh-movement giving rise to pied-piping, (43b).

(43)   a.

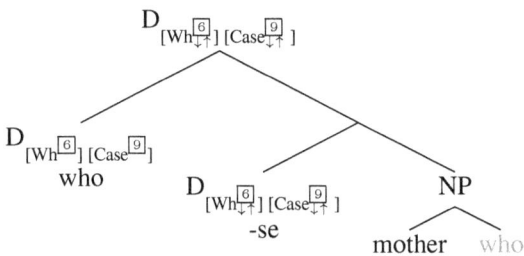

b.

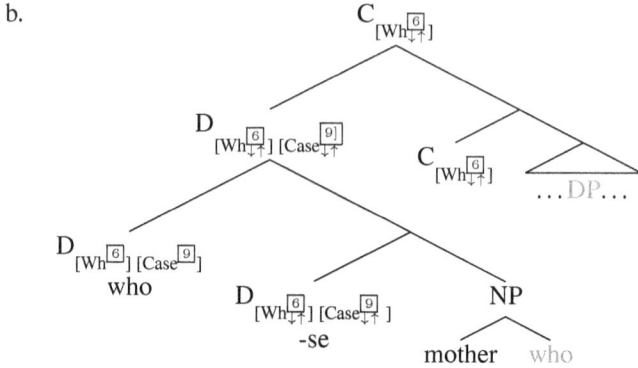

(42b) shows the iterated application this same strategy. The resulting structure for the DP is shown in figure 5.3. Since neither movement of *who* nor of *whose mother* is triggered by the Wh-feature, the resulting structure may undergo Wh-movement to Spec,CP without violating any conditions. Alternatively, the entire DP could be embedded under a preposition. In that case, the Wh-feature could be shared with the prepositional phrase giving rise to the mixed type of pied-piping observed in (44).

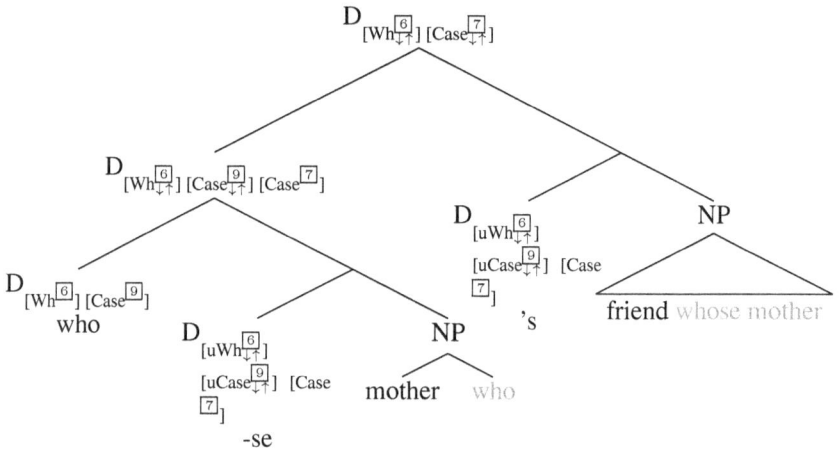

Table 5.3: Structure for recursive pied-piping from specifier position

(44)   German

Ich frage mich, mit wessen Mutter du   gesprochen hast.
I   ask   REFL with whose mother you spoken   have
I wonder whose mother you talked to.

The discussion so far derives the possibility of pied-piping from the specifier and complement positions of phase heads. The theory makes pied-piping optional in a certain sense. Nothing in the theory of feature-sharing and interpretation developed here forces the larger DP in (43b) to move. Moving *who* by itself is equally possible from the perspective of the theory of feature-sharing and interpretation. What rules out the counterpart of (43b) with extraction of *who* in English is the left-branch condition. Languages that allow violations of the left-branch condition, may therefore allow optional pied-piping. A good example is Tzotzil. Recall examples (23) in Chapter 3, which showed that pied-piping is optional in this language as long as extraction is possible in principle, (45).

(45) Tzotzil   Aissen, 1996, 481 ex. 97a, 485 ex. 103

    a. I-'ixtalaj s-kayijonal   y-osil   li j-tot-e.
        CP-ruin $A3^{rd}$-firelane $A3^{rd}$-land the $A.1^{st}$-father-ENC
        The firelane around my father's land was ruined.

    b. Buch'u i-'ixtalaj s-kayijonal   y-osil?
        who   CP-ruin $A3^{rd}$-firelane $A3^{rd}$-land

    c. Buch'u s-kayijonal   y-osil   i-'ixtalaj?
        who $A3^{rd}$-firelane $A3^{rd}$-land CP-ruin

    d. Buch'u y-osil   i-'ixtalaj s-kayijonal?
        who $A3^{rd}$-land CP-ruin $A3^{rd}$-firelane
        The fireland of whose land was ruined?

When direct extraction is impossible, pied-piping becomes obligatory, (46) (repeated from (37) in Chapter 3).

(46) Tzotzil   Aissen, 1996, p. 460

    a. Buch'u x-ch'amal y-elk'an   chij?
        whose $A3^{rd}$-child $A3^{rd}$-steal sheep?
        Whose child stole sheep

    b. *Buch'u y-elk'an   chij   x-ch'amal
        whose $A3^{rd}$-steal sheep $A3^{rd}$-child

The discussion gives us a simple solution for the Hungarian facts mentioned above. Recall that possessors in Hungarian may appear either in the nominative or in the dative. Dative possessors may be extracted or induce pied-piping, (47a). Nominative possessors may not be extracted, nor do they induce pied-piping, (47b).

(47) Hungarian   Heck, 2008, p. 92

    a. Dative possessor with optional pied-piping
       (i) [DP Kinek   a [kinek vendégét]] ismertétek?
            who.DAT the   guest   you.knew
            Whose guest did you know?

    (ii)   Kinek   ismertétek [DP kinek a [kinek vendégét]]
         who.DAT you.knew   the   guest
         Whose guest did you know?

  b.   Nominative possessors disallow pied-piping
    (i)   *[DP Ki   vendégét] ismertétek?
         who.NOM guest   you.knew
    (ii) *Ki   ismertétek [DP ki vendégét]?
         who.NOM you.knew   guest

The two types of possessors occupy distinct positions within the DP, with nominative possessors following the definite determiner and dative possessors preceding it:

(48)   Hungarian   Szabolcsi, 1994, ex. 2–3
  a.   (a) Mari   kalap-ja-i
       the Mari.NOM hat-POSS-PL.3^{rd}SG
       Mari's hats
  b.   Mari-nak a   kalap-ja-i
       Mari-DAT the hat-POSS-PL.3^{rd}SG
       Mari's hats

The D head that is associated with the nominative pattern does not raise the possessor to Spec,DP, as the possessor's positioning following D in (48a) shows. Therefore, this instance of D bearing [uNom↓] cannot undergo pied-piping by the possessor whether it bears an additional Wh-probe or not. The structure is schematized in (49). If D bore [uWh↓], pied-piping would be blocked by the generalization that all probes probing for the same feature must probe in the same way. Since the ultimate attractor of the Wh-phrase is [uWh↓↑], D_NOM must not bear any other type of probe. If D bore [uWh↓↑], then the possessor would move to Spec,DP, but this movement would be triggered by the Wh-feature and pied-piping would again be impossible.

(49)

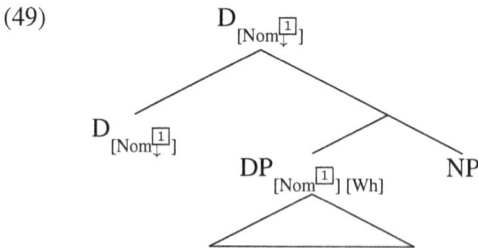

These considerations explain why (47b.i) is ungrammatical. To rule out the possibility of extraction of nominative possessors, (47b.ii), we need to assume in addition that, as a lexical property, the determiner bearing the nominative probe is incompatible with [uWh$_{\downarrow\uparrow}$]. This ensures that a Wh-possessor cannot move to Spec,DP$_{\text{NOM}}$. Movement past this determiner without a Wh-probe is then banned under the phase impenetrability condition. An alternative would be to allow D$_{\text{NOM}}$ to bear [uWh$_{\downarrow\uparrow}$] but to ensure that the DP is an island for extraction, even for elements in the specifier of DP.

By contrast, the determiner found in the dative pattern induces movement of the possessor, (49b). It bears [uDat$_{\downarrow\uparrow}$] and optionally also [uWh$_{\downarrow\uparrow}$], which, when present, is shared as a free-rider. This gives rise to the optional pied-piping pattern we observe, (47a).

The discussion so far has shown why pied-piping is possible but positionally restricted to complement and derived specifier positions. I have also shown why pied-piping is optional in the most general case and how obligatory pied-piping must be understood in terms of constraints on extraction (islands).

We can briefly take up the discussion of secondary movement from chapter 3. I distinguished there between apparent secondary movement and secondary movement proper and suggested that if a particular step of movement was allowed outside of pied-piping structures but forced in pied-piping structures, this should be classified as apparent secondary movement. English and Hungarian possessors are prime examples of this type. Since the relevant movements are licensed outside of pied-piping structures, they must have a trigger that is not related to pied-piping. For English and Hungarian, an implementation in terms of case-related features was suggested. The analytic idea here is that pied-piping is driven by some feature [F] and secondary movement by some other feature [G]. Pied-piping is licensed only if [F] can be shared as a free-rider under sharing of [G].

Secondary movement proper involves instances of movement that are not licensed outside of pied-piping contexts. These are cases where it looks as though even the movement step enabling pied-piping is driven by the same feature that gives rise to pied-piping.

In a strict theoretical sense, the current theory rules out secondary movement proper: Merger in the position from which pied-piping takes place must not be triggered by the feature [F] targeted by pied-piping. We can show this by a reductio ad absurdum argument. See also the discussion of (23) above. To set up the argument, assume that secondary movement could be triggered by the same feature that triggers pied-piping. The occurrence of the pied-piper would then be terminal for [F] and the position to which the pied-pipee moves would also count as terminal for [F]. [F] must therefore be interpreted in both positions in violation of the principle Interpret Once under Sharing. The only way to avoid a violation of Interpret Once under Sharing is to trigger the first of one of the two mergers by a different feature. These considerations derive the strong expectation that there cannot be any secondary movement proper. All secondary movement must reduce to apparent secondary movement.

As we saw in chapter 3, this expectation is borne out for the most part. Cases that even look like secondary movement proper are not easy to come by. One potential example was furnished by the French relative pro-PP *dont*—'of.whom'. I noted in the discussion that the relevant syntactic behavior is specific to *dont* and is not shared by other relative PPs such as *du-quelle*—'of.the-which'. Therefore, any implementation of the process that fronts *dont* within its containing DP will have to mention features other than [Rel] to be adequate. More precisely, the implementation will have to mention features or a feature combination specific to *dont*. On the reasonable assumption that whatever these features are (category or whatever), they are akin to selectional features and therefore below [Rel] on the hierarchy in (5), we find that an implementation of the behavior of *dont* will treat its movement as apparent secondary movement since the feature [Rel] will be shared as a free-rider.

Tzotzil possessors present us with a harder problem. Possessor fronting in the language is apparently impossible outside the contexts of Wh-movement and focus fronting. To make Tzotzil compatible with the claim that secondary movement proper does not exist, we need to find a feature [F], common to both Wh-movement and focus fronting structures but non-identical to either of them. We would then need to stipulate lexically that $[uF_{\downarrow\uparrow}]$ may co-occur with $[uFoc_{\downarrow\uparrow}]$ and $[uWh_{\downarrow\uparrow}]$ but may not occur in isolation. This would solve the problem the theory faces rather directly. Of course, the assumption of some unspecified feature F is not an analysis. Unfortunately, my knowledge of the syntax and interpretation of questions with pied-piping in Tzotzil and the other languages showing similar patterns does not allow me to make inferences about the nature of F. A possibility that comes to mind is the exhaustivity feature that I invoked in the discussion of Kîîtharaka above. The expectation would then be that exhaustivity is obligatorily found in questions with possessor fronting and in focus constructions with possessor fronting. I have to leave the question open.

Let me summarize the discussion of pied-piping up to this point. We have seen that and how the current theory derives the following expectations about pied-piping. Pied-piping should be optional. Recursive (specifier of specifier, complement of complement) as well as mixed (specifier of complement) pied-piping should be allowed. Secondary movement proper should be ruled out. All of these are indeed properties of pied-piping, which strengthens our confidence in the theory presented here.

What I have not commented on so far is the set of phrases that can be pied-piped. The discussion in this chapter was dedicated exclusively to DP and PP. The theory actually predicts that all phases (CP, PP, DP, vP) should participate in pied-piping in principle, because all phase heads can (optionally and subject to lexical availability in any given language) be endowed with any probe. In chapter 3, I gave examples of CP pied-piping, fulfilling a further expectation of the current system. I noted, however, that pied-piping of vP is rare. German provided a possible case. However, two of the examples that I mentioned as candidates for pied-piping from Spec,vP involve pied-piping of CP. The relevant examples are Basque under Arregi's (2002) analysis and Malayalam under Jayaseelan's (2001; 2003; 2004). Such pied-piping of XP from Spec,YP is disallowed under current assumptions, since it violates the generalization that all probes probing a particular feature must probe in the same way. This suggests that for Basque, the analysis in Ortiz de Urbina, 1989 is correct, which relies on pied-piping from Spec,CP. A similar analysis would have to be given for Malayalam.[12]

The scarcity of vP pied-piping is as much of a challenge for this theory as it is for other theories of pied-piping. Heck, 2008 suggests in response to this problem that vPs rarely if every pied-pipe because vPs are transparent for extraction. This response is coherent, because for Heck pied-piping happens only when extraction is impossible. By contrast, I have assumed that pied-piping is optional and opacity of a constituent may make pied-piping obligatory (possessor extraction in English) but transparency never inhibits pied-piping (optional extraction or pied-piping of possessors in Hungarian, (47a)). I can only offer the speculation that Spec,vP is too rarely the terminal landing site of relevant ulterior movements. Why this would be so, I don't know.

The theory of pied-piping presented here is based on sharing of relevant features between the head of the pied-piped constituent and the pied-piper. Heck, 2008 has criticized such theories on the grounds that they stipulate the relevant features exclusively to enable pied-piping. My hope is that the present system can escape this criticism by showing that there is converging if indirect evidence from various domains for the existence of the features in question.

5.5   Wh-movement in various languages

In the previous section I discussed how the current theory derives the main generalizations concerning partial movement, pied-piping, and secondary movement. It is now time to switch presentational mode once again and to show briefly how

---

[12]   If it turns out that there are irreducible cases of pied-piping of CP from Spec,vP, it might be necessary to redefine the notion of a terminal occurrence and/or the notion of which of a number of [uF$_\downarrow$] probes count as terminal, possibly making a distinction between triggering [uF$_\downarrow$] probes and free-riders along the lines of the distinction already present for [uF$_{\downarrow\uparrow}$] probes.

As things stand, Jayaseelan's (2001; 2003; 2004) analysis of Malayalam is a counterexample to the proposals made here and either that analysis or the proposals made here must be revised.

the present system can be used to describe the facts of Wh-movement in a variety of language types.

5.5.1 Single-Wh-movement languages: English, French, Italian

I start with English, as it has a fairly simple characterization. English will allow me to discuss a number of general points that come up but have not been addressed yet. After that I will briefly show how French and Italian can be handled. The former differs from English in having an optional Wh-in-situ strategy for direct questions. The latter differs from English in disallowing multiple Wh-questions (Adams, 1984; Calabrese, 1984).

All phase heads that are transparent for Wh-movement come in two flavors—one with and one without $[uWh_{\downarrow\uparrow}]$. This allows the following patterns in addition to some others to be discussed below. (For ease of reading I suppress showing the Wh-feature on the moving Wh-phrase and also suppress the superscripts indicating shared features.)[13]

(50) a. [$_C$ Who [$C_{[Wh_{\downarrow\uparrow}]}$ [who bought this book]]]?

b. [$_C$ What [[$_{C[Wh_{\downarrow\uparrow}]}$ did] [John did [$_v$ what [$_{v[Wh_{\downarrow\uparrow}]}$ buy] [buy what]]]]]

c. [$_C$ What [[$_{C[Wh_{\downarrow\uparrow}]}$ do] [you do [$_v$ what [$_{v[Wh_{\downarrow\uparrow}]}$ think] [think [$_C$ what [$C_{[Wh_{\downarrow\uparrow}]}$ [John [$_v$ what [$_{v[Wh_{\downarrow\uparrow}]}$ bought] [bought what]]]]]]]]]]]

This is as desired, but the system also allows the following versions of (50b) and (50c) as syntactically well-formed objects.

(51) a. [John [$_v$ [$_v$ bought] [buy what]]]

b. [John [$_v$ what [$_{v[Wh_{\downarrow\uparrow}]}$ buy] [buy what]]]

c. [You [$_v$ what [$_{v[Wh_{\downarrow\uparrow}]}$ think] [think [$_C$ what [$C_{[Wh_{\downarrow\uparrow}]}$ [John [$_v$ what [[$_{v[Wh_{\downarrow\uparrow}]}$ bought] [bought what]]]]]]]]]]

d. [You [$_v$ [$_v$ think] [think [$_C$ what [$C_{[Wh_{\downarrow\uparrow}]}$ [John [$_v$ what [$_{v[Wh_{\downarrow\uparrow}]}$ bought] [bought what]]]]]]]]

e. etc.

Example (51a) involves an in-situ Wh-phrase. These must be allowed syntactically in English to account for the syntax of multiple and echo Wh-questions. To the extent that there is anything wrong with (51a), it must be semantic. The same semantic considerations also rule out *Did you read what?* and *I wonder whether Joe read what.* as direct and indirect Wh-questions, respectively (see

---

[13] I indicate T-to-C movement as *[$_C$ T]* and verb movement of V to v as *[$_v$ V]*. This is meant merely as a convenient and short notation and not to be taken as suggestive of a particular analysis.

Adger, 2003, chapter 9). In other words, (51a) is syntactically well-formed but it cannot be interpreted as a regular Wh-question. A similar, simple reasoning applies to (51d). The verb *think* does not take questions as complements, but since the occurrence of *what* in Spec,CP is terminal for [Wh], the feature has to be interpreted there, which turns the CP into a question. The sentence cannot be interpreted.

The remaining examples pose a different challenge. Unlike (51a), they are unacceptable in all contexts and, unlike (51d), they do not improve under lexical replacement of the embedding verb. My suggestion to deal with such cases is to assume that they are semantically ill-formed: The Wh-feature would have to be interpreted on v but it cannot. Conceptually, this is similar to ideas found in Brody, 1997, where it is assumed that there are no uninterpretable features in the strict sense. All features are interpretable but they are not interpretable in all places. Wh-features happen to be uninterpretable on v the same way that θ-features are uninterpretable on C. In the current system, any feature that is uninterpretable on a particular category must be shared by a head which is terminal for that feature and where that feature is interpretable.

To a certain extent this clarifies what the distinction between phase heads and other heads in the current system is. Non-phase heads may bear only such features as dictated by their function. These features are interpreted on the heads that bear them. Phase heads on the other hand may bear any probe but only the features that related to the phase head's function can also be interpreted on the phase head. In other words, as far as interpreted features are concerned, phase heads are like any other head. But they are different in that they are possible bearers of features that are never interpreted on them.

To return to the narrow point under discussion, (51b) and (51c) are ill-formed because they do not have an interpretation. A question likely to arise at this point has to do with questions of look-ahead. The model suggested here provides numerous ways of creating syntactically well-formed structures that are semantically ill-formed.[14] Questions of look-ahead will also be raised about structures like the following:

(52)   *[$C_{[uWh_{\downarrow\uparrow}]}$ [John [$_v$ [$_v$ bought] [bought what]]]]

The structure has no well-formed continuation. [uWh$_{\downarrow\uparrow}$], borne by C, must be shared but C's complement does not bear [Wh]. The only bearer of the Wh-

---

[14] The examples in (51) are only the tip of the iceberg. All examples that violate the principle Interpret Once under Sharing and no other condition also fall in this category.

The issue can be syntacticized of course. The principle Interpret Once under Sharing can be replaced by the purely syntactic demand that every shared feature F determine a unique head for which that feature is terminal.

The cases discussed here could be dealt with by demanding that the unique head for which a shared Wh-feature is terminal must be C—and similarly for other features.

feature is buried in the complement of v and inaccessible by the phase impenetrability condition. What would have been required is the insertion of v bearing [uWh$_{\downarrow\uparrow}$]. But how can the grammar know this without looking ahead?

My answer to such questions is that the grammar doesn't look ahead. The grammar is a description of the function computed by the relevant module of the mind. In my understanding at least, the grammar is not a description at Marr's (1982) algorithmic level but a description at the computational level. First and foremost I am interested in characterizing correctly the set of acceptable and unacceptable sentences and to pair them correctly with meanings. Some of the conditions that I have appealed to (Last Resort and the virus theory of feature-sharing) follow naturally from a procedural view of creating sound-meaning relations, but the conclusions here are necessarily tentative. In other words, I set aside the question of how an efficient algorithm for the grammar can or should be formulated (see Abels, in preparation for further discussion).

Returning to English, there are a number of further facts to be captured. First, English allows only a single Wh-phrase to move to any given Spec,CP. This will be handled by the type of restriction discussed in section 5.3 in connection with the possibility of multiple movement: English Wh-probes are subject to the condition that they become inactive as soon as they are shared with a single target. Second, Wh-phrases in situ in multiple questions are therefore interpreted without establishing a syntactic link to the Wh-complementizer, (53). This, apparently correctly,[15] characterizes the second Wh-phrase in multiple questions as island-insensitive.

(53)   [Who$_{[Wh \boxed{5}]}$ [C$_{[Wh \boxed{5}]}$ [who [$_v$ [$_v$ bought] bought what]]]]?

The system readily allows Wh-movement in a language to alternate with Wh-in-situ. French is often cited as a relevant example. Unfortunately the description of what is and what is not possible in French Wh-in-situ questions vary widely. Thus, Cheng and Rooryck, 2000 describe the Wh-in-situ strategy as sensitive to strong and weak islands, restricted to root contexts, and, judging by Cheng and Rooryck, 2000, 12 ex. 20, as requiring that the Wh-phrase be a clausemate of its scope position (similarly Bošković, 1997b, p. 9, Bošković, 1998a, ex. 6).[16] Starke, 2001 agrees that Wh-in-situ is only available in direct

---

[15] The data in this area are not very clear. Kuno and Robinson, 1972 argue for a clausemate condition for multiple interrogation. Dayal, 2002 suggests that there might be a clausemate condition for pair-list readings but not for multiple questions in general. Other authors are much more permissive (e.g., Stroik, 2009). For discussion of even more complex data see Pesetsky, 2000.

The frequently used data concerning direct questions are potentially subject to contamination from echo questions—a point made in Heck, 2008 regarding the grammar of pied-piping. A systematic investigation of indirect multiple questions especially with predicates like *enumerate* or *agree* should be able to give greater clarity here.

questions, but claims that the construction shows weak- but not strong-island sensitivity under "the characteristic downfall intonation" (Starke, 2001, p. 23) and sensitivity neither to strong nor to weak islands with a "slight accent on the situ-wh" (Starke, 2001, p. 23).[17] I have nothing interesting to say about the root property of Wh-in-situ in French. Cheng and Rooryck, 2000, p. 13 suggest that this is a superficial property of French not observed European Portuguese (and possibly also Manglish). A fairly superficial account will do.[18]

For those speakers for whom Starke's description of Wh-in-situ in French holds, we can postulate that in addition to phase heads without Wh-probes and those with $[uWh_{\downarrow\uparrow}]$ there are also phase heads with $[uWh_{\downarrow}]$. This will allow strong-island insensitive Wh-in-situ subject only to Relativized Minimality. Intervention can be circumvented, as with overt movement, by enriching the Wh-phrase with additional content, which accounts for the effect of intonation. Those speakers who conform to the pattern described in Cheng and Rooryck, 2000 might have an almost identical grammar but with a generalized root restriction. Suppose that these speakers' grammar is identical to that of the speakers describe by Starke in that they, too, allow phase heads without Wh-probes, with $[uWh_{\downarrow\uparrow}]$ and with $[uWh_{\downarrow}]$. The difference may be that while Starke's speakers allow $C_{[uWh_{\downarrow}]}$ in embedded contexts, except if it is terminal for the Wh-feature, Cheng and Rooryck's speakers never allow embedded $C_{[uWh_{\downarrow}]}$.[19]

---

[16] It should be noted that the argument for strong-island sensitivity given in Cheng and Rooryck, 2000 is based on an example with a Wh-word in a position where it could not bear stress according to the nuclear-stress rule, whereas all the acceptable examples always involve Wh-phrases in roughly clause-final position where they could receive stress under the nuclear-stress rule. See Hamlaoui, 2011 for relevant discussion.

[17] Cheng and Rooryck, 2000, p. 4 claim that the French Wh-in-situ is characterized by a rising intonation. See Hamlaoui, 2011, 133 fn 4 and references cited there for reasons to be skeptical about this claim.

[18] The issue it seems to me is similar to why subject-auxiliary inversion is restricted to root contexts in standard English, why purely intonational polar interrogatives are restricted to root questions in English, and why direct polar interrogatives in English cannot be introduced by a complementizer.

[19] A direct prediction of the suggestion made here is that speakers of European Portuguese and Manglish, who allow Wh-in-situ in indirect questions, should not show the clausemate effects reported for French in Bošković, 1998a; Cheng and Rooryck, 2000. At least for Manglish, this expecation is borne out:

(i)   Manglish   Wong, 2012, 15 ex. 21
      a.   I want to know what Muthu believe Ali gave Meiling ah.
           I want to know what Muthu believe Ali gave Meiling Q
           I want to know what Muthu believes that Ali gave Meiling.
      b.   I want to know Muthu believe Ali gave Meiling what ah.
           I want to know Muthu believe Ali gave Meiling what Q

While French is a rather straightforward case of encoding an additional option in the grammar—with the root restriction as a quirk—an account of Italian Wh-questions pushes the system developed here to its very limit. I suspect that this is a good thing, as it shows that there are strict limits on the descriptive power of the current system. Italian is well known for having a ban against multiple questions (Adams, 1984; Calabrese, 1984; Dayal, 2006).[20]

(54) Italian   Dayal, 2006, 289 ex. 42
   a. *Chi ha scritto che cosa?
      who has written what thing
   b. *Chi é partito quando?
      who is left   when
   c. *Quale ragazza ha dato un bacio a quale ragazzo?
      which girl   has given a kiss to which boy

What we need to do to account for such patterns is to force all Wh-phrases to move and, at the same time, to restrict the number of Wh-phrases to one. The former goal can be achieved if we let all Wh-phrases bear some [uF]. This will ensure that the feature has to be shared with an appropriate probe, which will require movement of the bearer of [uF] whenever [uF$_{\downarrow\uparrow}$] is present higher in the structure. Restrictions on multiple movement were implemented above in terms of prohibitions on probes against multiple sharing. At first blush, the issue seems straightforward: Wh-elements bear [uWh] and phase heads bear [uWh$_{\downarrow\uparrow}$] which becomes inactive as soon as it is shared once.

Unfortunately, this 'solution' leads to a regress problem. Consider the well-formed single-Wh-question in (55).

(55) Italian

   Cosa ha   scritto?
   what has.3rdSG written
   What has he written

In the structure generated by the grammar we are entertaining as a hypothesis, unfortunately, the Wh-features remain unvalued. This should lead to ungrammaticality.

I want to know what Muthu believes that Ali gave Meiling.

[20] Moro, 2011 and a number of speakers that I have consulted disagree with the descriptions given in Adams, 1984; Calabrese, 1984; Dayal, 2006. I will accept the description of Italian as a language that disallows multiple Wh-questions to illustrate a possible linguistic type here. If this description is incorrect for Italian, then the account should apply to those other languages that have been claimed also ban multiple Wh-questions, like Irish (McCloskey, 1979) and Passamaquoddy (Bruening, 2007).

(56)

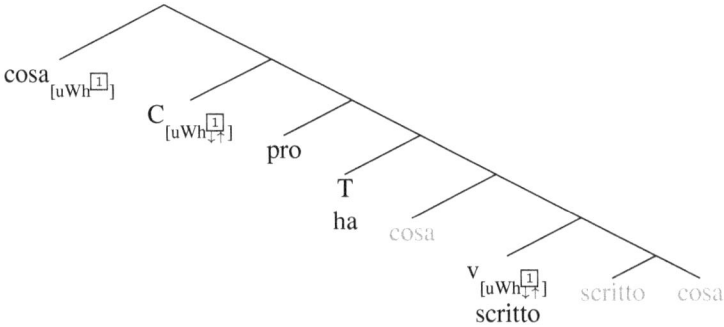

We cannot remedy the situation by merging a (null) head with a valued Wh-feature at the top of the tree, as in (57). The feature is not in a checking configuration with [uWh↓↑] on C. The valued Wh-feature could never become shared because [uWh↓↑] is no longer active.[21]

(57)

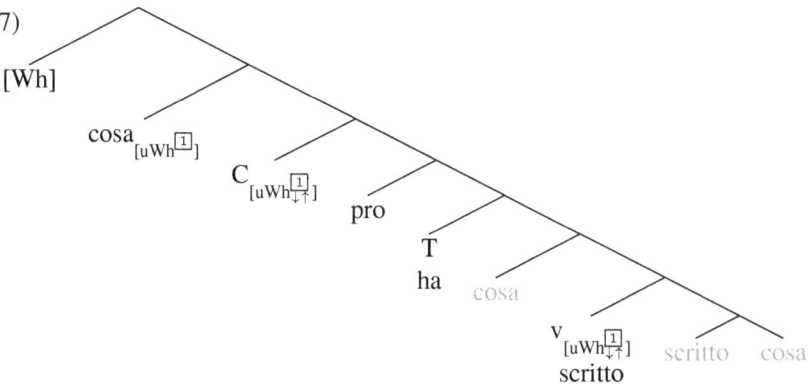

As an alternative we might consider merging [Wh] below C and valuing [uWh↓↑] under movement first, (58). Unfortunately, *cosa* and the Wh-probe on v still remain unvalued, eventually leading to a violation against the ban on unvalued features at the interface. Nothing can be done about this, since there is no active Wh-probe that could drive remerger of *cosa*. Notice that if *cosa* is not merged into the periphery of CP the violation of the ban against unvalued features will become irreparable because *cosa* will be inaccessible by the phase impenetrability condition.

---

[21] The same conclusion holds even if the Wh-feature were brought into a checking relation with [uWh↓↑] on C by merging it lower in the structure or by head-moving C past it.

(58)

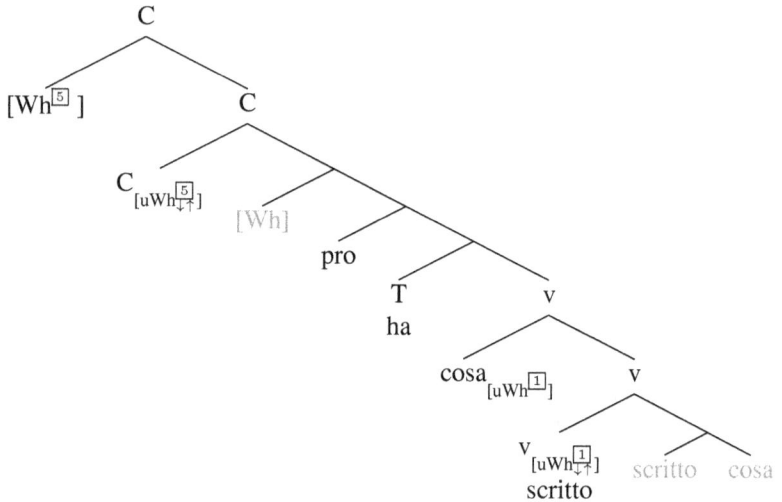

The problem is that there is always at least one unvalued feature. What we need to do instead is to use two different features—one to encode the obligatory nature of movement of Wh-phrases and one to encode the uniqueness restriction. We can assume for example that Wh-elements bear a valued Foc-feature and an unvalued Wh-feature ($cosa_{[Foc]\,[uWh]}$—'what') while the phase heads bear [uWh↑] which can agree multiple times and [uFoc↓↑] which can agree only a single time. Finally, a head bearing a valued Wh-feature needs to be assumed.

We now get the following result. *cosa* moves to Spec,vP in (59a). This movement is driven and triggered by the focus probe on v, which becomes inactive and unable to attract further targets as a result of feature-sharing with *cosa*. The Wh-probe on v enters into a sharing configuration with *cosa* as a by-product. The Wh-feature is shared as a free-rider. At the CP level, the same thing happens again, (59b). At this point, the Wh-features on *cosa* and C are still unvalued. However, the probe [uWh↑] on C remains active. We can therefore merge [Wh] and value the otherwise offending features, (59c).

(59)   a.

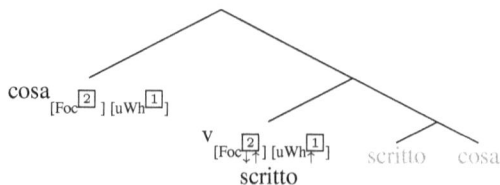

b.

cosa [Foc 2] [uWh 1] C [Foc 2 ↓↑] [uWh 1 ↑] pro T ha *cosa* v [Foc 2 ↓↑] [uWh 1 ↑] scritto *scritto* *cosa*

c.

[Wh 1] cosa [Foc 2] [Wh 1] C [Foc 2 ↓↑] [Wh 1 ↑] pro T ha *cosa* v [Foc 2 ↓↑] [Wh 1 ↑] scritto *scritto* *cosa*

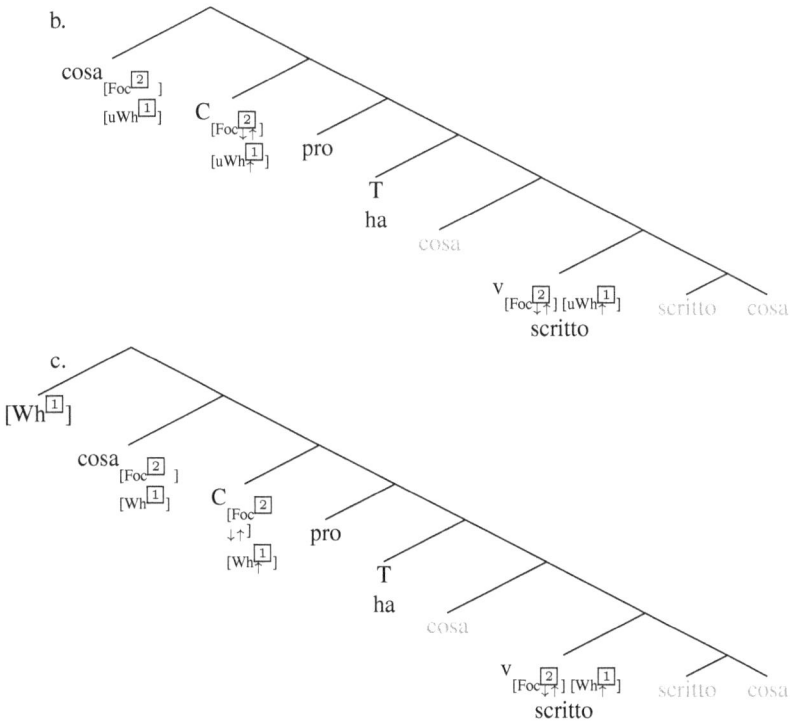

In this way we can generate examples with Wh-movement like (55). Multiple Wh-questions of the English type with the additional Wh-phrases in-situ are ruled out in Italian because those additional Wh-phrases all bear [uWh], which needs to be valued. However, it cannot be valued in situ since the only available Wh-probes are [uWh↑]. Multiple Wh-movement is also ruled out because this would require all Wh-phrases to move into a sharing configuration with a relevant probe. The only relevant probe that can drive movement (the Wh-probe on phase heads being ↑) is the [uFoc↓↑]-probe, which becomes inactive once it is shared.

I have shown in this section how the present system deals with various kinds of single-Wh-movement patterns. They fall within the descriptive power of the system. The difficulty we encounter in describing these patterns points to the healthy limitations the system imposes on what is and what is not a possible system.

5.5.2 Multiple-Wh-fronting languages

The discussion of Italian in the previous section has set the stage for a discussion of languages that do not tolerate Wh-phrases in situ. Rudin, 1988a,b distinguishes between two types of multiple-Wh-fronting languages. In a language like Bulgarian and Rumanian, the Wh-phrases are necessarily linearly adjacent:

(60)   Bulgarian   Bošković, 1997b, p. 2
   a.   Zavisi   ot tova, koj kogo prŭv e udaril
        depends on it   who whom first is hit
        It depends on who hits whom first
   b.   *Zavisi   ot tova koj prŭv kogo e udaril
        depends on it   who first whom is hit

All Wh-phrases obligatorily front to the scope position even in contexts of long Wh-movement:

(61)   Bulgarian   Rudin, 1988a, 7–8, ex. 20
   a.   Ksenija na kogo   kakvo kaza če   šte   donese?
        Ksenija to whom what   said that will bring.3^{rd}SG
        What did Ksenija say that she would bring to whom?
   b.   *Ksenija na kogo   kaza če   šte   donese   kakvo?
        Ksenija to whom said that will bring.3^{rd}SG what
   c.   *Ksenija kakvo kaza če   šte   donese   na kogo?
        Ksenija what   said that will bring.3^{rd}SG to whom
   d.   *Ksenija kakvo kaza na kogo šte   donese?
        Ksenija what   said to whom will bring.3^{rd}SG
   e.   *Ksenija na kogo   kaza kakvo šte   donese?
        Ksenija to whom said what   will bring.3^{rd}SG

These systems of multiple-Wh-fronting can be captured straightforwardly here. The system we need to assume is like my initial faulty suggestion about Italian with the one difference that the probes on the phase heads allow multiple feature-sharing. In other words, we need to assume that all Wh-words bear [uWh], that the phase heads bear [uWh$_{\downarrow\uparrow}$] which does not become inactive after sharing, and that there is a Wh-operator that gets externally merged at the edge of CP. Nothing further needs to be said to give a basic description of these languages.

A simple example will end up looking schematically as follows. *Whom* enters a feature-sharing relation with the preposition in situ, allowing pied-piping. [uWh$_{\downarrow\uparrow}$] on the preposition and the Wh-word remain unvalued. *To whom* moves to Spec,CP enabling feature-sharing between C and PP but leaving the feature unvalued. *What* also moves to Spec,CP enabling sharing between C and *what* but leaving the features still unvalued. The functional head bearing the valued Wh-feature merges. The merger is triggered by a categorial (selectional) C-feature on the head. Finally, C undergoes projection-internal head movement which enables sharing of C's [uWh$_{\downarrow\uparrow}$]-probe, finally valuing the feature.

(62)

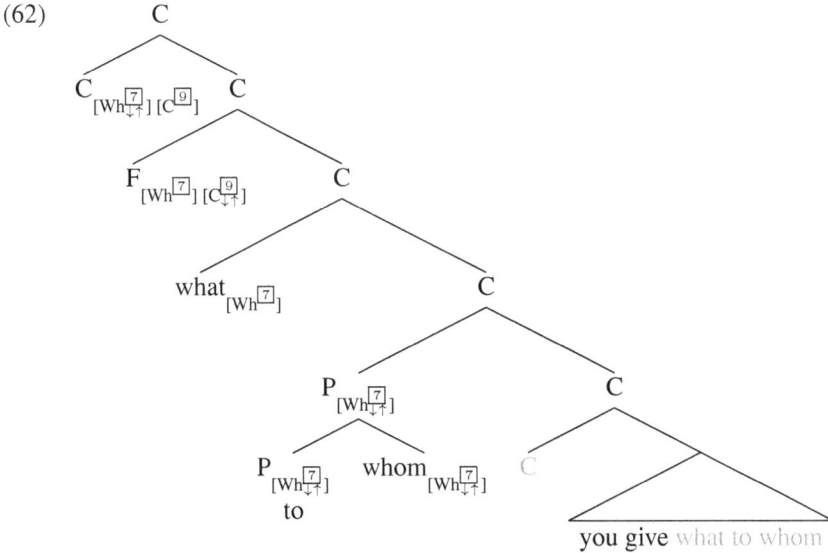

The adjacency requirement follows from this system, because interspersing merger of a non-Wh-related element with the Wh-related operations would require satisfying the ulterior feature [F] in between satisfaction of [Wh]. This entails the order of [Wh] $\ll$ [F] $\ll$ [Wh] on the Universal Constraint on the Ordering of Operations in Language. Such a conclusion violates the linearity assumption for that order (Abels, 2007).

The second type of multiple-Wh-fronting languages discussed by Rudin includes Serbo Croatian, Polish, and Czech. In these languages the Wh-phrases are not necessarily adjacent:

(63)   Serbo Croatian   Bošković, 1997b, p. 2
   a.   Zavisi   od toga ko   koga   prvi udari.
        depends on it   who whom first hits
        It depends on who hits whom first.
   b.   Zavisi   od toga ko   prvi koga   udari.
        depends on it   who first whom hits

In cases of long movement, the Wh-phrases need not—for other speakers must not—move together to the scope position.

(64)   Serbo Croatian   Rudin, 1988a, 9 ex. 25
   a.   Ko   želite   da vam šta   kupi?
        who want.2^{nd}PL to you what buy.3^{rd}SG
        Who do you want to buy you what?
   b.   Šta   želite   da vam ko   kupi?
        what want.2^{nd}PL to you who buy.3^{rd}SG

c. %Ko šta želite   da vam kupi?[22]
   who what want.2^{nd}PL to you buy.3^{rd}SG

d. *Šta ko želite   da vam kupi?
   what who want.2^{nd}PL to you buy.3^{rd}SG

e. *Ko želite   šta da vam kupi?
   who want.2^{nd}PL what to you buy.3^{rd}SG

f. *Šta želite   ko da vam kupi?
   what want.2^{nd}PL who to you buy.3^{rd}SG

In the present system there must be at least two different types of movement involved here, since in a single-feature system all movement must target the same position, the scope position, lest the structure violate the principle Interpret Once under Sharing. Indeed, Rudin, 1988a,b suggests that only one Wh-phrase moves to Spec,CP with the others targeting an IP-adjoined position. Similarly, Bošković, 1998b, 2000 claims that there is multiple focus movement at work here. I follow the latter implementation.

The grammar of speakers that follow the above pattern and disallow (64c) can be described by assuming that Wh-elements bear the following two features: [uFoc] and [Wh]. We then assume that there is a focus-fronting rule implemented using [uFoc$_{\downarrow\uparrow}$], which is set to allow multiple sharing. In addition we need to assume a valued inaudible [Foc] element, along the lines of the discussion of the Wh-operator invoked in the discussion of Italian in (59) above. Focus movement is clause-bounded. This is implemented as the lexical stipulation that [uFoc$_{\downarrow\uparrow}$] is never borne by C. Riding on the back of this multiple focus movement system is an English-type single-Wh-movement system which accesses the Wh-feature and provides [uWh$_{\downarrow\uparrow}$] probes on all relevant phase heads.

The other class of speakers also allow (64c). These speakers appear to be characterized by two additional facts. First, their [uWh$_{\downarrow\uparrow}$] allows multiple sharing. This assumption is necessary to allow (64c). Since these speakers also allow (64a-b), multiple fronting is strictly optional and, therefore, not implemented using [uWh] on Wh-elements. Second, the description in Bošković, 1997a, 1998b, 2000 suggests that the presence of [uWh$_{\downarrow\uparrow}$] on C is optional in direct questions and alternates on root C (and only there) with [uWh$_{\downarrow}$]. This gives rise to a pattern that is abstractly similar to the pattern discussed for French above.[23]

---

[22] Rudin gives '*' as the judgment for this example. There is actually a split between speakers, as Rudin's own and Bošković's (1997) discussion of such cases makes clear. I have adjusted the marking accordingly.

[23] If this analysis is on the right track, the Serbo Croatian of speakers who accept (64c) is a language with optional multiple-Wh-fronting, filling a gap in the existing typology noted in Dayal, 2006.

5.5.3   Wh-in-situ

The theory discussed in this and the previous chapter was developed for move-ment dependencies. I have left the tools for the analysis of in-situ dependencies much less developed and somewhat more blunt than the ones dealing with move-ment. This has to do with the main aim of this essay, which is to study movement relations, and should not be taken as a limitation in principle. As a consequence, the analytic possibilities for Wh-in-situ structures may be unduly limited. If this turns out to be true, there is an obvious way in which refinements can be intro-duced without touching the core of the movement theory. In section 5.2 above I introduced a distinction between features that count as triggers for movement and free-riders. This distinction was then used in the definition of when an oc-currence counts as terminal and, consequently, where to interpret a feature under sharing. If necessary, a similar distinction can be introduced for agreement, that is for probing features not inducing movement, which would moderately en-rich the descriptive apparatus for in-situ relations.[24] Without such revisions, the most obvious way to treat Wh-in-situ is what I suggested above for Kîîtharaka, namely, to assume that all phase heads between the Wh-element and the scope position bear $[uWh_\downarrow]$. This will allow long-distance Wh-dependencies which are locally mediated. Since they do not involve movement, they are insensitive to strong islands but, given that they involve feature-sharing, are subject to feature-based intervention effects. This is what we find in Wh-in-situ languages like Japanese. At a first pass, Wh-dependencies in the language are not sensitive to strong islands but various featurally defined interveners, including Wh-scope po-sitions, block the creation of the dependency.[25] This is seen most clearly for true Wh-adjuncts and other non-referential Wh-phrases and only with qualifications for argumental, referential Wh-phrases (see Watanabe, 2001 for an overview and references). The mitigation of weak-island effects by argumental Wh-phrases is,

---

[24]   The relevant definition would have to say something along the following lines. A feature shared by a $[uF_\downarrow]$ or a $[uF_\uparrow]$ probe on head H is a free-rider if and only if for all bearers B of [F] with which H shares [F] and which H c-commands there is a feature [G] such that (i) H shares [G] with B and (ii) [G] is lower on the hierarchy in (5) than [F]. We could then say that free-riders never force interpretation.

Such a revision might be necessary anyway to deal with what Heck, 2008 calls mas-sive pied-piping involving structures where the pied-piper is not in one of the canonical specifier or complement positions. A different analysis for such structures might in-volve a version of the null-operator analysis of Wh-in-situ discussed in the following two paragraphs but *with* rather than *without* pied-piping.

[25]   The relevant body of evidence is discussed under the heading of LF subjacency in Nishigauchi, 1986, 1990; Pesetsky, 1987 and as evidence for overt operator movement in Watanabe, 1992b. Watanabe, 2003 offers a discussion in terms of feature-based intervention very much in the spirit of what I have in mind.

of course, also found in movement dependencies and can be given a straightforward account under the assumptions of an articulated feature structure for syntax (for relevant discussion see Abels, 2012; Boeckx and Jeong, 2004; Rizzi, 2001c, 2004a; Starke, 2001). Since such accounts, in present terminology, trade on the locality conditions for feature-sharing, they apply equally well to the sharing by [uF$_{\downarrow\uparrow}$] and [uF$_{\downarrow}$] probes, that is, to in-situ and movement strategies alike.

A line of analysis for Wh-in-situ languages that has gained some popularity over the last 15 years involves dissecting the path between the Wh-element and the Wh-scope position into an island-sensitive upper part, where the relation is mediated by (operator) movement, and a strong-island insensitive lower part, where the relation is mediated in some non-movement way. A number of executions varying in detail of implementation exist (see Cable, 2010b; Hagstrom, 1998; Kishimoto, 2005; Watanabe, 1992a, 2001).

In order to implement such analyses in the current system, we would need to say that the lower part of the relation is mediated by $\downarrow$ probes linking the Wh-word with the point along the path where the operator is externally merged and signalling its presence.

In Japanese, Wh-words do double duty as indefinites and are sometimes called indeterminate phrases for that reaston. Let the feature probing for the presence of such items be an 'indeterminate'-feature ([uInd$_{\downarrow}$]). The indeterminate phrase itself would have to be analyzed as not carrying the Wh-feature, since otherwise we would expect it to have a regular Wh-syntax. We also need to postulate an operator (null or pronounced) that bears [uInd$_{\downarrow}$]. The [uInd$_{\downarrow}$] probe is needed to ensure that the operator cannot be inserted in a context not containing a Wh-word. I assume that the Ind-feature needs to be interpreted on the operator and that it is therefore inaccessible to further sharing without incurring a semantic violation.[26] The operator would also introduce the valued Wh-feature, possibly as one among other features. This Wh-operator could then be moved in the normal way.

Further assumptions will be needed to block pied-piping of the operator's sister. As in the case of the null operator discussed in Kîîtharaka above, the ban against pied-piping can be implemented as a second probe [uF$_{\downarrow\uparrow}$] on the operator which must be assumed to trigger the operator's merger in the first place.

It is clear from the brief remarks above that nothing in principle prevents this type of analysis. If this analysis is indeed deemed justified on empirical grounds, the nature of [F] and the feature I called [Ind] would need to be clarified.

We probably need to allow for the possibility of null-operator movement as a tool in the analysis of Wh-in-situ in addition. Van Valin, 1995, Van Valin and LaPolla, 1997, chapter 9 describe Lakhota as a Wh-in-situ language which

---

[26] This assumption is intended as a syntactic implementation of the intervention effects discussed prominently in Kratzer, 2005; Kratzer and Shimoyama, 2002; Shimoyama, 2001.

differs in its locality behavior substantially from Japanese or Chinese. According to these authors, Lakhota questions are formed with an interrogative particle and in-situ elements. The particle, *he*—'Q', marks both polar- and Wh-questions. The in-situ elements are ambiguous between an indefinite and a Wh-construal.

The following sentence is therefore ambiguous between a polar question with an indefinite and a Wh-question. I leave the indeterminate pronoun *táku* without a gloss.

(65) Lakhota   Van Valin and LaPolla, 1997, p. 617

Šų́ka ki táku yaxtáka   he?
dog   the 3^{rd}SGU.3^{rd}SGA.bite Q
What did the dog bite?
Did the dog bite something?

The ambiguity disappears when *táku* is embedded in a strong island.

(66) Lakhota   Van Valin and LaPolla, 1997, p. 616

Wičháša ki šų́ka wą táku yaxtáke   ki le
man   the dog a 3^{rd}SGA.3^{rd}SGU.bite the this
wą-yą́ka   he?
3^{rd}SGU-3^{rd}SGA.see Q?
Did the man see the dog which bit something?
*What did the man see the dog which bit?

This type of pattern can be described in terms of null-operator movement along the lines of the suggestion I made regarding Kîîtharaka partial movement. For Lakhota, one could assume that the indeterminate pronouns spell out structures that do or do not contain the Wh-feature. We can then assume a null operator made up of the features [uWh$_{\downarrow\uparrow}$] and an additional feature [X] which it does not share with the indeterminate pronoun. Merger of the operator with the indeterminate pronoun is triggered by the Wh-feature. The phase heads of Lakhota contain [uWh$_{\downarrow\uparrow}$] and [uX$_{\downarrow\uparrow}$] probes which can be valued either under movement of the operator alone or by pied-piping the entire constituent to which the operator attaches. However, pied-piping derivations are ruled out since otherwise both the operator itself and the operator phrase end up determining terminal occurrence for the Wh-feature, leading to a violation of the principle Interpret Once under Sharing. Pied-piping is therefore blocked. The X-feature serves the purpose of blocking derivations in which the operator is not merged with the indeterminate pronoun and in which the Wh-phrase undergoes independent overt Wh-movement. Based on the discussion in Van Valin, 1995; Van Valin and LaPolla, 1997 one might speculate that this feature might be identified with focus.

Finally, it has been claimed for Chinese, another Wh-in-situ language, that unlike Wh-arguments in the language, Wh-adjuncts are sensitive both to weak and to strong islands (Aoun and Li, 1993; Huang, 1982; Lasnik and Saito, 1992 among others). This suggests that Chinese uses the Japanese strategy (with [uWh$_\downarrow$]) for arguments and the Lakhota strategy with a null operator for its adjuncts.

5.6   Summary

In this chapter we have implemented the ideas regarding pied-piping and partial movement sketched informally at the end of chapter 3. We made crucial use of the idea that the position in which a feature is interpreted under sharing is a direct reflection of the instances of merge that were triggered by that feature. To give this assumption restrictiveness and make it comparable to Criterial Freezing and similar proposals, I adopted the assumption that features are interpreted once under sharing (adapted from Adger and Ramchand, 2005).

I showed what types of systems can be expected that manipulate a single feature. Then I went on to show how the main generalizations from chapter 3 follow from the current system. Finally, I briefly indicated how the existing typology of Wh-questions (no movement, single movement, multiple movement) can be described and derived in the present system. The section on the typology of Wh-questions was brief and intended mainly as a proof of concept: relevant generalizations can be expressed and existing language types can be described.

6   The phase heads v, C, P and the stranding generalization

In section 4.2 I used Last Resort to derive anti-locality, that is, the claim that movement is impossible if the launching and the landing site m-command each other. Given the phase impenetrability condition, anti-locality derives the stranding generalization, that is, the claim that movement can never separate the complement of a phase head from the phase head itself. If phases provide a unifying concept in the theory of movement, the hypothesis this essay investigates, then phase heads should never be separable from their complements even if their complements are independently movable categories. In this chapter I examine this prediction for v, C, and P.

6.1   VP immobility under v

In chapter 2 we saw evidence for the assumption that vP and CP are phases in the sense that they host intermediate traces of cyclic movement. We therefore expect them to be subject to the stranding generalization. The present section investigates this question for the case of v. In subsection 6.1.1 I show, based on German data, that VPs are movable in principle. In subsection 6.1.2 I use English data to show that VP, when embedded immediately under v, cannot move away stranding v. This immediately leads to the conclusion that v behaves as expected.

6.1.1   VPs are mobile

In German, verbs that take non-finite verbal complements select their complement in one of three morphological shapes. Some verbs select participles, some bare infinitives, and some infinitives with *zu*—'to'. Following Bech, 1955, 1957, the literature on German describes this distinction as *status government*. Bare infinitives always form a clearly monoclausal structure with the higher, selecting predicate. The two predicates create a unified domain for the application of scrambling, passive, reflexivization, and a number of other phenomena (see Reis and Sternefeld, 2004; Wöllstein-Leisten, 2001; Wurmbrand, 2001). The verb *empfehlen*—'recommend' in the following paradigm shows clear signs of a monoclausal structure, whereas the verb *bedauern*—'regret' shows clear signs of a biclausal structure.

(1)   German   Wurmbrand, 2001

      a.   ...weil   ihm Peter diesen   Turm zu besichtigen empfohlen
           ...because him Peter this.ACC tower to visit   recommended
           hat
           has
           ...because Peter recommended that he visit this tower.
      b.   ...weil   ihm dieser   Turm zu besichtigen empfohlen
           ...because him this.NOM tower to visit   recommended
           wurde
           was
           ...because it was recommended to him that he visit this tower.

(2)   a.   dass der Hans bedauert den Traktor repariert zu haben.
          that the Hans regrets   the tractor repaired to have
          that Hans regrets having repaired the tractor.
    b. *dass der   Traktor repariert zu haben bedauert wurde
          that the.NOM tractor repaired to have   regretted was
          intended: ...that they regretted that they had repaired the tractor

Observe that in (1b), the passive auxiliary *werden* selects the higher verb, *empfehlen*, which is therefore realized as the passive participle. The lowest embedded verb, *besichtigen*, does not show a passive-active alternation in (1). Nevertheless, the argument that is promoted to the clausal subject position is the internal argument of the embedded verb. We are faced with the slightly puzzling state of affairs where one verb morphologically alternates and a different verb's argument is promoted.

The pattern can be explained, Wurmbrand, 2001 suggests, on the assumption that *empfehlen*, which forms a tight monoclausal structure with its complement, selects VP. If accusative case is furthermore assigned by v, then the object in (1a), *diesen Turm*, is case-licensed not by v immediately above *besichtigen* but by v immediately above *empfehlen*. The passive morphology in (1b) suppresses the matrix verb's ability to assign accusative case to the embedded object, which therefore has to become the matrix subject in order to be properly case-licensed. As the matrix subject, it also triggers person and number agreement with the finite verb.

The pattern of agreement and case marking discussed above is optional. The matrix verb can also be passivized without triggering promotion of the most deeply embedded object:

(3)   German

  ... weil ihm diesen Turm zu besichtigen empfohlen wurde
  ... because him this.ACC tower to visit   recommended was
  ... because it was recommended to him that he visit this tower.

This simply shows that *empfehlen*, like other verbs that allow the long passive, select VP only optionally. The existence of this alternation does not affect the following argument.

I will assume that Wurmbrand's analysis of the long passive is essentially correct and that the long passive involves embedded infinitives no bigger than VP. The following example shows that the long passive is compatible with topicalization of the most-deeply embedded predicate. Since this predicate is a VP, the example shows that VPs can move.

(4)   German

  Zu besichtigen wurde ihm nur dieser Turm empfohlen.
  To visit   was him only this.NOM tower recommended.
  This is the only tower that he was recommended to visit.

6.1.2   VPs do not strand v

I will now demonstrate the ban against moving VP away from the embedding v on the basis of English topicalization. The crucial examples come from Huang (1993).

The anaphor *himself* in (5a) cannot take the matrix subject *John* as its antecedent, but when the object is topicalized, as in (5b), this becomes possible.

(5)   English

  a. John_i said that Bill_j likes pictures of $\text{himself}_{j\,|\,*i}$.
  b. John_i said that pictures of $\text{himself}_{j\,|\,i}$ Bill_j likes.

Huang observes that the pattern we find when verb and object are topicalized together is strikingly different. Again, in the base position, the anaphor *himself* cannot take the matrix subject as its antecedent, (6a). This situation does not change under topicalization of verb and object, (6b).

(6)   English

  a. (i) John_i said that Bil_j l would certainly wash $\text{himself}_{*i\,|\,\checkmark j}$.
    (ii) *John_i said that Mary would like pictures of himself_i
  b. (i) John_i said that wash $\text{himself}_{*i\,|\,\checkmark j}$ Bill_j certainly would.
    (ii) ?*John_i said that like pictures of himself_i Mary would.

Huang argues that this can be explained under the predicate-internal-subject hypothesis, since under this hypothesis the fronted constituent contains a trace of the subject. This trace will serve as the antecedent for the anaphor, whether the VP is topicalized or not, and block binding by the matrix subject.

The current standard formulation of the predicate-internal-subject hypothesis claims that the subject is generated in the specifier position a projection external to VP: Spec,vP (see Bowers (1993); Chomsky (1995c), Kratzer (1996) for proposals along these lines). For Huang's argument to work under this assumption, the structure of (5b) must be (7a), where the topicalizaed constituent is vP, rather than (7b), where it is VP.

(7)   a.   John said that [[$_{vP}$ Bill v [$_{VP}$ wash himself]] Bill certainly would VP

      b.   John said that [[$_{VP}$ wash himself] Bill certainly would [$_{vP}$ Bill v VP]

In other words, VP must not be allowed to strand v, as expected given anti-locality and the phase impenetrability condition.

A possible alternative account of (6) might be based on the idea that V undergoes overt head movement to v in English. On this view, if (6b.i) involved a fronted VP rather than a vP, the example should be realized as (8) instead, which is pronounced as (5b).

(8)   English
      John said that pictures of himself Bill would certainly like.

An immediate challenge for this view, according to which examples like (8) are structurally ambiguous between a DP topicalization and a VP topicalization structure, comes from the examples in (9). If headless VPs could be topicalized in English, then all of the (ii)-examples should be grammatical, contrary to fact.

(9)   English
      a.   (i)   John looked up Mary's phone number.
            (ii)   *Up Mary's phone number John looked.
      b.   (i)   John looked Mary's phone number up.
            (ii)   *Mary's phone number up John looked.
      c.   (i)   John gave Mary a pencil.
            (ii)   *Mary a pencil John gave.
      d.   (i)   The D.A. accused the defendants during the trials.
            (ii)   *The defendants during the trials the D.A. accused.
      e.   (i)   John told Mary that she should leave.
            (ii)   *Mary that she should leave John told.

Clearly then, the headless remnant VP must be prevented from being topical-ized. Anti-locality achieves this directly.[1]

In this section, I argued, based on Wurmbrand, 2001, that VPs can move in principle. I then claimed that VPs are stuck when they occur under v. On the assumption that v is a phase head, the reason why VP cannot strand v lies in the simultaneous action of the anti-locality constraint and the phase impenetrability condition. We find that vP has all the hallmarks of a phase in the sense in which the term is understood here: The edge of vP acts as an intermediate landing site of successive-cyclic movement (chapter 2); vP can be pied-piped (chapter 3 and possibly Huang's cases discussed above); movement of the complement of v is impossible; movement from the complement of v is possible.

6.2   TP immobility under C

This section follows the same general logic as the previous one. We saw in chapter 2 that there are good reasons to believe that CP hosts intermediate traces of successive-cyclic movement. In chapter 3 we also discussed examples of CP pied-piping. Both properties are expected if CP is a phase. If it is a phase, we expect C's complement, though mobile in principle, to be immobile when embedded under C.

The first subsection shows that there do not seem to be cases where a TP is separated from its embedding complementizer in a way that would suggest movement. I then argue that TPs are mobile in principle. Finally, I consider the interaction between the claims made here and Kayne's linear-correspondence axiom as well as the cartographic project for the left periphery. The final sub-section addresses the question why TPs appear never to move long distance.

6.2.1   TPs do not strand C

The fact that TPs do not strand their embedding complementizers in English is illustrated in (10) and (11).

(10)   English
      a.   Nobody believes that anything will happen.

---

[1]   Takano, 2000 claims that remnant movement of XP is generally impossible just in case the head of XP has moved out. However, Fanselow, 1991; Lenerz, 1995, Müller, 1998, p. 260–261, 265 discuss examples where a remnant created by head movement is itself displaced.

    b.   That anything will happen, nobody believes.

    c.   *Anything will happen, nobody believes that.

Examples (10a–b) show that the complement CP of the verb *believe* may be topicalized, but the embedded TP cannot be topicalized leaving the complementizer behind. The negative-polarity item *any* in the embedded clause was introduced to block the reading of *that* under which it functions as a demonstrative rather than a complementizer.

    The same point can also be made on the basis of (11).

(11)   English

    a.   John made the claim that Mary will arrive yesterday.

    b.   John made the claim yesterday that Mary will arrive.

    c.   *John made the claim that yesterday Mary will arrive.

Semantically, *yesterday* must be attached in the higher clause. This is possible in (11a–b) without any problems. The fact that (11c) has no sensible reading follows if extraposition of TP may not strand C.

    The same fact can be observed in German In German it is not necessary to introduce special controls (like the presence of the negative-polarity item in the English examples above) to force *dass*—'that' to act as a complementizer. The relevant effect is achieved simply because in (12c–d) *dass* follows the main verb, a position that is inaccessible to NP objects. Independently, the word order in the fronted clause in (12c) is the word order found in embedded clauses. (12b) is a control to show the bridge nature of *sagen*.

(12)   German

    a.   Ich habe gesagt, dass Peter gekommen ist.

        I   have said   that Peter come   has

        I said that Peter has come.

    b.   Wer hast   du gesagt, dass gekommen ist?

        Who have.2^{nd}SG you said   that come   is

        Who did you say has come?

    c.   *Peter gekommen ist, habe ich gesagt, dass.

        Peter come   is have I   said   that

    d.   *Peter ist gekommen, habe ich gesagt, dass.

        Peter is come   have I   said   that

    I interpret these data as evidence for the stranding generalization and the claim that C is a phase head. It might be objected, of course, that the *that*-trace effect could be invoked to rule out (11c) and (12c) on independent grounds. This objection has little force.

    First, *that*-trace effects are relatively weak or absent in German (see Bayer, Häussler, and Salzmann, 2011; Bayer and Salzmann, 2010; Featherston, 2005 for discussion).[2] This is already illustrated by the control in (12b).

Second, the null complementizer in English does not give rise to *that*-trace effects. Therefore, if the status of example (10c) were due to the *that*-trace effect, the example should improve when the complementizer is dropped. This expectation of the *that*-trace account of (10c) is not borne out, (13).

(13)   English
    a.   Nobody thought anything would happen.
    b.   *Anything would happen, nobody thought.

It should be noted that examples like (13b) are usually taken to show that CPs headed by a null complementizer cannot move, (14a), but the example is potentially ambiguous and the structure in (14b) needs to be ruled out as well. The stranding generalization achieves this directly.

(14)   a.   *[[$_{CP}$ $\emptyset_C$ [$_{TP}$ anything would happen]] [nobody thought CP]]
    b.   *[[$_{TP}$ anything would happen] [nobody thought [$_{CP}$ $\emptyset_C$ TP]]]

The point is reinforced by French, where the complementizer *que* induces *that*-trace effects while the complementizer *qui* does not, (15a) (though see Sportiche, 2011). Nevertheless, TP cannot strand C, (15d). As before, (15b–c) are controls to show that extraction from the clausal domain is in principle possible in the language.

(15)   French
    a.   l' homme que je crois qui viendra
        the man   that I know that came
        the man that I know arrived
    b.   Jean a   dit que Pierre a   acheté une maison
        Jean has said that Pierre has bought a   house
    c.   Que Jean a   dit que Pierre a   acheté?
        what Jean has said that Pierre has bought
    d.   *Pierre a   acheté une maison Jean a   dit {que | qui}.
        Pierre has bought a   house Jean has said that that

Finally, for Icelandic, the claim that *that*-trace effects are absent is fairly uncontroversial (Maling and Zaenen, 1978). Yet, Icelandic doesn't allow extraction of TP either, (15c).

(16)   Icelandic   Halldór Sigurðsson, pers. comm.

---

[2]   For English, Sobin, 1987 argued that the *that*-trace effect is subject to cross-dialectal variation. But there is no dialect that allows stranded complementizers.

a. Hver heldur þú að hafi   lesið þessa bók?
   who think   you that has.SUBJ read this   book
   lit: Who do you think that has read this book?

b. Jón heldur að María sé   að lesa.
   Jon thinks that Maria is.SUBJ to readINF
   Jon thinks that Maria is reading.

c. ?Að María sé   að lesa   heldur Jón.
   that Maria is.SUBJ to read.INF thinks Jon
   That Maria is reading, John thinks.

d. *María sé   að lesa   heldur Jón að.
   Maria is.SUBJ to read.INF believes Jon that

Of course, if the ban on TP stranding C is due to anti-locality, then we expect phrases smaller than TP to be be able to be extracted from CP. Standard cases of Wh- and other types of cross-clausal $\overline{\text{A}}$-movement show that this is true, of course. Examples of VP topicalization are more minimally paired with TP movement and its existence again makes the same point. Indeed, anti-locality explains a common property of predicate fronting (or predicate clefting as a lot of the literature calls it). Such constructions typically do not allow tensed verbs to be fronted. Aboh, 2006 alone lists Ewegbe, Gungbe, Tuki, Buli, Yiddish, Spanish, Brazilian Portuguese, Russian, and Hebrew, all of which show the relevant pattern.[3] Consider the following Kîîtharaka examples, which show that predicate fronting of a tensed predicate is impossible:

(17) Kîîtharaka   Abels and Muriungi, 2008, pp. 704–705

a. *I-kû*-gûra   Maria a-gur-ir-e   nyondo
   FOC-15-buy 1.Maria SM1-buy-PERF-FV 9.hammer
   Maria *bought* the hammer (she did not borrow it)

b. *N-a-gûr-ir-e   Maria   nyondo
   FOC-SM1-buy-PERF-FV 1.Maria 9.hammer
   Maria *bought* the hammer (she did not borrow it)

c. *N-a-gûr-ir-e   Maria a-gur-ir-e   nyondo
   FOC-SM1-buy-PERF-FV 1.Maria SM1-buy-PERF-FV 9.hammer
   Maria *bought* the hammer (she did not borrow it)

On the assumption that predicate clefting involves phrasal movement, (17b–c) are ruled out as anti-locality violations.

---

[3] In Abels, 2003c I gave Yoruba examples from Dekydtspotter, 1992 to make the same point. Dekydtspotter, 1992 claims that Yoruba disallows predicate fronting with certain predicates that he analyzes as inflected. However, Manfredi, 1993 contains very similar examples that are claimed to be acceptable. If Manfredi is right about the data, then I would have to analyze the relevant inflection as a lower aspectual head rather than as T to avoid a clash with anti-locality.

In this section we have seen evidence that TPs do not strand their embedding complementizer. I have argued that this is a property specifically of TP, since examples of minimally smaller projections moving out of CP abound. I have also argued that this effect cannot be reduced to the *that*-trace effect.[4]

6.2.2 TPs are mobile

Given the generalization that TPs do not strand their embedding complementizer, it is legitimate to ask whether TPs ever move. They do. Consider the examples in (18).

(18)   English

      a.   How likely to win the race is John?

      b.   How likely is John to win the race?

The infinitival *to win the race* is a raising infinitive, usually taken to be a TP. I assume that *to win the race* is generated as the complement of *likely* and that, prior to any movements, the structure is *[how [likely [to win the race]]]* rather than *[[how likely] [to win the race]]*.[5] On these assumptions, (18b) can only be derived if the TP *to win the race* moves out of the complement position. This is so, because the original constituent *[how [likely [to win the race]]]* is disrupted in a way easily compatible with movement of TP but hard to explain otherwise. The conclusion holds independently of whether the derivation is implemented in terms of rightward movement of TP or in terms of remnant movement of *how likely TP* or both. Such details of implementation are immaterial to the point under discussion.

Probably the most obvious alternative to a syntactic movement account would be an approach in terms of movement at PF of the infinitival clause or in terms of scattered deletion (Nomura, 2001). On such PF accounts, we would not expect movement of the infinitival TP to interact with genuinely syntactic processes. However, this direct prediction of PF-oriented accounts turns out to be wrong. To see this, observe the contrast between (19a) (Kroch and Joshi, 1985; Lasnik and Saito, 1992 among others) and (19b). Under Lasnik and Saito's analysis, moving the Wh-phrase *how likely to be a riot* in (19a) bleeds raising of the expletive. Movement of TP in (19b) would then counterbleed raising. Alternatively, under the analysis proposed in Abels, 2002, it is the presence of the degree

---

[4]   Note that if the reasoning invoked here is correct, this would provide and argument that right-node raising, which does target TPs, cannot be analyzed as movement.

[5]   In Abels, 2002 I give some arguments for this assumption, which is the standard view in any case—though see Boeckx (2002); Kuno (2003); Rosenbaum (1967) for the opposite view and Abels (2002) for counterarguments.

operator *how likely* that bleeds the establishment of the expletive-associate relation. The application of TP movement circumvents this bleeding effect.[6] We
can conclude then that example (19b) provides a bona fide case of syntactic TP
movement.

(19)　English

    a.　*How likely to be a riot is there?
    b.　How likely is there to be a riot?

So far in this section, I have argued that TPs are mobile in principle, but
that they never move away from an embedding complementizer. This appears
to be true across languages. On present assumptions this ban follows from the
combination of the last resort condition, which entails anti-locality and the phase
impenetrability condition.

It is of course independently known that extraction from the domain of TP
past the embedding complementizer is possible. We can summarize as in (20).

(20)　　a.　　possible to derive: $[C^0 [\ldots t \ldots]]$
      b.　　impossible to derive: $[C^0 \, t]$

Together with the fact that CP can undergo pied-piping and that C alternates
morphologically under the influence of successive-cyclic movement, we have
now established all the key properties of phases for CP. Before turning to PPs
and exploring their properties, I will briefly digress to consider the interactions
between the conclusions reached here and Kayne's linear-correspondence axiom
and Rizzi's theory of the fine structure of the left periphery.

---

[6]　The argument for an account where it is the presence of *how* that is responsible for the
degradation of (19a) comes from the fact that *how* interferes with the establishment of
the expletive-associate relation even in situ:

(i)　English

    a.　?*Who said that there is how likely to be a riot?
    b.　Who said that it is how likely that there will be a riot?

The idea that such intervention effects can be circumvented by moving larger units of
structure around the intervener has been aptly named *smuggling* by Collins and applied
to raising past experiencers and passives in various papers (Collins, 2005a,b; Gehrke
and Grillo, 2008; Grillo, 2009). Notice that the account of (19) is not complete unless
we guarantee that string vacuous extraposition of the infinitive is blocked in (ia). I
provide an account of this fact in Abels (2002).

6.2.3   The ban on C-stranding, word order, and cartography

The argument for the ban on C-stranding above came from the absence of cases where a complementizer is separated from its TP complement by material that belongs to the matrix clause. Of course, this does not mean that there is no variation in the positioning of complementizers with respect to their TP complement. Like other categories, complementizers may either precede or follow their complement. Since the current theory does not allow TP to leave its position as the complement of C, such variation must be described without invoking movement—in terms of the relative linearization of C and its complement. Linearization statements of the relevant kind are discussed in Abels and Neeleman, 2012b.

Much work following Kayne, 1994 has assumed that no variation in base-generated word order is possible, whether construed as a language-wide, category-, or item-specific parameterization. This line of thinking necessitates a movement account for final complementizers. Indeed, Kayne, 1994 suggests that (21), which obviously violates anti-locality, might be the correct analysis.

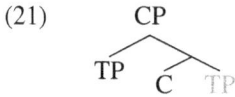

(21)

CP
TP   C   TP

The arguments Kayne advances for this analysis have been shown to be unconvincing in Bayer, 1999. Kayne, 1999, 2004 gives up this analysis, essentially without comment, in favor of an analysis that does not violate anti-locality:

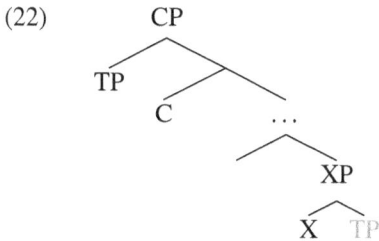

(22)

CP
TP   C   ...
XP
X   TP

While this new structure above obeys anti-locality, it still fails to offer an explanation for why C and TP are an inseparable unit. In particular, X is identified with the matrix verb in Kayne, 1999, 2004. This leads to the expectation that C and TP should be linearly separated by the matrix verb just in case TP fails to move. Separation of C and TP by the matrix verb is, of course, but a special instance of the general pattern of separation of C and TP by matrix material, which I have claimed above not to exist. Kayne's theory therefore clearly does not predict the inseparability of C and TP. If anything, it predicts the opposite. This failure cannot be remedied by identifying X with a position in the embedded clause: If the escape hatch position for long movement is below C, then

TP must pass through it on its way to Spec,CP in (22) and hence be eligible in principle for long extraction. If the escape hatch position for long movement is Spec,CP itself than TP can plainly reach this position and is eligible for further extraction. Finally, if the escape hatch position is above Spec,CP, then the theory provides no grounds for keeping TP and C together either. Therefore, the inseparability of TP and C cannot be predicted.

The ability of the present theory to explain the inseparability of TP and C provides an indirect argument against the antisymmetric program (for further discussion see Abels and Neeleman, 2012b). As the careful reader will no doubt have noticed, this argument is secure only if there is only a single complementizer position. If there are independent reasons to split the traditional complementizer into several distinct heads, the argument collapses.

Much work over the last fifteen years, inspired by Rizzi's (1997) seminal paper on the left periphery, has concluded that the assumption of a unified complementizer position cannot be maintained and that a multitude of functional positions constituting a 'C-domain' must be assumed instead (Benincà and Munaro, 2010; Panagiotidis, 2010; Rizzi, 2001a, 2004b among many others). If this line of work is correct, the above argument against the antisymmetric program collapses, as does the present account of the inseparability of C and TP.

Fortunately, the arguments for a multitude of functional heads in the left periphery of the clause are much weaker than is usually assumed. In Abels, 2012 I suggest that the articulated structure Rizzi proposed for the left periphery is not needed to account for the ordering of left-peripheral specifiers. In that paper I show that the facts described by Rizzi's sequence of functional heads is better accounted for by a version of Relativized Minimality coupled with a non-trivial syntactic feature structure. The approach allows (but does not force) all the features that are active in the left periphery of a given sentence to be represented on a single head. The relative ordering of the specifiers in accord with Rizzi's observations is derived from locality theory. The correct placement of the complementizer with respect to its specifiers can be achieved by movement (or its absence) of the head within its own projection, a device we have already made use of above. Locating all the relevant features on a single head is, of course, exactly what would be needed to reconcile the cross-linguistically valid ban on complementizer stranding with the cross-linguistically valid findings regarding the relative order of elements in the left periphery. The account of left-peripheral order given in Abels, 2012 thus suggests that the current approach is not fundamentally at odds with the *results* of cartography but only with an *implementation* in terms of local selection by (mostly null) functional heads.

There are independent reasons to suspect that the implementation of cartographic findings in terms of a sequence of functional heads ordered by local selectional relations will eventually be replaced by a deeper analysis without those heads.

First, Starke, 2004 has argued that this implementation creates unwanted theoretical redundancies and that the null functional heads usually employed should be given up.

In addition, there are also empirical difficulties. Bobaljik, 1999; Svenonius, 2002b point out a paradox that arises. Nilsen, 2003, p. 11 explains the paradox as follows: Bobaljik's "observation is that one finds phenomena where expressions of type X are rigidly ordered, and expressions of type Y are rigidly ordered, but where any $x \in X$ can precede or follow any $y \in Y$ as long as the ordering requirements internal to X and Y are both satisfied. It seems to follow that one cannot accommodate both X-type expressions and Y-type expressions in a unique linear [functional hierarchy]." Nilsen illustrates the issue with the following Norwegian paradigm.

(23)   Norwegian   Nilsen, 2003

    a.   Derfor   ga   **Jens Kari kyllingen**   tydeligvis ikke lenger
        therefore gave Jens Kari chicken.the evidently not any.longer
        kald
        cold

    b.   Derfor ga **Jens Kari** tydeligvis **kylingen** ikke lenger kald.

    c.   Derfor ga **Jens** tydeligvis **Kari kyllingen** ikke lenger kald.

    d.   Derfor ga **Jens** tydeligvis **Kari** ikke **kyllingen** lenger kald.

    e.   Derfor ga **Jens** tydeligvis **Kari** ikke lenger **kyllingen** kald.

    f.   Derfor ga **Jens** tydeligvis ikke lenger **Kari kyllingen** kald.

    g.   Derfor ga tydeligvis **Jens** ikke lenger **Kari kyllingen** kald.

    h.   Derfor ga tydeligvis ikke **Jens** lenger **Kari kyllingen** kald.

    i.   Derfor ga tydeligvis ikke lenger **Jens Kari kyllingen** kald.

    j.   *Derfor ga **Jens** ikke tydeligvis **Kari** lenger **kyllingen** kald.

    k.   *Derfor ga **Jens** tydeligvis ikke **kyllingen** lenger **Kari** kald.

The examples show arguments and adverbs with fixed relative orders in the Norwegian Mittelfeld. Both (23j) and (23k), where one of the orders is violated, are ungrammatical. However, the order of arguments relative to adverbs and of adverbs relative to arguments is fairly free. We learn from (23c–e) that *Kari* may immediately follow *tydeligvis* and from (23g) that *Jens* may immediately precede *ikke*. Nevertheless, the combination of these two options in (23j) must be ruled out. Likewise, we conclude from (23f–i) that *Kari* may appear to the right of *lenger* and from (23a–d) that *kyllingen* may appear to the left of *lenger*. But the combination of these two must be ruled out if we are to account for (23k). A single linearly ordered sequence of functional heads providing specifier positions is unable to account for all of these facts unless an independent constraint is invoked to ensure that the relative order of elements within each class remains constant under movement. But if such a constraint is available, the case for the linear sequence of positions melts away.

A second argument against a linear sequence of functional heads as the source of the ordering of elements found in cartographic work comes from Nilsen, 2003, 2004. Nilsen shows that the expectation that the order of elements is always transitive, an expectation which is entailed by the assumption of a unique functional hierarchy ordered by local selection, is not met. Examples (24a–b) are there to establish the rigid relative ordering between *muligens*—'possibly' and *ikke*—'not' and *ikke* and *alltid*—'always', respectively.

(24)   Norwegian   Nilsen, 2003, p. 10

    a.   (i)   Ståle har muligens ikke spist hvetekakene sine.
                   Ståle has possibly not eaten wheaties.the his
                   Stanley possibly hasn't eaten his wheaties.
       (ii)   *Ståle har ikke muligens spist hvetekakene sine.
                   Ståle has not possibly eaten wheaties.the his
    b.   (i)   Ståle hadde ikke alltid spist hvetekakene sine.
                   Ståle had not always eaten wheaties.the his
                   Stanley hadn't always eaten his wheaties.
       (ii)   *Ståle hadde alltid ikke spist hvetekakene sine.
                   Ståle had always not eaten wheaties.the his

Transitivity leads to the expectation that *muligens* has to precede *alltid*. But this expectation is not borne out. While the expected order does exist, the unexpected *alltid*-before-*muligens* order exists as well, (25). As indicated in the translation, the interpretation of the example gives *alltid* scope over *muligens*.[7]

(25)   Norwegian   Nilsen, 2003, p. 11

    Dette er et morsomt, gratis spill hvor spillerne alltid muligens
    this is a fun free game where the-players always possibly
    er et klikk fra å vinne $1000!
    are one click from to win $1000
    This is a fun, free game where you're always possibly a click away from
    winning $1000!

Ernst, 2009; Nilsen, 2003, 2004 propose an account of the order of such adverbs in terms of scope which does not require the assumption of a linear sequence of functional heads providing dedicated positions for them.[8]

While Bobaljik paradoxes and transitivity failures suggest that a sequence of functional heads linearly ordered by local selectional relations is too strong, there are also arguments to show that this assumption is too weak. Such evidence further strengthens the idea that the notion of scope is at work instead of the totally local relation of selection.

---

[7]   See also Craenenbroeck, 2006 for a different kind of example.
[8]   See Cinque, 2004 for possible ways around these arguments.

Cinque, 1999 observed that within a given clause, *already* precedes *no longer*, (26a).

(26)   English
      a.   He already no longer goes to school.
      b.   *He no longer already goes to school.

Both adverbs can be contained in a clause embedded by *it is the case*.

(27)   English
      a.   It is the case that he already goes to school.
      b.   It is the case the he no longer goes to school.

They may also both modify an *it is the case* matrix.

(28)   English
      a.   It is no longer the case that he goes to school.
      b.   It is already the case that he goes to school.

Crucially, the relative ordering of the adverbs is preserved across clauses, (29). This can straightforwardly be explained in terms of scope. Both *already* and *no longer* are phase quantifiers requiring a particular kind of event structure to give interpretable results. Since *it is the case* does not introduce its own event structure, both quantifiers operate on the event structure introduced by *go to school* and therefore behave as though they were contained in a single clause even when they are separated by a syntactic clause boundary (see also Biskup, 2010).

(29)   English
      a.   It is already the case that he no longer goes to school.
      b.   *It is no longer the case that he already goes to school.

This account in terms of semantic scope but not an account in terms of local selection then correctly predicts the contrast between (29) and (30): When the matrix predicate is not the bleached, stative *be the case* but a verb introducing its own event structure, the ordering of *no longer* and *already* is free across clauses.

(30)   English
      a.   He already said that she no longer goes to school.
      b.   He no longer says that she already goes to school.

Abels and Neeleman, 2012b make a similar point based on nominalization.

(31)   German

a. das die Haustür   dauernd   schnell schrubben
   the the house.door constantly quickly scrubbing
   the constant quick scrubbing of the front door
b. *das die Haustür   schnell dauernd   schrubben
   the the house.door quickly constantly scrubbing
c. das dauernd-e   schnelll-e die Haustür   schrubben
   the constant-AGR quick-AGR the house.door scrubbing
d. *das schnelll-e dauernd-e   die Haustür   schrubben
   the quick-AGR constant-AGR the house.door scrubbing
e. das dauernd-e   die Haustür   schnell schrubben
   the constant-AGR the house.door quickly scrubbing
f. *das schnelll-e die Haustür   dauernd   schrubben
   the quick-AGR the house.door constantly scrubbing

Abels and Neeleman, 2012b argue that if "the hierarchical ordering of the modifiers is determined by scope, there is a simple account for the data in [(31)]: As the nominalizing head makes no relevant semantic contribution, the relative order of modifiers is unaffected by its presence or absence. However, if hierarchical ordering effects are a consequence of local selection, an account of the data in [(31)] must rely on a conspiracy theory. First of all, there must be a close match between nominal and verbal functional sequences, such that heads in one have identifiable correspondents in the other. Second, there must be a series of nominalizing heads such that each has a position in the nominal functional sequence that corresponds to the position in the verbal functional sequence of the category it selects. Given that nominalization can take place quite freely, there must be such a category-changing head for every level of the verbal functional sequence. Nothing in the theory of selection links the properties of the selecting head to the properties of the selected category. Therefore, this arrangement would be an accident."

Theoretical and empirical reservations about the implementation of cartographic findings in terms of a linear sequence of functional heads converge with the requirements of the present theory. I will proceed on the assumption that the tension between the present work and cartographic studies is rooted strictly in the most common current implementations of cartography and will, hopefully, melt away once an implementation is found that overcomes these problems.

6.2.4   Is there long TP movement?

So far in this chapter I have looked at the properties of two well-established phase heads: C and v. The theory developed in chapter 4 predicts phase heads should obey the stranding generalization. The facts discussed so far support this view.

It turned out to be relatively difficult to find reasonably clear cases of TP and VP movement. This has to do with the fact that most TPs and VPs are embedded under C and v, respectively. The difficulty is compounded because it is often not clear whether a given structure is a bare TP rather than a CP with a null head.

As argued above, example (19b), repeated below as (32), does provide a bona fide example of syntactic TP movement.

(32)   English
        How likely is there to be a riot?

It turns out that the movement possibilities of such TPs are extremely restricted. (33) shows that they cannot be topicalized, for example.

(33)   English
        To be a riot there is likely.

Let's look at some further examples of TP movement.

Bošković, 1997c, p. 23 argues that control infinitivals may be TPs. Bošković observes that scrambling out of finite clauses, which are CPs by assumption, patterns with $\overline{\text{A}}$-movement in that it is subject to the weak crossover effect. Scrambling out of control clauses on the other hand patterns with A-movement in not being subject to the weak crossover effect in Serbo Croatian.[9]

If control clauses can be TPs, then an analysis might build on the idea that movement that has crossed a CP induces weak crossover effects. Indeed, we have reached similar conclusions above when discussing exceptional case marking in Romance languages, where we concluded that the A-property of receiving case is only possible at the first stopover for Wh-movement and in the discussion of complementizer agreement in Germanic, which targets subjects, even extracted ones, but only in the clause where they originate.[10] If the generalization is true, then control infinitives that allow A-scrambling out of them must be

---

[9]   Scrambling that is subject to the weak crossover effect is often referred to as $\overline{\text{A}}$-scrambling, while scrambling that is not subject to weak crossover is usually referred to as A-scrambling. A similar asymmetry between clause-bound A-scrambling and long $\overline{\text{A}}$-scrambling can be found in many languages (Kidwai, 2000; Mahajan, 1990 for Hindi, Nemoto, 1991; Ueyama, 2003 for Japanese, Karimi, 2005 for Persian, Haider, 2006; Haider and Rosengren, 1998, 2003 for German, and Abels, in press for a survey of some of the analytic issues.

[10] The generalization put forward here about $\overline{\text{A}}$-scrambling may be part of a larger pattern to the effect that A-relations in general cannot cross CP boundaries. I will not try to defend the broader claim here, though, since that would involve discussing a number of counterexamples. For example, exceptional case marking in Japanese (Bruening, 2001; Hiraiwa, 2002b) has been argued to cross a CP boundary (similarly for Belfast English if Davis, 1984 is on the right track). Hyperraising is another obvious potential counterexample.

TPs.

As an illustration, consider the Serbo Croatian examples (34a) and (34b). Example (34a) is a case of movement out of a CP, which is therefore subject to weak crossover, whereas (34b) is a case of movement out of a control infinitive (a TP) which is not subject to weak crossover.

(34) Serbo Croatian   Bošković, 1997c, p. 27

    a.   Svakoga$_i$ njegov$_{j \mid *?i}$ otac veruje da oni mrze
        everyone his   father believes that they hate
        Everyone, his father believes that they hate.

    b.   Svakoga$_i$ njegov$_i$ otac planira   kazniti
        everyone his   father is.planning PRO to.punish
        Everyone, his father is planning to punish.

    c.   Svakoga$_i$ njegov$_i$ otac kazniti planira
        everyone his   father to.punish is.planning
        Everyone, his father is planning to punish.

The infinitive itself can be moved in a very local way, as example (34c) shows, and it can be temporally modified. This is shown in example (35). Example (35a) represents the unmarked order. *Danas*—'today' can be understood to modify the verb *kazniti*—'to punish'. On the assumption that independent temporal modification requires the presence of TP (Wurmbrand, 2001 among others), this indicates that we are dealing with at least a TP.

Examples (35b) and (35c) where the infinitival has moved and *nekoga* is scrambled out are available on the same reading where *danas*—'today' modifies the embedded verb. The examples are marked and require special discourse contexts and intonation to be acceptable. This is, of course, not surprising. It is important though that the examples are acceptable at all. They illustrate again the claim that TPs are mobile in principle.

(35) Serbo Croatian

    a.   Svakoga$_i$ je njegov$_i$ otac planirao danas kazniti
        everyone is his   father planned today to.punish
        Everyone, his father planned to punish today.

    b.   Svakoga$_i$ je njegov$_i$ otac danas kazniti   planirao
        everyone is his   father today to.punish planned
        Everyone, his father planned to punish today.

    c.   Svakoga$_i$ je njegov$_i$ otac kazniti danas planirao
        everyone is his   father to.punish today planned
        Everyone, his father planned to punish today.

Interestingly, when the infinitive is moved to the clause initial position, A-scrambling from it becomes impossible, as the weak crossover effect in (36) shows.

(36) Serbo Croatian

　　??/* Kazniti   je svakoga$_i$ njegov$_i$ otac   planirao
　　to.punish is everyone his   father planned
　　Someone, his father was planning to punish.

The pattern indicates that TPs can move but that they cannot move to or through Spec,CP.

We can reach the same conclusion also for German. Wurmbrand, 2001 suggests that the classification of infinitives in German is not exhausted by the monoclausal-biclausal dichotomy (VP versus CP) discussed above. She suggests that there are several grades of clause union and that there is a class of verbs that take TP complements. These can be recognized on the one hand by their inability to occur with the long passive and their ability to be independently temporally modified—both of which distinguish them from the fully monoclausal construction discussed above—and on the other hand by the possibility of pronouns to move from the embedded infinitive to the matrix Wackernagel position—which distinguishes them from fully biclausal structures. A relevant verb is *beschliessen*—'decide', (37). (37b) shows the inability of the complement of *beschliessen* to occur in the long-passive construction. (37c) demonstrates independent temporal modification of the embedded predicate with simultaneous fronting of the object pronoun to the Wackernagel position.

(37) German

　　a. ...weil   der Hans den Traktor zu reparieren beschlossen hat
　　　...because the Hans the tractor to repair   decided   has
　　　...because Hans decided to repair the tractor.
　　b. *...weil   der   Traktor zu reparieren beschlossen wurde
　　　...because the.NOM tractor to repair   decided   was
　　　...because it was decided to repair the tractor.
　　c. ...weil   ihn der Hans morgen   zu reparieren beschlossen hat.
　　　...because it   the Hans tomorrow to repair   decided   has
　　　...because Hans decided to repair it tomorrow.

It turns out that *beschliessen* allows both TP complements and CP complements. The latter construal can be forced by topicalization of the complement; (38b) is grammatical, but although remnant topicalization is generally possible in German, (38a) is quite degraded. We can understand this if the topicalized infinitive cannot be a TP and must be a CP.[11]

---

[11] The same general pattern holds in Japanese where relevant examples can be constructed on the basis of Nemoto's (1991) discussion. Again, as in Serbo Croatian, A-scrambling out of the infinitival and fronting of it are mutually exclusive, although both options exist independently (Grewendorf, 2003; Hiraiwa, 2002a).

(38)   German

    a.   *Morgen   zu reparieren hat ihn der Hans beschlossen
        tomorrow to repair   has it the Hans decided
        Hans decided to repair it tomorrow.
    b.   Ihn morgen   zu reparieren hat der Hans beschlossen
        him tomorrow to repair   has the Hans decided
        Hans decided to repair it tomorrow.

All of this may indicate that TP cannot carry the features required for cross-clausal movement.[12] I will assume that something along these lines is correct and leave the issue here.

To recapitulate one more time: In this section we have seen that TPs don't ever strand their embedding complementizer despite the fact that CPs are transparent for movement and that TPs can move in principle. Together with the observation that CPs can be pied-piped and that the morphological shape of C is sensitive to successive-cyclic movement, we can conclude that C is a phase head. We have seen that the account of these facts developed here is at odds with the antisymmetric program but is consistent with the facts motivating cartographic approaches to the left periphery, though not with an implementation of these facts in terms of large hierarchies of functional heads. The discussion in the final subsection has shown that the account presented here is still too permissive in that TP movement is predicted where none exists. I leave the ultimate resolution of this problem open.

6.3   DP immobility under P

In this section I argue for the position that P is a phase head. This will allow me to interpret the cross-linguistically extremely common ban on P-stranding straightforwardly as an instance of the stranding generalization: If P is a phase

---

[12] Alternatively, the result of moving TP to Spec,CP, [TP_1 [C [$_{TP_2}$ ... TP_1 ...], might result in a deviant structure for other reasons. For example, if we switch notation from the familiar constituency structures to dependency structures (Brody, 2000), we discover the possibility of giving a definition of the notion *complement* in terms of functional selection and of the notion *specifier* as the elsewhere case (Abels, 2000; Adger, 2011; Bury, 2003, and for a related idea stated quite differently Drury, 2005). Under such assumptions, it cannot be determined easily which of the two daughters of C is the complement just in case both of them are TPs. This ambiguity might rule out such structures in general. Of course, such an account in terms of a fatal specifier-complement ambiguity derives the anti-locality constraint directly, which demonstrates the robustness of the idea.

head, it requires all movements out of PP to pass through Spec,PP. The complement of P cannot reach this escape hatch position because of Last Resort. Therefore, prepositions cannot be stranded. I have argued above that phase heads have a number of further properties. First, they should be able to undergo pied-piping. This is of course true for adpositions. Along with DPs, PPs are the canonical structure where we find pied-piping. Second, PPs should in principle be transparent for extraction. Transparency of PPs may, of course, be parameterized by movement type. Third, Spec,PP should be the target position for secondary movement in some languages and constructions.

The second expectation goes against a tradition that views PPs, at least in languages where adposition stranding is impossible, as islands for extraction. I will give an argument below that this traditional view is incorrect and that a better description of the facts can be built on the assumption that adpositions are phase heads.[13] The argument that the ban on P-stranding should derive from PP's phasehood and be interpreted as an instance of the stranding generalization comes from two sources. If the ban against P-stranding is not a straightforward island effect we expect extraction from the complement of P to be possible while at the same time extraction of the complement of P is impossible. Below I discuss data from Russian, German, Serbo Croatian, and French which show this prediction to be true.

The third expectation, that there should be secondary movement to Spec,PP is met and will be discussed on the basis of data from older stages of French and Tzotzil.

Taken together the arguments strongly suggest that prepositions are phase heads.

---

[13] In Abels, 2003c I provided an argument against the islandhood of PPs in non-P-stranding languages on the basis of sluicing. The argument was based on the assumption that islands are ameliorated under sluicing (Merchant, 2001 and in particular Lasnik, 2001b) but that P-stranding violations are not (Merchant, 2001). I reasoned that P-stranding violations cannot be island violations, since if they were, they would have to be ameliorated under sluicing.

I do not repeat the argument here. The second premise, that P-stranding violations are not repaired by sluicing still seems essentially correct to me, despite a number of superficial counterexamples (see Craenenbroeck, 2010; Nykiel and Sag, 2009; Rodrigues, Nevins, and Vicente, 2009; Sato, 2011; Stjepanović, 2008; Szczegielniak, 2005, 2008 among others). However, the assumption that islands are ameliorated by ellipsis in general and by sluicing in particular seems very questionable to me now (Abels, 2011; Abels, Panitz, and Starling, in progress; Fukaya, 2007), which is why I refrain from recasting the argument in the current context.

6.3.1 PP pied-piping

Pied-piping of PP by the complement of P is, of course, extremely common in the languages of the world and hardly needs to be exemplified. The following examples are typical.

(39) a. German
    Ich weiss nicht mit welchem Lehrer sie geredet hat.
    I know not with which.DAT teacher she spoken has
    I don't know which teacher she talked to.

    b. Russian
    Ja ne znaju s kem ona govorila.
    I not know.1^{st}SG.PRS with who.INST she spoke
    I don't know who she talked to.

    c. Spanish
    No sé con quién ha hablado.
    not know.1^{st}SG.PRS with who has.3^{rd}SG spoken
    I don't know who (s)he talked to.

The pattern is easily explained if P bears [uWh$_{\downarrow\uparrow}$]. Merger of the complement of P is triggered by selectional (categorial) features on P. [uWh$_{\downarrow\uparrow}$] can be shared with the complement as a free-rider and pied-piping at a later stage of the derivation is therefore licit. Recall that it is the privilege of phase heads that they and only they are able to bear uninterpreted probes.

While the possibility of PP pied-piping is common, we also find pied-piping from Spec,PP. According to Aissen, 1996, p. 468, Tzotzil has a semantically fairly bleached preposition *ta* which is used to mark spatial and temporal locations, instruments, and agents in the passive. This preposition cannot be stranded, (40a-b). Subextraction of a possessor is equally impossible, (40c), despite the fact that there is no general ban on extracting possessors in the language, (40d) repeated from above.

(40) Tzotzil   Aissen, 1996, 468 ex. 58–59a, 469 ex. 60, 485 ex. 103a

    a. I-kom ta s-na.
    CP-remain P A3^{rd}-houase
    He remained at his house.

    b. *K'usi nail i-kom ta k'usi nail?
    what house CP-remain P
    In which house did he remain?

    c. *Buch'u ch-a-bat ta s-na buch'u?
    who ICP-B2^{nd}-go P A3^{rd}-house
    Whose house are you going to?

    d. Buch'u i-'ixtalaj s-kayijonal y-osil?
    who CP-ruin A3^{rd}-firelane A3^{rd}-land

The firelane of whose land was ruined?

When the possessor of a DP which is the complement of *ta* is to be questioned, that possessor moves to the left edge of the PP and the entire PP undergoes Wh-movement.

(41) Tzotzil   Aissen, 1996, 470 ex. 63–64

    a. Buch'u ta s-na   ch-a-bat?
        who   P A3^{rd}-house ICP-B2^{nd}-go
        To whose house are you going?

    b. Buch'u ta s-na   av-ik'ta   komel l-a-bolsa-e?
        who   P A3^{rd}-house A.2nd-leave DIR   the-A.2nd-bag-ENC
        In whose house did you leave your bag?

Aissen points that "what is most striking about [(41)] is the visible reordering of the possessor within PP, over and above the preposing of the PP itself. The possessor of the object of the preposition comes to *precede* the preposition and cannot remain in situ, following the possessed noun" (Aissen, 1996, p. 470).

(42) Tzotzil   Aissen, 1996, 470–471 ex. 65–66

    a. *Ta s-na   buch'u ch-a-bat?
        P A3^{rd}-house who   ICP-B2^{nd}-go
        Whose house are you going to?

    b. *Ta s-na   buch'u av-ik'ta   komel l-a-bolsa-e?
        P A3^{rd}-house who   A.2nd-leave DIR   the-A.2nd-bag-ENC
        In whose house did you leave the bag?

In the context of present assumptions, these facts are strong evidence for the claim that prepositions are phase heads. The possessor undergoes secondary movement, that is movement driven by some feature other then the Wh-feature, to Spec,PP, where the Wh-feature can be shared as a free-rider. The entire PP can then undergo Wh-movement.

An abstractly similar pattern can be found in French. We discussed secondary movement of *dont*—'of which' in relative clauses above. Kayne, 1975, 112 note 57 notes (citing Grevisse, 1964, p. 479 and Haase, 1969, p. 74) that in older stages of French *dont*—'of which' could be moved to the edge of a containing PP and then pied-pipe that PP, (43). Again, the ability of *dont* to pied-pipe the containing PP indicates that the relevant feature is borne by P and, therefore, that P is a phase head.

(43) French   Kayne, 1975, 112 note 57

    la fille dont   au   frère   tu plais
    the girl of.which to.the brother you please
    the girl whose brother you please

206

Pied-piping from complement and specifier positions thus supports the claim that PPs are phases.

6.3.2 Subextraction

A second argument for the status of P as a phase head can be based on the fact that adpositions, in languages that do not allow P-stranding, obey the stranding generalization. In other words, while there are no patterns where the entire complement of P is extracted, there are cases where parts of the complement of P are extracted.

German *was-für* split

Abstracting away from R-pronouns, which will be discussed in the next chapter, German is clearly not a language that allows P-stranding. The ban on stranding prepositions under $\overline{\text{A}}$-movement is illustrated in (44). The possibility of pied-piping under $\overline{\text{A}}$-movement is illustrated in (44d).

(44) German

    a. *Was   hast du mit gerechnet?
       what$_{dat}$ have you with counted
       What did you expect?
    b. *Welchen Kandidaten hast du für gestimmt?
       which   candidate have you for voted
       Which candidate did you vote for?
    c. *Welchem Bett hast du {in | drin} geschlafen?
       which   bed have you in DR.in slept
       Which bed did you sleep in?
    d. Für welchen Kandidaten hast du gestimmt?
       for which candidate have you voted
       Which candidate did you vote for?

The ban on stranding prepositions under A-movement is illustrated below:

(45) German

    a. *Frank wurde vom Präsidenten mit geredet.
       Frank was by.the president with talked
       Frank was talked to by the president.

b. *Der Kandidat von den Grünen wurde am meisten für
   the candidate from the Greens was at.the most for
   gestimmt.
   voted.
   The candidate of the Green Party was voted for the most.

c. *Dieses Bett ist {in | drin} geschlafen worden.
   this bed is in DR.in slept been
   This bed has been slept in.

Data of this sort straightforwardly lead to a categorization of German as a non-P-stranding language: The DP complement of a preposition can never be extracted stranding the preposition.[14] Nevertheless, there are constructions where parts of PPs can be extracted. A first case comes from *was-für* split. A simple case of *was-für* split is given in (46) where (46a) is the unsplit version and (46b) the split version. (*was-für* split in Germanic is discussed in Beck, 1996; Bennis, Corver, and den Dikken, 1998; Besten, 1985; Corver, 1991; Diesing, 1992; Kratzer, 1996; Leu, 2003; Pafel, 1996; Vikner, 1995.)

(46) German

a. Was für Bücher hast du gelesen?
   what for books have you read

b. Was hast du für Bücher gelesen?
   what have you for books read
   What kind of books did you read?

There are two plausible analyses for *was-für* split, the direct-extraction analysis (47a) and the remnant movement analysis (47b).

(47) a. Direct Extraction: Was ... [$_{DP}$ was [für Bücher]]

b. Remnant Movement: [Was für Bücher] ... [für Bücher] was für Bücher[15]

Now consider what happens if a *was-für* DP is embedded within a PP. If we assume the direct-extraction analysis of *was-für* split, we expect the (i) examples in (48a–d) to be ungrammatical. The clause initial position must be occupied by a Wh-phrase or a Wh-phrase with pied-piped material. If *was* underwent direct extraction in *was-für* split constructions we would not expect it to form a constituent with the embedding preposition. Hence, the (i) examples cannot be generated. The (ii) examples may or may not be predicted to be grammatical, depending on whether extraction from PP is to be allowed. The remnant

---

[14] In certain northern dialects of German, bona fide P-stranding might be possible (Fleischer, 2002b). For discussion of the situation in West Frisian, see the next chapter.

[15] The trace within the trace is indicated by strike-out here.

movement analysis gives rise to exactly the opposite expectations. The actual judgments follow straightforwardly from the remnant movement analysis but are very problematic under the direct-extraction analysis.[16]

(48)   German

    a. (i)   Über was der   alles für Sachen bescheid weiß!
              about what the.M all   for things notice   knows

      (ii) *Was der   alles über für Sachen bescheid weiß!
             what theM all   about for things notice   knows

      (iii) Über was für Sachen der   alles bescheid weiß!
             about what for things the.M all   notice   knows
             All the things he knows about!

    b. (i)   Über was sich manche Leute nur für einen Quatsch
              about what REFL some   people only for a   nonsense
             aufregen!
             upset

      (ii) *Was sich manche Leute über für einen Quatsch
             what REFL some   people about for a   nonsense
             aufregen!
             upset

      (iii) Über was für einen Quatsch sich manche Leute
             about what for a   nonsense REFL some   people
             aufregen!
             upset
             What nonsense some people can get upset about!

    c. A: I didn't expect THIS kind of people to show up at my party.

      B: (i) Mit was hattest du denn für Leuten gerechnet?
             with what had   you PRT for people reckoned

         (ii) *Was hattest du denn mit für Leuten gerechnet?
             what had   you PRT with for people reckoned

         (iii) Mit was für Leuten hattest du denn gerechnet?
             with what for people had   you PRT reckoned
             What kind of people had you expected?

    d. (i)   An was hatten sie denn so für Preise gedacht?
              on what had   you then so for prizes thought

      (ii) *Was hatten sie denn so an für Preise gedacht?
             what had   you then so on for prizes thought

---

[16] For some speakers of Russian, the *čto-za* construction appears to behave similarly (Natasha Rakhlin, pers. comm.).

(iii) An was für Preise hatten sie denn so gedacht?
       on what for prizes had   you then so thought
       What kinds of prizes were you thinking about?

These examples, though perfectly acceptable with the right intonation, are not neutral. One class of examples that favors *was-für* split into PPs are exclamations, as in (48a) and (48b).[17] In these cases there is stress on the nouns *Sachen* and *Quatsch* respectively. The questions behave strikingly differently. Without sufficient context, the unsplit questions (48c.iii) and (48d.iii) are strongly preferred. In fact, (48c.i) and (48d.i) are unacceptable if they are given the intonation of standard examples of *was-für* split as in (46b), where stress falls on *Bücher*. In the questions, ((48c–d.i)), the nouns *Leute* and *Preise* cannot be stressed. Rather stress must fall on *denn* in (48c.i) and on *gedacht* in (48d.i). Nevertheless, the phenomenon seems to be real. Sigrid Beck (pers. comm.) points out that such examples are perfectly acceptable as indirect questions.[18]

Prepositions in German show the behavior that we would expect if they are phase heads. (i) Their complement may pied-pipe them. (ii) The complement cannot strand them. (iii) The complement domain is transparent for extraction.

---

[17] Case on the DP following *für* is assigned by the moved preposition. The only example that shows explicit case morphology on the DP is (48b). Some speakers find example (48b) degraded while accepting the others. This probably has to do with the licensing of overt case morphology.

[18] If German split partitives are derived via movement, they present further clear evidence for extraction out of PP. Compare (ia) with the split variant (ib) and (ic) with the split variant (id). However, the behavior of split partitives is quite distinct from the behavior of other extractions from DP in German, which casts some doubt on an extraction analysis.

(i)   German
       a. Viele von denen gefallen mir.
           many of them please me
           Many of them please me.
       b. Von denen gefallen mir viele   von denen.
           of them please   me many.
           Many of them please me.
       c. An die meisten von denen kann ich mich noch erinnern.
           on the most   of them can I   REFL still remember
           I can still remember most of them.
       d. Von denen kann ich mich noch [an die meisten von denen] erinnern
           of them can I   REFL still on the most   remember
           I can still remember most of them.

Notice that we can be quite sure that the ban against preposition stranding cannot be a PF effect attributable to prosodic weakness of prepositions (see Abels, 2003a,b for more detailed discussion). First, prepositions can appear without their complement in right-node raising structures, which is unexpected if preposition stranding were to be ruled out by a prosodic requirement:

(49)   German

     Ich habe für und du gegen den Vorschlag gestimmt.
     I   have for and you against the proposal   voted
     I voted for and you—against the proposal.

Second, even when prosodic requirements of the preposition are rendered irrelevant, because the preposition itself is not pronounced, the ban against P-stranding is observed. Elliptical constructions such as sluicing, (50), and stripping, (51), provide relevant test cases (see Merchant, 2001, 2003, 2004). If the preposition in (50) were to be stranded in the ellipsis site it would be deleted. An elided preposition presumably cannot cause a prosodic violation.

(50)   German

     Ich habe mit jemandem geredet, aber ich sage dir nicht *(mit)
     I   have with someone   spoken, but I   tell you not   with
     wem.
     whom
     I spoke with someone, but I won't tell you who.

Similarly, if the preposition could be stranded in the ellipsis site in (51), then (51b) ought to be ambiguous between the reading where *Sakis* is the subject and one where *Sakis* is the object. As a matter of fact, the example is unambiguous.

(51)   German
     a.   Ich habe gestern   mit Anna geredet und mit Sakis (auch).
           I   have yesterday with Anna spoken and with Sakis too
           I spoke with Anna yesterday and also with Sakis.
     b.   Ich habe gestern   mit Anna geredet und Sakis (auch).
           I   have yesterday with Anna spoken and Sakis too
           I spoke with Anna yesterday and Sakis did, too.

The fact that prepositions must be pied-piped even in elliptical contexts suggests strongly that the ban against P-stranding is a genuine syntactic constraint rather than a phonological one. On the assumption that P is a phase head, the stranding generalization captures the facts discussed here.

French *combien* split

A similar case can be made for French, another language that does not allow
P-stranding. We find the same kind of pattern that we have seen in the German
examples above. As is well known, *combien*—'how many' can under certain
conditions break away from its containing noun phrase.

(52)   French

    a.   Combien de livres as- tu   lu?
           how.many of books have you read
           How many books have you read?

    b.   Combien as- tu   lu   de livres?
           how.many have you read of books
           How many books have you read?

There are two plausible kinds of movement analysis for this pattern. Either
combien is extracted directly, as in (53a). The alternative is, again, a remnant
movement derivation, as in (53b).

(53)   a.   Direct Extraction: combien .... [combien de livres]

      b.   Remnant Movement: [combien de livres] ... [de livres] ... com-
bien de livres

French does not allow P-stranding as (54) indicates (for discussion see Kayne,
1984; King and Roberge, 1990; Roberge, 1998; Roberge and Rosen, 1999;
Zribi-Hertz, 1984 and references cited there).[19]

(54)   French

    a.   (i)   À quels photographes est-ce que tu as   parlé?
                to which photographers is-it   that you have talked
                Which photographers have you talked to?

        (ii)   *Quels photographes est-ce que tu as   parlé à?
                which photographers is-it   that you have spoken to

    b.   (i)   De combien de photos (est-ce que) tu as   besoin?
                of how.many of photos is-it   that you have need
                How many pictures do you need?

        (ii)   *Combien de photos (est-ce que) tu as   besoin de?
                how.many of photos is-it   that you have need   of

---

[19] On the phenomenon of 'orphan prepositions' in French see Roberge, 1998; Roberge
and Rosen, 1999; Zribi-Hertz, 1984; I will briefly touch upon orphan prepositions
below. The functional prepositions *à* and *de* used in the examples here, never occur as
orphan prepositions.

    c.   (i)   Pour quel candidat as-tu   voté?
               for   which candidate have-you voted
               Which candidate did you vote for?
        (ii) *Quel candidat as-tu   voté pour?
               which candidate have-you voted for

Kayne, 1983, chapter 3, p. 51–52; Starke, 2001, p. 45 note that *combien* split is possible with PPs. Thus, compare examples (54a–b) with (55a–b).[20]

(55)   French
    a.   (i)   Tu as   besoin de combien de photos?
               you have need   of how.many of photos
               How many photos do you need?
        (ii) De combien (est-ce que) tu as   besoin de photos?
               of how.many is-it that you have need   of photos
               How many photos do you need?
    b.   (i)   Tu as   parlé à combien de photographes?
               you have talked to how.many of photographers
               How many photographers have you talked to?
        (ii) À combien (est-ce que) tu as   parlé de photographes?
               to how.many is-it that you have talked of photographers
               How many photographers have you talked to?

Clearly, the partitive *de photo(graphe)s* must somehow have escaped from the containing PP headed by *à* and *de* respectively. Given our discussion of German above, the most plausible assumption is to follow Starke, 2001 and adopt the remnant movement analysis of *combien* split (53b).[21] Crucially, the examples show that material can escape a PP, just not the complement of P itself.

The arguments against a purely prosodic account of the ban on P-stranding in German carry over to French. Like German, French does not allow P-stranding under sluicing (Merchant, 2001) and it does allow prepositions without complements under right-node raising. French thus confirms the hypothesis that P is a phase head.

---

[20] These sentences are not equally acceptable in all varieties of French. The judgments given here are Starke's (p. 45), they are confirmed by Éric Mathieu (pers. comm.). Kayne, 1983 remarks (citing Obenauer, 1976, p. 17) that not all prepositions are equally acceptable with the construction. Michal Starke (pers. comm.) informs me that the cline is along the functional-lexical axis.

[21] We can assume that the first step of movement lands in a very low position and that the verb in French is obligatorily above this position.

Left-branch extraction in Serbo Croatian

The same kind of argument can also be based on left-branch extraction in Serbo Croatian. Serbo Croatian is typical of the situation in Slavic languages with the exception of Bulgarian, which does not allow left-branch extraction. (See Borsley and Jaworska, 1988; Corver, 1990; Siewierska, 1984 for Polish Mehlhorn, 2001; Sekerina, 1997 for Russian; and Siewierska and Uhlířová, 1998 for an overview of the Slavic situation.) Preposition stranding is strictly prohibited in Serbo Croatian, as (56) is intended to illustrate. A preposition cannot be fronted alone, as in (56b), nor can the complement of the preposition be fronted as a whole leaving the preposition behind, as in (56c).

(56) Serbo Croatian
    a. Prema velikoj kući je Jovan trčao
        towards big   house is Jovan run
        Jovan ran towards the big house.
    b. *Prema je Jovan trčao (velikoj) kući.
        towards is Jovan run   big   house
    c. *Velikoj kući je Jovan trčao prema.
        big   house is Jovan run   towards
    d. *Kući je Jovan trčao prema.
        house is Jovan run   towards
    e. *Prema je velikoj kući Jovan trčao
        towards is big   house Jovan ran

No permutation of these sentences that separates the preposition from its complement is allowed. Even the otherwise extremely intrusive second-position clitic *je* cannot intervene between the preposition and its complement, as shown in (56d). The same is true for all prepositions in the language: They cannot be stranded and second-position clitics can never separate them from their complement.

    Furthermore, it is easy to see that the ban against P-stranding is not prosodic in nature (for relevant data comparable to the German data given above see Abels, 2003a,b): Prepositions without overt complements are allowed in right-node raising structures and prepositions cannot be stranded even in elliptical constructions (Merchant, 2001).[22]

---

[22] It should be mentioned that the situation is empirically not quite as straightforward as Merchant, 2001 claims. For Polish, Szczegielniak, 2005, 2008 shows that the basic point remains untouched, though. For Serbo Croatian, Stjepanović, 2008 argues that there are severe complications but that the data remain compatible with what is claimed here.

214

Nevertheless, we find examples like (57), where the complement of the preposition *velikoj kući* does not form a contiguous unit any more.

(57)   Serbo Croatian

Prema velikoj je Jovan kući trčao.
toward big   is Jovan house run
Jovan ran towards the big house.

It is plausible to assume following (Ćavar and Wilder, 1994; Franks and King, 2000; Franks and Progovac, 1994 for Serbo Croatian and Zabrocki, 1984 for Polish) that the derivation of such sentences proceeds in two steps: First *kući* moves out of the containing PP, then the remnant PP *prema velikoj kući* is fronted, (58). Movement of *kući* involves extraction out of PP. If this analysis is correct, we have more evidence for the hypothesis that P is a phase head. It can be pied-piped by its complement. It cannot be stranded by its complement. Extraction of parts of its complement are licit.

(58)   [prema velikoj kući] ... kući ... prema velikoj kući

The examples above illustrate the interaction of left-branch extraction in Serbo Croatian with PPs. Obviously, an analysis of left-branch extraction which postulates direct movement of the adjective rather than remnant movement, predicts the unattested pattern (59), which makes it difficult to maintain.

(59)   Serbo Croatian

*Velikoj je Jovan trčao prema kući
big   is Jovan run   towards house

Further confirmation for the remnant movement analysis comes from (60).[23] On the remnant movement analysis *sobu* moves out of PP, then the remnant PP, *pravo u veliku sobu*, moves to the front of the clause. This predicts the word order in (60c). Example (60d) cannot be derived.

(60)   Serbo Croatian

a.   U veliku on udje   sobu.
     in big   he entered room
     He entered the big room.
b.   On udje   pravo u veliku sobu.
     he entered straight in big   room
c.   Pravo u veliku on udje   sobu.
     straight in big   he entered room
     He went straight into the big room.

---

[23] In Abels, 2003b example (60c) is erroneously reported to be ungrammatical.

d. *U veliku on udje pravo   sobu.
   in big   he went straight room

The contrast between (60c) and (60d) also argues against an alternative where the constituent *u veliko* is formed without extraction of *sobu* (Borsley and Jaworska, 1988; Bošković, 2003). Such an analysis wrongly expects (60c) to be ill-formed and may predict (60d) to be well-formed depending on further assumptions. The remnant movement analysis has no trouble with the examples.[24]

Wh-movement in Serbo Croatian behaves similarly, as the possibility of (61a) with *which* and (61b) with *whose* show.

(61)   Serbo Croatian   Bašić, 2004, 59 ex. 119ai, 119bi

a.   Iz   koje   je Jovan fioke   uzeo ključeve?
      from which is Jovan drawer took keys
      From which drawer did Jovan take the keys?
b.   Na čiju   je Marija poslala adresu   paket?
      to whose is Marija sent   address package
      To whose address did Maria send the package?

The Serbo Croatian situation concerning left-branch extraction with PPs is typical of the situation found more broadly in the Slavic languages (except for Bulgarian, which, as mentioned above, disallows left-branch extraction).

Whether the remnant movement analysis of left-branch extraction is accepted or not, the conclusion seems unavoidable that movement out of PP is allowed in some form or another, but that the complement of P cannot strand the preposition.

PP and DP subextraction

For German the following examples are discussed in the literature. They suggest that extraction of parts of PP is allowed.

(62)   German   Müller, 1999, 202 ex. 12.55

a.   Mit Norwegen befinden wir uns   allerdings [in einem
      with Noway   are   we ourselves however   in a
      langfristigen [Stellungskrieg mit Norwegen]].
      longterm   positional war
      We are engaged in long-term positional war with Norway.

---

[24] Bošković, 2003 discusses the remnant movement analysis and rejects it. For extensive argumentation supporting the remnant movement analysis of left-branch extraction in Serbo Croatian see Bašić, 2004.

b. Für ihren aus Altersgründen ausgeschiedenen
    for her for age reasons   retired
    Bundestagsvize   Burkhard Hirsch hat sie sich
    parliamentary vice president Burkhard Hirsch has she REFL
    noch [auf [keinen Nachfolger für ihren. . .]] einigen können.
    not yet on no   successor   agree   could
    It has not been able to agree on a successor for its parliamentary
    vice president Burkhard Hirsch, who retired because of his age.

Müller, 1999 suggests that the topicalized PPs are extracted from larger PPs, as
indicated. This analysis is not uncontroversial, however. Kuthy, 2002; Kuthy
and Meurers, 2001, for example, dispute the underlying assumption that the
topicalized PP necessarily originates as a nominal complement.

Relevant examples can also be found in other languages. Russian is a bona
fide non-P-stranding language. This is illustrated in (63).

(63) Russian

a. Ot čego sleduet otkazat'-sja?
    of what follows give up-REFL
    What should one give up?
b. *Čego sleduet otkazat'-sja   ot?
    what follows give up-REFL of

Subextraction out of PP is sometimes acceptable, or close to acceptable as shown
in (64)–(65). Such examples are rare. However, their existence suggests that PPs
are not inherently islands to movement.

(64) Russian

Za kakie prestuplenija on otkazal-sja ot otvetsvennosti?
for which crimes   he rid-REFL   of responsibility?
Which crimes did he reject responsibility for?

The sharp contrast between (65a) and (65c) shows that subextraction out of PP
and P-stranding are clearly different phenomena. (65b) is a control to show
that extraction must proceed from the domain of the PP headed by *o*—'about':
without the PP headed by *o* or the argument taking noun *argument*—'argument'
the sentence becomes unacceptable.

(65) Russian

a. ?Protiv kakoj točki zrenija ty ešče ne slyšal ob
    against which point view   you yet not heard about
    argumentax?
    arguments
    Which point of view haven't you heard about any arguments against?

    b. *Protiv kakoj točki zrenija ty ešče ne slyšal (o   nix)?
        against which point view   you yet not heard about them
        Which point of view haven't you heard about any arguments against?

    c. *Kakix argumentax protiv etoj točki zrenija ty ešče ne slyšal
        which arguments against this point view you yet not heard
        o?
        about

The examples may suggest that PPs can sometimes extract from PPs in Russian, while, at the same time the prepositions themselves cannot be stranded. This is precisely what we expect under the stranding generalization. Similar examples could be given from Czech (see Caha, 2010). The examples are generally less good than one would hope and the claims about underlying constituency maybe less well-motivated than is desirable. To increase our confidence, we now turn to some potentially stronger evidence from Şener, 2006 and Podobryaev, 2009.

Şener, 2006 looks at postpositions in Turkish. In Turkish, bare Ps like *için*— 'for' cannot be stranded, (66a–b), while subextraction of a possessor from the complement of the postposition is possible (66c).[25]

(66)   Turkish   Şener, 2006, 1 ex. 2a–b, p. 2 ex. 4,

    a. Biz   dün   Pelin-in   arkadaş-ı için para
        we.NOM yesterday Pelin-GEN friend-POSS for money
        topla-dı-k.
        collect-PST-1stPL
        Yesterday we collected money for Pelin's friend.

    b. *Biz   Pelin-in   arkadaç-ı   dün   için para
        we.NOM Pelin-GEN friend-POSS yesterday for money
        topla-dı-k
        collect-PST-1stPL

    c. Biz   Pelin-in   dün   arkadaç-ı için para
        we.NOM Pelin-GEN yesterday friend-POSS for money
        topla-dı-k
        collect-PST-1stPL

This is very direct confirmation that postpositions in Turkish obey the stranding generalization.

Things are slightly more interesting though, since there is another class of more complex postpositions which have an apparently nominal component and

---

[25] Şener, 2006 also gives examples from left-node raising showing that the ban on P-stranding in Turkish does not reduce to prosodic weakness of the relevant postpositions.

show agreement. For example *altında*—'under' is such a complex postposition. It should be analyzed as *alt-ın-da*—'bottom-AGR-LOC'. These postpositions can be stranded:

(67) Turkish   Şener, 2006, 3 ex. 9

Ben   Pelin-in   dün   yan-ın-da   knuş-tu-m.
I.NOM Pelin-GEN yesterday beside-3rdSG.AGR-LOC speak-PST-1stSG
I spoke (while I was) next to Pelin yesterday. (Not while I was behind her.)

If we assume that the structure of such postpositions is richer along the lines shown in (68), then the behavior of the more complex postpositions reduces to the behavior of postpositions more generally: extraction *of* the complement is impossible, but extraction *from* the complement is allowed.

(68)

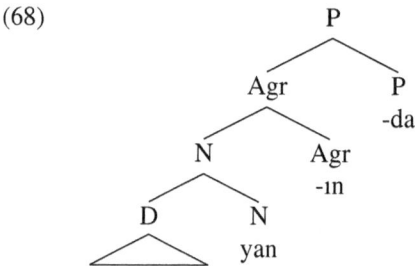

DP may extract from PP, because it can reach Spec,PP and thus escape the phase impenetrability condition without violating Last Resort. If Şener's analysis is on the right track, then the facts illustrate exactly the behavior that the stranding generalization would lead us to expect.

Podobryaev, 2009 makes a similar point about Russian, a language in which certain adpositions can be either pre- or postpositions. Some of the ones that may appear as postpositions may be stranded. A simple example is *navstreču*—'towards'.

(69) Russian   Podobryaev, 2009, ex. 15, 18

a. navstreču Pete
    towards   Petja.DAT

b. Pete   navstreču
    Petja.DAT towards

c. {Navstreču komu | Komu   navstreču} ty   bežal?
      towards   who.DAT who.DAT towards   you ran
    Who did you run towards?

d. Komu   ty   bežal navstreču?
    who.DAT you ran   towards

Who did you run towards?

Podobryaev, 2009 suggests that the relevant factor distinguishing between those adpositions that allow stranding and those that do not is complexity. The adpositions that allow stranding have nominal substructure. The adposition *navstreču*, for example, is clearly composed of the simple preposition *na*—'on' and the noun *vstreča*—'meeting'. Podobryayev then suggests an analysis which can be rendered as follows and which is fully in line with the stranding generalization. Simple prepositions only have a prepositional layer. Their apparent complement is their real complement. They are phase heads and obey the stranding generalization. The strandable adpositions, which are ambiguous between pre- and postpositions, have the following structure.[26]

(70)

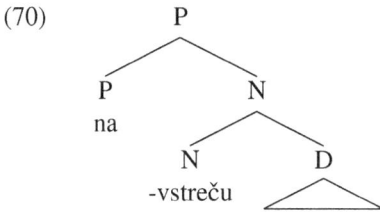

This structure allows the DP to move to Spec,PP without violating last resort. From this position they can then either pied-pipe the entire PP in a postpositional pattern or extract in the stranding pattern.

Subcomparatves into PP

A final plausible case of extraction out of PP is furnished by subcomparatives. As has been noted in the literature (Corver, 1990; Kennedy, 2002), subcomparatives are possible into PPs even in languages that do not allow P-stranding.

The Czech example (71) illustrates that comparatives cannot be formed on the complement of a preposition. Presumably this is due to the fact that comparatives require movement of the (abstract) comparative operator, but since Czech does not allow P-stranding this movement is ungrammatical. Example (71) then merely shows that comparative movement patterns with other kinds of movement in obeying the ban against P-stranding.

---

[26] There are also some unstrandable adpositions that act either as pre- or as postpositions. These would have to be treated as P-heads whose linearization to the left or to the right of the complement is not specified by the grammar.

220

(71)   Czech   Kennedy, 2002, p. 560
        *Bydlel   jsem ve vice městech   než ty jsi
        live.PST.1^{st}SG aux in more cities.GEN.PL than you aux
        bydlel   v.
        live.PST.2^{nd}SG in
        I have lived in more cities than you have lived in.

Example (72) is somewhat surprising. It shows that subcomparison into a
PP is possible. We can understand the pattern if full comparative movement
is movement of the complement of PP and if subcomparatives are formed by
moving the degree operator only.

(72)   Czech
        Chci   bydlet ve   více   amerických městech
        want.PRS.1^{st}SGlive.INF in   more American city.GEN.PL than
        než jsem   bydlel v   europských městech.
        aux lived.PST.1^{st}SG in   European cities
        I want to have lived in more American cities than I have lived in Euro-
        pean cities.

If this is true, comparative movement in (71) represents the categorically disallowed movement *of* the complement of a phase head while the subcomparative
example (72) represents the licit extraction *from* the complement of a phase head.
It is fairly common for a language that has clausal comparatives and subcomparatives to disallow comparatives involving the complement of P but to allow
subcomparatives into PP: the pattern is also found in Russian, German, Dutch
(Corver, 1990), and Hebrew (Yael Sharvit, pers.comm.) to name but a few.[27]

Wrapping up P

In summary, we have seen ample evidence in this section that adpositions in
languages that disallow adposition stranding obey the stranding generalization.
Their complements are frozen in place while extraction of parts of the complement is not categorically ruled out.

(73)   a.   possible: [P [...t ...]]
        b.   impossible: [P t]

In addition, the complement and specifier of adpositions may pied-pipe PP. All
of this strongly suggests that adpositions are phase heads.

---

[27] French does not seem to allow the pattern (see Kayne, 1984, p. 53).

6.4   Conclusion

This chapter has provided reasons to believe that the stranding generalization, according to which phase heads can never be stranded by their complements, holds true for v, C, and P.

(74)   a.   possible: [H [... t ...]]
       b.   impossible: [H t]

The stranding generalization is interesting to the extent that the complements of phase heads are independently known to be movable and to the extent that the phases are not islands for extraction.

The first point is not easy to establish beyond reasonable doubt regarding the complements of C and v, TP and VP, respectively. Numerous open theoretical and descriptive problems regarding the range of possible VP and TP movements remain. Nevertheless, if what I have suggested here is on the right track, it yields an argument against Kayne's (1994) linear-correspondence axiom and against the implementation of cartographic insights invoking a proliferation of null functional heads.

The second point, lack of islandhood, might not have been immediately obvious regarding the category P, because of a tradition that links the ban on P-stranding with the purported islandhood of PPs. The data presented in the final section of this chapter severs this link. The section on adpositions also demonstrated that PPs may not only be pied-piped but may also be the target of secondary movement. Both properties are expected of phase heads and they are expected to cluster in the way they actually do. The next chapter discusses languages that allow P-stranding and theories of P-stranding.

I have not in any detail researched the question whether D obeys the stranding generalization. My impression is that determiners are not strandable across languages (apparent counterexamples even in German notwithstanding – see Riemsdijk, 1989), that DPs are in principle transparent for extraction (some examples for the latter assumptions were given above), and that their complement is a movable category. Similarly, Abels and Neeleman, 2012b raise the possibility that the degree head might head a phase. Detailed investigation of these questions will have to await another occasion.

7   On adposition stranding

In the previous chapter I argued that adpositions have the properties expected of phase heads. Adpositional phrases undergo pied-piping and they are the target of secondary movement. PPs can be extracted from. They have movable complements but cannot be stranded. All of this points to the phasal nature of P. If this conclusion is accepted, it raises the question of what is going on in languages like English, where adpositions can be stranded.

A number of analytic possibilities present themselves immediately. First, one could give up the assumption made implicitly so far that the set of phase-defining categories is invariant across languages: Maybe in languages that allow adposition stranding, adpositions are simply not phases. However, giving up the idea that the inventory of phase heads is universal would represent a substantial weakening of the theory and should therefore be avoided.

It might therefore be preferable to pursue the idea that adposition stranding is an illusion. For example, if it could be shown that apparent stranding really involves null resumptive pronouns, then the parameterization of the phasal nature of P could be avoided. However, I will show in the next section that this solution is unlikely to be successful. In the remainder of the chapter I then pursue an alternative way of avoiding the brute force parameterization of the phasal nature of P. This alternative takes its cue from the discussion of those adpositions in Turkish and Russian that can be stranded. Recall that Şener, 2006 and Podobryaev, 2009 account for the mixed stranding behavior by exploiting the link created by the stranding generalization between stranding behavior and additional structure present only in the strandable adpositions. I show how this approach deals with the main facts of adposition stranding. Finally, I briefly discuss previous approaches to preposition stranding.

7.1   Trace or null resumptive?

In the introductory remarks to this chapter I suggested the possibility that adposition stranding might be the superficial reflex not of a strategy of movement from PP but of a covert resumption strategy. In this section I argue that this analytic option must be rejected.

As is well known, in languages that allow resumptive pronouns, the structures with resumptives are often less sensitive to island constraints than those without (see Boeckx, 2001 for examples, discussion, and relevant qualifications). This well-known fact leads to the expectation that in languages that allow adposition stranding, structures with adposition stranding might be less sensitive to islands than structures with bona fide extraction. However, in English and the other Germanic P-stranding languages, extraction is island-sensitive whether it originates from object position or from the complement position of a preposition. We therefore have no positive evidence of a resumptive strategy. Not to be misunderstood, there is no entailment relation between the existence of a resumptive strategy and island-insensitivity. The argument just given is therefore relatively weak: There is no positive evidence for the assumption of a resumptive strategy from island effects.

Second, the literature on resumptive pronoun has sometimes noted that languages do not have special pronominal paradigms for resumptive pronouns (Boeckx, 2001; McCloskey, 2002). If P-stranding involved a null resumptive strategy, then we would expect such languages to have null pronouns with the relevant functions independently of P-stranding. Again the Germanic P-stranding languages including English fail this expectation.

It might be useful to contrast English with a language like Irish. Irish has null pronominals as complements of P. They co-occur with agreement on P. These null pronouns are used resumptively where otherwise a movement chain would terminate as the complement of a preposition (McCloskey, 1990b, p. 207). The fact that such dependencies into PPs involve resumptives rather than traces can be demonstrated on the basis of the complementizer alternation, which, as discussed, is sensitive in Irish to the distinction between movement chains and resumptive chains.[1]

This second consideration strongly suggests that P-stranding does not in general involve null resumption; P-stranding would otherwise violate the robust generalization about the morphology of resumptive pronouns.

Third, resumptive pronouns tend strongly to be associated with *de re* interpretations where traces are compatible with both *de re* and *de dicto* readings (Doron, 1982). This is illustrated by the following two examples. (1a) has a relative chain ending in a gap and is compatible with the *de dicto* and *de re* interpretations of the relative clause while (1b) contains a resumptive pronoun and is compatible only with the *de re* interpretation. The same holds in many other languages.

(1)   Hebrew   Doron, 1982, p. 26 ex. 49, 50

    a.   dani yimca   et   haiSa   Se hu mexapes
        Dani find.FUT ACC the.woman that he seeks

---

[1]   See Willis, 2000 for discussion of related Welsh facts that suggest that colloquial Welsh does allow P-stranding.

b. dani yimca   et   haiSa   Se hu mexapes ota
    Dani find.FUT ACC the.woman that he seeks   her
    Dani will find the woman that he seeks.

If the foot of a superficial P-stranding chain in English were a null resumptive pronoun, then we would expect only *de re* readings for such chains. In other words, there should be a relevant contrast between (2a), which should only have a *de re* reading and (2b), which should also admit a *de dicto* reading. This expectation is, of course, not borne out.

(2) English
     a. Dan will find the woman that he is looking for.
     b. Dan will find the woman that he is seeking.

Examples like the above constitute a direct argument against the assumption that P-stranding gaps are filled by a null resumptive.

We might add the following consideration here. According to Postal, 1998, there are certain contexts where weak definite pronouns are impossible. Postal calls these *antipronominal*. The complement position of a preposition can be antipronominal in this sense when it acts as a predicate nominal. Thus, Postal gives (3a) as ungrammatical. He argues that there are extractions that systematically rely on a null resumptive at the tail of the chain and he claims that those extractions are incompatible with antipronominal contexts. A relevant example is given in (3b).

(3) English   Postal, 1998, 34 ex. 37c, 28 ex. 12d, and 28, ex. 11d
     a. *Frank turned into it.
     b. *A vicious werewolf, Frank immediately turned into.
     c. What sort of thing did he turn into?

Now, if the complement position of a stranded preposition were systematically filled with a null resumptive pronoun, then prepositions which do not allow weak definite pronouns as their complements should be incompatible with extraction. (4c) shows that this expectation is not borne out. If Postal's generalizations are correct, they constitute clear evidence against the analysis of P-stranding gaps as systematically filled by a null resumptive. It should be noted that there is a certain tension between this argument and the morphological considerations mentioned above.

Fourth, the category of resumptives is generally assumed to be restricted to pronouns (see Pesetsky, 1998), but elements that are not nouns can be the head of a chain that strands prepositions, (4). This further undermines the idea that there might be a resumptive pronoun at the site of all P-stranding gaps.

(4) English
     Where did that come from?

Lastly, resumptive pronouns appear to be incompatible with comparatives, more precisely with comparatives of inequality, while traces are compatible with all standard $\overline{\text{A}}$-movement constructions.

In many languages the distribution of resumptive pronouns is much narrower than the distribution of traces. True resumptive pronouns often occur only in relative clauses (see Boeckx, 2001 for much pertinent discussion). There appears to be an implicational hierarchy whereby resumption in Wh-questions entails resumption in relative clauses. Be that as it may, the following set of Hebrew data exemplify the ban on resumption in a comparative construction in a relatively permissive language with resumption. Example (5a) shows that a D-linked Wh-phrase in an interrogative can be resumed by a pronoun. Example (5b) shows the same for a relative clause.

(5)   Hebrew   Yael Sharvit, pers. comm.
     a.   eyze   sfarim dani kara (otam)
           which books Dani read them
           Which books did Dani read?
     b.   ha-sfarim Se   Dani kara (otam)
           the-books that Dani read them
           the books that Dani has read

On the other hand, resumptive pronouns are impossible in comparatives:

(6)   Hebrew   Yael Sharvit, pers. comm.
     a.   Dani kara yoter sfarim me-aSer Yosi kara (*otam)
           Dani read more books than-that Yosi read   them
           Dani has read more books than Yosi has read.
     b.   Dani diber al   yoter sfarim me-aSer Yosi kara (*otam)
           Dani talked about more books than-that Yosi read   them
           Dani has talked about more books than Yosi has read.

In Hebrew preposition stranding is impossible. Therefore, whenever a chain would terminate in the complement of a preposition, the resumptive strategy must be used:[2]

(7)   Hebrew
     a.   eyze   sfarim dani diber al*(-eyhem)
           which books Dani talked on-3^{rd}PL
           Which books did Dani talk about?

---

[2] I follow Shlonsky, 1997 and assume that there is a null pronoun in the complement of the preposition, which, in that case, is inflected. The facts discussed in this section are also compatible with the analysis where the inflection on the preposition is treated as a clitic. See section 7.3.1 for the reason to assume Shlonsky's analysis.

b. ha-sfarim Se Dani diber al*(-eyhem)
    the-books that Dani talked on-3^{rd}PL
    the books that Dani has talked about?

Since prepositions require resumptive pronouns and since resumptive pronouns are incompatible with the comparative, there is no grammatical variant for the clausal comparatives in (8a–b). The intended meaning of (8a) must be expressed as in (8c).

(8) Hebrew
    a. *Dani diber al   yoter sfarim me-aSer Yosi diber al(-eyhem).
        Dani talked about more books than-that Yosi talked on-3^{rd}PL
        Intended: Dani has talked about more books than Yosi has talked about.
    b. *Dani kara yoter sfarim me-aSer Yosi diber al(-eyhem)
        Dani read more books than-that Yosi talked on-3^{rd}PL
        Intended: Dani has read more books than Yosi has talked about.
    c. Dan diber al   yoter sfarim me-aSer Yosi
        Dan talked about more books than-that Yosi
        Dani talked about more books than Yosi.

The same restriction against resumptive pronouns in comparatives seems to hold more generally (Ur Shlonsky (pers. comm.) for Arabic and Arsalan Kahnemuyipour (pers.comm.) for Persian).[3]

We might ask why resumptives do not occur in comparatives. I would like to suggest, albeit tentatively, that this has to do with the interpretation of the traces in comparative clauses. A standard analysis of comparatives (see Corver, 2006) assumes that an example like (9a) derives from a structure like (9b).

(9) English
    a. John has taken out more books from the library than he will read.
    b. John has taken out [[-er many] books] from the library than we will read [[x-many] books]

The position of the gap is interpreted as *x-many books*. What is both crucial and obvious is such an interpretation is not available to regular pronouns.

---

[3] Zribi-Hertz, 1984 has argued that when prepositions in French occur without a complement, so called orphan prepositions, the complement of the preposition is occupied by a null pronominal pro. pro can act as a resumptive pronoun. It is tempting to try to show that the generalization made here holds for French. A number of factors interfere with a straightforward construction of the relevant examples. (I would like to thank Mélanie Jouitteau and Anne Zribi-Hertz for discussion of this issue.) To the extent that the relevant examples can be constructed in certain dialects of French, the expectation appears to be borne out.

This is important, since Sharvit, 1999 argues that resumptive pronouns can have only such denotations that the pronoun could also have in its non-resumptive, non-A'-bound use. If Sharvit's generalization is true, we have a straightforward explanation for why resumptive pronouns do not occur in comparatives.

The incompatibility of resumptives with comparatives seems both well supported and non-accidental. Therefore, the fact that in P-stranding languages comparatives are possible into the complement position of an adposition is a strong argument against a resumptive analysis of P-stranding.

There are some facts from Irish that require a slight refinement of the generalization that resumptive pronouns never occur in comparatives. McCloskey (1979, pp. 135, 156) had claimed that resumptive pronouns are indeed incompatible with the comparative. However, McCloskey, 1990b gives examples where resumptive pronouns terminate a comparative chain. The relevant examples are very rare (Jim McCloskey, pers. comm.) and of two kinds.

The first kind is exemplified in (10).

(10)   Irish

> níos mó mine ná a raibh gnaithe acu fiin   leis
> more   meal than AN was need   at.themselves with.it
> more corn meal than they needed themselves

This type of example doesn't seriously threaten the generalization that resumptive pronouns are incompatible with comparatives. The putative comparative clause might be analyzed as a headless relative clause (for this suggestion in different contexts, see Beck, Oda, and Sugisaki, 2002; Besten, 1978, 1981). Indeed the string is independently attested as a headless relative meaning *all that they themselves needed* (Jim McCloskey, pers. comm.).

The second type of comparative with a resumptive pronoun is shown in examples like (11a) (from McCloskey (1990b, p. 239)) and (11b–c) (Jim McCloskey, pers. comm.). These examples are truly problematic for the generalization that resumptives never occur in comparatives.

(11)   Irish

> a.   Do fuair sé leaba chó math agus ar lui   sé riamh uirthi.
>   get.PST he bed as good as   AN lie.PST he ever on3^{rd}SG.F
>   He got a bed as good as he ever lay on (it).
> b.   fairrge comh fiadhain agus comh garbh agus a gcualaidh mi a
>   sea   as wild   and as   rough as C heard   I its
>   tuairisc
>   report
>   a sea as wild and as rough as I have ever heard tell of
> c.   phíosa brea coirce chomh maith agus ar leag fear nó bean súil
>   piece fine corn as   good as C laid man or woman eye

ariamh air
ever   on.it
as fine a patch of corn as man or woman ever laid eyes on

d.   capall comh scsipeamhail a's shuidh tú   ar a mhuin ariamh
horse as   lively   as sat   you on its back   ever
a horse as lively as you ever rode

Notice, though, that all of the examples are equatives and that the Hebrew examples above were all comparisons of inequality. Equatives have a somewhat different syntax from comparatives of inequality (see Price, 1990 for pertinent discussion of Spanish comparative constructions). The Irish facts suggest that the following more fine-grained generalization might still hold universally: Resumptive pronouns never occur in comparatives of inequality.

This refinement does not affect our conclusions about P-stranding gaps in languages like English: English allows P-stranding in comparatives of inequality, therefore, P-stranding gaps cannot be null resumptives.

The five arguments given in this section seem sufficiently strong to reject the idea that the complement position of a stranded preposition or postposition is systematically occupied by a null resumptive pronoun.

Excursus on Frisian and P-stranding creoles

For some languages, the question whether they show a P-stranding or a resumption strategy has been difficult to answer. The brief discussion that follows shows that using criteria based on the arguments given above allows for a fairly direct resolution of the question. I first discuss Frisian and then turn to some creoles.

Whether Frisian does or does not allow preposition stranding has been somewhat controversial. Unlike Dutch, which does not generally allow preposition stranding, (12a), and which, therefore, does not allow preposition stranding in comparatives of inequality (Besten, 1978, 1981; Riemsdijk, 1978b), (12b), Frisian does allow superficial cases of preposition stranding, (13a) (see also Fleischer, 2002a), and does allow comparatives of inequality with preposition stranding (Hoekstra, 1995, pp. 107–109), (13b).

(12)   Dutch
a.   *Hoevel   geld   had ze op gerekend?
how.much money has she on counted
b.   *Jan heeft meer geld   verdiend dan zijn vrouw op gerekend had.
Jan has   more money earned   than his wife   on counted   had
intended: Jan made more money than his wife had expected.

If the reasoning above is correct, the comparative, (13b), is more telling than

230

simple Wh-movement, (13a), and we have a clear case of real preposition stranding in Frisian.[4]

(13)   Frisian
    a.   Hoefolle jild   hie se op rekkene?
          how.much money has she on counted
          How much money did she count on?
    b.   Jan hat mear jild   fertsjinne as   dat syn frou op rekkene hie.
          Jan has more money earned   than that his wife on counted had
          Jan made more money than his wife had expected.

A second piece of evidence pointing to the same conclusion comes from the following example, which is modeled on the Hebrew examples from Doron, 1982 discussed above.

(14)   Frisian   Eric Hoekstra, pers. comm.
        Pyt sil grif   de dreamfrou   fine dêr='t   hy nei op syk   is
        Pyt will surely the dreamwoman find there=COMP he to on search is
        Pyt will surely find the dreamwoman he is on a search for.

According to Hoekstra, the example has both a *de dicto* and a *de re* reading. If Frisian used a null resumptive strategy, only the *de re* reading would be expected.

A number of creole languages pose a similar challenge. For Papiamentu, Muysken, 1977 argues that prepositions can be stranded but that the trace in the complement position of P is then spelled out with a special morpheme and that this does not represent a resumptive strategy in the language. This theory has been adopted also for a number of other creoles (for São Tomense see Hagemeijer, 2000, for Cape Verdean Creole see Alexandre, 2009 and for discussion of further candidate languages see also Alexandre and Hagemeijer, 2002). From the perspective of the above discussion, Muysken's theory is supported by an observation in Dijkhoff, 1983, where it is claimed that spelled out traces may occur in comparatives.

The most systematic investigation to date is Alexandre's 2009 study of Cape Verdean Creole. The language has a resumptive strategy, in which the resumptive pronouns agree in phi features with their antecedent but the language also allows the third person singular pronoun to spell out a trace, no matter what the phi features of the antecedent are.[5] This non-agreeing spelled-out trace is restricted

---

[4]   Hoekstra, 1995, where the examples come from reaches the opposite conclusion, but on grounds that don't seem compelling to me. See Abels, 2003c, pp. 186–191 for details.
[5]   I will return to the analysis of this element below, after discussing R-pronouns in German. Eventually, I will not adopt the idea that the element in question spells out a trace, but I use Alexandre's terminology here for ease of exposition.

to the complement position of prepositions. Alexandre, 2009 shows that agreeing resumptive pronouns ameliorate island violations but that the non-agreeing spelled-out trace does not. Abels and Alexandre, in progress probe whether spelled-out traces differ from resumptive pronouns in Cape Verdean Creole in their ability to allow *de dicto* readings and to occur in comparative clauses. The preliminary results support Alexandre's 2009 conclusion that spelled-out traces are not resumptive pronouns.

The discussion in this excursus suggests that Frisian and at least Cape Verdean Creole should be added to the list of languages that allow preposition stranding.

7.2   P-stranding in German and Dutch

As discussed by Riemsdijk, 1978a German and Dutch do not have bona fide examples of extraction of full DPs from the complement position of P. Example (15) illustrates the ban for Wh-movement again.

(15)   German

    a. *Was   hast du mit gerechnet?
        what.DAT have you with counted
        What did you expect?

    b. *Welchen Kandidaten hast du für gestimmt?
        which   candidate   have you for voted
        Which candidate did you vote for?

    c. *Welchem Bett hast du {in | drin} geschlafen?
        which   bed have you in DR.in slept
        Which bed did you sleep in?

Example (16) does the same for A-movement. I concentrate on (my variety of) German in the discussion, but most of it carries over to Dutch directly.

(16)   German

    a. *Frank wurde vom   Präsidenten mit geredet.
        Frank was   by.the president   with talked
        Frank was talked to by the president.

    b. *Der Kandidat von den Grünen wurde am   meisten für
        the candidate from the Greens was   at.the most   for
        gestimmt.
        voted.
        The candidate of the Green Party was voted for the most.

    c. *Dieses Bett ist {in | drin} geschlafen worden.
        this   bed is in DR.in slept   been
        This bed has been slept in.

Data of this sort straightforwardly lead to a categorization of German as a non-stranding language. This conclusion can be corroborated by looking at comparatives, where German behaves like other non-stranding languages. Compartives of inequality on the complement of a preposition are impossible:

(17)   German

    a. *Ich habe gegen mehr Kandidaten gestimmt als du für
        I   have against more candidates voted   than you for
        gestimmt hast.
        voted   have
        I voted against more candidates than you voted for.
    b. *Ich bin mit mehr Typen ausgegangen als du mit
        I   am with more guys gone.out   than you with
        ausgegangen bist.
        gone.out   are
        I have gone out with more guys than you have gone out with.
    c. *Ich habe mehr Bücher gelesen als du {dar- | dr- | ∅-} über
        I   have more books read   than you dar- DR-   about
        gehört hast.
        heard have
        I have read more books than you have heard about.

Subcomparatives of inequality are somewhat better, (19).

(18)   German

    ?Ich habe nach mehr Büchern über die französische Revolution gefragt,
    I   have after more books   over the French   revolution asked
    als du nach Büchern über die englische (Revolution) gefragt hast.
    than you after books   about the English revolution   asked has
    I have asked about more books on the French revolution than you asked
    about books on the English revolution.

In many ways then German and Dutch look like typical examples of non-stranding languages. However, there are cases where certain prepositions can occur without an overt complement and that give the appearance of preposition stranding as in (i) and (ii) of (19a–c).[6]

---

[6]   I should note again that the judgments reported here are my own. Fleischer, 2002a discusses a number of variations on the pattern given here. I grew up in the village of Borgholzhausen (between Bielefeld and Osnabrück) but do not speak the local Low

(19)   German

   a.   Wh-question
        (i)   Wo   hast du   mit gerechnet?
               where have you with counted
               What did you count on?
        (ii)   Wo   hast du   für gestimmt?
               where have you for voted
               What did you vote for?
        (iii) Wo   hast du   {*in | drin} geschlafen?
               where have you   in DR.in slept
               What did you sleep in?

   b.   Topicalization
        (i)   Da   habe ich nicht mit gerechnet.
               there have I   not   with counted
               I didn't expect that.
        (ii)   Da   hat Peter gestern   auch für gestimmt?
               there has Peter yesterday also for voted
               Peter also voted for that yesterday.
        (iii) Da   hat niemand {*in | dr=in} geschlafen.
               there has nobody   in DR=in slept
               Nobody has slept in it.

   c.   Relativization
        (i)   Das ist das Ergebnis, wo   keiner mit gerechnet hat.
               this is the result   where nobody with reckoned has
               This is the result that nobody expected
        (ii)   Das ist der Vorschlag, wo   Peter auch für gestimmt hat.
               this is the proposal where Peter also for voted   has
               This is the proposal that Peter also voted for.
        (iii) Das ist das Zelt, wo   niemand {drin | *in} geschlafen
               this is the tent where nobody   DR.in   in slept
               hat.
               has
               This is the tent that nobody has slept in.

The (i)- and (ii)-examples look like preposition stranding, as they involve a
gap within PP and there is a displaced overt element that can be associated with
this gap. The displaced elements here are the locatives *wo*—'where' and *da*—

German basilect. The pattern where there is doubling of moved *wo* or *da* by *da* with
prepositions that are consonant initial (e.g., *Da habe ich nicht damit gerechnet.* for
(19b.i)) sound marked but not impossible under topicalization and relativization and
impossible in Wh-questions. My judgments therefore fall within the range of dialects
discussed by Fleischer, although basilectal data with my judgement pattern might have
been expected somewhat further south.

'there'. Riemsdijk, 1978a calls these elements R-pronouns, but I will use the more neutral term R-words.[7] In other dialects R-words may also be the indefinite and negative locative quantifiers *somewhere* and *nowhere* (Fleischer, 2002a; Hoekstra, 2006; Riemsdijk, 1978b). Van Riemsdijk assumes that the R-words, despite their independent life as adverbial modifiers, are proforms for the DP complement of prepositions and are thus pronouns. There are two independent claims here: (i) R-wordss are pronouns, that is, proforms for DPs; and (ii) R-words originate in the complement position of P. In the literature on German and Dutch, claim (i) is often rejected (but see Müller, 2000; Riemsdijk, 1978a) while claim (ii) is fairly commonly adopted (Bayer, 1990; Bennis and Hoekstra, 1984; Besten and Webelhuth, 1990; Corver, 1990; Fanselow, 1983, 1991; Grewendorf, 1990; Koopman, 1997; Müller, 2000; Riemsdijk, 1978a, 1985, 1990). I will follow Oppenrieder, 1991; Trissler, 1993 and reject both (i) and (ii).

I first give two reasons for rejecting (i) (see Bennis and Hoekstra, 1984; Trissler, 1993). The first argument is based on an observation in Riemsdijk, 1978b. The second argument is directly from Bennis and Hoekstra, 1984; Trissler, 1993. I then briefly illustrate the reasons that lead Trissler to reject (ii) as well.

7.2.1 R-words are not pronouns

Riemsdijk, 1978b discusses an effect that arises with R-words in Dutch and that we can understand as a Relativized Minimality effect. The same effect is found in German. The analysis as a Relativized Minimality effect implies that R-words are not pronouns.

As noted, all R-words have homophonous locative adverbials. This is a coincidence if we treat R-words as pro*nouns*, that is, as proforms for DPs. Interestingly, R-words interact for locality with their homophonous locative adverbials rather than interacting with pronouns. Consider example (20). The example only has the reading given in (20a-i) but not the reading in (20a-ii). There are two potential R-words in the sentence. Only the closer one, *da*, can be construed with the gap in the PP. When the locative *da* is absent as in (20b), the question is about the gap in the PP.

(20)   German

      a.   Wo   hat er da   gestern   drüber   nachgedacht?
           where has he there yesterday DR.about thought
          (i)   Where did he think about that yesterday?
          (ii) *What did he think about there yesterday?

---

[7]   They are called R-words, because in Dutch they all contain an /r/-phoneme absent in other pronominal forms.

b. Wo   hat er gestern   drüber   nachgedacht?
    where has he yesterday DR.about thought
    What did he think about yesterday?

The example shows something like an intervention effect between locative proforms but not between locative proforms and regular pronouns. If there were an interaction between the latter two, *wo* should not be able to be construed with the gap in PP in (20b) since there is a subject pronoun intervening between PP and *wo*.

We can make sense of this observation by appealing to Relativized Minimality (Rizzi, 1990). If *wo* and *da* belong to the same class of items, then they should not be able to cross. Of course, *wo* is a Wh-word and might thus be expected to cross the non-Wh-word *da* without any problems. As discussed in Riemsdijk, 1978a, R-words can move from the PP where they originate into a position in the upper Mittelfeld of the clause, immediately following weak pronouns (21). Call this *R-position* and *R-movement*, respectively:

(21)   German

      ... weil   er ihr da   gestern   [da drüber]   berichtet hat
      ... because he her there yesterday   DR.about reported has
      ... because he reported to her about that yesterday.

Suppose that Wh-movement of *wo* in (20) is a two-step process. First *wo* undergoes movement to the R-position, and from there it undergoes *wh*-movement. Movement to the R-position is triggered by features shared by all locative proforms. R-movement is therefore sensitive to intervention by other locative proforms but Wh-movement to Spec,CP is not. This way, we can block construals of *wo* with PP in (20a). Two elements that belong to different classes do not interfere with each others' movements, which accounts for the lack of any effect of the subject pronoun in (20b).

Corroborating evidence comes from the fact that regular pronouns never intervene with R-movement, (22), which shows that R-words and regular pronouns belong to different classes.

(22)   German

      ... weil   er da   gestern   IHR drüber   berichtet hat.
      ... because he there yesterday her   DR.about reported has
      ... because he reported to HER about it yesterday.

The above data suggest that pronouns and R-words belong to different classes. We can also show that traces of R-words and traces of DPs belong to different classes. The data are taken from Trissler, 1993, pp. 260–261, who in turn adapts an argument about Dutch from Bennis and Hoekstra, 1984. The argument has to do with a structure that is sometimes interpreted as involving parasitic gaps in the German Mittelfeld (Felix, 1983, 1985; Webelhuth, 1992, among others) and sometimes as a coordinate structure without a regular conjunction (Fanselow, 2001; Haider, 1993; Haider and Rosengren, 2003; Kathol, 2001, among other). In my own view, the parasitic gap analysis is most likely incorrect, but the argument given here is independent of it.[8]

(23) German   Trissler, 1993, 261 ex. 29

    a. ein wichtiges Buch, das   statt   nur ___ zu zitieren
        an important book which instead.of only   to quote
        jeder   ___ kaufen sollte
        everybody   buy   should
        an important book that everybody should buy instead of just citing it

    b. ??ein Vorhaben, wo   er statt   dauernd [___ von] zu reden
        a   project   which he instead.of always   about to talk
        mal besser [___ mit] anfangen sollte
        PRT better   with start   should
        a project that he should start with instead of constantly talking about it

    c. ??ein wichtiges Buch, wo   statt   nur ___ zu zitieren
        an important book where instead.of only   to quote
        jeder   ___ kaufen sollte
        everybody   buy   should
        an important book that everybody should buy instead of just citing it

    d. **ein wichtiges Buch, das   statt   dauernd [___ von] zu
        an important book which instead.of always   about to
        reden jeder   ___ kaufen sollte
        talk everybody   buy   should
        an important book that everybody should by instead of just talking about it

    e. *ein wichtiges Buch, wo   statt   dauernd [___ von] zu
        an important book where instead.of always   about to
        reden jeder   ___ kaufen sollte
        talk everybody   buy   should
        an important book that everybody should buy instead of just talking about it

Example (23a) shows that the relative pronoun *das*—'which' can be related

---

[8] I reproduce the judgments given in Trissler, 1993 here. My own dialect doesn't allow relative clauses with *wo*—'where' as a relative particle as a general strategy. For this reason (23c) is worse for me than indicated.

to two object gaps. Example (23b) shows that the R-word *wo* can marginally be related to two gaps inside of PP. (23c) shows that the relative particle *wo*— 'where' the relative particle *wo*—'where', which is presumably associated with a null operator in Spec,CP, can also, equally marginally, be related to two object gaps. Finally, (23d) and (23e) show *das* and *wo* relate to two gaps, one of which is inside of PP and the other one of which is an object. The examples are sharply ungrammatical. But if the gap inside of the PP and the object gap had the same status, it would not be obvious why this should be so, since, in English objects of verbs and objects of PPs can be mixed in across-the-board, (24a), and in parasitic-gap constructions, (24b).

(24)　　English
　　　　a.　　This is the child that I talked to ___but ended up frightening ___.
　　　　b.　　This is the child that my attempt to talk to ___ended up frightening
　　　　　　___.

As argued by Bennis and Hoekstra, 1984 and Trissler (1993, p. 261), these data suggest that traces of R-words and traces of DP complements belong to different categories.

We have seen two sets of data that suggest that R-words are not DP proforms.

7.2.2　R-words are not complements of P

Above I mentioned two assumptions from Riemsdijk, 1978a: (i) R-words are pronouns, that is, proforms for DPs; and (ii) R-words originate in the complement position of P. We have now seen reasons to reject (i). This leaves the option of assuming (ii) while rejecting (i). Rejecting (i) amounts to claiming that there are significant inherent differences between pronouns (and DPs more generally) and R-words. In certain theoretical settings this move alone might be sufficient to derive or at least describe the fact that DPs never strand P while R-words apparently do.

However, the general claim, developed throughout this essay, is that the absence of P-stranding in general and in German in particular follows from the stranding generalization. The stranding generalization does not allow for exceptions: the complement of a particular head is either frozen or not depending on whether the head is a phase head or not. The category of the complement is irrelevant for the operation of the stranding generalization. It follows straightforwardly from this logic that R-words cannot be externally merged as complements of P.[9] In other words, the logic of my account forces me to reject

---

[9]　The only way this conclusion could be avoided, as far as I can see, is if we allow for a category to project a phase when it takes one kind of complement but not when it

hypothesis (ii).[10]

This theoretical argument against R-words as the complement of P is nicely buttressed by empirical ones. Oppenrieder, 1991; Trissler, 1993 argue that no significant generalizations are captured by making assumption (ii) while rejecting (i). If R-words are regular complements of prepositions, then their exceptional behavior (positioning to the left of the preposition, stranding of prepositions,...) cannot be derived but has to be stipulated.

The following is an illustrative example of Trissler's general line of argumentation: Bennis and Hoekstra, 1984 had claimed that R-words are complements to adpositions but appear to their left because they are case-resistant and because adpositions in German and Dutch assign case to the right. In other words, adpositions in German and Dutch can take complements in either direction; the place where the complement actually appears is dictated, if at all, by other factors. Ideally these other factors are inherent properties of the complement itself. The relevant property here is the need for case or the inherent resistance to it. The system is intended to derive the following pattern.

(25)   German
        a.   mit dem Mann
              with the man
        b.   damit
              there.with
        c.   *dem Mann mit
              the man   with
        d.   *mit da
              with there

Trissler asks how general this account is. Prepositions can take PPs as their complements. If prepositional phrases do not require case marking but are not case resistant, we would expect PPs to be able to occur on either side of their embedding adpositions. If we assume that PPs, like R-words under Bennis and Hoekstra's account, are case resistant, they should occur only to the left of their embedding adposition. Neither of these options gives the right results, as the status of (26b) shows. Full PPs behave just like regular DPs. Under Bennis and Hoekstra's account we must therefore embrace the conclusion that PPs, just like DPs, require case. Such a conclusion would contradict traditional case theory,

---

takes another kind of complement. I am not going to explore this avenue since such a parameterization would unnecessarily weaken the theory.

[10] The observant reader will notice that the question of the category discussed in the previous subsection plays only a minor role in the argument given here. Nevertheless, I began by clarifying the categorial status of R-words, because rejecting the notion that they are DP proforms somewhat simplifies the discussion.

of course, and would seem entirely ad hoc.

(26)   German

    a.   von vor   der Wahl
        from before the elections
    b.   *vor   der Wahl   von
        before the elections from

As though this wasn't bad enough, Željko Bošković (pers. comm.) notices a difficulty in implementing this proposal. He reasons that adpositions either assign case obligatorily or they don't. If P obligatorily assigns case, then (25b) cannot be generated, because P has nothing to assign case to. On the other hand, if P assigns case only optionally, it becomes unclear why (25d) is ungrammatical. This is clearly a problem for the case-resistance account of the distribution of R-words.

Consider the question now whether *da* can truly be case-resistant. The preposition *von*—'from' in its directional use assigns dative case to its complement (27a). The DP *dem Bahnhof* designates the origin of the movement. In place of the DP we can use *da* to refer to the origin. In this case, *da* must follow the embedding adposition, (27b) and (27d). The reverse order in (27c) is grammatical but does not have the directional interpretation. In its locative use, *da* cannot be extracted, (27e).

(27)   German

    a.   {von dem | vom}   Bahnhof
         from the.DAT   from.the.DAT station
    b.   von da
        from there
    c.   davon
        there.from
    d.   Das Auto kam von da.
        the car   came from there
        The car came from there.
    e.   *{Da | Wo}   kam das Auto von.
        there where came the car   from

There are two possible conclusions: locative *da* is a homophone of the R-word *da* with substantially different properties; or the idea that *da* as an R-word is the leftward complement of the adposition is wrong. Taking the first option creates a conflict with the evidence from section 7.2.1, where I showed that R-words and locative pro-forms are substantially the same category. This leaves us with the second option, that is, to give up the idea that *da* can be a leftward complement of adpositions; we also give up the case-resistance account; finally,

240

we give up the notion that *da* can be extracted from the complement of P.

I concur with Trissler that for the paradigms just discussed, no significant generalizations are captured by assuming that R-words are leftward complements of adpositions. Trissler shows that similar problems arise not only under Bennis and Hoekstra's version of the thesis that R-words are as complements of adpositions but under every existing implementation of that assumption. Given that we gain little or nothing by assuming that R-words are generated as the complements of prepositions, I will reject this assumption.

7.2.3 So what are R-words? And where?

In the preceding discussion I have ignored a fact that becomes relevant now. I illustrated the extraction pattern from PPs in my variety of German above, (19a)–(19c). I indicated that the preposition *in*—'in' must appear in the unexpected form *drin* in extraction contexts. The same is true for other vowel initial prepositions. *Über*—'over' appears as *drüber*, *unter*—'under' appears as *drunter*, *auf*—'on' appears as *drauf*, and so on. Consonant initial prepositions appear in their regular form in extraction contexts or, somewhat marginally, are prefixed with *da*: *da=mit*—'there=with', *da=durch*—'there=through', *da=nach*—'there=after', and so on.

The morphology is not so much indicative of extraction as it is indicative of the presence of the R-word, as we find almost identical morphological effects also when the R-word forms a constituent with the preposition. Thus we have *auf*—'on', *wo-(d)r-auf*—'where-DR-on', and *wo...dr-auf*—'where...DR-auf', *in*—'in', *wo-(d)r-in*—'where-DR-in', and *wo...dr-in*—'where...DR-in', and so on. Similar triplets can also be given with *da*—'there': *auf*—'on', *da-(d)r-auf*—'there-DR-on', *da...dr-auf*—'there...DR-on'.[11]

A similar morphological reflex of the presence of R-words is also found in Dutch and Afrikaans, though the distinction is marked only on two prepositions in Dutch and on three in Afrikaans. For Dutch we have *met*—'with' without R-words vs. *mee* with R-word and in extraction contexts and *tot*—'to' vs. *toe*. In Afrikaans (Ponelis, 1979, p. 172) *met*—'with', *tot*—'to', and *vir*—'for' alternate with *mee*, *toe*, and *voor* when occurring with R-words and in extraction contexts.

Any account of the facts needs to take these morphological alternations into account.

Gallmann, 1997, p. 36 suggests the following structure for *da-dr-an*—'there-DR-at' and the (mostly southern German) *da-da-mit*—'there-DR-with'.

---

[11] See Fleischer, 2002a for detailed discussion of how these elements are realized in various dialects.

(28)
```
              PP
          ┌────┴────┐
        DP          P'
         │      ┌────┴────┐
        D⁰     P⁰        DP
        da  ┌───┴───┐
        da D⁰    P⁰
           da   mit
           dr    an
```

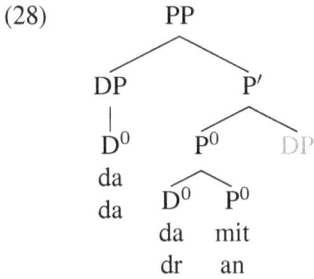

Under Gallmann's analysis, *da* in Spec,PP is a DP which moves there from the complement position of P. The element adjoined to P, *da/dr*, is an agreement morpheme in structures like these. Based on the discussion so far, I would like to suggest the following slight modification of this structure:

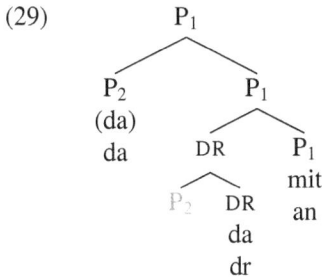

(29)
```
              P₁
          ┌────┴────┐
        P₂          P₁
       (da)     ┌────┴────┐
        da     DR        P₁
           ┌────┴───┐    mit
          P₂   DR    an
               da
               dr
```

Similarly for *woran* and *womit*:

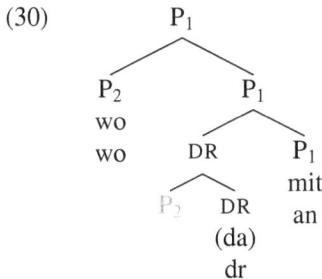

(30)
```
              P₁
          ┌────┴────┐
        P₂          P₁
        wo      ┌────┴────┐
        wo     DR        P₁
           ┌────┴───┐    mit
          P₂   DR    an
              (da)
               dr
```

The structure is based on the following assumptions. First, DR selects R-words and nothing else. Second, DR realizes the case assigned by P. The further selectional properties of P ($[uF_{\downarrow\uparrow}]$) are satisfied not by DR but by the R-word; this requires movement of the R-word to Spec,PP. Such movement does not violate the anti-locality constraint, because of the presence of DR intervening between P and the R-word. There is a specific linearization statement (see Abels and Neeleman, 2012b for the general idea) according to which DR is realized to the left of its sister.[12] Finally, we need to stipulate allomorphy rules to ensure that DR is realized as *dr* when occurring with vowel initial adpositions and as ∅ (or *da* depending on dialect), when occurring with constant-initial ones. The initial /d/ of *dr* is subject to optional deletion when occurring immediately after *da* or *wo*. As is to be expected, the morphological realization rules are subject to substantial cross-dialectal variation (see Fleischer, 2002a). As far as I can see, this correctly describes the facts. An immediate, correct prediction is that movement of R-words is subject to regular locality constraints.

In the structure, *wo* and *da* occupy Spec,PP. Their merger in that position is triggered by selectional features. Wh-features or features related to topicalization can be shared as free-riders enabling optional pied-piping, as desired.

An alternative, suggested in Abels, 2003c was to assume that *drauf*, *drüber*, *drunter*, *drin*, etc.— the prepositional adverbs of descriptive grammars—are lexical items different from the regular prepositions *auf*, *über*, *unter in*, etc. The idea was that prepositions take complements and prepositional adverbs do not. In such a structure the R-word is still the sister of the prepositional adverb, a fact which can be used to explain why the prepositional adverb can be pied-piped.

The advantage of the lexical description was that it easily captures the fact that only certain prepositions combine with R-words. *Wegen*—'because of', *trotz*—'despite', *ohne*—'without', *seit*—'since', *mittels*—'by means of' and, in fact, most prepositions that are not of the oldest stock of German prepositions (see Müller, 2000) do not combine with R-words. A way of reconciling the two positions might be to assume that the syntactic structure in (30) was the correct analysis at some earlier stage of the language and that the lexical analysis is correct synchronically.

A third alternative, also discussed in Abels, 2003c, however cannot be reconciled with current assumptions. I suggested that maybe DR is the complement of the adposition, (31).

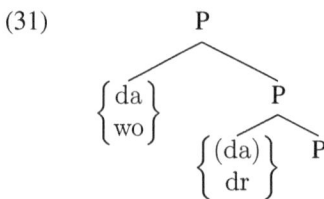

(31)

$$
\begin{array}{c}
\text{P} \\
\left\{\begin{matrix} da \\ wo \end{matrix}\right\} \qquad \text{P} \\
\qquad \left\{\begin{matrix} (da) \\ dr \end{matrix}\right\} \quad \text{P}
\end{array}
$$

In such a structure, *da* and *wo* cannot share [uF$_{\downarrow\uparrow}$] with P, which would rule out pied-piping, counter to fact. For this reason, the structure in (31) must be rejected here. I suggested that examples like (32) could be used to argue that

---

[12] Such a specific linearization statement will override the more general statement that P precedes its complement in German. This is a simple application of the Pāṇini principle. Item-specific linearization statements are needed independently for the few postpositions that German and even English has (e.g., *ago*).

R-words need to be externally merged in Spec,PP independently of the constructions under discussion here.

(32)   German

>   Wo   im   Hals   tut   es dir denn weh?
>   where in.the throat does it you then hurt?
>   Where is the pain located in your throat?

The same analysis was to be applied also to Dutch cases like the following:

(33)   Dutch   Corver, 1990, 71 fn 38 ex. (i)

>   Ergens   (diep) (bij   Marie) (achter) in de keel   zit een zweer
>   somewhere deep with Marie   back   in the throat sits an abscess
>   There is an abscess somewhere far back in Mary's throat.

However, *wo* is clearly locative in (32) and so is the R-word *ergens*—'somewhere' in (33). Comparable examples with a preposition under a non-locative use are sharply ungrammatical, (34). There is no strong reason to assume that *wo* is in Spec,PP in (33) rather than PP being adjoined to *where*.

(34)   German

>   *Ich habe da=((d)r-)über das Problem nachgedacht.
>   I   have there=DR-over the problem thought
>   I have thought about the problem.

I should note that the conditions under which *da* and *wo* can be moved from Spec,PP are not entirely clear. A generalization that is often claimed to restrict the occurrence of R-words in German is that P must be left-adjacent to the verb before and after movement of the R-word. As shown in Fleischer, 2002a,b, Oppenrieder, 1991, and Trissler, 1993, there are counterexamples to this generalization.

(35)   German   Trissler, 1993, p. 288

>   a.   Da   hat er ihm mit   auf den Kopf geschlagen.
>   there has he him with on the head hit
>   He hit him on the head with that.
>   b.   Da   ist er doch hoffentlich mit   zum   Arzt   gegangen.
>   there is he PRT hopefully   with to.the doctor went
>   Hopefully he went to see a doctor about this.

Examples from actual use like those in (36) corroborate Trissler's judgment and are discussed in Fleischer, 2002b, 2002:135. The East Franconian example (37b) is Fleischer's (p. 136) example (12c'). Fleischer notes that Abraham, 1995, p. 337 judges this type of example to be ungrammatical.[13]

(36)   German

    a.   Da   will ich nichts   mehr hören von.
          there want I   nothing more hear   from
          I don't want to hear anything about this any more.
    b.   då   håt er niks   gsåcht driwer
          there has he nothing said   DR.about
          He didn't say anything about it.

If the structure in (29) is accepted as the correct analysis either for contemporary German and Dutch or for some older stage of the languages, then these languages provide some evidence for linking extraction from PP to the presence of an additional piece of syntactic structure interposed between the preposition and its superficial complement. The fact that such structures are in a historical and dialectal continuum with true adposition stranding (in Frisian) suggests that languages with true stranding always license a (null) counterpart of DR and that a parameter regarding the phasehood of P is not necessary.

In this light, recall the discussion of P-stranding in Papiamentu and Cape Verdean Creole above. In these languages, a special element appears in place of a gap in P-stranding constructions. Previous research had classified these elements as spelled-out traces. Such a view is not easily compatible with modern syntactic theory, which assumes the copy theory of movement and has no invariant trace. It is therefore unclear why the arbitrarily complex and variable structure at the site of the gap should be spelled out uniformly. Under the current approach, by contrast, it is natural to treat such elements along the lines of DR in German: as a piece of structure separating the preposition from its apparent complement and enabling extraction. Since such a morpheme is in no sense a copy of the moving element, the problem of invariance and, for Cape Verdean Creole, ϕ-feature mismatch are solved.

There are, of course, two important differences between DR in German and the elements from creole languages under discussion now: First, DR in German appears both when *da* and *wo* form a constituent with the preposition (*wo-(d)r-über*—'where-DR-about') and when they are separated, while the 'spelled-out traces' occur only when the notional complement of P has moved away. Second, DR in German restricts the category of its sister in such a way as to exclude regular DPs, while this is not the case for 'spelled-out traces.' Recall that for German I assumed that movement of *da* and *wo* to Spec,PP in German is triggered by an unvalued category feature ($[uF_{\downarrow\uparrow}]$). To describe the first difference, all we need to say is that the selectional features of P are $[uF_\downarrow]$ in Papiamentu and

---

[13] Corver (1990, p. 42) provides Dutch examples where PP is a complement of AP and can be stranded by R-movement if it is either left- or right-adjacent to the adjective, but not if it is extraposed out of AP. This suggests that speakers who allow the patterns in the examples in the text might generate them without extraposition.

Cape Verdean Creole. Treating them as [uF$_\downarrow$] will prevent them from triggering movement themselves and allow them to be checked only as free-riders, namely, when independently motivated movement passes through Spec,PP. The second difference can be encoded simply by dropping the very restrictive selectional features that we assumed for German DR.

7.3 P-stranding languages

In section 7.1 I discussed and rejected the possibility that the complement position of prepositions in P-stranding languages is always occupied by a null resumptive pronoun rather than a trace. Section 7.2 discussed the restricted P-stranding patterns found in German and Dutch. I argued that the key to understanding these patterns is provided by the morphological changes that prepositions in German undergo when stranded. This morphological key is the morpheme DR, which separates prepositions and R-words, allowing the latter to extract. The same logic, I claimed, would also explain the extraction patterns found in various creole languages and provide a good explanation of the appearance of 'spelled-out traces' in those languages.

From this perspective, English and other stranding languages might simply represent the case where the morpheme separating the preposition from its notional complement is phonologically empty, (37). An ultimate theory of P-stranding will have to determine whether the null DR-morpheme in (37) is restricted to movement contexts, as in the creoles discussed at the end of the last section, or whether it may, as in German and Dutch, or must occur outside of movement contexts as well.

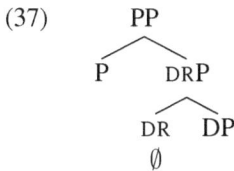

(37)
```
        PP
       /  \
      P    DRP
          /  \
        DR    DP
        ∅
```

The current section investigates this proposal by asking how well it accounts for known facts about adposition stranding. It is heartening that the process reveals no incompatibilities between the theory pursued here and the facts. Unfortunately, although a number of generalizations from the literature would, if true, have supported the theory developed here directly, none of them stand up to scrutiny. As a result, while the facts seem compatible with the present account of P-stranding in terms of a null separating morpheme, they do not lend direct support for it over a competitor where the phasehood of adpositional phrases is parameterized. In the face of such a null result, the main reason for embarking on the discussion is to show that the theory of adposition stranding in terms of a null morpheme is not without content or predictions, subtle though they might be.

7.3.1 Special clitics as the complement of adpositions

It is widely assumed that there are clitic pronouns in natural languages that must be characterized in terms of a syntax that differentiates them from full DPs as well as strong and weak pronouns. This special syntax is often characterized in terms of additional syntactic movement operations that clitic pronouns are subject to and that weak pronouns, strong pronouns, as well as full DPs are exempt from (see for example Cardinaletti and Starke, 1999). Barring the possibility of pied-piping of the preposition by the clitic,[14] we expect special clitics not to be able to occur as the complement of P in non-P-stranding languages but we do expect them to be possible as apparent complements of P in P-stranding languages.

Nothing in what I have said so far rests on the particulars of the theory of adposition stranding proposed here. The expectation that special clitics are impossible as the complements of prepositions in non-stranding languages simply follows from the ban on P-stranding in those languages. As I show below, this general expectation fits the facts rather well. A second, more detailed empirical expectations specifically of the current account is that a language that disallows special clitics as the complement of preposition might allow this pattern just in case a separating DR-morpheme is interposed between the adposition and the clitic in its externally merged position. It is less clear that the prediction regarding DR-morphemes is borne out. Potential examples and counterexamples will be presented after a brief discussion of the basic case.

For non-P-stranding languages, special clitics should be banned from the complement position of adpositions. Serbo Croatian and Spanish provide typical examples:

---

[14] Under current assumptions, pied-piping of the adposition by special clitics might be barred because the clitics' special syntax rests on the moving element being ambiguous between a head and a phrase (Chomsky, 1995a).

Alternatively, the features that are involved in triggering movement of P cannot be shared with P as free-riders but are the features that trigger merger of the preposition and its complement to begin with. This would probably be true if the relevant feature is the category feature [D] of the clitic.

(38) a. Serbo Croatian
         Prema {*=joj | njoj} trče.
         toward =her her run
         They run towards her.
      b. Spanish
         Sobre {*=la | ella} habló Pedro.
         about =her her talked Pedro
         Pedro talked about her.

In both languages, the clitics have a special syntax. Purely prosodic approaches cannot explain the facts above. I discuss Serbo Croatian in some detail here.

There are two main approaches to clitics in Serbo Croatian: (i) clitics in the language are located at surface structure in a designated syntactic (Wackernagel) position,[15] (ii) the second-position requirement is a prosodic filter.[16]

Under the syntactic theory of cliticization in Serbo Croatian, clitics must move overtly to a designated position. (39) gives the two candidate structures that would give rise to the word order in (38a). The trees in (39) are unlabeled (except for the PP) because it is unclear (and irrelevant to my point) what the exact landing site of clitics should be under a syntactic approach to clitics in Serbo Croatian.

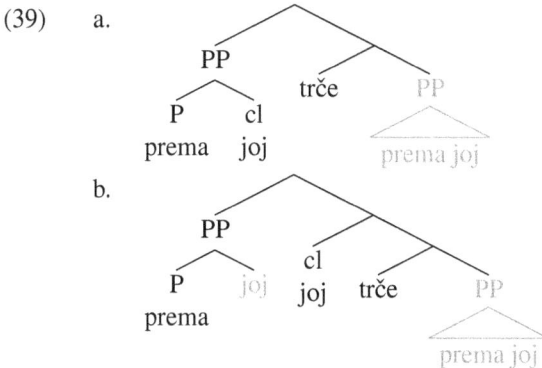

(39) a.

        PP
       / \   trče   PP
      P   cl
    prema joj   prema joj

      b.

        PP
       / \   cl
      P   joj   joj   trče   PP
    prema
                        prema joj

The structure in (39a) directly violates the syntactic theory of second-position

---

15 Theories along these lines are Franks, 1998; King, 1996; Progovac, 1996; Schütze, 1994; Tomic, 1996; Wilder and Ćavar, 1994 among many others. For criticism see, e.g., Bošković, 1995, 2001; Franks, 1998; Radanovic-Kocic, 1988; Stjepanović, 1998.
16 For different versions of a prosodic approach to the second-position effect, cf. Bošković, 2001; Embick and Noyer, 2001; Franks, 1998 and references cited there.
    The characterization in the text is obviously painted with a very broad brush, but for my purposes the present dichotomy is sufficient.

cliticization, because the clitic is presumably not in the right position.[17] The structure in (39b) does not obviously violate the positioning requirement, but it does violate the ban against preposition stranding. We have already seen in (56a) on page 213 that Serbo Croatian allows remnant PPs to front. We have also seen that such fronted remnant PPs can host second-position clitics in the language. The relevant example is repeated here.

(40)   Serbo Croatian

Prema velikoj je Jovan kući trčao.
toward big   is Jovan house run
Jovan ran towards the big house.

Prema velikoj is a remnant PP from which *kući* has extracted. *Je* is a second-position clitic hosted by the remnant PP *prema velikoj*. Given this, the syntactic account of second-position clitics in Serbo Croatian rules out (39a) as a violation of the syntactic positioning requirements and (39b) as a violation of the ban on preposition stranding operative in the language.

Under a purely prosodic account, the second-position effect arises as the result of a prosodic filter that rules out sentences with clitics that are not in a prosodically defined second position. Such a purely prosodic approach cannot account for the status of (38a) with a clitic.

Consider example (41a). The example contains *ispod*—'below', which can act both as a transitive preposition and as an intransitive preposition (an adverb in a different way of categorizing elements). There is no reason to believe that prosodically the transitive preposition *ispod* behaves differently from its intransitive twin. In its intransitive use, *ispod* can host-second position clitics—the clitic auxiliary *sam* in (41b).

(41)   Serbo Croatian   Alex Perovic, pers. comm.

a.   Gledao sam ispod.
     looked was underneath
     I was looking around underneath.
b.   Ispod   sam gledao.
     underneath was looked
     I was looking around underneath.

Even transitive *ispod* can host clitics. (42) is an example of left-branch extraction where the complement of the preposition *mi dostojanstva*—'my.DAT dignity.GEN' is split. The clitics *mi* and *je* are again hosted by *ispod*. Given examples like these, there appears to be no prosodic reason why clitics should not be hosted by prepositions—at least by polysyllabic ones.

---

[17] Recall that we need to assume that the features of either the clitic or the host position—the features that are involved in clitic movement—cannot be satisfied via pied-piping.

(42) Serbo Croatian   Wayles Browne, pers. comm.

Ispod=mi=je   dostojanstva, da idem
below=me.DAT=is dignity   that go.1stSG
It is below my dignity to go.

Nevertheless, examples where the clitic acts as the complement of the preposition *ispod* are ungrammatical, (43a–b). The tonic pronoun must be used instead, (43c-d). The difference between the grammatical examples with *ispod* hosting clitics, (41b) and (42), and the ungrammatical ones, (43a-b), lies in the syntax not in the prosody. *Ispod* and other prepositions in Serbo Croatian can host clitics but not take them as complements.

(43) Serbo Croatian   Alex Perovic, pers. comm.
   a. *Ispod=ga=je Jovan ostavio čekić.
       below=it=is Jovan left   hammer
   b. *Jovan=je ostavio čekić   ispod=ga.
       Jovan=is left   hammer below=it
   c. Jovan=je ostavio čekić   ispod njéga.
       Jovan=is left   hammer below it
       Jovan left the hammer below it.
   d. Ispod njéga=je Jovan ostavio čekić.
       below it=is   Jovan left   hammer
       Jovan left the hammer below it.

The facts discussed here show that an at least partially syntactic account of second position cliticization in Serbo Croatian is unavoidable and that such an account necessarily involves the ban against preposition stranding.

The filter against special clitics as the complements of pronouns does not hold universally, though. There are languages that violate it. Gbadi is probably the clearest example:

(44) Gbadi   Koopman, 1984, 54 ex. 27d

wa y=É-ɓÒ   klÚ jÍÌÉĒ
they PERF=it-Q [PP É on] put-Q
Have they put food on it?

In Gbadi (44) the pronominal clitic É has moved out of its containing postpositional phrase across the question marker ɓÒ and has merged with the perfect auxiliary. Clearly, Gbadi has special clitics. Their ability to appear in postpositional phrases is fully consistent with the fact that Gbadi allow postposition stranding quite generally:

(45)   Gbadi   Koopman, 1984, 54 ex. 27a–c

    a.   Pied-piping of P
       [táɓlĒ klÚ] yɪ̀ wà kÉ-lÒ   lm̄lÈ táɓlĒ klÚ jɪ̀lÉ
       table on Wh they FUT-FOC food   put
       It is on the table they will put food.

    b.   P-stranding under Wh-movement
       táɓlĒ yɪ̀ wà kÉ-lÒ   lm̄lÈ táɓlĒ klÚ jɪ̀lÉ
       table Wh they FUT-FOC food   on put
       It is on the table they will put food.

    c.   P-stranding under A-movement
       táɓlĒ kÉ   lm̄lÈ táɓlĒ klÚ jɪ̀lm̄Ò
       table FUT-FOC food   on put
       The food will be put on the table.

In other languages the situation is less clear. Thus, the P-stranding languages English, Swedish, Icelandic, and Norwegian allow weak or clitic pronouns as the complements prepositions, but it is not entirely clear whether these are special clitics in the relevant sense (see Abels, 2003c for discussion of these patterns and references). On the other hand, there are also non-P-stranding languages that superficially allow clitics as the complements of P (for discussion of Greek see Terzi, 2001, for Bulgarian *pomeždu*—'between' see Hauge, 1999, Arabic also allows the pattern). The P-stranding languages are, of course, unproblematic. For the non-P-stranding languages, there are a number of analytic options. First, the clitics that act as the complement of P might not be *special* clitics. Second, the clitics that act as the complement of P might be agreement morphemes that agree with a silent pronoun in the true complement position of P (an analysis along these lines for Irish was proposed in McCloskey and Hale, 1984). Third, the putative adpositions might not be adpositions after all (for a suggestion along these lines, see Terzi, 2007).

A case that would provide crucial support for the present theory would be a language that does not allow special clitics as the complements of P when P is morphologically unchanged but which does allow the pattern just in case a DR-morpheme, a morpheme that separates the preposition from the clitic, is inserted. There are cases where morphemes that have no other function are inserted between prepositions and their clitic complements. For example, Old Church Slavonic did not allow preposition stranding, yet, it has a clitic *i* (*$*jь$) (3^{rd}SG.M.ACC) which can appear as the complement of prepositions. Grammars of Old Church Slavonic state that "[a]fter prepositions an *n* is prefixed to the stem [of the clitic]" (Lunt, 1959, p. 281). Thus, *$*jь$ becomes *$*njь$ when it precedes prepositions like *na*—'on'. On current assumptions, it is tempting to interpret *n*- as a DR-morpheme that provides the necessary separation between the preposition and the clitic for the clitic to be mobile.

(46)

```
        PP
       ╱  ╲
      P    DRP
          ╱  ╲
        DR   clitic
        n-
```

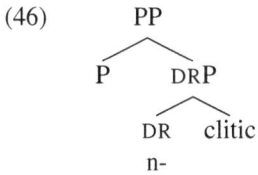

A similar example is provided by Hausa. The language does not generally allow clitic pronouns to occur as the complements of P (Tuller, 1986, pp. 280–1):

(47)   Hausa   based on Tuller, 1986, p. 280

    da   {*=shi | shii}
    with   =him   him
    with him

However, clitic pronouns may appear as the complement of the preposition *ga*—'to/by', but in this case the morpheme *-ree* is added to the preposition (Tuller, 1986, p. 281).

(48)   Hausa   Tuller, 1986, 281 ex. 82c

    ga-ree {=ni | =mu | ...}
    P-ree   =me =you ...

Again it is tempting to analyze *-ree* as a DR-morpheme providing space between the preposition and the clitic. The problem with interpreting the Old Church Slavonic and Hausa examples as direct evidence for the present theory is that it is not clear that the clitics in question are special clitics and, hence, in need of a DR-morpheme to enable their escape (presumably at LF under such an approach) from PP. Nor is it the case that the alternative theory, which characterizes prepositions in non-P-stranding languages as non-phasal, is unable to deal with these facts, since under such a theory one could claim that Old Church Slavonic *n-* and Hausa *-ree* provide the PP-internal landing sites required by the clitics. Indeed, this move would make the Old Church Slavonic and Hausa facts compatible with a theory under which PPs are islands in non-P-stranding languages.

In this subsection I have discussed what behavior would be expected of special clitics under the theory of P-stranding developed here. In general, the expectation that special clitics do not act as the complement of P is borne out. There is some suggestive evidence for the further prediction, specific, prediction that special clitics may occur as the thematic complement of P only when accompanied by a DR-morpheme, but the facts are compatible with other interpretations as well.

252

7.3.2 *Was für* split

I now discuss a generalization relating the word order patterns found in *was-für* split to the presence and absence of adposition stranding in the language. The generalization is due to Leu, 2007, who takes it to show that in adposition-stranding languages there is more hidden structure below the preposition than in non-stranding languages. Obviously, such a conclusion would provide welcome support for the present theory. However, I show below that Leu's correlation is factually incorrect and that *was-für* split therefore does not provide such crucial support.

Recall the discussion of *was-für* split in German in 6.3.2 on page 206. Above, I interpreted examples like those below as providing evidence for the possibility of subextraction from prepositional phrases. (49a) shows that pied-piping of the entire PP is possible, (49b) illustrates that preposition stranding is impossible. (49c) is the pattern that I analyzed above as subextraction followed by remnant movement, and (49d) is the disallowed direct-extraction pattern.

(49)   German

     a. Mit was für Leuten hast du   denn gerechnet?
         with what for people have you PRT reckoned
         What kind of people did you expect?

     b. *Was für Leuten hast du   denn mit gerechnet?
         what for people have you PRT with reckoned

     c. Mit was hast du   denn für Leuten gerechnet?
         with what have you PRT for people reckoned
         What kind of people did you expect?

     d. *Was hast du   denn mit für Leuten gerechnet?
         what have you PRT with for people reckoned

Leu, 2007 discusses *was-für* split in various Germanic languages. He makes the observation that in Norwegian and Swedish—both of which are preposition-stranding languages—the *was-für* split pattern with prepositions looks very different, (50). Danish, another P-stranding language, is similar.[18]

(50)   Swedish   Leu, 2007, 6–7, ex. 12–14, attributed to Börjars

     a. Med vad   för en hund jagar han?
         with what for a dog   hunt he

     b. Vad   för en hund jagar han med?
         what for a dog   hunt he   with

     c. *Med vad   jagar han för en hund?
         with what hunt he   for a dog

---

[18] Thanks to Jeff Parrott for help with the Danish facts.

d. Vad jagar han med för en hund?
   what hunt he with for a dog
   What (type of) dog does he hunt with?

Leu claims that the difference between Swedish and German is linked to the possibility of preposition stranding in Swedish and its impossibility in German. He suggests that PPs should bbe split into (at least) three projections, which I will call *X*, *Y*, and *Z*, (51). Under Leu's approach, the difference between the stranding languages and the non-stranding languages lies in the position of the preposition: it is positioned in Z in non-stranding languages and in X in stranding languages. According to Leu, *was-für* split in both P-stranding and non-P-stranding languages involves a step of moving the *for* phrase, *for a dog*, to Spec,YP followed by movement of ZP to Spec,CP in the clausal left periphery.[19]

---

[19] A very similar idea regarding the structural difference between PPs in stranding vs. non-stranding languages is proposed in Sugisaki, 2002 on independent grounds. Sugisaki suggests that the availability of P-stranding might be linked to the syntax of a pP layer above PP ([pP p [PP P DP]]). In essence, the proposal holds that DP never strands P and PP is always pied-piped when DP moves. However, there are two paramaters regulating the syntax of pP: (i) In some languages pP is absent altogether, thus P and DP are always kept together. (ii) P-to-p movement exists but is subject to parameterization. Stranding is allowed in all and only those languages that have a pP layer and that exhibit P-to-p movement. The semantic diagnostic for the presence of the pP layer comes from the well-known difference between French and English illustrated in (ia–b).

(i)   a.   English
           The bottle floated under the bridge.
           ✓the bridge=location, ✓ the bridge=goal
      b.   French
           La bouteille a flotté sous le pont.
           the bottle has floated under the bridge
           The bottle floated under the bridge
           ✓the bridge=location; *the bridge=goal

On Sugisaki's proposal, the p-layer present in English supports the goal interpretation. Its absence in French prevents the goal interpretation (see Cinque and Rizzi, 2010 for much pertinent discussion). The account predicts a typological implication from the absence of goal readings to the absence of P-stranding. The prediction remains to be tested against data from stranding languages outside of Germanic.

The structural aspects of the proposal are obviously rather similar to Leu's if we let Z=P and X=p. On both proposals DP never strands P=Z.

This entails that PP=ZP occupies the subject position in pseudo passives. Such PP subjects would have to trigger agreement obligatorily. This conclusion is problematic since Bresnan and Kanerva, 1992; Conway, 1996 have argued that PPs never occupy subject position in English. Even if they do, they would not be expected to agree.

(51)

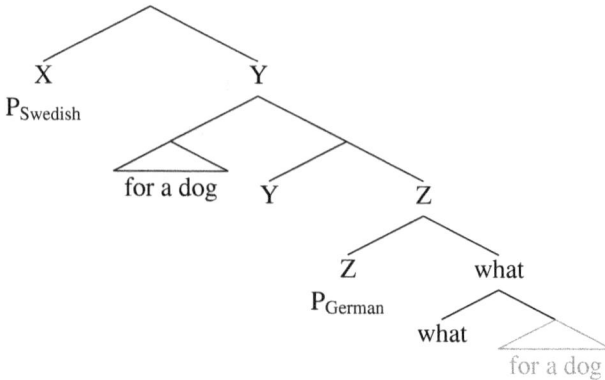

Such a derivation gives rise to the order *[z ∅ what]...[x P for a dog]* in Swedish and *[z P what]...[x ∅ for a dog]* in German. In other words, the difference between the languages is implemented in terms of an additional position (Spec,YP), which is available *below* the preposition in stranding languages and unavailable (or rather available *above* the preposition) in non-stranding languages. Obviously, this is very close in spirit to the parameterization in terms of additional structure below the preposition in stranding languages that we are considering here and, if true, might provide crucial support for this account.

An immediate consequence of Leu's suggestion is that all stranding languages should pattern with Swedish and all non-stranding languages should pattern with German. While the stranding languages Norwegian and Danish behave as expected, both expectations are falsified in a larger sample of languages.

I argued above that Frisian has preposition stranding. Leu therefore predicts that it should pattern like Swedish. However, the crucial order (*what...P for...*) is ungrammatical:

(52) Frisian   Jarich Hoekstra , pers. comm.

    a. Mei wat foar lju   hasto   dan rekkene?
        with what for people have.you PRT reckoned
        What kind of people did you expect?

    b. *Mei wat hasto   dan foar lju   rekkene?
        with what have.you PRT for people reckoned

    c. Wat foar lju   hasto   dan mei rekkene?
        what for people have.you PRT with reckoned

    d. *Wat hiest   dan mei foar lju   rekkene?
        what have.you PRT with for people reckoned

As the examples show, Frisian also fails to pattern with non-stranding German. Frisian would therefore continue to be a counterexample even if we re-classified it as a non-stranding language.

The other half of the expectation is also not borne out. The Dutch examples below indicate that not all non-stranding languages pattern with German. Dutch therefore falsifies the second of the two expectations from Leu's account.

(53)   Dutch Ad Neeleman, Hans van de Koot, Hedde Zeijlstra , pers. comm.

    a.   Op wat voor mensen heb je   gerekend?
        on what for people have you reckoned
        What kind of people did you expect?

    b.   *Op wat heb je   voor mensen gerekend?
        with what have you for   people reckoned

    c.   ??Wat voor mensen heb je   op   gerekend?
        what for   people have you with reckoned

    d.   *Wat heb je   op   voor mensen gerekend?
        what have you with for   people reckoned

The distinction between German and Dutch suggests that the movement of the *für* phrase in the German example (49c) is related to scrambling. As is well known, scrambling is much more liberal in German than in Dutch. As we saw above in example (62) in Chapter 6, scrambling may subextract prepositional phrases from prepositional phrases in German (we also noted, of course, that this analysis is somewhat controversial). An appeal to scrambling as the operation that licenses the PP-external landing site of the *für* phrase in German would be consistent with other claims made by Leu and would remove the false expectation that Dutch should pattern with German.

This leaves us with Frisian. Assuming that scrambling in Frisian is equally restrictive as in Dutch, we can explain why (52b) is ungrammatical. We still need to explain why Frisian fails to conform to Leu's expectation when it comes to (52d). The most obvious difference between Frisian on the one hand and Swedish, Danish, and Norwegian on the other is that Frisian is OV, while the other languages are all VO varieties. This observation becomes relevant in the following way. Leu discusses altogether three positions of the *für*-phrase in German.

(54)   German

    Was (für Bücher) hast du (für Bücher) gelesen (für Bücher)?
    what for books   have you for books   read   for books
    What (kind of books) have you read?

In an OV language the distinction between the position of the *für* phrase in the Mittelfeld, before the main verb, and in extraposed position, after the main verb, is easy to discern. We expect the same three positions to be available in VO varieties as well. However, it will be much more difficult to establish whether the *für* phrase is extraposed or not in a VO language, because we cannot use the position of the verb as a signpost; extraposition in a VO language may be string-vacuous.

VP-final adverbs may be used to signal extraposition in an unambiguous way. (55) shows that variably placed adjuncts have three positions under *was-für* split. The crucial example is (55b), where the adverb *alltid*—'always' intervenes between the preposition and the *für* phrase.

(55)   Norwegian   Øystein Nilsen , pers. comm.
    a.   Hva jakter han alltid   med for en hund?
         what hunts he   always with for a   dog
         What kind of a dog does he always hunt with?
    b.   Hva jakter han med alltid   for en hund?
         what hunts he   with always for a   dog
    c.   Hva jakter han med for en hund alltid?
         what hunts he   with for a   dog always

The example indicates that extraposition from PP must be considered as an option in deriving the Scandinavian *what...P for...*-pattern. This opens up the possibility that the *für* phrase is always extraposed from the containing PP, followed by remnant movement of *hva for en hund* to Spec,CP, stranding the preposition:

(56)   [Hva for en hund] jakter han med hva for en hund (alltid) for en hund
         (alltid)

Notice that if we assume that the *what...P for...*-pattern in Scandinavian involves obligatory but often string-vacuous extraposition of the *für* phrase, we have an immediate account of the Frisian data. Frisian being OV, extraposition is not string vacuous and could never land in the Mittelfeld position taken up by the *für* phrase in the problematic example (52d).

Overall it then seems that both in the P-stranding and the non-stranding varieties, when a DP inside a PP undergoes *was-für* split, the *für* phrase moves out of the PP first. This is followed by fronting of the Wh-phrase with or without pied-piping of P, depending on whether the language allows or disallows P-stranding. Scrambling provides the first step for this derivation in German, while restrictions on scrambling bar it in Dutch and Frisian. Extraposition from PP—often string-vacuous—open this derivational sequence in Swedish, Norwegian, and Danish.

This analysis, which accounts for all the known facts, removes the need for an additional PP-internal position in all and only the P-stranding languages and therefore fails to lend unequivocal support to the specific analysis of stranding advocated here.[20]

---

[20] Bošković, 2004 argues for a rich PP-internal structure in P-stranding languages based

7.3.3 Adposition stranding and D-to-P incorporation

Law, 1998, 2006b; Salles, 1997 suggest that the existence of suppletive forms combining determiners and prepositions (for example, French *de le*—'of the' becomes *du* and German *an dem*—'at the.DAT' becomes *am*) is evidence of D-to-P incorporation. The underlying assumption is that two heads must form a syntactic constituent for morphological suppletion to be possible. According to Law, D-to-P incorporation is a completely general phenomenon in the languages that show such suppletion; D-to-P incorporation applies even in structures where no suppletive form is used. He claims that languages that show D-P suppletion disallow adposition stranding.[21] Together with a few ancillary assumptions this explains why French and other Romance languages and German and other Germanic languages that have determiner-preposition suppletion disallow preposition stranding.

Consider this state of affairs from the current perspective. If Law's generalization turned out to be true and no language that allows preposition stranding had suppletive determiner-prepositions forms, we could interpret this directly in terms of an analysis where there is additional structure interposed between P and its apparent complement DP in standing languages but not in non-standing languages, (57). The additional head X could be held responsible for blocking D-to-P incorporation and hence for blocking suppletion.

---

on quantifier placement patterns. Unfortunately, the argument is equally inconclusive.

He claims that there is a contrast between English and Icelandic regarding the possibility of having PP-internal quantifier float:

(i) Icelandic and English   Bošković, 2004, 716, ex. 88–89
  a. ?Ég talaði við stúdentana alla.
      I   talked with students.the all
  b. *I talked with the students all.

Under Bošković's approach to quantifier float, the examples entail that there is a landing site for movement of the DP within PP available in Icelandic that is not available in English. It would be tempting to identify this position, a landing site for object shift, according to Bošković, with the position Y in (51) above.

The problem with this move is that both English and Icelandic allow preposition stranding and should, therefore, both license Y. We can avoid this problem by allowing Y to have different feature content in different languages. In other words, Y may be subject to the same kind of parametric variation that we find everywhere else in the lexicon, but we do not have a clear case of structural covariation with preposition stranding.

[21] For Law, 2006a R-words in German and Dutch are principled exceptions that prove the rule. See Law's discussion.

(57) a. Stranding

[P [$_X$ X [$_D$ D NP]]]

b. Non-stranding

[P [$_D$ D NP]]

Law's analysis runs up against considerable technical difficulties and empirical problems. Some of them are discussed in Law, 2006b. The most severe problem is that there are counterexamples to the implicational universal expected under Law's account. Law predicts that no language with preposition stranding should have suppletive forms combining determiners and prepositions.

Consider Prince Edward Island French (King and Roberge, 1990). Prince Edward Island French appears to show the regular French pattern of P-D contraction. At the same time preposition stranding is allowed. (58a) is an example of a pseudopassive in Prince Edward Island French and (58b) of a relative clause with preposition stranding. The examples also contain suppletive determiner-preposition combinations: *au* in (58a) and *du* in (58b).

(58) Prince Edward Island French King and Roberge, 1990, p. 356 ex. 7c, p. 362 ex. 22b

a. Robert a   été   parlé beaucoup de Robert au   meeting.
Robert has been talked much   of   at.the meeting
Robert was talked about a lot at the meeting.

b. Ça fait   trois locataires qu' on a   du   trouble avec
that makes three tenants   that one has of.the trouble with
We have had three tenants whom we had trouble with.

Similarly, if we are to conclude that Papiamentu allows P-stranding in the relevant sense, as argued above, then Papiamentu also counterexemplifies the generalization. The preposition *di*—'of' and the definite article *é* can be contracted to *dje* as shown in (59). (The example is from the web. For further examples see Birmingham, 1970, pp. 41, 108). Presumably this counts as a suppletive form, but then Papiamentu should not allow preposition stranding under Law's theory.[22]

(59) Papiamentu

e porta dje Jeep a   habri
the door of.the Jeep ASP open

---

[22] Law, 2006b, p. 646 is quite loose in his use of thhe term 'suppletion' and lists perfectly regular, transparent contractions, such as *auf das*—'on the.N', which is realized as *auf's*, as 'suppletive'. Under such a loose understanding of suppletion, Frisian also constitutes a counterexample, since, in Frisian the definite determiner *de* "is often rendered *'e* in prepositional phrases like *op 'e mar*—'on the lake'" (Hoekstra and Tiersma, 1994, p. 513). I argued above that Frisian allows preposition stranding turning it into another counterexample.

The door of the Jeep opened.

Although it would thus be fairly easy to incorporate Law's generalization about determiner-preposition suppletion into the current system, I will not pursue this option here, since the generalization appears to be false.

7.3.4   The pseudo passive

There are two types of adposition-stranding languages: those that allow stranding only under Ā-movement and those that allow stranding both under A- and Ā-movement. Preposition stranding under A-movement usually goes by the name of 'prepositional passive' or 'pseudo passive'. An example is given in (60).

(60)   English
       This bed has been slept in (by Napoleon).

Of course, pseudo passives must obey regular constraints on passivization. The question of whether pseudo passives are subject to restrictions over and above those imposed on regular passives has been somewhat contentious. (See Åfarli, 1989; Lørdrup, 1991; Mills, 2007; Takami, 1992; Truswell, 2009; Ziv and Sheintuch, 1981 among others for discussion.)

As far as I know, no language has ever been reported to allow adposition stranding only under A-movement but not under Ā-movement. The languages that allow both types of stranding include English, Norwegian (Åfarli, 1989; Lørdrup, 1991; Merchant, 1999, 2001; Vikner, 1995), Swedish (Maling and Zaenen, 1985a; Merchant, 1999, 2001; Takami, 1992; Vikner, 1995), Vata with postpositions (Koopman, 1984), Gbadi with postpositions (Koopman, 1984), and Prince Edward Island French (King and Roberge, 1990; Roberge, 1998; Roberge and Rosen, 1999).[23]   Stranding only under Ā-movement is allowed in Icelandic (Maling and Zaenen, 1985a,b, 1990), Frisian (Hoekstra, 1995),[24]

---

[23]   There do not appear to be pseudo middles in any P-stranding language.

(i)   *This bed sleeps {in well. | sleeps well in.}

I do not have an explanation for this.

[24]   Arguments for the availability of P-stranding under Ā-movement in Frisian (contra Hoekstra) were given above in section 7.1. Pseudo passives are not available in the language:

(i)   Frisian   Hoekstra, 1995, 116n4

       *De bern   wurde   net nei harke.
       the children were.PL not to   listened
       The children were not listened to.

Danish (Herslund, 1984; Merchant, 1999, 2001; Takami, 1988, 1992; Vikner, 2007), Faroese (Truswell, 2009), and possibly Papiamentu (Muysken, 1977), São Tomense (Hagemeijer, 2000), and Cape Verdean Creole (Alexandre, 2009).

In Abels, 2003c I suggested that there is a simple logic that explains this implication on the assumption that the phasehood of adpositions is subject to parametric variation. On this assumption, adpositional phrases are transparent for all kinds of extraction in stranding languages. The ability to Ā-extract follows directly from this parameter setting. The availability of a pseudo passive in such a language does not. Pseudo-passivization relies on an additional parameter under that theory, a parameter which allows adpositions not to assign case to their complements. I argued that the second parameter has a discernible effect only in those languages that allow adposition stranding; in a stranding language, if an adposition doesn't assign case to its complement, the structure can be saved if the adposition's complement undergoes A-movement and has its case requirements satisfied by a different head; in a language without adposition stranding on the other hand, a DP without case is trapped inside of the PP. It can never satisfy its case requirements and all such structures are therefore ungrammatical, which renders this combination of parameter settings either impossible or empirically invisible.[25]

Truswell, 2009 is the only attempt aside from Abels, 2003c where a grammar theoretic implication between stranding under A- and Ā-movement is created while at the same time the possibility of subextraction from adpositional phrases even in non-stranding languages is taken into account. Truswell suggests that there is a parameterized operation suppressing features on phase heads, which, under the phase-theoretic assumptions he makes (essentially those of Abels, 2003c), derives why A-extraction from adpositional phrases and Ā-extraction from adpositional phrases pattern together in languages that have feature suppression. The ability to Ā-extract from adpositional phrases (without A-extraction) depends on a separate parameterization of prepositions as phase heads. Together, these two parameters explain the implication.

Truswell, 2009 further claims that a language allows Ā-extraction from bare present participle adjuncts, (61), if and only if that language allows pseudo passives.

---

[25] The reasoning is watertight only on the additional assumption that adpositions cannot be pied-piped in A-movement constructions even in non-P-stranding languages, where, by assumption, P is a phase head. The ban on pied-piping adpositions under A-movement needs to be stipulated and does not follow from existing theories of pied-piping, including the one developed above. (A possible exception is Cable, 2010a,b.)

(61)   English

    a.   What did Joe arrive [whistling what]?

    b.   What did Joe drive Mary insane [whistling what]?

Truswell, 2009 derives this biconditional from structural assumptions about bare present participle adjuncts together with his mechanism of feature suppression. This mechanism allows suppression of essentially any feature on a phase head. The theory of the phase impenetrability condition in terms of Relativized Minimality from Abels, 2003c then predicts that movement involving the suppressed feature may bypass the escape hatch position at the edge of the phase.

Therefore, if a language allows feature suppression, it should show no signs of obeying the phase impenetrability condition. Such a language should, for example, not show signs of obeying the stranding generalization. English and Norwegian, which allow pseudo passives and extraction from bare present participle adjuncts, should therefore show no signs of obeying the stranding generalization.

We saw above that the stranding generalization holds for C and v in English. (Though I haven't shown this, the same is true for Norwegian.) It seems to me therefore that the feature suppression mechanism would have to be carefully restricted to be descriptively adequate. It is not obvious that a restricted version of feature suppression would still yield the implications that Truswell attempts to derive.

These skeptical remarks should not detract from the great interest that Truswell's generalization about the availability of pseudo passives and extraction from bare present participle adjuncts holds. If the generalization is true, it needs to be accounted for and creating such an account might yield important results regarding the nature of grammar, as suggested by Truswell.

Returning to the main line of the discussion, there does not seem to be a natural grammar theoretic account of the implication from P-stranding under A-movement to P-stranding under $\overline{\text{A}}$-movement on present assumptions. Consider why. For a stranding language to allow the pseudo passive, a suitable DR-morpheme has to be available separating the adposition from its notional complement and, independently, the adposition needs to bear unvalued and uninterpreted features relevant for the passive (case, phi,...). For a stranding language to allow $\overline{\text{A}}$-extraction from PP, a suitable DR-morpheme has to be available and the adposition needs to bear unvalued and uninterpreted features relevant for $\overline{\text{A}}$-movement. Parameterizations for A-related and $\overline{\text{A}}$-related features on a phase head are independent. Complementizers typically carry relevant $\overline{\text{A}}$-related features and v in many languages carries both. However, I suggested that, in Tagalog, v bears only A-related features and lacks $\overline{\text{A}}$-related ones. The parameterizations for A- and $\overline{\text{A}}$-related features are therefore independent of each other. Hence, the implication from pseudo passivization to adposition stranding under $\overline{\text{A}}$-movement cannot be made to follow from the theory.

I submit, however, that there is a plausible account of the implication (at least in Germanic) that makes a theoretical deduction superfluous. An immediately striking fact about all of the languages that allow pseudo passives is that they have very rudimentary case systems. In these languages case is expressed only on pronouns. This observation suggests a historical link between $\bar{\text{A}}$-extraction of the complements of adpositions and A-extraction of these complements.

Consider the history of English. Old English had well-developed case morphology, impersonal passives without expletive subjects (much like modern German, (62), for Old English see Bennett, 1980), topicalization, and preposition stranding in various $\bar{\text{A}}$-movement constructions (including topicalization).

(62)   German

    a.   Dem   kann geholfen werden.
        him.DAT can helped become
        He can be helped.

    b.   Denen   kann geholfen werden.
        they.DAT can helped become
        They can be helped.

While Old English did not know the pseudo passive yet, it did have preposition stranding. We therefore expect that examples much like the modern German (63a) would have been possible. We also expect examples like (63b) to have been possible, since Old English, unlike modern German, did allow full DPs to strand prepositions under topicalization.[26]

(63)   German

    a.   Mit großem Andrang muss gerechnet werden.
        with big.DAT crowding must reckoned be
        Heavy crowding is to be expected.

    b.   *Großem Andrang muss mit gerechnet werden.
        big.DAT crowding must with reckoned be

Such examples are analyzable in a grammar with P-stranding under topicalization. There would have been no examples that would have suggested a grammar with a pseudo passive to the learner. However, when case and agreement morphology were getting lost, relevant examples could be interpreted by learners as evidence either for topicalization in an impersonal passive without expletive

---

[26] I assume that relevant structures were possible in Old English, although they were apparently rare. Bennett, 1980, p. 106 claims that "[t]here are no impersonal passives of this type from O[ld] E[nglish] to be discussed."

None of the modern Germanic languages that allow pseudo passives have retained impersonal passives without expletives, English has lost the impersonal passive altogether.

or as evidence for the existence of a pseudo passive structure. The analytical ambiguity—from the learner's perspective—is present in modern Frisian examples like (64).

(64)   Frisian

    De jonge wurdt net nei harke.
    the boy   is.SG not to listened
    The boy, people didn't listen to him.
   *The boy wasn't listened to.

In addition to the analytically ambiguous examples like (64), there is also unambiguous evidence for P-stranding topicalization in impersonal passives in Frisian:

(65)   Frisian   Hoekstra, 1995, p. 97 ex. 3a
    De bern   wurdt   net nei harke.
    the children was.SG not to   listened
    The children, one didn't listen to them.

The only unambiguous evidence *against* the existence of a pseudo passive for the learner would be negative evidence: the ungrammaticality of (i) in 24 above. The analytical uncertainty surrounding examples of the type in (64) might have given rise to the pseudo passive in the history of English and the Mainland Scandinavian languages. It seems plausible that the decline of the impersonal passive without expletive could have forced an analysis of examples like (64) as pseudo passives. Frisian has retained the impersonal passive without an expletive and has, therefore, not followed this derivational path.

Evidence for this line of argumentation comes from the fact that pseudo passives begin to occur in the Middle English period as early as the first half of the 13th century (Bennett, 1980, p. 106). However, I must leave it to experts on the history of English and the Scandinavian languages to support or refute this account in detail. The suggestion made above seems plausible enough to me and I offer it as an account of the implication from pseudo passives to preposition stranding under $\bar{\text{A}}$-movement. If the suggestion is on the right track, we do not require a formal (grammar theoretic) implication and can maintain the present theory, which, as we saw, fails to derive such an implication.

7.3.5   Adposition stranding and verbal particles

A final connection is often made between adposition stranding and verbal particles. Concretely, there is work suggesting that all languages with adposition stranding also have particles (Stowell, 1982, see also Sugisaki, 2002; Sugisaki

264

and Snyder, 2001a,b, who discuss this implication from the perspective of the acquisition of English).

Relevant evidence concerning Germanic can be found in Åfarli, 1985; den Dikken, 1992; Herslund, 1984; Holmberg, 1986; Neeleman, 1994, 2001; Svenonius, 2002a among many others, Vata and Gbadi are discussed by Koopman, 1984, and Prince Edward Island French in King and Roberge, 1990. The existence of verbal particles (or separable prefixes, as they are usually called in the Germanic OV languages) is a familiar fact. I illustrate the existence of particles here for Prince Edward Island French, which departs significantly from standard French both regarding preposition stranding (see above) and in the availability of verbal particles.

(66)   Prince Edward Island French   King and Roberge, 1990, pp. 366–367

    a.   Il a   pluggé {in le computer | le computer in}.
        he has plugged in the computer the computer in

    b.   Plugge {le | le computer} in!
        plug   it the computer in

    c.   Ils avont layé {off le monde | le monde off} à la factorie
        they have layed off the people the people off at the factory

    d.   Il y   a   une tapée de femmes qui travaillont out
        it there has a   lot of women who work   out
        There are a lot of women who work outside the home.

Given that the set of languages that allow adposition stranding is so heavily skewed towards Germanic and since all Germanic languages have verbal particles, the generalization in the form presented above might not be particularly significant. Even the fact that both preposition stranding and particles are found in Prince Edward Island French is not too impressive in view of the fact that Prince Edward Island French is heavily influenced by English. Unfortunately, too little is known about particles in the other stranding languages (Vata, Gbadi, Papiamentu, Cape Verdean Creole,...).

However, it might be possible to sharpen the generalization about particles further. Particles and separable prefixes are not all created equal. Svenonius, 2002a argues that particle constructions in Swedish, Danish, Norwegian, and English and separable prefixes in Dutch, German, Yiddish, and Afrikaans are substantially different.

The languages in the second group have separable-prefix verbs where the object of the verb represents either the figure or the ground argument of the particle, (67).

(67)   German   Svenonius, 2002a, ex. 2

    a.   Er lädt die Koffer   ab.
        he loads the suitcases off

He loads off the suitcases.

b. Er lädt den Gepäckwagen ab.
   He loads the baggage cart off
   He unloads the baggage cart.

The languages in the first group on the other hand, as a general pattern, only allow particles with the figure argument, (68). (For examples from the other languages mentioned, see Svenonius, 2002a.)

(68)   Danish   Svenonius, 2002a, ex. 6

a. Han tog frakken av.
   he took coat.the off
   He took off his coat.
b. *Han tog barnet av.
   He took child.the off

It will be noted that all the languages with the restricted particle construction are languages that allow generalized P-stranding in the sense that full DPs may strand prepositions. The languages with the more liberal construction are languages where prepositions may only be stranded by R-words. Thus, among the languages discussed by Svenonius, we observe that the adposition-stranding languages have a more restricted particle construction than the non-stranding languages.

Of course, there is an alternative generalization. All of the languages that have the more liberal particle construction are OV languages while all of the more restricted languages are VO languages. A possible exception here is Yiddish, whose status as either OV or VO is notoriously difficult to determine. (See Vikner, 2001, chapter 2 and references cited there for discussion.)

Frisian provides the test case to distinguish between the two formulations of the generalization. If the correct generalization has to do with the basic OV order, then Frisian should pattern with Dutch and German and other OV languages in having the more liberal construction. On the other hand, if the correct generalization has to do with adposition stranding, then Frisian should pattern with English and Danish and the other adposition stranding languages and only have the more restricted particle construction. Empirical work is required here. Initial probing suggests that Frisian patterns with the other P-stranding languages.[27]

Given the substantial gaps in our knowledge about Svenonius's parameter, we need to proceed with caution. I will now speculate on how Svenonius's parameter could be related to the stranding parameter on the assumption that

---

[27] Of course, the conclusions above regarding Frisian might still be wrong. This would be unfortunate, because then there would be no Germanic OV language with stranding leaving an important but, in view of the existence of Vata and Gbadi, probably not theoretically relevant gap in the attested typology within Germanic.

the relevant property distinguishing the two types of languages is the *obligatory* presence of a null DR-morpheme in the stranding languages and its absence in the non-stranding languages, (69).[28]

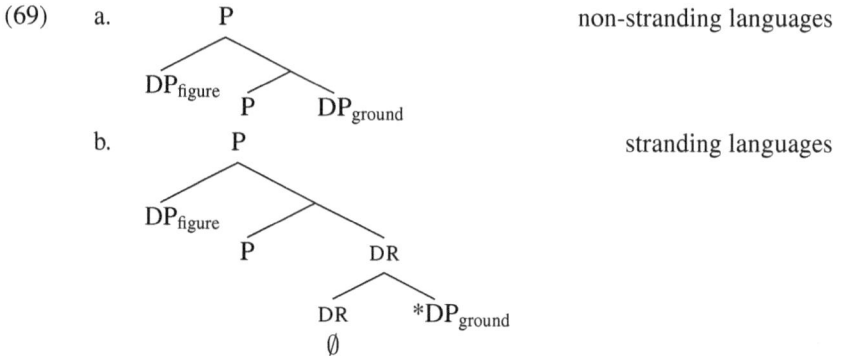

(69)　　a.　　　　　P　　　　　　　　　　　　non-stranding languages

DP_{figure}

P　　DP_{ground}

　　　b.　　　　　P　　　　　　　　　　　　stranding languages

DP_{figure}

P　　　　DR

DR　　$*DP_{ground}$

∅

Support for the structure in (69) comes from the longstanding observation (see Sugisaki, Lasnik, and Snyder, 2001) that children acquiring English produce the order V DP Prt significantly earlier than the order V Prt DP. The structure in (69b) accounts for this fairly directly. Recall that Svenonius argues that English only allows figure DPs in particle constructions. The figure is the specifier of the particle. Therefore, the late-acquired order V Prt DP has a more complex structure, as it requires either leftward movement of the particle or rightward movement of the figure DP.[29]

Suppose that the particle construction with ground DPs, that is, the construc-

---

[28] If the relevant parameter has to do with the VO versus OV nature of the language, then the ideas contained in Haider, 2000, 2005; Janke and Neeleman, 2012; Neeleman and Weerman, 1999 regarding the construction of shell structures in VO but not in OV languages might provide the distinctions relevant for constructing an account.

[29] Sugisaki, Lasnik, and Snyder's own account of the acquisitional sequence rests on the claim that the order V Prt DP is the base order and that V DP Prt is derived by object shift. On this view, object shift is obligatory at early stages of development and becomes optional later. Sugisaki, Lasnik, and Snyder go on to claim that the possibility of preposition stranding relies on the (optional) absence of object shift and thus on the availability of the V Prt DP order. This is in conflict with the cross-linguistic record: Danish allows preposition stranding but disallows the V Prt DP order (Svenonius, 1996)—an impossible state of affairs under Sugisaki, Lasnik, and Snyder's theory.

Stowell, 1982 suggests that there is a link between the syntax of the verb-particle construction and the availability of pseudo passives. In particular, there is an implication in Germanic from the availability of the pseudo passive to the availability of the order V Prt DP. This is not a biconditional, since Icelandic allows the order V Prt DP (Svenonius, 1996, ex. 35) but has no pseudo passive.

tion which is absent in stranding languages rests on P moving out of its base-generated position. In the relevant structures, the particle need not assign case: the ground argument freely becomes the subject of a personal passive, in which case it appears in the nominative, (70a) and triggers verbal agreement, (70b).

(70)   German

    a.   Der   Gepäckwagen ist abgeladen worden.
          the.NOM baggage cart   is off.loaded been
          The baggage cart has been unloaded.

    b.   Die Gepäckwagen sind abgeladen worden.
          the baggage carts are off.loaded been
          The baggage carts have been unloaded.

In examples like (70), the object of the particle transparently moves away. This would be impossible if the phrases projected by particles were phases. The phasehood of particles must therefore be voided. This may be achieved if particles undergo head movement to the main verb, since on certain theories of phases such movement would extend the phase, which would allow the ground DP to move away from the complement position of (the trace of) P without violating either the last-resort or the . In other words, case assigning and locality properties of the verb and the particle are unified in the structures in question. Let us assume provisionally that this is indeed brought about by movement of the particle to the verb.

We can now relate the absence of this type of particle construction to the presence of stranding using the structure in (69b). If in stranding languages the null DR-morpheme must be present and if this head is in need of an overt licenser, then movement of P to a higher position might destroy the relevant licensing condition.[30]

In this subsection I have discussed the relation between the possibility of generalized adposition stranding in a language and the syntax of verbal particles in that language. The first generalization in this area is that all adposition-stranding languages have verbal particles (Stowell, 1982). Although it seems to be true,

---

[30] Head movement would have to bleed licensing of the null DR-morpheme. This might be a bit surprising, since Baker 1988 claimed that incorporation is head movement and that the government transparency corollary holds. It says that government relations are maintained under head movement. The difference between the cases discussed by Baker and the present one might lie in the intrinsically phonological nature of the licensing of DR: Syntax proper is arguably not sensitive to phonological content of an item. The licensing condition for null DR would therefore have to hold at the syntax-morphology interface or in the phonology proper. It is at least conceivable that traces of (head) movement are no longer visible at that point.

The account suggested here is inspired by Pesetsky, 1995.

the very restricted data available do not allow us to determine whether this implication is theoretically significant. I did not try to account for it.

I suggested that a potentially more significant generalization might emerge from Svenonius, 2002a—though here, too, significant questions about the generalization remain. I developed, very tentatively, the bare outline of an account of the hypothesized correlation between the lack of adposition stranding and the availability of a more permissive particle construction in Germanic based on the idea that stranding languages obligatorily have null DR-morphemes in need of the adposition as a local licensor. It is difficult to see how the correlation could be captured on the assumption that adpositions are not phase heads in languages that allow adposition stranding.

7.3.6   Implications

In this section I have discussed a number of properties that seem to correlate in one way or another with the generalized availability of adposition stranding. In the final analysis, it is not clear how strong or how theoretically significant the generalizations really are. Empirically, this has to do with the fact that almost the entire body of data on generalized preposition stranding comes from the Germanic VO languages. Many of the purported correlations might therefore reflect historical accidents or confound properties of OV languages with properties of non-stranding languages.

On the basis of comparative constructions and *de dicto* readings, I had argued in section 7.1 (contra Hoekstra, 1995) that Frisian is an OV language with stranding, but it would be good to have more facts to distinguish Hoekstra's resumptive analysis from the present movement analysis more clearly. Once the question of whether Frisian allows stranding is resolved, it may be possible to revisit the generalizations discussed in the present section (to the extent that they hold up otherwise) and find out whether they distinguish adposition-stranding languages from non-stranding language or whether they distinguish OV languages from VO languages. I must also leave it to future research to determine to what extent the claimed correlations hold outside of Germanic.

Regardless, I have shown that the generalizations discussed above, if true, do not threaten the theory of adposition stranding in terms of a null DR-morpheme. The one exception is the implication from stranding under $\overline{\text{A}}$-movement to stranding under A-movement, which I consequently suggested to treat as a historical accident.

7.4   Conclusion

At the start of this chapter I introduced three hypotheses that would make the existence of superficial adposition stranding compatible with the facts that we observed in section 6.3. The first was to analyze adposition stranding away in terms of null resumptives. I rejected this hypothesis on strong empirical grounds. The second idea was to parameterize the phasehood of prepositional phrases. I rejected this approach on conceptual grounds. The final hypothesis held that stranding languages have null DR-morphemes, separating the adposition from its apparent complement, thus licensing movement to Spec,PP in conformity with the phase impenetrability and the last resort conditions. The hypothesis is indirectly supported by the stranding patterns found in German, Dutch, and Cape Verdean Creole. I tested how it squares with known facts about generalization adposition stranding and found no contradictions.

I finnish this chapter by relating the present theory of adposition stranding to three older strands of research on the topic.[31] On the first approach, preposition stranding is analyzed in terms of the availability of an escape hatch position only in stranding languages (Koopman, 1997; Riemsdijk, 1978a, 1990). The second type of approach distinguishes stranding languages from non-stranding languages in terms of the availability of a reanalysis rule only in stranding languages (Hornstein and Weinberg, 1981; Stowell, 1982). The third type of approach makes the ability of prepositions to govern subject to parametric variation (this tradition was inspired by Kayne 1981, 1984, chapter 5).

The first class of theories is similar to the approach developed here and those in Leu, 2007; Sugisaki, 2002 in that they relate the availability of P-stranding to the internal structure of adpositional phrases in the language. In essence, Koopman, 1997; Riemsdijk, 1978a, 1990 propose that an escape hatch position is available within PP in all and only the stranding languages. The main problem with this approach is that in non-stranding languages PPs should not have escape hatches and are therefore predicted to be islands for all types of extraction. No distinction between extraction *of* the complement of PP and extraction *from* the complement of PP can be made. We saw in subsection 6.3.2 above that such a distinction is empirically necessary.[32]

---

[31] This is not intended as a general overview of the literature. For discussion of the approach to P-stranding in terms of category neutralization, which was proposed in Pollock, 1989; Rizzi, 1990, the reader is referred to Newmeyer, 1998. More recent approaches to P-stranding (Law, 2006b; Leu, 2007; Sugisaki, 2002; Truswell, 2009) were already discussed above.

[32] It should be noted that Riemsdijk, 1978a treats $\overline{\text{A}}$-movement from PPs as indicated in the text. A-movement from PPs is analyzed in terms of V-P reanalysis under adjacency.

270

The second approach (Hornstein and Weinberg, 1981) assumes a universal filter from which it follows that the complement position of P may not be empty. P-stranding languages get around this problem because they have a process of reanalysis, absent in non-stranding languages. The reanalysis rule feeds syntactic movement processes and reanalyzes a verb structurally with the head of a PP, as long as the PP is attached within the verb's maximal projection. The precise formulation of the reanalysis rule is then intended to capture the conditions under which adposition stranding is possible in stranding languages and those under which it is blocked.

This proposal is similar to the current approach in that it entails a universal ban on traces as the complements of adpositions. This also means that Hornstein and Weinberg do not make the prediction that extraction *of* and *from* the complement of P should behave the same way. This makes their proposal in principle compatible with the data in 6.3.2, which led me to reject proposals based on the availability of escape hatches. An important difference between the present account and that of Hornstein and Weinberg is that under the present approach the ban on traces as the complement of P is connected to the phase impenetrability and to last- resort conditions. In Hornstein and Weinberg, 1981 by contrast, it derives from the filter in (71).

(71)   *[$_{NP}$ e   ]
              oblique

On the assumption that adpositions assign oblique case, (71) entails a ban on empty complements of adposition. Notice that the filter is more general than that: It rules out all empty oblique NPs; it thus also bans null pronouns as the complement of adpositions as well as traces and null pronouns in oblique object positions. These predictions seem far too strong. Even languages that clearly disallow adposition stranding like French allow null pronouns as the complement of P (Zribi-Hertz, 1984). Furthermore, many languages allow oblique NPs to $\overline{\text{A}}$-move in violation of (71). The approach adopted here is much more specific in that it derives a ban against traces as the complement of P and therefore

---

The adjacency condition is an attempt to give a syntactic implementation for the fact that there needs to be a closer relation between the verb and the preposition for pseudo passives than for P-stranding $\overline{\text{A}}$-movement.

The strict-adjacency condition between the verb and the preposition is too restrictive. (For relevant examples from English, see Truswell, 2009, ex. 81a-c, 84a,b, Mills, 2007, ex. 2a,c, Ziv and Sheintuch, 1981, 3, ex. 8a citing Bolinger, 1975, p. 59) and from Norwegian, see Åfarli, 1989, 105 ex. 16a,b, Lørdrup, 1991, 118, ex. 2, 120, ex. 10, 127, ex. 47, and Taraldsen, 1979, p. 49.)

What exactly the correct conditions are under which the pseudo passive is licit remains an open question. (See Mills, 2007; Newmeyer, 1998; Truswell, 2009; Ziv and Sheintuch, 1981 for some comments).)

does not encounter these problems.

The way stranding languages avoid violating (71) is through P-to-V incorporation. Such incorporation turns the erstwhile object of P into an object of V with concomitant structural rather than oblique case marking.[33] The reanalysis proposal faces substantial technical and empirical difficulties (Baltin and Postal, 1996; Couper-Kuhlen, 1979; Cruz and Saameno, 1996; Donaldson, 1982; Duarte, 1994; Inada, 1981; Levine, 1984; Maling and Zaenen, 1985a,b; Newmeyer, 1998; Salles, 1997; Siegel, 1983; Takami, 1988, 1992), some of which will be reviewed below.

Nevertheless, Hornstein and Weinberg make the important point that formulating a stranding parameter is by itself not a complete theory of preposition stranding. Even in a stranding language further constraints need to be imposed to regulate which adpositions can be stranded and under what conditions. The details of the reanalysis rule and the additional conditions on pseudo passives are intended to provide the relevant constraints.

The observation that a stranding parameter by itself does not provide a complete analysis of adposition stranding and that stranding needs to be constrained further is correct, of course. Given that stranding involves movement, a number of locality constraints on movement will be immediately relevant to adposition stranding. With this in mind, consider Hornstein and Weinberg's condition on reanalysis whereby PP must be an immediate daughter of VP for P-to-V reanalysis to be possible. In other words, a preposition can be stranded only when it is an immediate daughter of VP. This condition strongly resembles the family of constraints held responsible for condition-on-extraction-domain effects (see Cattell, 1976; Chomsky, 1981, 1986; Cinque, 1990b; Huang, 1982; Kayne, 1981; Truswell, 2011; Uriagereka, 1999, among others). Since the constraint holds generally, it should be stated as a constraint on movement rather than as a special condition on P-stranding.

The strategy suggested in the previous paragraph is to reduce constraints on adpositition stranding to general constraints on movement. We can illustrate the strategy further using the following contrast:

(72)   English   Hornstein and Weinberg, 1981, 59 ex. 19

      a.   Who did you speak to Harry about yesterday?

      b.   *Who did you speak to Harry yesterday about?

Hornstein and Weinberg, 1981 account for these data in terms of their reanalysis rule: The application of reanalysis bleeds rightward shift of the PP. However, there are alternative, more general accounts of this. Rightward shift in general

---

[33] The suggestion in subsection 7.3.5 above directly contradicts Hornstein and Weinberg, 1981, as I claimed there that P-to-V incorporation is allowed in particle constructions in non-stranding languages and disallowed in stranding languages.

272

is often claimed to create islands for extraction because of the freezing principle (Ross, 1967; Wexler and Culicover, 1980). An alternative approach might say that rightward shift is illicit unless the shifted constituent is focal.[34] We need not decide the matter, since extraction in (72b) is illicit either way. The derivation of (72b) either violates the freezing principle or the discourse conditions on rightward shift. Clearly, invoking special constraints on adposition stranding to account for (72) is neither necessary nor desirable.

Truswell, 2009 considers the issue at some length and concludes that adposition stranding in English is subject to regular conditions on extraction that also governs extraction from other categories. No assumptions specific to adposition stranding appear to be necessary.

The point can be strengthened if we consider cases of adposition stranding that are ruled out under Hornstein and Weinberg's formulation of the reanalysis rule but that are nevertheless licit and obey run-off-the-mill constraints on movement:

(73)   English
        Tell me which suspect Mary will send a picture of to inspector Smithers.

The example is problematic for Hornstein and Weinberg's analysis since the PP projected by the stranded preposition *of* is not directly dominated by VP. (73) is therefore incorrectly predicted to be ungrammatical.

I now turn to some of the more technical objections to Hornstein and Weinberg, 1981. To account for the significant differences between P-stranding under A- and under $\overline{\text{A}}$-movement, (74), Hornstein and Weinberg, 1981, p. 65 assume that there are general conditions which ensure that a reanalysed word in the case of A-movement is also a 'semantic word'. This condition does not apply to reanalysis in the case of $\overline{\text{A}}$-movement.

(74)   English
        a.   Who did Sam talk to Harry about?
        b.   *John was talked to Harry about.

---

[34] Kayne, 1994 gives examples like (ia–d)

(i)   English
        a.   the problem which I explained part of to John
        b.   ?*the problem which I explained to John part of
        c.   ?the problem which I explained to John only part of   Kayne, 1994, p. 74
        d.   the problem which I explained to John only the first part of

and uses them to argue that there is no freezing effect arising from rightward shift. The argument is consistent with the second of the two approaches mentioned in the text.

Again, there are difficulties in clarifying the notion of semantic word, but I set this issue aside here. The conditions under which pseudo-passivization is allowed remain elusive under any approach.

However, even if we ignore the issue of semantic words, there are still substantial problems for the reanalysis proposal. An important class of problems for the reanalysis account comes from the lack of positive evidence for it. Concretely, the problem is that the putative reanalyzed strings do not behave as words for processes like gapping (Åfarli, 1989; Baltin and Postal, 1996; Christensen, 1986; Koster, 1986; Lørdrup, 1991; Newmeyer, 1998, among others). It must be possible to reanalyze *look at* to derive example (75a). The question is then why the verb *[ᵥ look at]* cannot be gapped (75b).

(75) English

    a.   Who did you look at?

    b.   John looked at Mary and Bill ___*(at) Sue.

A second class of problems (noted already in Hornstein and Weinberg, 1981, 74 fn. 21 and attributed there to Henk van Riemsdijk and Edwin Williams) has to do with multiple P-stranding, (76). I indicate the output of the reanalysis rule by bracketing *[ᵥ ...]*. To derive (76a) the string *talk to Harry about* must be reanalysed as a verb. To derive (76b), *talk to* must be reanalyzed as a verb. So far, this is unproblematic.

(76) English

    a.   Who did you [ᵥ talk to Harry about] who?

    b.   Harry has been [ᵥ talked to] Harry about this issue.

    c.   Which problems has Harry been [ᵥ [ᵥ talked to Harry] about] which problems?

    d.   Who would you like to be [ᵥ [ᵥ sung to] you by] who?

    e.   Which person was the book [ᵥ given the book to] which person

However, to derive (76c), both reanalyses must be done simultaneously and, more worryingly, *Harry* must move out of the larger reanalysed verb *talk to Harry about*, an option that Hornstein and Weinberg must exclude for their account of (72b) to work.[35] The same problem of movement out of a reanalyzed constituent arises for a derivation of (76d) and even for the simple (76e), where only a single instance of reanalysis has applied.

Consider example (77) next. The example poses a very serious problem for Hornstein and Weinberg's analysis because it necessarily involves the applica-

---

[35] In this connection Hornstein and Weinberg, 1981, 74 fn. 21 discuss the question whether it is possible to have several competing reanalyses in the same phrase marker. They endorse the conclusion that this is possible but seem to miss the real point of the example, namely, that movement out of a reanalyzed string must be allowed.

tion of transformations within the reanalyzed verb: relativization in (77a) and (77b), passivization and relativization in (77c).

(77)   English
   a.   What did you talk to the guy [$_{CP}$ who [$_{IP}$ who was here yesterday]] about what?
   b.   What did you talk to the guy who Peter kissed who on the face about what?
   c.   What did you talk to the guy who who was kissed who on the face about what?

We are led to the conclusion that movement transformations feed reanalysis. However, if this conclusion is accepted, the proposal loses its restrictiveness, since it now allows examples like (74b). In sum, while reanalysis rules do not seem to be the right way to go, the discussion has served to highlight an important point: The internal structure of PPs does not provide a complete analysis of extraction from PP; locality theory is crucially involved as well.

Finally, let me briefly remark on the government-based approaches to P-stranding, going back to Kayne, 1984.[36] Kayne suggests a system where two parameters are involved. The first parameter concerns the question whether an adposition governs its complement structurally or only in the sense of sub-cateogrization. Together with the empty category principle, this parameter is responsible for the basic dichotomy between stranding and non-stranding languages. Since traces need to be properly governed, only those adpositions can be stranded that structurally govern their complement.[37] The second parameter

---

[36] Across a number of papers Kayne moves further and further from a reanalysis approach to one strictly in terms of government. The formulations used in the process are sometimes a bit misleading. Consider the following quote: "We shall accept the existence of a Reanalysis rule in English, while following Vergnaud's (1979) suggestion that [...] what is involved is not so much reanalysis qua constituent as reanalysis in terms of government [...]" Kayne, 1984, pp. 114–115. *Reanalysis in terms of government* boils down to co-superscripting under government for the formation of a *percolation projection* Kayne, 1984, p. 58.

[37] The conclusion holds only if Spec,PP is not available as an escape hatch in non-stranding languages. It turns out that Kayne seems to assume that there is a third parameter regulating the availability of an escape hatch at the edge of PP. The following quote suggests as much (Kayne, 1984, p. 116):

"Van Riemsdijk's [(1978a)] analysis of Dutch preposition stranding seems essentially correct, and does not involve reanalysis. (That is, the R-word 'escape hatch position' obviates the need for reanalysis; the ECP still imposes government [...].)"

Assuming this third parameter amounts to a substantial weakening of the overall system, which now allows two different analyses for adposition stranding. All comments

concerns the question whether adpositions assign structural accusative or structural oblique case to their complement. Pseudo passive is allowed only in those languages where adpositions assign structural accusative. The second parameter is a sub-parameter of the first in the sense that it is active, or maybe relevant, only in case prepositions govern structurally.

Unlike Hornstein and Weinberg's or the present theory and like Riemsdijk's, Kayne's theory contains a parameter regulating whether the complement of P may or may not be occupied by a trace. Unlike in Riemsdijk's or the present theory, the P-stranding parameter involves a change in the nature of the adposition rather than the geometry of the phrase structure. In this particular sense, Kayne's proposal is most closely related to a parameterization of the phasehood of P, which I have tried to eschew.

The central concept in Kayne's theory is the empty-category principle. This principle specifically regulates the distribution of phonologically empty elements in syntax. Such a principle is suspect in modern theories of syntax, which construe movement traces as copies and assume that phonological content is inserted post-syntactically. This makes all nodes phonologically empty and traces, qua copies, indistinguishable from their antecedents.[38] This alone would be sufficient grounds to search for an alternative.

Kayne explicitly makes the two following predictions about cross-linguistic variation:

(78) a. All languages that allow double-accusative constructions will also allow pseudo passives.
      b. All languages that have prepositional complementizers of the English (case marking) type also allow pseudo passives.

Both of these predictions have been discussed in the literature and should be rejected.[39]

In addition, Kayne's proposal encounters the problem, familiar from the discussion of Riemsdijk, 1978a above, that subextraction from PP is ruled out in non-stranding languages, since in languages where adpositions do not govern

---

about van Riemsdijk's analysis of adposition stranding under $\bar{A}$-movement carry over to this extension of Kayne's proposal. I have nothing further to say about it here.

[38] For further discussion of related issues, see Abels and Neeleman, 2012a.

[39] For discussion and counterexamples to (78a), see King and Roberge, 1990; Sugisaki, 2002; Sugisaki and Snyder, 2001a; Zhang, 1990).

For discussion and counterexamples to (78b), see King and Roberge, 1990, Mensching (2000, p. 162) on Tallerman, 1998. For further discussion of the situation in Celtic see also Borsley, 1986; Harlow, 1992; Hendrick, 1988; Rouveret, 1990, 1994. (78b) is claimed to find some support in data from the acquisition of English (Sugisaki, 2002; Sugisaki and Snyder, 2001b), but given the cross-linguistic record, there are reasons to be skeptical.

structurally, percolation projections do not, as it were, pass through PPs. As a consequence, all extraction from PP is blocked in non-stranding languages. Given the facts from section 6.3.2, the government-based proposal can be rejected also on empirical grounds.

This concludes my brief comparison of the current approach to adposition stranding with the three most well-known alternatives. The present approach makes sense of the distinction between extraction *of* and extraction *from* the complement of an adposition. It does this in a principled way using notions and assumptions that are independently justified. Once general locality effects are taken into account, the theory achieves a good coverage of the empirical data (Truswell, 2009).

The question driving this chapter can now be answered. I asked whether there are counterexamples to the generalization that adpositions can never be stranded by their complement. No clear counterexamples have been found. While the syntax of stranding languages is incompatible with an analysis of stranding in terms of null resumption, the analysis in terms of null DR-morphemes, (37) on page 245, encountered no serious obstacles. This allows me to hold on to the restrictive assumption that adpositional phrases are phases universally.

8 Phases

I opened this essay with the claim that if the concept of the phase is as fundamental in universal grammar as minimalist work would have it, then it should provide the grounds for a unifying formulation of different aspects of the theory of grammar and of syntactic theory in particular.

Much recent work has looked at phases from the perspective of the interfaces of syntax with other parts of the grammar or with external systems. The present essay has ignored that perspective completely. If phases are central, then their centrality should become apparent by investigating the internal workings of syntax alone.

Here I have applied this idea to movement theory. I investigated a number of logically unrelated properties of movement and claimed that there is an empirical generalization tying together successive-cyclic movement, pied-piping, secondary movement, partial movement, and stranding. The generalization that I am suggesting is that the phrases that can be pied-piped also provide intermediate landing sites for successive-cyclic movement; the phrases that provide intermediate landing sites for successive-cyclic movement also provide landing sites for secondary and partial movement; and the heads of those phrases can never be stranded by their complements.

None of these claims are uncontroversial, of course. I have entered into some of the controversies directly in the preceding chapters and set others aside more or less without comment. For example, I have assumed without comment that pied-piping exists despite the arguments in Cable, 2007, 2010a,b to the contrary. The main reason for this move is the following: Cable builds his analysis of pied-piping in part on Kratzer and Shimoyama, 2002. Though much work in semantics has discussed the merits and demerits of Kratzer and Shimoyama's system, the syntactic assumptions implicit in that work have not been investigated carefully. For a first step in that direction, the reader is referred to Martí and Abels, 2011.

If the generalizations and idealizations made here are accepted, then it turns out that there are some phrases for which the properties mentioned above cluster. This warrants singling them out as special: the phrases projected by these heads are the phases. These phrases play a central role in the phenomenology of movement. The list includes C, v, P, and D.

The theory developed in the preceding chapters ties the phenomenology together with two crucial assumptions about phases and their heads. First, phase heads but not other heads may bear probes whose content is not intrinsically related to the category or the interpretation of the phase head. Second, phases are subject to the phase impenetrability condition. All remaining assumptions are not tied specifically to phases and their heads. They should have support outside of the range of phenomena that cluster around phases. Although I have not systematically argued the point here, it seems to me that most of the assumptions made here are either natural conceptually, or well-supported empirically, or both.

What remains a stipulation is that phase heads are associated with the two properties just mentioned. I should add that most work on the interface properties of phases assumes in addition that they have a third property: phases (or some well-defined subpart) but not other constituents are transferred to the interface. Obviously, the reasons for this clustering must lie outside of syntax proper. I do not know what the reasons may be, but I hope that this essay has shed some new light on the syntactic properties of phases and that such clarification will ultimately lead to an understanding of why the properties of phases cluster in the way that they do.

9 Bibliography

Abels, Klaus (2000). *Move?* Ms. University of Connecticut.

– (2002). "On an Alleged Argument for the Proper Binding Condition". In: *Proceedings of HUMIT 2001. MIT Working Papers in Linguistics 43*. Ed. by Tania R. Ionin, Heejeong Ko, and Andrew Nevins. Cambridge, MA., pp. 1–16.

– (2003a). "A note on clitics and P-stranding". In: *Proceedings of FASL 11*. Ann Arbor: Michigan Slavic Publishers.

– (2003b). "*[P clitic]! - Why?" In: *Investigations into Formal Slavic Linguistics: Contributions of the Fourth European Conference on Formal Description of Slavic Languages – FDSL IV*. Ed. by Peter Kosta et al. Vol. 2. Potsdam, Germany: Peter Lang, pp. 443–460.

– (2003c). "Successive Cyclicity, Anti-locality, and Adposition Stranding". Ph.D dissertation. University of Connecticut.

– (2007). "Towards a Restrictive Theory of (Remnant) Movement". In: *Linguistic Variation Yearbook* 7, pp. 53–120.

– (2009). "Some implications of improper movement for Cartography". In: *Alternatives to Cartography*. Ed. by Jeroen van Craenenbroeck. Berlin & New York: De Gruyter, pp. 325–359.

– (2011). *Don't repair that island! It ain't broke.* Talk presented at Islands in Contemporary Linguistic Theory.

– (2012). "The Italian Left Periphery: A view from locality". In: *Linguistic Inquiry* 43.2, pp. 229–254.

– (in preparation). "A reply to Hornstein: 'Three grades of Grammatical Involvement'". In: *Mind and Language*.

– (in press). "Word Order". In: *Syntax - An international handbook of contemporary research*. Ed. by Artemis Alexiadou and Tibor Kiss. 2nd ed. Berlin: de Gruyter. Chap. 40.

Abels, Klaus and Nélia Alexandre (in progress). *Spelled out trace or resumptive pronoun? – The case of non-agreeing 'el' in Cape Verdian Creole.* ms. UCL and Universidade da Lisboa.

Abels, Klaus and Kristine Bentzen (2009). "A note on the punctuated nature of movement paths". In: *Catalan Journal of Linguistics* 8, pp. 19–40.

– (2010). "A note on the punctuated nature of movement paths". In: *Local Modelling of Non-Local Dependencies in Syntax*. Ed. by Artemis Alexiadou, Tibor Kiss, and Gereon Müller. Linguistische Arbeiten. Tübingen: Max Niemeyer Verlag.

Abels, Klaus and Luisa Martí (2010). "A unified approach to split scope". In: *Natural Language Semantics* 18.4, pp. 435–470.

Abels, Klaus and Peter Muriungi (May 2008). "The focus particle in Kîîtharaka: Syntax and Semantics". In: *Lingua* 118.5, pp. 687–731.

Abels, Klaus and Ad Neeleman (Mar. 2012a). *e.* Talk presented at the Workshop on empty categories, GLOW 35.

– (2012b). "Linear asymmetries and the LCA". In: *Syntax* 15.1, pp. 25–74.

Abels, Klaus, Ezekiel Panitz, and George Starling (in progress). *Resumptives and sluicing in Welsh and Hebrew*. ms. UCL.

Aboh, Enoch Oladé (2006). "When verbal predicates go fronting". In: *ZAS Papers in Linguistics* 46, pp. 21–48.

Abraham, Werner (1995). *Deutsche Syntax im Sprachvergleich. Grundlegung einer typologischen Syntax des Deutschen*. Studien zur deutschen Grammatik 41. Tübingen: Gunter Narr Verlag.

Adams, Marianne (1984). "Multiple Interrogation in Italian". In: *The Linguistic Review* 4.1, pp. 1–27.

Adger, David (2003). *Core Syntax: A Minimalist Approach*. Oxford: Oxford University Press.

– (2011). *A syntax of substance*. Ms. Queen Mary University of London.

Adger, David and Gillian Ramchand (2005). "Merge and Move: *Wh*-Dependencies Revisited". In: *Linguistic Inquiry* 36.2, pp. 161–194.

Aelbrecht, Lobke (2008). *Dutch modal complement ellipsis and English VPE*. Talk presented at CGSW 23, Edinburgh.

– (July 2009). "You have the right to remain silent". PhD thesis. Brussels: Katholieke Universiteit Brussel.

– (2010). *The Syntactic Licensing of Ellipsis*. Ed. by Werner Abraham and Elly van Gelderen. Vol. 149. LA. Amsterdam and Philadelphia: John Benjamins Publishing Company.

Åfarli, Tor A. (1985). "Norwegian Verb Particle Constructions as Causative Constructions". In: *Nordic Journal of Linguistics* 8, pp. 75–98.

– (1989). "Passive in Norwegian and in English". In: *Linguistic Inquiry* 20.1, pp. 101–107.

Aissen, Judith (1996). "Pied-Piping, Abstract Agreement, and Functional Projections in Tzotzil". In: *Natural Language and Linguistic Theory* 14, pp. 447–491.

Alexandre, Nélia (2009). "Wh-Constructions in Cape Verdean Creole: extensions of the theory of movement". PhD thesis. Lisbon: Universidade de Lisboa.

Alexandre, Nélia and Tjerk Hagemeijer (2002). "Pronomes Resumptivos e Abandono de Preposi cao nos Crioulos Atlanticos de Base Portuguesa". In: *Working Papers of the Portuguese Linguistics Society*.

Algeo, John (2006). *British or American English? A handook of word and grammar patterns*. Ed. by Merja Kytö. Studies in English Language. Cambridge: Cambridge University Press.

Aoun, Joseph and Yen-Hui Audrey Li (1993). "Wh-elements in situ: Syntax or LF?" In: *Linguistic Inquiry* 24.2, pp. 199–238.

Arregi, Karlos (2002). "Focus on Basque Movements". PhD thesis. Cambridge, MA: MIT.

– (2003). "Clausal Pied-Piping". In: *Natural Language Semantics* 11 (2), pp. 115–143.

Baker, Carl Leroy (1984). "Two observations on British English *do*". In: *Linguistic Inquiry* 15.1, pp. 155–157.

Baker, Mark (1988). *Incorporation*. Chicago, Illinois: University of Chicago Press.

Baltin, Mark (2007). *Deletion Versus Pro-Forms: A False Dichotomy?* Ms. NYU.

– (2010). *Deletion Versus Pro-Forms: An overly simple dichotomy*. Ms. NYU.

Baltin, Mark and Chris Collins, eds. (2001). *The Handbook of Contemporary Syntactic Theory*. Oxford: Blackwell.

Baltin, Mark and Paul Postal (1996). "More on Reanalysis Hypotheses". In: *Linguistic Inquiry* 27.1, pp. 127–45.

Barker, Chris and Geoffrey K. Pullum (1990). "A theory of command relations". In: *Linguistics and Philosophy* 15, pp. 1–34.

Barss, Andrew (1986). "Chains and anaphoric dependence: On reconstruction and its implications". Doctoral dissertation. MIT.

Bašić, Monika (2004). "Nominal Subextractions and the Structure of NPs in Serbian and English". MA thesis. Tromsø, Norway: Universitetet i Tromsø.

Bayer, Josef (1984). "COMP in Bavarian syntax". In: *The Linguistic Review* 3, pp. 209–274.

– (1990). "Interpretive Islands". In: *Scrambling and Barriers*. Ed. by Günther Grewendorf and Wolfgang Sternefeld. Amsterdam: Benjamins, pp. 341–421.

– (1999). "Final complementizers in hybrid languages". In: *Linguistics* 35, pp. 233–271.

Bayer, Josef, Jana Häussler, and Martin Salzmann (2011). That-*trace effects without traces. An experimental investigation*. Paper presented at GGS 2011.

Bayer, Josef and Martin Salzmann (2010). That-*trace effects and resumption as the result of Improper Movement*. Ms., University of Konstanz.

Bech, Gunnar (1955). *Studien über das detusche verbum infinitum, 1. Band*. Vol. 35. Historisk-filologiske Meddelelser 2. København: Det Kongelige Danske Videnskabernes Selskab.

– (1957). *Studien über das detusche verbum infinitum, 2. Band*. Vol. 36. Historisk-filologiske Meddelelser 6. København: Det Kongelige Danske Videnskabernes Selskab.

Beck, Sigrid (1996). "Quantified structures as barriers for LF movement". In: *Natural Language Semantics* 4, pp. 1–56.

Beck, Sigrid and Shin-Sook Kim (2006). "Intervention Effects in Alternative Questions". In: *Journal of Comparative Germanic Linguistics* 9.3, pp. 165–208.

Beck, Sigrid, Toshiko Oda, and Koji Sugisaki (2002). "Comparative Constructions in Japanese vs. English". In: *NELS 33*. Cambridge, MA.

Belletti, Adriana (1988). "The Case of unaccusatives". In: *Linguistic Inquiry* 19, pp. 1–34.

Benincà, Paola and Nicola Munaro, eds. (2010). *Mapping the Left Periphery*. Vol. 5. The Cartography of Syntactic Structures. Oxford University Press.

Bennett, Paul A. (1980). "English passives: a study in syntactic change and Relational Grammar". In: *Lingua* 51, pp. 101–114.

Bennis, Hans, Norbert Corver, and Marcel den Dikken (1998). "Predication in Nominal Phrases". In: *The Journal of Comparative Germanic Linguistics* 1.2, pp. 85–117.

Bennis, Hans and Teun Hoekstra (1984). "Gaps and Parasitic Gaps". In: *The Linguistic Review* 4.1, pp. 29–87.

Bentzen, Kristine (2007). "Order and Structure in Embedded Clauses in Northern Norwegian". PhD thesis. University of Tromsø, Norway.

Bentzen, Kristine, Jason Merchant, and Peter Svenonius (May 2012). *Deep properties of surface pronouns: Pronominal predicate anaphors in Germanic*. Talk presented at CGSW 27.

Bergvall, Victoria Lee (1987). "Focus in Kikuyu and Universal Grammar". PhD thesis. Cambridge, MA: Harvard University.

Besten, Hans den (1978). "On the Presence and Absence of Wh-Elements in Dutch Comparatives". In: *Linguistic Inquiry* 9, pp. 641–671.

– (1981). "Marking Wh-Movement in Afrikaans". In: *Generative Studies in Creole Languages*. Ed. by Pieter Muysken. Dordrecht: Foris, pp. 141–179.

– (1985). "The ergative hypothesis and free word order in Dutch and German". In: *Studies in German Grammar*. Ed. by Jindra Toman. Dordrecht: Foris, pp. 23–65.

Besten, Hans den and Gert Webelhuth (1990). "Stranding". In: *Scrambling and Barriers*. Ed. by Günther Grewendorf and Wolfgang Sternefeld. Amsterdam and Philadelphia: Academic Press, pp. 77–92.

Bianchi, Valentina (2004). "Resumptive Relatives and LF Chains". In: *The Structure of CP and IP*. Ed. by Luigi Rizzi. Oxford: Oxford University Press, pp. 76–114.

Bianchi, Valentina and Roberto Zamparelli (2004). "Edge Coordinations: Focus and Conjunction Reduction". In: *Peripheries: Syntactic Edges and their Effects*. Ed. by David Adger, Cécile de Cat, and George Tsoulas. Dordrecht, The Netherlands: Kluwer Academic Publishers, pp. 313–327.

Birmingham, J.C. (1970). "The Papiamentu language of Cura cao". Ph.D. thesis.
Biskup, Petr (2010). "The Phase Model and Adverbials". PhD thesis. Leipzig: Universität Leipzig.
Bobaljik, Jonathan D (1999). "Adverbs: the hierarchy paradox". In: *GLOT International* 4.9, pp. 27–28.
Boeckx, Cedric (2001). "Mechanisms of Chain Formation". Doctoral Dissertation. Storrs: University of Connecticut.
– (2002). "Agree or Attract? A Relativized Minimality solution to a Proper Binding Condition puzzle". In: *Theoretical Approaches to Universals*. Ed. by Artemis Alexiadou. Amsterdam: John Benjamins, pp. 41–64.
– (2008). *Understanding Minimalist Syntax: Lessons from Locality in Long-Distance Dependencies*. Vol. 9. Generative Syntax. Blackwell Publishing.
Boeckx, Cedric and Kleanthes Kostas Grohmann (2007). "Remark: Putting Phases in Perspective". In: *Syntax* 10.2, pp. 204–222.
Boeckx, Cedric and Youngmi Jeong (2004). "The Fine Structure of Intervention in Syntax". In: *Issues in Current Linguistic Theory: A festschrift for Hong Bae Lee*. Ed. by Chungja Kwon and Wonbin Lee. Seoul: Kyungjin, pp. 83–116.
Bolinger, Dwight (1975). "On the passive in English". In: *LACUS* 1, pp. 57–80.
Borsley, Robert D (1986). "Prepositional complementizers in Welsh". In: *Journal of Linguistics* 22, pp. 67–84.
Borsley, Robert D and Ewa Jaworska (1988). "A note on prepositions and Case marking in Polish". In: *Linguistic Inquiry* 19, pp. 685–691.
Bošković, Željko (1994). "D-structure, theta-criterion, and movement into theta-positions". In: *Linguistic Analysis* 24, pp. 247–286.
– (1995). "Participle Movement and Second Position Cliticization in Serbo-Croatian". In: *Lingua* 96, pp. 245–266.
– (1997a). "Coordination, object shift and V-movement". In: *Linguistic Inquiry* 28.2, pp. 357–365.
– (1997b). "Superiority Effects with Multiple Wh-fronting in Serbo-Croatian". In: *Lingua* 102, pp. 1–29.
– (1997c). *The syntax of nonfinite complementation: An economy approach*. Cambridge, MA: MIT Press.
– (1998a). "LF Movement and the Minimalist Program". In: *Proceedings of the North East Linguistic Society*. Ed. by Pius N. Tamanji and Kiyomi Kusumoto. University of Toronto: Graduate Linguistic Student Association, pp. 43–58.
– (1998b). "Multiple WH-Fronting and Economy of Derivation". In: *Proceedings of the sixteenth West Coast Conference on Formal Linguistics*. Ed. by Emily Curtis, James Lyle, and Gabriel Webster. Stanford, CA: CSLI, pp. 49–63.

284

Bošković, Željko (1999). "On Multiple Feature Checking: Multiple *Wh*-Fronting and Multiple Head Movement". In: *Working Minimalism*. Ed. by Samuel David Epstein and Norbert Hornstein. MIT Press, pp. 159–188.

– (2000). "Sometimes in SpecCP, sometimes in-situ". In: *Step by step: Essays on minimalism in honor of Howard Lasnik*. Ed. by Roger Martin, David Michaels, and Juan Uriagereka. Cambridge, MA: MIT Press.

– (2001). *On the Nature of the Syntax-Phonology Interface: Cliticization in South Slavic*. London: Elsevier North-Holland.

– (2002a). "A-movement and the EPP". In: *Syntax* 5.3, pp. 167–218.

– (2002b). "Expletives don't move". In: *Proceedings of North East Linguistic Society 32*. Ed. by Masako Hirotani. Vol. 1, pp. 21–40.

– (2003). "On left branch extraction". In: *Proceedings of the 4th European Conference on Formal Description of Slavic Languages*. Ed. by Peter Kosta et al. Frankfurt am Main: Peter Lang, pp. 543–577.

– (2004). "Be careful where you float your quantifiers". In: *Natural Language and Linguistic Theory* 22, pp. 681–742.

– (2007). "On the locality and motivation of Move and Agree: An even more minimal theory". In: *Linguistic Inquiry* 38, pp. 589–644.

– (2008). "On Successive Cyclic Movement and the Freezing Effect of Feature Checking". In: *Sounds of Silence: Empty Elements in Syntax and Phonology*. Ed. by Jeremy Hartman, V Hegedus, and Henk van Riemsdijk. Amsterdam: Elsevier North-Holland, pp. 195–233.

Bouma, Gosse, Robert Molouf, and Ivan A. Sag (2001). "Satisfying Constraints on Extraction and Adjunction". In: *Natural Language and Linguistic Theory* 19.1, pp. 1–65.

Bowers, John (1993). "The syntax of predication". In: *Linguistic Inquiry* 24, pp. 591–656.

Bresnan, Joan W and Jonni M. Kanerva (1992). "The thematic hierarchy and locative inversion in UG". In: *Syntax and Semantics 26: Syntax and Lexicon*. Ed. by Eric Wehrli and Timothy Stowell. New York: Academic Press, pp. 53–101.

Broadwell, George Aaron (2001). "Optimal Order and Pied-Piping in San Dionico Zapotec". In: *Formal and Empirical Issues in Optimality Theoretic Syntax*. Ed. by Peter Sells. Studies in Constraint-Based Lexicalism. Stanford, CA: CSLI Publications, pp. 197–223.

– (2005). *Pied-piping and optimal order in Kiche (K'iche')*. Ms. SUNY Albany.

Brody, Michael (1997). "Towards Perfect Chains". In: *Elements of Grammar, a Handbook of Syntax*. Ed. by Liliane Haegeman. Kluwer.

– (2000). "Mirror Theory. Syntactic Representation in Perfect Syntax". In: *Linguistic Inquiry* 31.1, pp. 29–57.

Bruening, Benjamin (2001). "Syntax at the Edge: Cross-Clausal Phenomena and The Syntax of Passamaquoddy". Doctoral dissertation. MIT.

– (2007). "Wh-in-situ does not Correlate with *Wh*-Indefinites or Question Particles". In: *Linguistic Inquiry* 38.1.

Bury, Dirk (2003). "Phrase Structure and Derived Heads". PhD thesis. London: University College London.

Cable, Seth (2007). "The Grammar of Q: Q-Particles and the Nature of Wh-Fronting, as Revealed by the Wh-Questions of Tlingit". PhD thesis. Cambridge, Massachusetts: Massachusetts Institute of Technology.

– (2010a). "Against the Existence of Pied-Piping: Evidence from Tlingit". In: *Linguistic Inquiry* 41.4, pp. 563–594.

– (2010b). *The Grammar of Q: Q-Particles, Wh-Movement and Pied-Piping*. Oxford University Press.

Caha, Pavel (2009). "The nanosyntax of case". PhD thesis. Tromsø, Norway: Universitetet i Tromsø.

– (2010). *Case syncretism and the ban on P-stranding*. Ms. Universitet i Tromsø.

Calabrese, Andrea (1984). "Multiple Questions and Focus in Italian". In: *Sentential Complementation*. Ed. by Wim de Geest and Yvan Putseys. Dordrecht: Foris, pp. 67–74.

Cardinaletti, Anna and Michal Starke (1999). "The Typology of Structural Deficiency". In: *Clitics in the Languages of Europe*. Ed. by Henk van Riemsdijk. Berlin and New York: Mouton de Gruyter, pp. 145–234.

Carstens, Vicki (2003). "Rethinking Complementizer Agreement: Agree with a Case-checked Goal". In: *Linguistic Inquiry* 34.3, pp. 393–412.

Castillo, Juan Carlos, John Edward Drury, and Kleanthes Kostas Grohmann (1999). "Castillo, Juan Carlos, John E. Drury & Merge over Move and the Extended Projection Principle". In: *University of Maryland Working Papers in Linguistics* 8, pp. 63–103.

– (2009). "Merge over Move and the Extended Projection Principle: MOM and the EPP revisited". In: *Iberia* 1.1, pp. 53–114.

Cattell, Ray (1976). "Constraints on movement rules". In: *Language* 52, pp. 18–50.

– (1979). "On extractability from quasi-NPs". In: *Linguistic Inquiry* 10.1, pp. 168–172.

Ćavar, Damir and Chris Wilder (1994). "Clitic third in Croatian". In: *Eurotyp Working Papers, Grammatical Models Selection* 6, pp. 19–61.

Cheng, Lisa Lai-Shen and Johan Rooryck (2000). "Licensing *Wh*-in-situ". In: *Syntax* 3.1, pp. 1–19.

Chierchia, Gennaro (1993). "Questions with quantifiers". In: *Natural Language Semantics* 1.3, pp. 181–234.

Chomsky, Noam (1977). *Essays on form and interpretation*. New York: Elsevier North-Holland, Inc.

– (1981). *Lectures on government and binding*. Dordrecht: Foris.

Chomsky, Noam (1986). *Barriers*. Vol. 13. Linguistic Inquiry Monograph. Cambridge, MA: MIT Press.

– (1993). "A minimalist program for linguistic theory". In: *The view from Building 20*. Ed. by Kenneth Hale and Samuel J. Keyser. Cambridge, MA: MIT Press, pp. 1–52.

– (1995a). "Bare phrase structure". In: *Government and binding theory and the minimalist program*. Ed. by Gert Webelhuth. Oxford: Basil Blackwell, pp. 383–439.

– (1995b). "Categories and transformations". In: *The Minimalist Program*. Cambridge, MA: MIT Press. Chap. 4, pp. 219–394.

– (1995c). *The minimalist program*. Cambridge, MA: MIT Press.

– (2000). "Minimalist Inquiries: The Framework". In: *Step by Step: Essays on minimalism in honor of Howard Lasnik*. Ed. by Roger Martin, David Michaels, and Juan Uriagereka. Cambridge, MA: MIT Press, pp. 89–155.

– (2001). "Derivation by Phase". In: *Ken Hale: a Life in Language*. Ed. by Michael Kenstowicz. Cambridge, MA.: MIT Press, pp. 1–52.

– (2004). "Beyond Explanatory Adequacy". In: *Structures and beyond*. Ed. by Adriana Belletti. Vol. 3. Oxford studies in comparative syntax The cartography of syntactic structures. Oxford and New York: Oxford University Press, pp. 104–131.

– (2008). "On Phases". In: *Foundational issues in linguistic theory: Essays in Honor of Jean-Roger Vergnaud*. Ed. by Robert Freidin, Carlos Otero, and Maria-Luisa Zubizarreta. Cambridge, MA: MIT Press, pp. 133–166.

Chomsky, Noam and Howard Lasnik (1993). "The theory of principles and parameters". In: *Syntax: An international handbook of contemporary research*. Ed. by Joachim Jacobs et al. Vol. 1. Berlin: Walter de Gruyter, pp. 506–569.

Christensen, Kirsti Koch (1986). "Complex Passives, Reanalysis, and Word Formation". In: *Nordic Journal of Linguistics* 9, pp. 135–162.

Cinque, Guglielmo (1978). "Towards a unified treatment of island constraints". In: *Proceedings of the Twelfth International Congress of Linguists. Innsbrucker Beiträge zur Sprachwissenschaft*. Ed. by W. U. Dressler and W. Meid, pp. 344–348.

– (1990a). *Types of A'-dependencies*. Cambridge, MA: MIT Press.

– (1990b). *Types of A'-dependencies*. Cambridge, Massachusetts: MIT Press, p. 223.

– (1999). *Adverbs and Functional Heads - A Cross-Linguistic Perspective*. New York and Oxford: Oxford University Press.

– (2004). "Issues in adverbial syntax". In: *Lingua* 114.6, pp. 683–710.

– (2005). "Deriving Greenberg's Universal 20 and its Exceptions". In: *Linguistic Inquiry* 36 (3), pp. 315–332.

Cinque, Guglielmo and Luigi Rizzi, eds. (2010). *Mapping Spatial PPs*. Vol. 6. The cartography of syntactic structures. Oxford and New York: Oxford University Press.

Cole, Peter and Gabriella Hermon (1998). "The typology of wh-movement. Wh-questions in Malay". In: *Syntax* 1.3, pp. 221–258.

Collins, Chris (2005a). "A Smuggling Approach to Raising in English". In: *Linguistic Inquiry* 36.2, pp. 289–298.

– (2005b). "A smuggling approach to the passive in English". In: *Syntax* 8.2, pp. 81–120.

Comrie, Bernard and Edward Keenan (1979). "Noun Phrase Accessibility Revisited". In: *Language* 55.3, pp. 649–664.

Conway, Laura (1996). *NPs in disguise*.

Coon, Jessica (2009). "Interrogative Possessors and the Problem with Pied-Piping in Chol". In: *Linguistic Inquiry* 40.1, pp. 165–175.

Corver, Norbert (1990). "The Syntax of Left Branch Extractions". PhD thesis.

– (1991). "The internal syntax and movement behavior of the Dutch 'wat voor'-construction". In: *Linguistische Berichte* 133, pp. 190–228.

– (2006). "Comparative deletion and subdeletion". In: *The Blackwell Companion to Syntax*. Ed. by Martin Everaert and Henk van Riemsdijk. Vol. I. Malden, MA: Blackwell Publishers. Chap. 15, pp. 582–637.

Couper-Kuhlen, Elizabeth (1979). *The prepositional passive in English: A semantic-syntactic analysis, with a lexicon of prepositional verbs*. Tübingen: Max Niemeyer Verlag.

Craenenbroeck, Jeroen van (2006). "Transitivity failures in the left periphery and foot-driven movement operations". In: *Linguistics in the Netherlands 2006*. Ed. by Jeroen van de Weijer and Bettelou Los. Vol. 23. John Benjamins, pp. 52–64.

– (2010). "Invisible Last Resort: A note on clefts as the underlying source for sluicing". In: *Lingua* 120.7, pp. 1714–1726.

Craenenbroeck, Jeroen van and Marcel den Dikken (2006). "Ellipsis and EPP Repair". In: *Linguistic Inquiry* 37.4, pp. 653–664.

Cresti, Diana (1995). "Extraction and reconstruction". In: *Natural Language Semantics* 3.1, pp. 79–122.

Cruz, Juan de la and Emilio Saameno (1996). "The Middle English Prepositional Passive: Analogy and GB". In: *Neuphilologische Mitteilungen* 97.2, pp. 169–186.

Culicover, Peter (2001). "Parasitic gaps: A History". In: *Parasitic gaps*. Ed. by Peter Culicover and Paul Postal. Cambridge, MA: MIT Press, pp. 3–68.

Culicover, Peter and Paul Postal, eds. (2001). *Parasitic gaps*. Cambridge, MA: MIT Press.

Cysouw, Michael (2004). *Interrogative words: an exercise in lexical typology*. Presentation at "Bantu grammar: description and theory workshop".

Davies, William D. and Stanley Dubinsky (2004). *The Grammar of Raising and Control*. Blackwell.

Davis, A (1984). "Behind the for-to filter: for-to infinitives in Belfast English and the theory of government". In: *Scheffield Working Papers in Linguistics* 1, pp. 56–71.

Dayal, Veneeta (2002). "Single-Pair versus Multiple-Pair Answers: *Wh*-in-situ and scope". In: *Linguistic Inquiry* 33.3, pp. 512–520.

– (2006). "Multiple-*Wh*-Questions". In: *The Blackwell Companion to Syntax*. Ed. by Martin Everaert and Henk van Riemsdijk. Vol. 3. Malden, MA: Blackwell Publishers. Chap. 44, pp. 275–326.

Dekydtspotter, Laurent (1992). "The syntax of predicate clefts". In: *Proceedings of the North Eastern Linguistic Society*. Vol. 22. Amherst: GLSA, University of Massachusetts, pp. 119–133.

den Dikken, Marcel (1992). "Particles". Ph.D. Thesis.

– (2006a). *A reappraisal of* vP *being phasal – a reply to Legate*. Ms. CUNY.

– (2006b). *Relators and Linkers*. MIT Press.

– (2009a). "Arguments for successive-cyclic movement through SpecCP : A critical review". In: *Linguistic Variation Yearbook* 9, pp. 89–126.

– (2009b). *On the nature and distribution of successive cyclicity*. Ms. CUNY.

Diesing, Molly (1992). *Indefinites*. Cambridge, MA.: MIT Press.

Dijkhoff, Marta B. (1983). "Movement Rules and the Resumptive Pronoun Strategy in Papiamentu". Unpublished M.A. thesis. Rijksuniversiteit Groningen.

Donaldson, Anne (1982). "On Restructuring and Preposition Stranding". In: *Cahiers linguistiques d'Ottawa* 10, pp. 81–100.

Doron, Edit (1982). "On the syntax and semantics of resumptive pronouns". In: *Texas Linguistic Forum 19*. Ed. by Robert Bley-Vroman, pp. 1–48.

– (1999). "V-Movement and VP Ellipsis". In: *Fragments : Studies in Ellipsis and Gapping*. Ed. by Shalom Lappin and Elabbas Benmamoun. New York and Oxford: Oxford University Press, pp. 124–140.

Drury, John Edward (2005). "Alternative Directions for minimalist inquiry: Expanding and contracting phases of derivation". PhD thesis. College Park, MD: University of Maryland.

Duarte, Yara (1994). "Constructions with Unaccompanied Prepositions in English". In: *Revista de Documentacao de Estudos em Linguistica Teorica e Aplicada* 10.2, pp. 409–420.

Embick, David and Rolf Noyer (2001). "Movement Operations after Syntax". In: *Linguistic Inquiry* 32.4, pp. 555–595.

– (2007). "Distributed Morphology and the syntax/morphology inerface". In: *The Oxford handbook of linguistic interfaces*. Ed. by Gillian Ramchand and Charles Reiss. Oxford: Oxford University Press, pp. 289–324.

Engdahl, Elisabet (1980). "The Syntax and Semantics of Questions in Swedish". PhD thesis. Amherst, MA: University of Massachusetts.

– (1986). *Constituent Questions -The Syntax and Semantics of Questions with Special Reference to Swedish*. Dordrecht et al.: Reidel.

Epstein, Samuel David and T. Daniel Seely (1999). *SPEC-ifying the GF "subject"; eliminating A-Chains and the EPP within a Derivational Model*.

Epstein, Samuel David et al. (1998). *A derivational approach to syntactic relations*. Oxford: Oxford University Press.

Ernst, Thomas (2009). "Speaker-oriented adverbs". In: *Natural Language and Linguistic Theory* 27.3, pp. 497–544.

Everaert, Martin and Henk van Riemsdijk, eds. (2006). *The Blackwell Companion to Syntax*. Malden, MA: Blackwell Publishers.

Fanselow, Gisbert (1983). "Zu einigen Problemen von Kasus, Rektion und Bindung in der deutschen Syntax". M.A. Thesis. Universität Konstanz.

– (1991). "Minimale Syntax". In: *Groninger Arbeiten zu germanistischen Linguistik* 32.

– (2001). "Features, θ-Roles, and Free Constituent Order". In: *Linguistic Inquiry* 32.3, pp. 405–437.

– (2004). "The MLC and derivational economy". In: *Minimality Effects in Syntax*. Ed. by Arthur Stepanov, Gisbert Fanselow, and Ralf Vogel. Vol. 70. Studies in Generative Grammar. deGruyter, pp. 73–124.

– (2006). "Partial *wh*-movement". In: *The Blackwell Companion to Syntax*. Ed. by Martin Everaert and Henk van Riemsdijk. Vol. 3. Malden, MA: Blackwell Publishers. Chap. 47, pp. 437–492.

Featherston, Sam (2005). "*that*-trace in German". In: *Lingua* 115.9, pp. 1277–1302.

Felix, Sascha (1983). "Parasitic Gaps in German". In: *Groninger Arbeiten zur Germanistischen Linguistik* 22, pp. 1–46.

– (1985). "Parasitic Gaps in German". In: *Erklärende Syntax des Deutschen*. Ed. by Werner Abraham. Tübingen: Gunter Narr Verlag, pp. 173–200.

Felser, Claudia (2001). "*Wh*-expletives and secondary predication: German partial *wh*-movement reconsidered". In: *Journal of Germanic Linguistics* 13, pp. 5–38.

Fitzpatrick, Justin (2002). "On Minimalist Approaches to the Locality of Movement". In: *Linguistic Inquiry* 33.2, pp. 443–464.

Fleischer, Jürg (2002a). *Die Syntax von Pronominaladverbien in den Dialekten des Deutschen*. ZDL-Beiheft 123. Wiesbaden: Franz Steiner Verlag.

– (2002b). "Preposition Stranding in German Dialects". In: *Syntactic Microvariation*. Ed. by Sjef Barbiers, Leonie Cornips, and Susanne van der Kleij. Amsterdam: Meertens Institute.

Fox, Danny (2000). *Economy and Semantic Representation*. Cambridge, MA: MIT Press and MITWPL.

Frampton, John (1999). "The Fine Structure of Wh-Movement and the Proper Formulation of the ECP". In: *The Linguistic Review* 16.1, 43–61w.

Frampton, John and Sam Gutmann (2000). *Agreement is feature sharing*. Ms. Northeastern University.

Franks, Steven (1998). "Clitics in Slavic". In: *Comparative Slavic Morphosyntax Workshop*. Bloomington, ID.

Franks, Steven and Tracy Holloway King (2000). *A handbook of Slavic clitics*. New York: Oxford University Press.

Franks, Steven and Ljiljana Progovac (1994). "On the placement of Serbo-Croatian clitics". In: *Proceedings of the 9th Biennial Conference on Balkan and South Slavic Linguistics, Literature, and Folklore (=Indiana Linguistic Studies 7)*. Bloomington: Indiana University Linguistic Club, pp. 69–78.

Fukaya, Teruhiko (2007). "Sluicing and Stripping in Japanese and Some Implications". PhD thesis. Los Angeles, CA: University of Southern California.

Fukui, Naoki (1997). "Attract and the A-over-A Principle". In: *UCI working papers in Linguistics (3)*. Ed. by Chen Sheng Liu and Kazue Takeda. Irvine, CA: Irvine Linguistics Students Association, pp. 51–67.

Gallmann, Peter (1997). *Zur Morphosyntax und Lexik der w-Wörter*. Arbeitspapiere des Sonderforschungsbereichs 340 107. Tübingen: Universität Tübingen.

Gärtner, Hans Martin (2002). *Generalized Transformations and Beyond: Reflections on Minimalist Syntax*. Berlin: Akademie Verlag.

Gehrke, Berit and Nino Grillo (2008). "How to become passive". In: *Explorations of Phase Theory: Features, Arguments, and Interpretation at the Interface*. Ed. by Kleanthes Kostas Grohmann. Berlin: de Gruyter.

Georgopoulos, Carol (1991). *Syntactic variables: Resumptive pronouns and binding in Palauan*. Dordrecht: Kluwer.

Giorgi, A and Giuseppe Longobardi (1991). *The Syntax of Noun Phrases*. Cambridge: Cambridge University Press.

Goldberg, Lotus Madelyn (2005). "Verb-Stranding VP Ellipsis: A Cross-Linguistic Study". PhD thesis. Montreal: McGill University.

Grevisse, M (1964). *Le bon usage*. 8th ed. Gembloux: J. Duculout.

Grewendorf, Günther (1990). *Ergativity in German*. Vol. 35. Studies in Generative Grammar. Dordrecht: Foris.

– (2003). "Improper Remnant Movement". In: *Gengo Kenkyu* 123, pp. 47–94.

Grewendorf, Günther and Joost Kremers (2009). "Phases and Cycles. Some Problems with Phase Theory". In: *The Linguistic Review* 26.4, pp. 385–430.

Grillo, Nino (2009). "Generalized Minimality: Feature impoverishment and comprehension deficits in agrammatism". In: *Lingua* 119, pp. 1426–1443.

Grohmann, Kleanthes Kostas (2000). "Prolific Peripheries: A Radical View from the Left". Doctoral Dissertation. University of Maryland, College Park.

– (2003). *Prolific Domains : On the Anti-Locality of Movement Dependencies*. Vol. 66. Linguistik Aktuell. Amsterdam & Philadelphia: John Benjamins Publishing Company.

Grosu, Alexander (1988). "On the Distribution of Genitive Phrases in Ruma-nian". In: *Linguistics* 26, pp. 931–949.

Gruber, Bettina (May 2008). "Complementiser Agreement : New Evidence from the Upper Austrian Variant of Gmunden". MA thesis. Vienna: Universität Wien.

Haase, A (1969). *Syntaxe Française du XVIIéme Siécle*. Paris: Delgrave.

Haddican, Bill (2007). "The structural deficiency of verbal pro-forms". In: *Linguistic Inquiry* 38.3, pp. 539–547.

Haegeman, Liliane (1992). *Theory and description in generative grammar. A case study in West Flemish*. Cambridge: Cambridge University Press.

Hagège, C (2008). "Towards a typology of interrogative verbs". In: *Linguistic Typology* 12.1, pp. 1–44.

Hagemeijer, Tjerk (2000). "Serial Verb Constructions in Sao-Tomense". MA Thesis. University of Lisbon.

Hagstrom, Paul (1998). "Decomposing questions". Doctoral dissertation. MIT.

Haider, Hubert (1993). *Deutsche Syntax- generativ: Vorstudien zur Theorie einer projektiven Grammatik*. Tübingen: Gunter Narr Verlag.

– (2000). "OV is more basic than VO". In: *The Derivation of VO and OV*. Ed. by Peter Svenonius. Philadelphia, PA: John Benjamins, pp. 45–67.

– (2005). "How to turn German into Icelandic - and derive the OV-VO con-trasts". In: *The Journal of Comparative Germanic Linguistics* 8 (1-2), pp. 1–56.

– (2006). "Mittelfeld phenomena (Scrambling in Germanic)". In: *The Blackwell Companion to Syntax*. Ed. by Martin Everaert and Henk van Riemsdijk. Vol. 3. Malden, MA: Blackwell Publishers. Chap. 43, pp. 204–274.

Haider, Hubert and Inger Rosengren (1998). "Scrambling". In: *Sprache und Pragmatik* 49.

– (2003). "Scrambling: Nontriggered Chain Formation in OV Languages". In: *Journal of Germanic Linguistics* 15.3, pp. 203–267.

Halle, Morris and Alec Marantz (1993). "Distributed Morphology and the Pieces of Inflection". In: *The View from Building 20*. Ed. by Kenneth Hale and Samuel Jay Keyser. Cambridge, Massachusetts: MIT Press, pp. 111–176.

Hamlaoui, Fatima (2011). "On the role of phonology and discourse in Francilian French *wh*-questions". In: *Journal of Linguistics* 47.1, pp. 129–162.

Harley, Heidi and Rolf Noyer (1999). "Distributed Morphology". In: *GLOT* 4.4, pp. 3–9.

Harlow, Stephen (1992). "Finiteness and Welsh sentence structure". In: *Structure de la Phrase et Thorie du Liage*. Ed. by Hans-Georg Obenauer and Anne Zribi-Hertz. Prais: Presses Universitaires Vincennes, pp. 93–119.

Harris, Alice C. (1993). "Georgian". In: *Syntax - Ein internationales Handbuch zeitgenössischer Forschung*. Ed. by Joachim Jacobs et al. Vol. 2. HSK. Berlin: de Gruyter, pp. 1377–1397.

292

Hauge, Kjetil Ra (1999). *A Short Grammar of Contemporary Bulgarian*. Bloomington, ID: Slavica Publishers.

Heck, Fabian (2004). "A Theory of Pied-Piping". PhD thesis. Tübingen: Universität Tübingen.

– (2008). *On Pied-Piping : Wh-movement and Beyond*. Vol. 98. Studies in Generative Grammar. Berlin: Mouton de Gruyter.

– (2009). "On Certain Properties of Pied-Piping". In: *Linguistic Inquiry* 40.1, pp. 75–111.

Heck, Fabian and Gereon Müller (2000). "Successive cyclicity, long-distance superiority, and local optimization". In: *Proceedings of the West Coast Conference on Formal Linguistics* 19, pp. 218–231.

Heim, Irene and Angelika Kratzer (1998). *Semantics in generative grammar*. Malden, MA.: Blackwell Publishers.

Hendrick, Randall (1988). *Anaphora in Celtic and Universal Grammar*. Dordrecht, The Netherlands: Kluwer Academic Publishers.

Henry, Alison (1995). *Belfast English and Standard English: Dialect Variation and Parameter Setting*. New York, Oxford: Oxford University Press.

Hermon, Gabriella (1985). *Syntactic Modularity*. Vol. 20. Studies in Generative Grammar. Foris Publications.

Herslund, Michael (1984). "Particles, prefixes and preposition stranding". In: *Topics in Danish syntax*. Ed. by Finn Sorensen and Lars Heltoft. Copenhagen: Akademisk Forlag, pp. 34–71.

Hiraiwa, Ken (2002a). "Movement and Derivation: Eliminating the PBC". In: *Penn Linguistics Colloquium 26*. Philadelphia, PA.

– (2002b). *Raising and Indeterminate-Agreement*.

Hoekstra, Jarich (1995). "Preposition Stranding and Resumptivity in West Germanic". In: *Studies in Comparative Germanic Syntax*. Ed. by Hubert Haider, Susan Olsen, and Sten Vikner. Kluwer Academic Publishers, pp. 95–118.

– (2006). "Jürg Fleischer, Die Syntax von Pronominaladverbien in den Dialekten des Deutschen: Eine Untersuchung zu Preposition Stranding und verwandten Phänomen." In: *Journal of Comparative Germanic Linguistics* 9, pp. 209–215.

Hoekstra, Jarich and Peter Meijes Tiersma (1994). "Frisian". In: *The Germanic Languages*. Ed. by Ekkehard König and Johan van der Auwera. London and New York: Routledge, pp. 505–531.

Holmberg, Anders (1986). "Word order and syntactic features in the Scandinavian languages and English". Ph.D. Dissertation. University of Stockholm.

Hornstein, Norbert, Howard Lasnik, and Juan Uriagereka ((2003) 2007). "The dynamics of islands: Speculations on the locality of movement". In: *Linguistic Analysis* 33, pp. 149–175.

Hornstein, Norbert and Amy Weinberg (1981). "Case theory and preposition stranding". In: *Linguistic Inquiry* 12, pp. 55–91.

Horvath, Julia (2006). "Pied-Piping". In: *The Blackwell Companion to Syntax*. Ed. by Martin Everaert and Henk van Riemsdijk. Vol. III. Malden, MA: Blackwell Publishers. Chap. 50, pp. 569–630.

Houser, Michael, Line Mikkelsen, and Maziar Toosarvandani (2007). "Verb phrase Pronominalization in Danish: Deep or Surface Anaphora?" In: *Proceedings of the Thirty-Fourth Western Conference on Linguistics*. Ed. by Erin Brainbridge and Brian Agbayani. Fresno, CA: University of California, pp. 183–195.

Huang, C.-T. James (1982). "Logical relations in Chinese and the theory of grammar". Doctoral dissertation. MIT.

– (1993). "Logical Form". In: *Government and Binding Theory and the Minimalist Program: Principles and Parameters in Syntactic Theory*. Ed. by Gert Webelhuth. Oxford and Cambridge: Blackwell, pp. 125–176.

Huddleston, Rodney and Geoffrey K. Pullum (2002). *The Cambridge Grammar of the English Language*. Cambridge: Cambridge University Press.

Hyams, Nina, Dimitris Ntelitheos, and Cecile Manorohanta (2006). "Acquisition of Malagasy voicing system: implications for the adult grammar". In: *Natural Language and Linguistic Theory* 24.4, pp. 1049–1092.

Inada, Toshiaki (1981). "Problems of reanalysis and preposition stranding". In: *Studies in English Linguistics* 9, pp. 120–131.

Janke, Victoria and Ad Neeleman (2012). "Ascending and Descending VPs in English". In: *Linguistic Inquiry* 43.2.

Jayaseelan, Karattuparambil A. (1990). "Incomplete VP deletion and gapping". In: *Linguistic Analysis* 20, pp. 64–81.

– (2001). "IP-Internal Topic and Focus Phrases". In: *Studia Linguistica* 55.1, pp. 39–75.

– (2003). "Question words in focus positions". In: *Linguistic Variation Yearbook* 3, pp. 69–99.

– (2004). "Question movement in some SOV languages and the theory of feature checking". In: *Language and linguistics* 5.1, pp. 5–27.

Johnson, Kyle (2001). "What VP ellipsis can do, and what it can't, but now why". In: *The Handbook of Syntactic Theory*. Ed. by Mark Baltin and Chris Collins. Oxford: Blackwell, pp. 439–480.

Joos (1964). *The English Verb: Form and Meanings*. Madison: University of Wisconsin Press.

Karimi, Simin (2005). *A Minimalist Approach to Scrambling*. Vol. 76. Studies in Generative Grammar. Berlin & New York: De Gruyter.

Kathol, Andreas (2001). "On the Nonexistence of True Parasitic Gaps in Standard German". In: *Parasitic gaps*. Ed. by Peter Culicover and Paul Postal. Cambridge, MA: MIT Press, pp. 315–338.

Kayne, Richard (1975). *French syntax: The transformational cycle*. Cambridge, MA.: MIT Press.

294

Kayne, Richard (1981). "Two notes on the NIC". In: *Theory of markedness in generative grammar - Proceedings of the 1979 GLOW Conference*. Ed. by Adriana Belletti, Luciana Brandi, and Luigi Rizzi. Pisa: Scuola Normale Superiore, pp. 317–346.

- (1983). "Connectedness". In: *Linguistic Inquiry* 14. [Reprinted in Kayne 1984], pp. 223–249.
- (1984). *Connectedness and binary branching*. Dordrecht: Foris.
- (1994). *The antisymmetry of syntax*. Cambridge, MA.: MIT Press.
- (1999). "Prepositional complementizers as attractors". In: *Probus* 11, pp. 39–73.
- (2004). "Prepositions as Probes". In: *Structures and Beyond: The Cartography of Syntactic Structures*. Ed. by Adriana Belletti. Vol. 3. Oxford: Oxford University Press, pp. 192–212.
- (2005). *Movement and Silence*. Oxford Studies in Comparative Syntax. Oxford and New York: Oxford University Press.

Keenan, Edward (2008). "Voice and relativization without movement in Malagasy". In: *Natural Language and Linguistic Theory* 26.3, pp. 467–497.

Keenan, Edward and Bernard Comrie (1977). "Noun phrase accessibility and Universal Grammar". In: *Linguistic Inquiry* 8, pp. 63–99.

- (1979). "Data on the Noun Phrase Accessibility Hierarchy". In: *Language* 55.2, pp. 333–351.

Kennedy, Chris (2002). "Comparative deletion and optimality in syntax". In: *Natural Language and Linguistic Theory* 20.3, pp. 553–621.

Kidwai, Ayesha (2000). *XP-adjunction in universal grammar: scrambling and binding in Hindi-Urdu*. Oxford: Oxford University Press, p. 181.

King, Ruth and Yves Roberge (1990). "Preposition Stranding in Prince Edward Island French". In: *Probus* 3, pp. 351–369.

King, Tracy Holloway (1996). "Slavic clitics, long head movement, and prosodic inversion". In: *Journal of Slavic Linguistics* 4, pp. 274–311.

Kishimoto, Hideki (2005). "WH-in-situ and Movement in Sinhala Questions". In: *Natural Language and Linguistic Theory* 23.1, pp. 1–51.

É. Kiss, Katalin (2001). "Parasitic Chains Revisited". In: *Parasitic gaps*. Ed. by Peter Culicover and Paul Postal. Cambridge, MA: MIT Press, pp. 99–124.

Kitahara, Hisatsugu (1997). *Elementary operations and optimal derivations*. Cambridge, MA: MIT Press.

Klamer, Marian (Nov. 2002). "Ten years of synchronic Austronesian linguistics (1991–2002)". In: *Lingua* 112.11, pp. 933–965.

Koopman, Hilda (1984). *The syntax of verbs: From verb movement rules in the Kru languages to Universal Grammar*. Studies in Generative Grammar; 15. Dordrecht: Foris.

- (1997). *Prepositions, Postpositions, Circumpositions and Particles: The Structure of Dutch PPs*.

Koster, Jan (1986). *Domains and Dynasties: The radical autonomy of syntax.* Studies in Generative Grammar 30. Dordrecht: Foris.
– (1987). *Domains and Dynasties.* Dordrecht: Foris Publications.
Kratzer, Angelika (1996). "Severing the external argument from its verb". In: *Phrase Structure and the Lexicon.* Ed. by Johan Rooryck and Laurie Zaring. Dordrecht, The Netherlands: Kluwer Academic Publishers, pp. 109–137.
– (1998). "Scope or pseudoscope? Are there wide-scope indefinites?" In: *Events and grammar.* Ed. by Susan Rothstein. Dordrecht: Kluwer Academic Publishers, pp. 163–196.
– (2005). "Indefinites and the Operators they depend on: From Japanese to Salish". In: *Reference and quantification: The Partee effect.* Ed. by Gregory N Carlson and Francis J Pelletier. Stanford, CA: CSLI Publications, pp. 113–142.
Kratzer, Angelika and Junko Shimoyama (2002). "Indeterminate pronouns: The view from Japanese". In: *Proceedings of the Tokyo conference on psycholinguistics.* Ed. by Yukio Otsu. Vol. 3. Tokyo: Hituzi Syobo, pp. 1–25.
Kroch, Anthony and Aravind Krishna Joshi (1985). *The linguistic relevance of Tree Adjoining Grammar.*
Kroeger, Paul (1993). *Phrase Structure and Grammatical Relations in Tagalog.* Dissertations in Linguistics. Stanford: CSLI Publications.
Kuno, Masakazu (2003). *A New Perspective on "How-Likely" Puzzle.*
Kuno, Susumu and Jane J. Robinson (1972). "Multiple wh-questions". In: *Linguistic Inquiry* 3, pp. 463–487.
Kuthy, Kordula de (2002). *Discontinuous NPs in German: A Case Study of the Interaction of Syntax, Semantics, and Pragmatics.* Studies in Constraint-Based Lexicalism. Stanford, CA: CSLI Publications.
Kuthy, Kordula de and Walt Detmar Meurers (2001). "On partial constituent fronting in German". In: *The Journal of Comparative Germanic Linguistics* 3.3, pp. 143–205.
Lasnik, Howard (1995a). "A note on pseudogapping". In: *Papers on minimalist syntax, MIT working papers in linguistics* 27, pp. 143–163.
– (1995b). "Case and expletives revisited: On Greed and other human failings". In: *Linguistic Inquiry* 26.4, pp. 615–633.
– (1995c). "Last resort". In: *Minimalism and linguistic theory.* Ed. by Shosuke Haraguchi and Michio Funaki. Tokyo: Hituzi Syobo, pp. 1–32.
– (1999). "On feature strength: Three minimalist approaches to overt movement". In: *Linguistic Inquiry* 30.2, pp. 197–217.
– (2001a). "A note on the EPP". In: *Linguistic Inquiry* 32.2, pp. 356–362.
– (2001b). "When can you save a structure by destroying it?" In: *Proceedings of the North East Linguistic Society 31.* Ed. by Minjoo Kim and Uri Strauss. Georgetown University: GLSA, pp. 301–320.

Lasnik, Howard and Myung-Kwan Park (2003). "The EPP and the subject condition under sluicing". In: *Linguistic Inquiry* 34, pp. 649–660.

Lasnik, Howard and Mamoru Saito (1991). "On the subject of infinitives". In: *Papers from the 27th regional Meeting of the Chicago Linguistic Society Part One: The General Session*. Ed. by Lise M. Dobrin, Lynn Nichols, and Rosa M. Rodriguez. Chicago: Chicago Linguistic Society, University of Chicago, pp. 324–343.

– (1992). *Move α: Conditions on its application and output*. Cambridge, MA: MIT Press.

Law, Paul (1998). "A unified Analysis of P-stranding in Romance and Germanic". In: *Proceedings of NELS 28*. Ed. by Pius N. Tamanji and Kiyomi Kusumoto. Amherst, MA: GLSA.

– (2006a). "Adverbs in A-Not-A Questions in Mandarin Chinese". In: *Journal of East Asian Linguistics* 15.2, pp. 97–136.

– (2006b). "Preposition Stranding". In: *The Blackwell Companion to Syntax*. Ed. by Martin Everaert and Henk van Riemsdijk. Vol. 3. Malden, MA: Blackwell Publishers. Chap. 51, pp. 631–684.

Lebeaux, David (1991). "Relative clauses, licensing and the nature of the derivation". In: *Syntax and Semantics 25: Perspectives on phrase structure*. Ed. by Susan Rothstein. New York: Academic Press, pp. 209–239.

Lechner, Winfried (to appear). "Evidence for Survive from Covert Movement". In: *The Survive Principle in a Crash Proof Syntax*. Ed. by Michael T Putnam. Amsterdam: John Benjamins.

Legate, Julie Anne (2003). "Some Interface Properties of the Phase". In: *Linguistic Inquiry* 34.3, pp. 506–515.

Lenerz, Jürgen (1995). "Klammerkonstruktionen". In: *Syntax, Vol. II*. Ed. by Joachim Jacobs et al. Berlin: Mouton de Gruyter, pp. 1266–1276.

Leu, Thomas (2003). *What moves where and what for. An account of Swiss German was für*.

– (2007). "A note on *what for* split". In: *NYU Working Papers in Linguistics* 1.

Levin, Nancy (1978). "Some identity-of-sense deletions puzzle me. Do they you". In: *Proceedings of the Fourteenth Annual Meeting of the Chicago Linguistic Society*. Chicago: Chicago Linguistic Society, Chicago Univerisity, pp. 229–240.

– (1986). *Main-verb ellipsis in spoken English*. New York: Garland Publishing, Inc., p. 217.

Levine, Robert D. (1984). "Against Reanalysis Rules". In: *Linguistic Analysis* 14.1, pp. 3–30.

Lohndal, Terje (2011). "Freezing effects and objects". In: *Journal of Linguistics* 47, pp. 163–199.

Longobardi, Giuseppe (1991). "Extraction from NP and the proper notion of head government". In: *The Syntax of Noun Phrases*. Cambridge: Cambridge University Press. Chap. 2, pp. 57–112.

Lørdrup, Helge (1991). "The Norwegian Pseudopassive in Lexical theory". In: *Working Papers in Scandinavian Syntax* 47, pp. 118–129.

Lunt, Horace G. (1959). *Old Church Slavonic Grammar*. Second, revised edition. Slavistic Printings and Reprintings. 'S-Gravenhage: Mouton & Co.

Lutz, Ulrich (Dec. 2001). "Studien zu Extraktion und Projektion im Deutschen". Ph.D. dissertation. Tübingen: Universität Tübingen.

Lutz, Ulrich, Gereon Müller, and Arnim von Stechow, eds. (2000). Wh-*scope marking*. Vol. 37. Linguistik aktuell. Amsterdam: John Benjamins.

Mackenzie, J. Lachlan (2009). "Content interrogatives in a sample of 50 languages". In: *Lingua* 119.8, pp. 1131–1163.

Mahajan, Anoop (1990). "The A/A-bar distinction and movement theory". Doctoral dissertation. MIT.

Maling, Joan and Annie Zaenen (1978). "The Nonuniversality of a Surface Filter". In: *Linguistic Inquiry* 9.3, pp. 475–497.

– (1985a). "Preposition-Stranding and Oblique Case". In: *Cornell Working Papers in Linguistics* 7, pp. 149–161.

– (1985b). "Preposition-Stranding and Passive". In: *Nordic Journal of Linguistics* 8.2, pp. 197–209.

– (1990). "Preposition-stranding and passive". In: *Syntax and Semantics 24: Modern Icelandic syntax*. Ed. by Joan Maling and Annie Zaenen. [Reprint of Maling and Zaenen (1985)]. New York: Academic Press.

Manfredi, Victor (1993). "Verb Focus in the Typology of Kwa/Kru and Haitian". In: *Focus and Grammatical Relations in Creole Languages*. Ed. by Francis Byrne and Donald Winford. Vol. 12. Creole Language Library. John Benjamins, pp. 3–51.

Marr, David (1982). *Vision : A Computational Investigation into the Human Representation and Processing of Visual Information*. New York: Freeman.

Martí, Luisa and Klaus Abels (Oct. 2011). *Propositions or Choice Functions: What do Quantifiers Quantify Over?* Ms. UCL and QMUL.

Martin, Roger (1992). *Case theory, A-chains, and expletive replacement*.

Mayr, Clemens (2010). "On the Necessity of Phi-features: The Case of Bavarian Subject Extraction". In: *The Complementizer Phase*. Ed. by E. Phoevos Panagiotidis. Vol. 30. Oxford Studies in Theoretical Linguistics. Oxford, UK: Oxford University Press, pp. 117–142.

McCloskey, James (1979). *Transformational Syntax and Model Theoretic Semantics: A Case Study in Modern Irish*. Synthese Language Library. Dordrecht, Boston, and London: D. Reidel Publishing Company.

McCloskey, James (1990a). *Clause structure, ellipsis and proper government in Irish*. Santa Cruz, CA: Syntax research center, Cowell College, University of California at Santa Cruz.

– (1990b). "Resumptive Pronouns, A'-Binding, and Levels of Representation in Irish". In: *The Syntax of the Modern Celtic Languages. Syntax and Semantics 23*. Ed. by Randall Hendrick. San Diego: Academic Press, pp. 199–248.

– (2002). "Resumption, successive cyclicity, and the locality of operations". In: *Derivation and Explanation in the Minimalist Program*. Ed. by Samuel David Epstein and T David Seely. Malden, MA and Oxford, UK: Blackwell, pp. 184–226.

– (2004). "Questions in a Local English". In: *GURT*.

– (2006). "Questioning and Questions in a Local English". In: *Crosslinguistic Reserach in Syntax and Semantics: Negation, Tense, and Clausal Architecture*. Ed. by Raffaella Zanuttini et al. Washington, DC: Georgetown University Press, pp. 87–126.

McCloskey, James and Ken Hale (1984). "On the syntax of person number marking in Modern Irish". In: *Natural Language and Linguistic Theory* 1, pp. 487–533.

Mehlhorn, Grit (2001). "Kontrastierte Konstituentedn im Russischen. Experimentelle Untersuchungen zur Informationsstruktur". PhD thesis. Universität Leipzig.

Mensching, Guido (2000). *Infinitive Constructions with Specified Subjects: A Syntactic Analysis of the Romance Languages*. Oxford Studies in Comparative Syntax. Oxford: Oxford University Press.

Merchant, Jason (1999). "The Syntax of Silence - Sluicing, Islands, and Identity of Ellipsis." Ph.D. dissertation. UCSC.

– (2001). *The Syntax of Silence: Sluicing, Islands, and the Theory of Ellipsis*. Oxford: Oxford University Press.

– (2003). "Remarks on stripping". Ms. University of Chicago.

– (2004). "Fragments and Ellipsis". In: *Linguistics and philosophy* 27.6, pp. 661–738.

Miller, Philip H. (2000). "*Do* auxiliaire en anglais: un morphème grammatical sans signification propre". In: *Travaux Linguistiques de Cerlico* 13, pp. 119–147.

– (2002). "Les emplois non finis de *do* auxiliaire". In: *Construire et reconstruire en linguistique anglaise. Syntax et sémantique*. Ed. by Claude Delmas and Louis Roux. Vol. 107. Centre Interdisiplinaire d'Études et de Recherches sur l'Expression Contemporaine. Publications de l'Université de Saint-Étienne, pp. 185–198.

Mills, Jillian (2007). "Objects in the Pseudopassive : The syntax and semantics of bare-NP complements". In: *Proceedings of the 2007 annual conference of the Canadian Linguistic Association*.

Miyagawa, Shigeru (2010). *Why Agree? Why Move? : Unifying Agreement-Based and Discourse Configurational Languages*. Vol. 54. Linguistic Inquiry Monograph. Cambridge, MA: MIT Press.

Moro, Andrea (2000). *Dynamic Antisymmetry*. Linguistic Inquiry Monograph 38. Cambridge, MA: MIT Press.

– (2011). "Clause Structure Folding and the "Wh-in-Situ Effect"". In: *Linguistic Inquiry* 42.3, pp. 389–411.

Müller, Gereon (1996a). "A constraint on remnant movement". In: *Natural Language and Linguistic Theory* 14, pp. 355–407.

– (1996b). "Partial wh-movement and Optimality Theory". In: *Papers on wh-scope marking*. Ed. by Ulrich Lutz and Gereon Müller. Stuttgart/Tübingen: Universität Stuttgart/Universität Tübingen/IBM Deutschland, pp. 179–230.

– (1998). *Incomplete Category Fronting: A Derivational Approach to Remnant Movement in German*. Dordrecht, Boston: Kluwer Academic Publishers.

– (2000). "Das Pronominaladverb als Reparaturphänomen". In: *Linguistische Berichte* 182, pp. 139–178.

– (2004). "Phrase impenetrability and Wh-intervention". In: *Minimality Effects in Syntax*. Ed. by Arthur Stepanov, Gisbert Fanselow, and Ralf Vogel. Berlin: Mouton de Gruyter, pp. 289–325.

– (2010). "On Deriving CED Effects from the PIC". In: *Linguistic Inquiry* 41.1, pp. 35–82.

Müller, Gereon and Wolfgang Sternefeld (1994). "Scrambling as A-bar movement". In: *Studies on scrambling*. Ed. by Norbert Corver and Henk van Riemsdijk. Vol. 41. Studies in Generative Grammar. Berlin: De Gruyter, pp. 331–386.

Müller, Stefan (1999). *Deutsche Syntax deklarativ*. Vol. 394. Linguistische Arbeiten. Tübingen: Niemeyer.

Muriungi, Peter (2003). "Wh-Questions in Kiitharaka". MA thesis. Johannesburg: University of the Witwatersrand.

– (2005). "Wh-Questions in Kiitharaka". In: *Studies in African Linguistics* 34, pp. 43–104.

Muysken, Pieter (1977). "Movement rules in Papiamentu". In: *Amsterdam Creole Studies* 1, pp. 80–102.

Neeleman, Ad (1994). "Complex Predicates". PhD thesis. Utrecht, NL: Universiteit Utrecht.

– (2001). *Particle Placement*.

Neeleman, Ad and Hans van de Koot (2002). "The Configurational Matrix". In: *Linguistic Inquiry* 33.4, pp. 529–574.

– (2010). "A local encoding of syntactic dependencies and its consequences for the theory of movement". In: *Syntax* 13.4, pp. 331–372.

Neeleman, Ad and Fred Weerman (1999). *Flexible Syntax*. Kluwer Academic Publishers.

Nemoto, Naoko (1991). "Scrambling and conditions on A-Movement". In: *Proceedings of the West Coast Conference on Formal Linguistics*. Vol. 10. Stanford, CA: Stanford Linguistic Association, Stanford University, pp. 349–358.

Newmeyer, Frederick J. (1998). "Preposition Stranding: Parametric Variation and Pragmatics". In: *Languages and Linguistics* 1, pp. 1–24.

Ngonyani, Deo (1998). "V-to-I Movement in Kiswahili". In: *Swahili Forum V*. Ed. by Rose Marie Beck, Thomas Geider, and Werner Graebner. Vol. 55. Afrikanistische Arbeitspapiere. Köln: Institu für Afrikanistik, pp. 129–144.

Nilsen, Øystein (2003). *Eliminating Positions: Syntax and semantics of sentence modification*. Utrecht, NL: LOT.

– (2004). "Domains for adverbs". In: *Lingua* 114.6, pp. 809–847.

Nishigauchi, Taisuke (1986). "Quantification in syntax". Doctoral dissertation. University of Massachusetts.

– (1990). *Quantification in the Theory of Grammar*. Vol. 37. Dordrecht, The Netherlands: Kluwer Academic Publishers, p. 239.

Nissenbaum, Jon (2000). "Investigations of covert phrase movement". PhD thesis. Cambridge, Massachusetts: Massachusetts Institute of Technology, p. 243.

– (2001). "Investigations of Covert Phrasal Movement". Ph. D. Dissertation. MIT.

Nomura, Masashi (2001). *Extraposition or Scattered Deletion?*

Noonan, M (1997). "Functional Architecture and Wh-Movement: Irish as a Case in Point". In: *Canadian Journal of Linguistics* 42, pp. 111–139.

Nunes, Jairo (2004). *Linearization of Chains and Sideward Movement*. Linguistic Inquiry Monographs, 43. Cambridge, MA: MIT Press.

Nykiel, Joanna and Ivan A. Sag (2009). "Sluicing and stranding". In: *Paper presented at the 83rd LSA Meeting*. San Francisco, CA.

Obenauer, Hans-Georg (1976). *Etudes de syntaxe interrogative de francais*. Tübingen: Niemeyer.

Ochi, Masao (1998). "Move or Attract?" In: *Proceedings of the West Coast Conference on Formal Linguistics*. Vol. 16. Stanford, CA: CSLI, Stanford University.

Oppenrieder, Wilhelm (1991). "Preposition Stranding im Deutschen? - Da will ich nichts von hören!" In: *Strukturen und Merkmale Syntaktischer Kategorien*. Ed. by Gisbert Fanselow and Sascha Felix. Tübingen: Gunter Narr, pp. 159–173.

Ortiz de Urbina, Jon (1989). *Parameters in the Grammar of Basque : A GB Approach to Basque*. Dordrecht: Foris.

Pafel, Jürgen (1996). "Die syntaktische und semantische Struktur von was für-Phrasen". In: *Linguistische Berichte* 161, pp. 37–67.

Panagiotidis, E. Phoevos, ed. (2010). *The Complementizer Phase: Subjects and Operators*. Vol. 30. Oxford Studies in Theoretical Linguistics. Oxford, UK: Oxford University Press.

Pesetsky, David (1987). "Wh-in situ: Movement and unselective binding". In: *The representation of (in)definiteness*. Ed. by Eric J. Reuland and Alice G. B. ter Meulen. Cambridge, MA: MIT Press, pp. 98–129.

– (1992). *Zero Syntax Vol. 2*.

– (1995). *Zero syntax*. Cambridge, MA: MIT Press.

– (1998). "Some Optimality Principles of Sentence Pronunciation". In: *Is the Best Good Enough? - Optimality and Competition in Syntax*. Ed. by Pilar Barbosa et al. Cambridge, MA: MIT Press, pp. 337–383.

– (2000). *Phrasal Movement and Its Kin*. Linguistic Inquiry Monograph 37. Cambridge, MA: MIT Press.

Pesetsky, David and Esther Torrego (2007). "The Syntax of Valuation and the Interpretability of Features". In: *Phrasal and Clausal Architecture : Syntactic Derivation and Interpretation*. Ed. by Simin Karimi, Vida Samiian, and Wendy K. Wilkins. Vol. 101. Linguistik Aktuell. John Benjamins Publishing Company, pp. 262–294.

Podobryaev, Alexander (2009). ""Postpostion Stranding" and related phenomena in Russian". In: *Studies in Formal Slavic Phonology, Morhphology, Syntax, Semantics and Information Structure*. Ed. by Gerhild Zybatow et al. Vol. 21. Linguistik International. Frankfurt am Main: Peter Lang, pp. 197–208.

Pollard, Carl (1984). "Generalized Phrase Structure Grammar". PhD thesis. Stanford University.

Pollard, Carl and Ivan A. Sag (1994). *Head-Driven Phrase Structure Grammar*. Chicago: University of Chicago Press.

Pollock, Jean-Yves (1989). "Opacity, genitive subjects, and extraction from NP in English and French". In: *Probus* 1, pp. 151–162.

Ponelis, F. A. (1979). *Afrikaanse Sintaksis*. Pretoria: J.L. Van Schaik.

Postal, Paul (1974). *On raising: One rule of English grammar and its theoretical implications*. Cambridge, MA: MIT Press.

– (1994). "Parasitic and pseudoparasitic gaps". In: *Linguistic Inquiry* 25, pp. 63–117.

– (1998). *Three investigations of extraction*. Current Studies in Linguistics Series 29. Cambridge, MA: MIT Press.

Potts, Christopher (2002). "The syntax and semantics of as-parentheticals". In: *Natural Language and Linguistic Theory* 20.3, pp. 623–689.

Preminger, Omer (2009). "Breaking Agreements: Distinguishing Agreement and Clitic Doubling by Their Failures". In: *Linguistic Inquiry* 40.4, pp. 619–666.

Price, Susan (1990). *Comparative constructions in Spanish and French syntax*. London: Routledge.

Progovac, Ljiljana (1996). "Clitics in Serbian/Croatian: Comp as the Second Position". In: *Approaching Second: Second Position Clitics and Related Phe-*

nomena. Ed. by A Halpern and A Zwicky. Stanford: CSLI Publications, pp. 411–428.

Pullum, Geoffrey K. and Deidre Wilson (1977). "Autonomous Syntax and the Analysis of Auxiliaries". In: *Language* 53.4, pp. 741–788.

Putnam, Michael T, ed. (2009). *Towards a derivational syntax : survive minimalism*. Vol. 144. Linguistik Aktuell. Amsterdam & Philadelphia: John Benjamins Publishing Company.

Rackowski, Andrea and Norvin W. III Richards (2005). "Phase Edge and Extraction: A Tagalog Case Study". In: *Linguistic Inquiry* 36.4, pp. 565–599.

Radanovic-Kocic, Vesna (1988). "The grammar of Serbo-Croatian clitics: A synchronic and diachronic perspective". Doctoral dissertation. University of Illinois.

Rappaport, Gilbert C. (2001). "Extraction from Nominal Phrases in Polish and the Theory of Determiners". In: *Journal of Slavic Linguistics* 8.3.

Reinhart, Tanya and Eric Reuland (1993). "Reflexivity". In: *Linguistic Inquiry* 24.4, pp. 657–720.

Reis, Marga (2006). "Gibt es interrogative VPs? Zu einem ungelösten Pied-Piping Rätsel des Deutschen". In: *2006-4-26 Between 40 and 60 puzzles for Krifka*. Ed. by Hans-Martin Gärtner et al. Berlin: ZAS.

Reis, Marga and Inger Rosengren (1992). "What do *wh*-imperatives tell us about *wh*-movement". In: *Natural Language and Linguistic Theory* 10.1, pp. 79–118.

Reis, Marga and Wolfgang Sternefeld (2004). "Susanne Wurmbrand: Infinitives. Restructuring and Clause Structure. Studies in Generative Grammar 55. Berlin: Mouton de Gruyter, 2001. vi + 371 pp." In: *Linguistics* 42.2, pp. 469–508.

Richards, Marc David (2007). "On feature inheritance: An argument from the Phase Impenetrability Condition". In: *Linguistic Inquiry* 38.3, pp. 563–572.

– (2011). "Deriving the Edge: What's in a Phase?" In: *Syntax* 14.1, pp. 74–95.

Riemsdijk, Henk van (1978a). *A case study in syntactic markedness: The Binding Nature of Prepositional Phrases*. Lisse: The Peter de Ridder Press.

– (1978b). "On the Diagnosis of Wh Movement". In: *Recent Transformational Studies in European Languages*. Ed. by Samuel Jay Keyser. Cambridge, MA: MIT Press, pp. 189–206.

– (1985). "On Pied-Piped Infinitives in German Relative Clauses". In: *Studies in German Grammar*. Ed. by Jindrich Toman. Dordrecht, The Netherlands: Foris Publications, pp. 165–192.

– (1989). "Movement and regeneration". In: *Dialect variation and the theory of grammar*. Ed. by Paola Beninca. Dordrecht: Foris, pp. 105–136.

– (1990). "Circumpositions". In: *Unity in Diversity. Papers Presented to Simon Dik on his 50th Birthday*. Ed. by Harm Pinkster and Inge Genee. Dordrecht: Foris, pp. 229–241.

Rizzi, Luigi (1982). *Issues in Italian syntax*. Dordrecht: Foris.

– (1990). *Relativized minimality*. Vol. 16. Linguistic Inquiry Monograph. Cambridge, MA: MIT Press.

– (1997). "The Fine Structure of the Left Periphery". In: *Elements of Grammar: Handbook in Generative Syntax*. Ed. by Liliane Haegeman. Dordrecht: Kluwer, pp. 281–337.

– (2001a). "On the Position of Interrogative in the Left Periphery of the Clause". In: *Current Studies in Italian Syntax. Essays Offered to Lorenzo Renzi*. Ed. by Guglielmo Cinque and Giampaolo Salvi. Oxford: Elsevier North-Holland.

– (2001b). "Reconstruction, Weak Island Sensitivity and Agreement". In: *Semantic Interfaces : Reference, Anaphora and Aspect*. Ed. by Carlo Cecchetto, Gennaro Chierchia, and Maria Teresa Guasti. Stanford, CA: CSLI Publications, pp. 145–176.

– (2001c). "Relativized Minimality Effects". In: *The Handbook of Syntactic Theory*. Ed. by Mark Baltin and Chris Collins. Oxford: Blackwell, pp. 89–110.

– (2004a). "Locality and left periphery". In: *Structures and Beyond: Cartography of Syntactic structures*. Ed. by Adriana Belletti. Vol. 3. New York: Oxford University Press, pp. 223–251.

– ed. (2004b). *The Structure of CP and IP*. Vol. 2. Oxford studies in comparative syntax: The cartography of syntactic structures. Oxford: Oxford University Press.

– (2006). "On the form of chains: Criterial positions and ECP Effects". In: *Wh-movment: moving on*. Ed. by Lisa Lai Shen Cheng. Ms. University of Siena. Cambridge, MA: MIT Press, pp. 97–134.

Roberge, Yves (1998). "Les prépositions orphelines dans diverses variétés de fran cais d'Amérique du Nord". In: *Fran cais d'Amérique: variation créolisation, normalisation*. Ed. by P Brasseur. Avignon: Presses de l'Université d'Avignon.

Roberge, Yves and Nicole Rosen (1999). "Preposition Stranding and Que-Deletion in Varieties of North American French". In: *Linguistica Atlantica* 21, pp. 153–168.

Rodrigues, Cilene, Andrew Ira Nevins, and Luis Vicente (2009). "Cleaving the interactions between sluicing and preposition stranding". In: *Romance Languages and Linguistic Theory 2006: selected papers from "Going Romance," Amsterdam, 7–9 december 2006*. Ed. by L. Wetzels and Jeroen van der Weijer. John Benjamins, pp. 175–198.

Rosenbaum, Peter S. (1967). *The grammar of English predicate complement constructions*. Cambridge, MA: MIT Press.

Ross, John (1967). "Constraints on variables in syntax". PhD thesis. Massachusetts Institute of Technology.

Ross, John Robert (1973). "Slifting". In: *The formal analysis of natural languages : Proceedings of the first international conference*. Ed. by Maurice Gross, Morris Halle, and Marcel-Paul Schützenberger. The Hague: Mouton, pp. 133–169.

Rouveret, Alain (1990). "X-bar theory, minimality, and barrierhood in Welsh". In: *The Syntax of the Modern Celtic Languages: Syntax and Semantics 23*. Ed. by Randall Hendrick. New York: Academic Press, pp. 27–79.

– (1994). *Syntaxe du Gallois: Principes Généreaux et Typologie*. Paris: CNRS éditions.

Rudin, Catherine (1988a). "Multiple questions in South Slavic, West Slavic and Romanian". In: *Slavic and East European Journal* 32, pp. 1–24.

– (1988b). "On multiple questions and multiple wh-fronting". In: *Natural Language and Linguistic Theory* 6, pp. 445–501.

Runner, Jeffrey T, Rachel S Sussman, and Michael K. Tanenhaus (2002). "Logophors in Possessed Picture Noun Phrases". In: *WCCFL 21 Proceedings*. Ed. by Line Mikkelsen and Chris Potts. Cascadilla Press, pp. 401–414.

Sabel, Joachim (2000). "Partial *wh*-movement and the typology of *wh*-questions". In: Wh-*scope marking*. Ed. by Ulrich Lutz, Gereon Müller, and Arnim von Stechow. Vol. 37. Linguistik aktuell. Amsterdam: John Benjamins, pp. 409–446.

– (2006). "Typologie des W-Fragesatzes". In: *Linguistische Berichte*, pp. 147–206.

Sag, Ivan A. (1983). "On Parasitic Gaps". In: *Linguistics and Philosophy* 6, pp. 35–45.

Saito, Mamoru (1992). "Long distance scrambling in Japanese". In: *Journal of East Asian Linguistics* 1, pp. 69–118.

Saito, Mamoru and Keiko Murasugi (1999). "Subject predication within IP and DP". In: *Beyond Principles and Parameters: Essays in Memory of Osvaldo Jaeggli*. Ed. by Kyle Johnson and Ian Roberts. Dordrecht: Kluwer Academic Publisher, pp. 167–188.

Salles, Heloisa Maria Moreira-Lima (1997). "Prepositions and the Syntax of Complementation". Ph.D. Dissertation. University of Wales.

Sato, Yosuke (2011). "P-Stranding under sluicing and repair by ellipsis: why is Indonesian (not) special?" In: *Journal of East Asian Linguistics* 20, pp. 339–382.

Sauerland, Uli (1996). "The Interpretability of Scrambling". In: *Formal Approaches to Japanese Linguistics 2*. Ed. by Masatoshi Koizumi, Masayuki Oishi, and Uli Sauerland. Vol. 29. MIT Working Papers in Linguistics. MIT-WPL, pp. 213–234.

– (1998). "The Meaning of Chains". PhD thesis. Cambridge, MA: MIT.

– (2004). "The interpretation of traces". In: *Natural Language Semantics* 12, pp. 63–127.

Schneider-Zioga, Patricia (2009). "Wh-agreement and bounded unbounded move-ment". In: *Merging Features: Computation, Interpretation and Acquisition.* Ed. by Josep M Brucart, Anna Gavarrò, and Jaume Solà. Oxford: Oxford University Press, pp. 46–60.

Schütze, Carson (1994). "Serbo-Croatian second position clitic placement and the phonology-syntax interface". In: *MIT Working Papers in Linguistics* 21, pp. 373–473.

Schwarz, Florian (2003). "Focus Marking in Kikuyu". In: *Questions and Focus.* Ed. by Regine Eckardt. Vol. 30. ZAS Papers in Linguistics. Berlin: Zentrum fur allgemeine Sprachwissenschaft, pp. 41–118.

Sekerina, Irina A (1997). "The Syntax and Processing of Scrambling Construc-tions in Russian". PhD thesis. State University of New York at Stoney Brook.

Şener, Serkan (2006). "Strandability of a P is about its extendability". Handout from the Workshop on Antilocality, Havard, April 22.

Sharvit, Yael (1999). "Resumptive Pronouns in Relative Clauses". In: *Natural Language and Linguistic Theory* 17.3, pp. 587–612.

Shima, Etsuro (2000). "A preference for Move over Merge". In: *Linguistic In-quiry* 31.2, pp. 375–385.

Shimoyama, Junko (2001). "Wh-constructions in Japanese". PhD thesis. Am-herst, MA: University of Massachusetts.

Shlonsky, Ur (1994). "Agreement in Comp". In: *The Linguistic Review* 11.3-4, pp. 351–376.

– (1997). *Clause Structure and Word Order in Hebrew and Arabic: An Essay in Comparative Semitic Syntax.* New York: Oxford University Press.

Shuyler, Tamara (2002). "Wh-Movement out of the Site of VP Ellipsis". MA thesis. Santa Cruz, CA: UCSC.

Siegel, Muffy E. A. (1983). "Problems in Preposition Stranding". In: *Linguistic Inquiry* 14.1, pp. 184–188.

Siewierska, A (1984). "Phrasal Disontinuity in Polish". In: *Australian Journal of Linguistics* 4, pp. 57–71.

Siewierska, A and L Uhlířová (1998). "An overview of word order in Slavic lan-guages". In: *Constituent Order in the Languages of Europe.* Ed. by A Siewier-ska. Berlin, New York: de Gruyter, pp. 105–149.

Sobin, Nicholas (1987). "The Variable Status of Comp-Trace Phenomena". In: *Natural Language and Linguistic Theory* 5, pp. 33–60.

Sportiche, Dominique (1998). *Partitions and Atoms of Clause Structure : Sub-jects, agreement, case and clitics.* London and New York: Routledge.

– (2011). "French Relative *Qui*". In: *Linguistic Inquiry* 42.1, pp. 83–124.

Stabler, Edward P. (2004). "Varieties of crossing dependencies: structure depen-dence and mild context sensitivity". In: *Cognitive Science* 28, pp. 699–720.

Starke, Michal (2001). "Move Dissolves into Merge: a Theory of Locality". Doctoral dissertation. University of Geneva.

Starke, Michal (2004). "On the Inexistence of Specifiers and the Nature of Heads". In: *Structures and Beyond: The Cartography of Syntactic Structures*. Ed. by Adriana Belletti. Oxford University Press. Chap. 8.

– (2009). "Nanosyntax – A short primer to a new approach to language". In: *Nordlyd* 36.1, pp. 1–6.

Stepanov, Arthur (2007). "The End of CED? Minimalism and Extraction Domains". In: *Syntax* 10.1, pp. 80–126.

Stjepanović, Sandra (1998). "On the Placement of Serbo-Croatian Clitics: Evidence from VP-Ellipsis". In: *Linguistic Inquiry* 29.3, pp. 527–537.

– (2008). "P-Stranding under Sluicing in a Non-P-Stranding Language?" In: *Linguistic Inquiry* 39.1, pp. 179–190.

Stowell, Timothy (1982). "Conditions on Reanalysis". In: *MIT Working Papers in Linguistics* 4, pp. 245–269.

Stroik, Thomas S (1999). "The Survive Principle". In: *Linguistic Analysis* 29.3-4, pp. 282–309.

– (2009). *Locality in Minimalist Syntax*. Vol. 51. Linguistic Inquiry Monograph. Cambridge, MA: MIT Press.

Sugisaki, Koji (2002). "Innate Constraints on Language Variation: Evidence from Child Language". Doctoral Dissertation. University of Connecitut.

Sugisaki, Koji, Howard Lasnik, and William Snyder (Nov. 2001). *Obligatory Object Shift in Child English and its Consequences*.

Sugisaki, Koji and William Snyder (2001a). "Preposition Stranding and Double Objects in the Acquisition of English". In: *Proceedings of the Second TCP*.

– (Nov. 2001b). *Preposition Stranding in the Acquisition of English and the Theory of Parameters*.

Svenonius, Peter (1996). *The verb-particle alternation in the Scandinavian languages*. Ms. Universitet i Tromsø.

– (2002a). *Limits on P: filling in holes vs. falling in holes*.

– (2002b). "Subject Positions and the placement of adverbials". In: *Subjects, expletives, and the EPP*. Ed. by Peter Svenonius. Oxford and New York: Oxford University Press, pp. 201–242.

Szabolcsi, Anna (1994). "The Noun Phrase". In: *The Syntactic Structure of Hungarian*. Ed. by Ferenc Kiefer and Katalin É. Kiss. Vol. 27. Syntax and Semantics. San Diego: Academic Press, Inc., pp. 179–274.

Szczegielniak, Adam (2005). *All sluiced up, but no alleviation in sight...* ms. Boston College.

– (2008). "Islands in Sluicing in Polish". In: *Proceedings of the 27th West Coast Conference on Formal Linguistics*. Ed. by Natasha Abner and Jason Bishop. Cascadilla Proceedings Project, pp. 404–412.

Takahashi, Daiko (1994a). "Minimality of movement". Doctoral dissertation. University of Connecticut.

– (1994b). "Sluicing in Japanese". In: *Journal of East Asian Linguistics* 3.3, pp. 265–300.

Takami, Ken-ichi (1988). "Preposition Stranding: Arguments against Syntactic Analyses and an Alternative Functional Explanation". In: *Lingua* 76.4, pp. 299–335.

– (1992). *Preposition Stranding: From Syntactic to Functional Analyses*. Berlin: Mouton de Gruyter.

Takano, Yuji (2000). "Illicit Remnant Movement: an argument for feature-driven movement". In: *Linguistic Inquiry* 31.1, pp. 141–156.

Tallerman, Maggie (1998). "The uniform Case-licensing of subjects in Welsh". In: *The Linguistic Review* 15, pp. 69–133.

Taraldsen, Knut Tarald (1979). "Remarks on some central problems of Norwegian syntax. Review article of T. Freheim (ed.) *Sentrale problemer i norsk syntaks*". In: *Nordic Journal of Linguistics* 2, pp. 23–54.

– (2010). "The nanosyntax of Nguni noun class prefixes and concords". In: *Lingua* 120.6, pp. 1476–1501.

Tellier, Christine (1990). "Subjacency and Subject Condition Violations in French". In: *Linguistic Inquiry* 21.2, pp. 306–311.

Terzi, Arhonto (2001). "Complex Prepositions as Small Clauses". In: *The 22nd Linguistics meeting of the University of Thessaloniki*. Thessaloniki, GR.

– (2007). "Locative Prepositions, Predicate Inversion and Full Interpretation". In: *Selected Papers from the 17th International Symposium on Theoretical and Applied Linguistics of Thessaloniki*. Ed. by E Agathopoulou, M Dimitrakopoulou, and D Papadopoulou, pp. 210–219.

Thoms, Gary (2011). *From economy to locality: do-support as head movement*. Ms. Strathclyde University.

– (to appear). "'Verb Floating' and VPE: towards a movement theory of ellipsis licensing". In: *Linguistic Variation Yearbook*.

Tomic, Olga Miseska (1996). "The Balkan Slavic Clausal Clitics". In: *Natural Language and Linguistic Theory* 14.4, pp. 811–872.

Toosarvandani, Maziar (2009). "Ellipsis in Farsi Complex Predicates". In: *Syntax* 12.1, pp. 60–92.

Torrego, Esther (1983). "More effects of successive cyclic movement". In: *Linguistic Inquiry* 14, pp. 561–565.

– (1984). "On inversion in Spanish and some of its effects". In: *Linguistic Inquiry* 15, pp. 103–129.

Trissler, Susanne (1993). "P-Stranding im Deutschen". In: *Extraktion im Deutschen I*. Ed. by Franz-Josef d' Avis et al. Arbeiten des Sonderforschungsbereichs 340 34. Universität Tübingen, Universität Stuttgart, pp. 248–291.

– (2000). *Syntaktische Bedingungen für W-Merkmale : Zur Bildung interrogative w-Phrasen im Deutschen*. Arbeitspapiere des Sonderforschungsbereich 340 151. Tübingen: Universität Tübingen.

Truswell, Robert (2007a). "Extraction from Adjuncts and the Structure of Events". In: *Lingua* 117, pp. 1355–1377.

– (2007b). "Locality of Wh-movement and the individuation of events". PhD thesis. London: University College London.

– (2009). "Preposition Stranding, Passivisation, and Extraction from Adjuncts in Germanic". In: *Linguistic Variation Yearbook* 8, pp. 131–177.

– (2011). *Events, phrases, and questions*. Oxford University Press.

Tuller, L A (1986). "Bijective Relations in Universal Grammar and the Syntax of Hausa". Ph.D. Dissertation. University of California.

Ueyama, Ayumi (2003). "Two Types of Scrambling Construction in Japanese". In: *Anaphora: A Reference Guide*. Ed. by Andrew Barss. Malden, MA: Blackwell Publishing, pp. 23–71.

Uriagereka, Juan (1999). "Multiple Spell-Out". In: *Working minimalism*. Ed. by Norbert Hornstein and Samuel D. Epstein. Cambridge, MA: MIT Press, pp. 251–282.

Uribe-Echevarria, María (1992). "On the structural positions of subjects in Spanish, and their consequences for quantification". In: *Syntactic theory and Basque syntax*. Ed. by Joseba A. Lakarra and Jon Ortiz de Urbina. San Sebastian: ASJU, pp. 447–493.

van Koppen, Marjo (2005). "One probe – two goals : aspects of agreement in Dutch". PhD thesis. Leiden, The Netherlands: Leiden University.

Van Valin, Robert D (1995). "Toward a fucntionalist account of so called 'extraction constraints'". In: *Complex Structures : A functionalist Perspective*. Ed. by Betty Devriendt, Louis Goossens, and Johan van der Auwera. Berlin: Mouton de Gruyter, pp. 29–60.

Van Valin, Robert D and Randy J LaPolla (1997). *Syntax : Structure, Meaning, and Function*. Cambridge: Cambridge University Press.

Vergnaud, Jean-Roger (1979). *Case and Binding*. Paper given at the Pisa Workshop.

Vikner, Sten (1995). *Verb movement and expletive subjects in Germanic languages*. Oxford: Oxford University Press.

– (2001). *Verb Movement Variation in Germanic and Optimality Theory*. Neuphilologische Fakulta Universitat Tubingen.

– (Oct. 2007). *The SVO/SOV-question and verb particles in Danish, German and Yiddish*. Handout of a talk presented in Salzburg.

Watanabe, Akira (1992a). "Subjacency and S-structure movement of *wh*-in-situ". In: *Journal of East Asian Linguistics* 1.3, pp. 255–291.

– (1992b). "Wh-in-situ, Subjacency, and chain formation". In: *MIT Occasional Papers in Linguistics* 2.

– (2001). "*Wh*-in-situ Languages". In: *The Handbook of Syntactic Theory*. Ed. by Mark Baltin and Chris Collins. Oxford: Blackwell. Chap. 7, pp. 203–225.

- (2003). "Wh and operator constructions in Japanese". In: *Lingua* 113.4-6, pp. 519 –558.

Webelhuth, Gert (1992). *Principles and parameters of syntactic saturation*. New York: Oxford University Press.

Weiß, Helmut (1998). *Syntax des Bairischen : Studien zur Grammatik einer natürlichen Sprache*. Vol. 391. Linguistische Arbeiten. Tübingen: Max Niemeyer Verlag.

Wexler, Kenneth and Peter Culicover (1980). *Formal principles of language acquisition*. Cambridge, MA: MIT Press.

Wilder, Chris and Damir Ćavar (1994). "Long head movement? Verb movement and cliticization in Croatian". In: *Lingua* 93, pp. 1–58.

Williams, Edwin S. (2002). *Representation Theory*. Cambridge, MA: MIT Press.

- (2011). *Regimes of Derivation in Syntax and Morphology*. New York: Routledge.

Willis, David (2000). "On the Distribution of Resumptive Pronouns and wh-trace in Welsh". In: *Journal of Linguistics* 36.3, pp. 531–573.

Wöllstein-Leisten (2001). *Die Syntax der dritten Konstruktion : Eine repräsentationelle Analyse zur Monosententialität von 'zu'-Infinitive im Deutschen*. Tübingen: Stauffenburg.

Wong, Deborah (May 2012). *Wh-Questions in Colloquial Malaysian English*. Long Essay, UCL.

Wurmbrand, Susanne (2001). *Infinitives. Restructuring and Clause Structure*. Studies in Generative Grammar 55. Berlin and New York: Mouton de Gruyter.

Zabrocki, T (1984). "on the Nature of Movement Rules in English and Polish". In: *Contrastive Linguistics: Prospects and Problems*. Ed. by Jacek Fisiak. Amsterdam: Mouton.

Zhang, Shi (1990). "Correlations between the Double Object Construction and Preposition Stranding". In: *Linguistic Inquiry* 21.2, pp. 312–316.

Ziv, Yael and Gloria Sheintuch (1981). "Passives of Obliques over Direct Objects". In: *Lingua* 54.1–17.

Zribi-Hertz, Anne (1984). *Orphan Prepositions in French and the Concept of 'Null Pronoun'*.

Zwart, Jan-Wouter C. (2001). "Syntactic and Phonological Verb Movement". In: *Syntax* 4.1, pp. 34–62.

10 Index

www.ingramcontent.com/pod-product-compliance
Lightning Source LLC
Chambersburg PA
CBHW070018100426
42740CB00013B/2543